STRANGERS IN OXFORD

CE

STRANGERS IN OXFORD

A Side Light on the First Civil War 1642 – 1646

by

MARGARET TOYNBEE
M.A., Ph.D., F.S.A., F.R.Hist.S.

and

PETER YOUNG
D.S.O., M.C., M.A., F.S.A., F.R.Hist.S., F.R.G.S.

PHILLIMORE

1973
Published by
PHILLIMORE & CO. LTD.
London and Chichester
Head Office: Shopwyke Hall,
Chichester, Sussex, England

ISBN 0 85033 035 1

Thanks are due to the generous help of the Marc Fitch Fund in enabling this volume to be published

Made and printed by Eyre & Spottiswoode Ltd.,
Her Majesty's Printers,
at Grosvenor Press, Portsmouth

This study of the Strangers and their landlords living in St. Aldate's parish, Oxford, during the First Civil War, we dedicate to the memory of Norman Tucker, who first inspired us to undertake it.

Margaret Toynbee
Peter Young

CONTENTS

LIST OF ILLUSTRATIONS

ABBREVIATIONS

Ashburnham's *Accompt*	Account of Charles I's Receipts and Expenses April 1642-October 1643: Appendix to Vol. II of *A Narrative by John Asburnham* (1830)
C.A.M.	*Calendar of the Proceedings of the Committee for the Advance of Money*, 3 vols. (1888)
Cart. H. St J.B.	*A Cartulary of the Hospital of St John the Baptist*, ed. H. E. Salter, Oxford Historical Society, 5 vols. (1914-16)
Cart. Oseney Abbey	*Cartulary of Oseney Abbey*, ed. H. E. Salter, Oxford Historical Society, 6 vols. (1929-36)
Carte	T. Carte, *The Life of James Duke of Ormond*, 2nd edn., 6 vols. (1851)
C.B.	*Complete Baronetage*
C.C.C.	*Calendar of the Proceedings of the Committee for Compounding*, 5 vols. (1889-92)
C.C.S.P.	*Calendar of the Clarendon State Papers*, 4 vols. (1869-1932)
C.J.	*Journals of the House of Commons*
Clarendon	*History of the Rebellion and Civil Wars in England*, ed. W. D. Macray, 6 vols. (1888)
C.P.	*Complete Peerage*, new edn.
C.S.P.D.	*Calendars of the State Papers Domestic*
C.S.P.I.	*Calendars of the State Papers relating to Ireland*
C.S.P.V.	*Calendars of the State Papers Venetian*
C.T.B.	*Calendars of Treasury Books*
Dalton	C. Dalton, *English Army Lists and Commission Registers*, 1661-1714, 6 vols. (1892-1904)
D.N.B.	*Dictionary of National Biography*

Dugdale	*The Life, Diary and Correspondence of Sir William Dugdale*, ed. William Hamper (1827)
H.M.C.	Historical Manuscripts Commission
I.O.	*A List of [Indigent] Officers* (1663)
Keeler	M. F. Keeler, *The Long Parliament A Biographical Study of its Members*, American Philosophical Society (1954)
L.C. 3/1	P.R.O., List of his Maties seruants in ordinary of the Chamber 1641
L.J.	*Journals of the House of Lords*
Luke	*Journal of Sir Samuel Luke*, ed. I. G. Philip, Oxfordshire Record Society, 3 vols. (1950-3)
Nicholas Papers	*Correspondence of Sir Edward Nicholas*, ed. Sir G. F. Warner, 4 vols. (1886-1920)
O.C.A.	*Oxford City Council Acts* 1583-1626, ed. H. E. Salter, Oxford Historical Society, Vol. LXXXVII (1928), 1626-1665, ed. M. G. Hobson and H. E. Salter, Vol. XCV (1933), and 1666-1701, ed. M. G. Hobson, N.S Vol. II (1939)
O.C.P.	*Oxford City Properties*, ed. H. E. Salter, Oxford Historical Society, Vol. LXXXIII (1926)
P.C.C.	Prerogative Court of Canterbury
Peacock	Edward Peacock, *Army Lists of the Roundheads and Cavaliers*, 2nd edn. (1874)
Phillips	J. R. Phillips, *Memoirs of the Civil War in Wales and the Marches*, 1642-1649, 2 vols. (1874)
P.R.O.	Public Record Office
Register	*Register of the University of Oxford*, ed. C. W. Boase and A. Clark, 2 vols. (Vol. II in 4 Parts), Oxford Historical Society (1885, 1887, 1888, 1889)
Register of the Visitors	*The Register of the Visitors of the University of Oxford*, 1647-1658, ed. M. Burrows, Camden Society (1881)
R.C.H.M.	Royal Commission on Historical Monuments
R.O.P.	*The Royalist Ordnance Papers*, Part I, ed. Ian Roy, Oxfordshire Record Society, Vol. XLIII (1964)
Rushworth	John Rushworth, *Historical Collections*, 8 vols. (1659-1701)

S. and T.	*Surveys and Tokens*, ed. H. E. Salter, Oxford Historical Society, Vol. LXXV (1920)
Shaw	W. A. Shaw, *Letters of Denization and Acts of Naturalisation* (1911)
S.P.D.	State Papers Domestic
Stevens	*The Papers of Captain Henry Stevens*, ed. Margaret Toynbee, Oxfordshire Record Society, Vol. XLII (1961)
Survey of South-West Ward	H. E. Salter, *Survey of Oxford*, ed. W. A. Pantin and W. T. Mitchell, O.H.S., N.S., Vol. XX (1969), pp. 1-132
Survey of South-West Ward	H. E. Salter, *Survey of Oxford*
Symonds	Richard Symonds, *Diary of the Marches of the Royal Army*, ed. C. E. Long, Camden Society (1859)
Symonds, MS. Harleian 986	Notebook of Richard Symonds
V.C.H.	*The Victoria History of the Counties of England*
Walker	Sir Edward Walker, *Historical Discourses* (1705)
Warburton	E. G. B. Warburton, *Memoirs of Prince Rupert and the Cavaliers*, 3 vols. (1849)
Wood, *C. of O.*	*Wood's City of Oxford*, ed. A. Clark, Oxford Historical Society, 3 vols. (1889, 1890, 1900)
Wood, *L. and T.*	*The Life and Times of Anthony Wood*, ed. A. Clark, Oxford Historical Society, 5 vols. (1891, 1892, 1894, 1895, 1900)

ACKNOWLEDGMENTS

To Bodley's Librarian for permission to print the Survey of St Aldate's Parish, Oxford, upon which this study is based, as well as other items from the Heath Papers.

To the Keeper of the Oxford University Archives for permission to quote from Wills and Inventories proved in the Court of the Chancellor of the University.

To the Governing Bodies of the following Oxford Colleges for permission to consult and print extracts from documents preserved in their archives and for help generously given in directing our researches: All Souls, Balliol, Brasenose, Christ Church, Lincoln, Magdalen, Merton, New College, Oriel, Pembroke, Queen's, St John's, and University.

To the Oxford City Librarian for permission to consult and quote from documents preserved in the City Archives, and to Mr C. J. H. Walker for invaluable help in locating them.

To the Rector of St Aldate's Church, the Revd. Canon O. K. de Berry, for permission to consult and quote from documents in the Parish Chest.

To the Director of the Shakespeare Birthplace Trust, Dr Levi Fox, O.B.E., for permission to consult and print extracts from items in the Willoughby de Broke MSS.

Other acknowledgments are made in the notes.

Mr L. C. Nagel compiled the Index and Mr R. G. Sharp made the plan of St Aldate's.

INTRODUCTION

In the autumn of 1961 the late Mr Norman Tucker, the historian of North Wales in the Civil War, called our attention to the significance of the seventeenth-century document of three pages which provides the subject of this study. A cursory investigation convinced us of its importance, and we decided to edit it in the form of an article. After several years' intensive research, the projected paper has turned into a sizeable book.

The document is entitled 'An Exact Accompt of all psons being strangers now resident with the pish of St Aldates Oxon', to which has been added slightly lower in another hand: 'Taken 23° Jan: 1643' (i.e. 1643/4). It forms folios 46, 48, and 49 of the Bodleian Library MS. Add. D. 114. This manuscript is a tall volume, bound in boards, with a leather spine, measuring 15 1/8 inches by 10 inches, and consisting of 179 numbered folios, of which many are blanks to which the original documents contained in it are loosely attached. It is entitled on f.4: 'A COLLECTION OF ORIGINAL PAPERS relative to THE SEIGE [sic] of OXFORD, &c', and below is written: 'Presented to the Bodleian Library, by Wm Hamper, F.S.A. of Birmingham, Decr. 10th 1825'. Folios 1-2 consist of the following letter with address and seal:

> 'Highgate near Birmingham, Decr. 10th 1825.
>
> My dear Sir,
>
> I beg to thank you for your friendly Letter, and, in consequence of it, have placed my Dugdalian Volume in the hands of Harding & Leopard, who are proceeding to print it immediately. There will be two original Portraits, as well as some other Embellishments, to lard the leanness of my meagre performance, and render it palatable to the Black Letter Dogs; so that I hope it may go down without much grumbling.
>
> I enclose the Vol. of Oxford Papers which you will please to deposit in the Bodleian Library, as a small token of my Affection:
>
> "The gift is small
> "But love is all".
>
> With my kind Regards to Dr. Bandinel,[1] I am,
> My dear Sir
> Yrs very faithfully
> Wm Hamper
> Revd. Dr. Bliss.'[2]

William Hamper (1776-1831) was an assiduous antiquary, of whom an account will be found in *D.N.B.* The 'Dugdalian Volume' to which he refers is his *Life, Diary and Correspondence of Sir William Dugdale*, published in 1827, his most valuable work. A note made in 1890 inside the cover of MS. Add. D. 114, by Falconer Madan, Bodley's Librarian from 1912 to 1919, states that 'fol. 74-101 were added in 1883 from MSS. bought in about 1880'. These folios are 137-171 of the present pagination.

It is unfortunate that Hamper does not record where he obtained the documents which compose the 'Seige of Oxford' volume. Of these the majority are manuscripts, but there are also some printed Proclamations and Articles. Their value for the student of the history of the Royalist capital in the Civil War in general is very great: reference is made to the collection in the Introduction to *The Papers of Captain Henry Stevens.*[3] Yet until we came to tackle the question for the purposes of this study, no attempt seems to have been made to discover their original ownership.

The fact that the St Aldate's survey of 'strangers' was entrusted to Edward Heath, of Cottesmore, Rutland, and the pronounced emphasis of the documents on St Aldate's parish, suggested to us that they had once belonged to Heath himself. A large number are written in the same educated hand, including two memoranda couched in the first person singular. Fortunately, a voluminous collection of the

Heath family's official and private papers are preserved amongst the Egerton MSS. in the British Museum.[4] A smaller, but highly important, collection of Heath accounts and correspondence has been deposited by Lord Willoughby de Broke in the Record Office of the Shakespeare Birthplace Trust at Stratford-upon-Avon.[5] Comparison of holographs of Edward Heath contained in these collections with photographic copies of some of the above-mentioned manuscripts in the 'Seige of Oxford' volume has proved beyond a shadow of doubt that the latter constitutes a part, if not the whole, of his official Wartime papers.

EDWARD HEATH

Edward Heath was the eldest of the five sons of Sir Robert Heath (1575-1649), of Brasted, Kent, judge and Recorder of London, who was appointed Chief Justice of the King's Bench late in 1642.[6] Edward's mother was Margaret, daughter and heiress of John Miller, of Tonbridge. He was born at Crabbet House in the parish of Worth, Sussex, 2nd September 1612, and baptized at Worth on the 15th.[7] Edward and his next brother, John (born 2nd May 1614), matriculated as Fellow Commoners from Clare College, Cambridge, in Easter Term 1626. There exists among the Heath Papers in the British Museum a careful and neatly-written 'Note of all our Expences at Cambridge' from Midsummer 1626 to Christmas 1628, kept by Edward.[8] The boys' tutor was Richard Love (1596-1661), Fellow of Clare, who became Master of Corpus Christi College, Cambridge, in 1632.[9] When, in January 1628/9, Edward went to reside at the Inner Temple, to which he and John had been admitted in November 1625 when their father was Treasurer of the Society, he began a meticulous record of his quarterly expenses. This he continued until Shrove Monday 1630/1, when 'I was married and then I gaue ouer yis account'.[10] Methodical habits had been formed for a lifetime and were to stand Edward in good stead when he was commissioned to do official work for King Charles I at Oxford during the Civil War.

On 21st February 1630/1 Heath married at All Hallows, Bread Street, Lucy, only surviving child and heir of Paul Ambrose Croke, barrister of the Inner Temple.[11] Croke, who died 25th August 1631, was the fourth son of Sir John Croke, of Chilton, Buckinghamshire: in 1619/20 he had purchased the manor of Cottesmore. Lucy's mother, her father's second wife, was Susan, or Susanna, second daughter of Thomas Coe, of Boxford, Suffolk, successively widow of Thomas Tasker, of Walthamstow and Bury St Edmunds, and Humphrey Milward, vintner, of the parish of St Christopher-le-Stocks, London.[12] Although Milward was only buried on 7th January 1608/9, Susan married Croke at St Helen's, Bishopsgate, on the following 24th June.[13] Lucy Croke was born 5th January 1617/8, and baptized at Hackney on the 17th.[14] She and her brother, Samuel (died 1630), are named in the Will of their maternal grandfather, made 27th July 1622.[15]

In his Will, made 4th April 1631,[16] Croke enjoined that after his wife and daughter had taken their choice of his English books, his son-in-law was to have 'the rest of all my bookes except lawe bookes'. Catalogues of those received by Heath from Croke's study in the Inner Temple in 1631 and those taken out of his study at Cottesmore in 1634 are extant.[17] Susan Croke was to enjoy the manor of Cottesmore until her death, but she resided, partially at least, at her house in St Bartholomew's Close, London, where she died 17th January 1634/5.[18] On her death-bed Mrs Croke appointed Edward Heath her sole executor. She directed: 'All the rest of my goods and Chattells (excepting only my Cupboard of gilt plate which I give to the Childe wch my daughter nowe goeth withall (yf it lyve) (whether it be sonne or daughter) All the rest I say . . . I doe give to my daughter Lucye the wife of Edward Heath Esqr yf she doth lyve or her Childe But yf it shall happen that my daughter and her Childe doe both dye Then I give to my said sonne in lawe Mr Edward Heath Cll and my two Coach horses'.[19]

In spite of the cautious provision made by Croke in his Will for his daughter if she 'shalbe in any want during the life of her husband Edward Heath Esq' by any unkinde vsage of him or his parents', the marriage turned out very well: their fourteen years of happy married life are recorded in the draft of their memorial inscription drawn up by Sir John Heath, Edward's executor, after his death.[20] According to her brother-in-law, Lucy was 'Vxor casta, Parens felix, Matrona pudica: Sarah Viro, Mundo Martha, Maria Deo'. Her husband described her as 'a good wife, a good friend and a good woman'.[21] Twice in his Will Edward refers to her as 'my deare wife', and although he survived her for twenty-four years, he paid her the compliment of remaining a widower.

Nevertheless, it is clear from four undated letters[22] written by Lucy to her husband in the years before the outbreak of the Civil War that Edward was a somewhat neglectful husband, who was frequently absent from home. In one letter, written from London, she refers to his breach of promise, declaring that 'this is not the first time that you have broken to me', and begs him to make haste to town. In another letter Lucy tells Edward that she is unable 'to endure your absence any longer without spoileing my selfe with too much malenchollie'.

The Heaths do not appear to have settled permanently at Cottesmore, although two children were born to them there in 1635 and 1639.[23] When their third daughter, Margaret, was born on 29th October 1636, her parents were living in Verulam House in the parish of St Michael, a suburb of St Albans:[24] this is described as 'our parish' by Edward Heath when recording the burial of a premature daughter in the chancel of the church in January 1638/9.[25] The Heaths' youngest daughter, Lucy, was born at Purleigh, in Essex, 5th August 1641.[26] On the eve of the outbreak of the War, a son, Robert, was born at Cottesmore 7th August 1642.[27]

In 1634 Edward and his brother John were called to the bar, and in 1639 the former became a J.P. In 1634 also Sir Robert Heath was temporarily disgraced. Restored to favour, Sir Robert supported the King, and in 1642 followed him first to York and then to Oxford, where Edward Heath and his wife and his brothers, John,[28] the Revd. George,[29] Robert and Francis,[30] also repaired. In April 1644 Edward was lodging in St Martin's parish,[31] but in May 1645 he and Lucy were living in a house in the parish of Holywell.[32] As will be seen, the surviving Heath children, Margaret, Lucy, and Robert, were left behind.

Early in the War a central and co-ordinating board, known as the Lords Commissioners, had been charged with the direction of a host of committees set up at Oxford.[33] Both Sir Robert Heath and his eldest son were appointed committee Commissioners.[34] Edward's chief duty during the summer of 1643 was to help to oversee the work being executed on the city fortifications. He was the Commissioner responsible for St Aldate's labour, and, together with Thomas Smyth, one of the leading inhabitants, for the contributions in money due from parishioners. On 5th June Heath and Smyth were ordered, in common with the Commissioners and their assistants from the other parishes, to take the names of 'all the inhabitants and resiants' in their parish,[35] and on 7th June the 'Returnes of the Names of the Inhabitants & Lodgers within each seu'all parish from 16 to 60' were made.[36] Only the numbers have been preserved: that for St Aldate's was 395, being surpassed only by St Michael's (402). A week later (14th June) the names of the defaulters in St Aldate's from the work on the fortifications were noted and listed in a detailed house-to-house survey.[37] This, which is in Heath's handwriting, we have reproduced after the 'Accompt' itself, to which it forms an invaluable supplement. Thus Heath was experienced in the compilation of parochial surveys when he was called upon to make the exhaustive one of January 1643/4.

Other documents included in the 'Seige of Oxford' collection are accounts or returns 'for the parish of St Aldates working at the fortifications' between 14th June and 25th August 1643;[38] a number of receipts for money handed over by the St Aldate's collectors;[39] and tables setting out the St Aldate's rota at the bulwarks, all also for the summer of 1643.[40] Of the two memoranda in the first person singular to which reference has been made, one is concerned with 'the seuerall accounts dureing my being a Commissioner' for the fortifications; the other states that 'these seuerall retournes were delivered weekely under my hand & the 2 constables of the parish to a provost marshall appointed from the governor, one David woodfield & vpon the comeing of this governor to his place, the ordering of the works & oversight of the parishes was disposed of by him in another way, since that time what hath been donne I know not'.[41] The Governor in question was Sir Arthur Aston, appointed in August 1643, so it would appear that thenceforward Heath ceased to be concerned with St Aldate's share in the fortifications.

In February 1643/4 a grant was made by their father to Edward and Francis Heath of 'custos brevium et clericus de Nisi Prius' in the Court of King's Bench.[42]

In common with other landed gentry who followed the King to Oxford, Edward Heath had cause for constant anxiety about the fate of his family and tenants, his house, his estates, and his rents. Fortunately, in Katharine Wirdnam the Heaths possessed a devoted member of their household whose letters to her master, written in a small clear script, give a vivid picture of conditions at Cottesmore during his absence.[43]

From these reports we learn that only Margaret, who sent regular messages to her parents, was living at Cottesmore. The two infants, Lucy and Robert, were at nurse at Collyweston in Northamptonshire, where Edward owned the manor. On 12th November 1643 Katharine Wirdnam communicated bad news. Forces from the Parliamentarian garrison of Rockingham Castle had seized Edward's rents and plundered the house of bedding, corn, and halberds.

On 5th December following Lucy Heath addressed a pathetic appeal[44] to Sir Gilbert Pickering, of Titchmarsh, Northamptonshire. He was an M.P. for that county and a strong Parliamentarian, but he had apparently already done Lucy numerous favours. In this letter she states that 'all our estate is sequestered' and tells Pickering of her fears for her children:

'I haue found it a great trouble to me to be so long debarred the comfort of my children haueing when I took my iorney into these partes lefte them behinde me as I supposed for their safety and good, but now to my unspeakable greife besides the itterated losses in my husbands estate I am certainly informed the garrison at Rockingham castle are resolued not onely to fetch away all our goods but to turne my childe that is in my house and family out of doores and make my house a quarter for souldiers'.

Lucy goes on to beg that Pickering

'would be pleased to grante a safe passage through all your forces for foure coach horses and a coach man of my auntes the Lady Crokes[45] to my house and back againe with my coach and childe my waiteing woman one mayde a man on horseback and a footman to attend on her to my auntes at Waterstock in Oxfordshire'.

This appeal was successful. Margaret duly joined her father and mother in Oxford, where she still was in January 1645/6[46] and where she probably remained until the surrender of the city. Lucy and Robert stayed on at Collyweston, where the latter died on 2nd April 1644: he was buried at Cottesmore.[47]

An unsigned draft of a letter from Lucy Heath[48] to a friend, a Mrs Horsman, which must belong to early April 1644 since it refers to the recent death of Robert, gives further particulars of the family's sufferings.

Lucy's correspondent, there can be little doubt, was Elizabeth, wife of Robert Horsman, of Stretton, Rutland, and an aunt of Sir Gilbert Pickering.[49] Stretton lies only a short distance from Cottesmore, and, from what Lucy says, it is clear that the Crokes and Horsmans had been friends as well as neighbours. The Horsmans, however, were Parliamentarians. A Captain Robert Horsman was in command of a troop of Cromwell's in October 1644[50] and he addressed a letter from Rockingham Castle to the Northamptonshire Committee in February

1644/5.[51] He was probably Elizabeth's eldest son, who was named Robert. Horsman may have been responsible for the orders issued from Rockingham in 1643, since Lucy complained to Pickering of the 'hard vsage especially from them whoe I had hoped had soe well loved my dead father and me' that they would have protected the Heath household.

To Mrs Horsman Lucy writes:

'I know you cannot but heare of the rigor is used against me and my husband in the sequestrating of all the estate not leauing any thing for me and my inoccente children but denying so much as might bury my deare babe I haue now newly lost and to this is added this time when I most neede them being big with childe the takeing away of all my lennin even to my very baby clouts and mantels all which I confess I much more prize in regard they were the gift of my deare mother you very [sic] knew'.

Mrs Horsman is entreated to use her influence to get the garments restored.

On 10th June 1644 Edward Heath drafted a letter[52] for his wife to write to Sir Samuel Luke, Governor of Newport Pagnell in Buckinghamshire, with whom she could claim distant kinship through the Crokes. The object of this letter was to beg for a free passage and return for a servant to

'goe to Colliweston in Northamptonshire to enquire after the welfare of a child which I have there at nurse . . . About 2 months since it pleased god to take out of this world a child of mine then at nurse in that place, which was a great griefe to me, since that time I have not heard how my other child there doeth, which makes me so desirous to bee satisfied now therein'.

Whether Luke proved compassionate or not we do not know, but there are numerous references to Lucy, 'very full of talke and a sweet child', in later letters to Edward Heath from Katharine Wirdnam. Lucy eventually went home to Cottesmore.

The child whom Lucy Heath told Elizabeth Horsman that she was expecting was born on 11th October 1644 at Oxford, where he was baptized by the name of John by his uncle George Heath the next day. On 26th November the infant died 'at nurse at Peter Wrenche his house in Great Milton and was buried the next day in Waterstock chancill neere the body of his Great Unkle Sr George Croke, kt'.[53] On the 15th of the month Lady Croke, who included 'Littil pegge' in her respects, wrote[54] to the child's father that she had sent someone to see him and that he was then very well.

Six months later Edward lost his wife, probably worn out by her many pregnancies and maternal disappointments, at the early age of twenty-seven. She died at the Heaths' house in Holywell, Oxford, on Ascension Eve, 14th May 1645, and was buried in All Saints' church on the night of the 16th. A note in the earliest Baptismal Register (1559-1810), written between the entries for 13th and 21st July 1645, records: 'Memorandu' that the 16 day of May 1645 the body of Lucy Heath wife of Edward Heath Esq' was deposited in the vault on the north side of All Hallowes Church in the city of Oxon (being comended thither by a full congreaon, & wth the vse of the publike prayers of the church, and particularly those appointed for buriall by the minister &) there to remaine vntill the sayd Edward Heath, or any of her ffriends shall require the same to be deliuer'd out, & then to be deliu'd accordingly — Witnesse the Hands of us the minister & churchwardens. 1645'.[55] In his *Diarium* Edward relates Lucy's wish to be buried eventually at Cottesmore and yet not to be embalmed, and gives minute details of the arrangements accordingly made for the preservation of her body.[56] The removal 'after the surrender of Oxford was p'formed by divers of my tenents of Cotsmore, Barrow and Colliweston going with a coach thither for the corps, which accordingly was brought and leyd in Cotsmore church vault according to her desire on Friday the 31 day of July 1646'. Her coffin plate was discovered in the vault in 1860.[57] Edward stayed on in Oxford until the surrender, a public catastrophe which followed hard upon his personal tragedies. On 4th September 1646 he begged to compound on the Oxford Articles for Delinquency in going there. He renewed his petition on 27th February 1646/7, having been hindered in prosecuting his composition by the embezzlement of many of his writings. He was admitted to compound on the Oxford Articles and was fined £700 on 1st April 1647.[58]

After the War Heath retired to Cottesmore. In September 1646 motherless ten-year-old Margaret was dispatched to school at Richmond.[59] In December 1656 Edward was assessed as a Delinquent at £80.[60] The Heath Papers shew that he suffered imprisonment during the Interregnum, being discharged from restraint 27th August 1659.[61] In a petition which he addressed to Charles II in 1661 he describes himself as having been 'for his constant loyalty during the late Rebellion . . . heavily persecuted with Sequestration Decimation & Imprisonments'.[62] It is possible that the Edward and George Heath for whose apprehension a warrant was issued on 29th March 1650 were Edward and his brother George.[63] With other Rutland gentlemen he joined in signing an address of congratulation to Charles II on his restoration, 26th June 1660,[64] and was created K.B. on the occasion of the Coronation 23rd April 1661. He died 30th August 1669[65] and on 5th September was buried at Cottesmore,[66] 'in the vault there belonging to my house and upon the body of my deare wife Lucy Heath', so runs the wish expressed in his Will.

Sir Edward's Will was made 6th July 1668 and proved on 15th September 1670.[67] His daughter Lucy having died at Cottesmore at the age of six, 11th November, 1647,[68] there was only one surviving child, Margaret, wife of Sir Thomas Fanshawe (1628-1705), of Jenkins, Barking, Clerk of the Crown, whom she had married in 1656/7 without her father's consent or approbation.[69] Lady Fanshawe died in 1674, leaving a daughter, Susanna, who, in 1682, married the Hon. Baptist Noel, third son of Baptist Noel, third Viscount Campden (1611-1682), the well-known Cavalier, and ancestor of the present Earl of Gainsborough. The manor of Cottesmore passed to the Fanshawes and their descendants. When making his numerous bequests, Heath directed that 'one full Tenth part of the cleare yearely revenue of my share . . . of my adventure in the lands woods and Iron works about Ennyscorthy in Ireland' should annually be applied 'in the first place towards the reliefe of the widowes or children of any Orthodox sequestered ministers within the Kingdome of England and dominion of Wales. And afterwards towards the reliefe of any truly loyall officers or souldiers or their widowes being in want'. Sir Edward's gift to 'the Rector of the parish Church of Cotsmoor for the tyme being and to his successors forever of my greate Polyglot Bible published by Doctor Walton being bound vp in six volumes in folio with the deale box wherein they are' has unfortunately disappeared, as the Rector informs us. His direction that 'the somme of one hundred and fiftie pounds be bestowed on the erecting of a decent monument for my deare wife Lucy Heath to be placed over the Vault in Cotsmore Church where she lyes buried with her owne father and mother' met with an equally unlucky fate. As has been seen, Sir John Heath composed a draft for a memorial inscription to Sir Edward and his wife but the monument seems never to have been executed. No more fitting words with which to end this brief biographical sketch can be found than those used of Heath by his brother: 'Vir, Deo Pius, Regi Fidus, Propinquiis Benignus, omnibus Probus, sibi Castus'.

THE ACCOMPT

From its compiler we now turn to a consideration of the 'Accompt' itself. This for the student of Oxford's 'evacuee' population during the Civil War, scrutinized in conjunction with closely-related documents in the 'Seige of Oxford' collection, affords a unique source of information.

The presence of 'strangers' in Oxford during the War years has been taken too much for granted: the subject has never been explored in detail. Exactly what kind of people besides the military, came? Who housed these civilians, and the soldiers, too? What sort of billets did they have? To provide answers to these questions is one of the main purposes of this study.

At least as early as May 1643 King Charles shewed awareness of the problem of the evacuees. In an order dated the fifteenth of the month and addressed to Sir Christopher Hatton, later Comptroller of the Household, seven other knights, and four esquires, of whom one was Edward Heath, he states:

'Whereas in our Citty of Oxford besides the Vniuersity and the Members of the Colledges and Halls thereof and besides the naturall Inhabitants of the Citty, there are now there residing not onely Our owne Court and part of our Army, but also many others come thither from seuerall parts of the kingdome some out of their good affections to attend Vs, and some out of iust cause of feares and daungers for the defence and protection of their owne persons, And all of them being heere must necessarily be prouided for of Victualls before hand, if this place should be put to any streight, which would be perillous for them . . . We thinke it fitt that a Magazine of Corne and other Victualls should be prouided before hand proportionable to the persons who are to be sustayned in this place'.[70]

This Proclamation was followed up by the appointment by the Commissioners of two sets of surveyors of provisions. The first was to survey the provisions of 'strangers' lodging in colleges and halls: the second was to act in the same capacity in the parishes, taking into account both inhabitants and evacuees.[71] The overseers appointed for St Aldate's were Sir George Benyon and Mr Thomas Nevill. Benyon, a London mercer, was himself lodging in the parish. Nevill, a City of London draper, was a brother-in-law of the Secretary of State, Sir Edward Nicholas.

At this period the King was concerned with the matter of supplies. Eight months later it was the question of billets which was exercising his mind. On 22nd December 1643 Charles had issued a Proclamation 'for the Assembling the Members of both Houses at Oxford, upon the occasion of the Invasion by the Scots'.[72] Obviously, accommodation would be needed for these important persons: of the forty-five peers and well over a hundred commoners who initially responded, many would have been newcomers. The 'Lords & other his Mats Commissrs for the fortifying Victualing & Cleansing the City of Oxford' were accordingly commanded in January 1643/4 to make a survey of all persons lodging in colleges, halls, and private houses. For this purpose the Commissioners divided up the parishes, colleges, and halls among themselves. Were all their 'accompts' extant, we should, of course, possess a complete inventory of the Royalist evacuees in Oxford when Parliament opened on 22nd January. As it is, only one 'accompt' — that for St Aldate's parish — has, by good chance, survived, to cast a beam of light amidst much darkness. That the survivor should be for St Aldate's is fortunate. Not only was it one of the largest parishes, but the presence within its boundaries at Christ Church of the King and Court caused the billeting there of an exceptional number of notable soldiers and civilians, as well as officers and men of the Lifeguard of Foot, and many Royal servants.

The instructions issued to Heath for making his survey were both clear and cogent. They read as follows:

'Die Sabbati 13° Januarij 1643

Whereas a Strickt and exact Accompt is by his Ma:ts Comaund to be taken and presented to him of the names & quallities of all Lodgers and Inmates with their Children and Servants, of both Sexes, wch lye in any Colledge, Hall, or private Howse in the aforesaid Cittie This Board to the end the same may be performed accordingly, Hath divided the service amongst themselves, and ordered, That Edward Heath esq' shall visit the pish of St Aldates Pembrock Colledge and New Inne hall And to Call to him for Assistance ye Constables, Churchwardens, or any other pson or psons he shall thinke fitt, And to the end this may be performed wth that exactness his Matie requires, It is thought fitt to beare this Order about him, to the end the respective Maisters of Colledges, Halls, and Inhabitants of this Cittye may take notice thereof Who (in case they doe not Clearly & faithfully giue a note in writeing vnder their hands to be returned to this Board, of all Lodgers & Inmates as aforesaid in their seuerall Colledges, halls, or howses, wth their Quallities Retineues (and Ages, if Children) neither exempting any of the Kinges, or Queenes servants &c. Comanders, Officers or other Souldiers) their neglect wilbe interp'ted as a high Contempt of his Mats Authority, and they proceeded against as harboror' of Spies & persons ill affected to his Mats service.'[73]

Although no streets are named in the 'Accompt', our study of the householders listed in it, has enabled us to follow Heath as, armed with this formidable warrant, he made his round on 23rd January 1643/4. He began his task at the most northerly house in St Aldate's parish on the west side of Fish Street (the modern St Aldate's Street). Then, as still today, the parish boundary ran across the street several doors south of Carfax: but whereas in the seventeenth century St Aldate's marched with St Martin's, the latter has now been incorporated in All Saints'. Heath proceeded south as far as Pennyfarthing Street (the modern Pembroke Street). This he turned down, following the north side of the street as far as the boundary with St Ebbe's parish, when he crossed and retraced his steps along the south side back to Fish Street. Going south again, he called at the long-since demolished houses which masked the east end of St Aldate's church, passed the Christ Church Almshouses (now absorbed by Pembroke College), left the city by the South Gate and then entered Sleying Lane (the modern Brewer Street) in order to interrogate the owners of the only two houses situated there: these were both on the southern side, facing the city wall which formed the lane's northern boundary. When he regained the main thoroughfare, Heath found himself at Tower Hill, and shortly afterwards in Grandpont or Grandpool, the suburban continuation of Fish Street, which he followed down to Folly Bridge. In doing so he had to cross over the shire brook which then separated the counties of Oxfordshire and Berkshire, a few houses in St Aldate's parish actually lying in the latter. Stopping short at the bridge, Heath crossed the street and called at the Wharf House, after which he traversed the east side of Grandpont, Tower Hill, and Fish Street, skirting the façade of Christ Church and crossing New Lane (the modern Blue Boar Street) to reach the last house in the parish on that side before the boundary with St Martin's parish. Thus Heath ended up at a spot exactly opposite that from which he had started.

In the great majority of cases the houses are listed in the 'Accompt' in the order in which they actually stood: in a few instances neighbouring tenements are wrongly placed, which suggests that Heath did not always find the owner in at his first call and had to go back again. But only one house, that of John Dunte, a basketmaker in Grandpont, appears among houses on the opposite side of the street. It is legitimate to guess that Heath met Dunte across the way from his home and took particulars there and then.

We have seen that Heath's instructions empowered him to enlist the help of parish officials and others. It is probable that he was accompanied on his perambulation by one of the constables or churchwardens of St Aldate's. It also seems likely that the householders had been notified of the day of the visitation and that some of them, at any rate, would have had the required information ready. When all the notes had been collected, they would have been written up into the 'Accompt' as we have it for the use of the King and the Governor of Oxford, Heath having a fair copy made for himself for reference purposes. It is this fair copy which has been preserved among his papers. With the exception of the words which follow the heading, 'Taken 23° Jan: 1643', and the last two paragraphs of notes at the end, the document is not in Heath's hand.

A striking feature of the 'Accompt' is the over-all accuracy with which the 'strangers' ' names are recorded. A few blunders occur: 'Colonel Henderforde' for 'Colonel Sir John Henderson', 'Sir Henry Radcliffe' for 'Sir Henry Radley', 'The Lord Wray' for 'Mr Edward Wray' are some exceptions which prove the rule.

THE STRANGERS

The Royalists billeted in St Aldate's constitute, as has already been said, a particularly interesting set of evacuees, and cannot therefore be regarded as completely typical of those who during the years 1642 to 1646 came to Oxford 'from seuerall parts of the Kingdome' to be accommodated in private houses as distinct from colleges and halls. Beginning at the top end of the scale, and taking into account the Defaulters' List of June 1643 as well, the 'Lord Generall', Patrick Ruthven, Earl of Forth, was undoubtedly the most important person lodging in the parish. Other high-ranking officers include Sir John Henderson, (Sir) George Lisle, Sir Richard Cave, Colonel David Scrymgeour, Major William Legge, Sir Charles Vavasour, Sergeant-Major Leighton, and Sergeant-Major Markham. The nobility is represented, among others, by the Earls of Bath, Carlisle, and Lindsey (Lord High Chamberlain), Lord Arundell, Lord Spencer, and Lord Wentworth. A French lord, St Paul, and his brother also appear. There are, too, a number of baronets and knights, of whom Sir Francis Windebank, ex-Secretary of State, deserves special mention. Several members of the Lower House were lodged in St Aldate's: of these Sir Frederick Cornwallis, Sir Richard Lee, and Sir John Price spring readily to mind. Special groups, as has been noted, are the officers and men of the Lifeguard of Foot, who have a separate section devoted to them in Part II, and the Royal servants. Of these latter the Messengers, whose profession in Wartime had become distinctly more hazardous, form an especially interesting category. Among individual servants, mention may be made of the King's surgeon, Michael Andrewes, his tailor, Andrew Morrison, his barber, Thomas Davies, his apothecary, John Wolfgang Rumler (a native of Augsburg, who can little have expected to find himself quartered in a tailor's house in Oxford), and the King's sempstress, Mrs Julian Elliot. The tracing of obscurer figures has proved a rewarding task: William White, a poulterer to the King, Lawrence Ball and George Wild, the King's bakers, William Langley, who provided wax-lights, Samuel Nurse, a coal-carrier to the Court, and many more. The number of Scots amongst the servants is noticeable.

In connexion with the Royal servants one point must be emphasized. The Stuarts, and Charles II in particular, have often been accused by those who like to make sweeping generalisations, of wholesale ingratitude towards those who had served them faithfully. To follow Charles I to Oxford did often call for 'good affections', fidelity, and self-sacrifice. Historians have thought too little of the upheaval which leaving London must have meant for these men, their wives, and sometimes quite young families. But generalisations about the ingratitude meted out to this loyalty simply will not bear investigation. Anyone who has taken the trouble to study the *Calendars of Treasury Books*, cannot escape the stubborn evidence of Charles II's appreciation of loyalty in those dark Oxford days, which he was never, incidentally, ashamed to recall in prosperity. Wherever possible, we have followed the post-Restoration careers of the surviving Royal servants billeted in St Aldate's. It is remarkable how large a proportion regained their positions and had their sons associated with them in their offices. Claims and credentials were clearly conscientiously investigated. Naturally, among the avalanche of petitions which descended upon the King and his advisers in 1660 and the years immediately following, some were bound to go unanswered. William Langley had a difficult struggle to regain his post in the Royal Chandry, and one has much sympathy with Peter Maber, a blind man, who was passed over when the list of Royal Messengers was drawn up.

A major problem for Charles II at the Restoration was the question of the arrears of salaries and wages due from his father. During the Civil War, and indeed in many cases since the outbreak of hostilities with the Scots in 1639,[74] these had perforce often gone unpaid, and it can only be supposed that the Household lived largely on credit, a source of suffering all round. It is true that in 1649 Parliament had ordered the sale of the Royal Collection of pictures and other possessions largely with a view to meeting with the proceeds the claims of the late King's servants and creditors who were not Delinquents.[75] Examination of the lists of warrant-holders upon the lists of 1649/50 and 1651 and the warrants themselves, preserved in the Public Record Office, has revealed that few of the servants lodging in St Aldate's in 1643/4 benefited by such relief as was afforded. A serious situation remained to confront the new King: with this, handicapped by inadequate resources, he did his best to cope. The faithful Thomas Davies received his back pension (for seven years) and a handsome expenses allowance. The widow of Michael Andrewes, who, when he died in 1646, was owed six years' pension, amounting to £900, was less fortunate. She received her husband's salary for one quarter in 1661.

In the chapter on 'Military Orders' in his *Siege of Oxford* (1932) F. J. Varley states that 'the practice of "billeting" generally did not result in ready money payment, but a system of "billeting tickets" was in vogue which, if the tickets were not readily convertible into cash or its equivalent, would differ little from "free quartering".' It seems likely that the method employed for billeting soldiers may have been used in the case of civilians: Heath's papers shed no light on this point. What can be said is that, either by official direction, or in some cases owing to personal application, a certain amount of discrimination was employed by the billeting officers in the placing of the 'strangers'. On the whole, the more substantial landlords tended to lodge the better-class 'strangers', while the poorer householders took in humbler folk. Lord Forth, for example, lodged with the prosperous Thomas Smyth, Edward Heath's colleague in 1643, who was elected mayor of Oxford in September of that year. Corporals and private soldiers had to be content with the accommodation of small craftsmen's houses. Families of all ranks were kept together, and more distant connexions received consideration in this matter. In 1643 Lord Forth had his two sons-in-law with him; in 1643/4 Dr Clayton, Master of Pembroke College, was housing his son's mother-in-law (and no one else!); brothers-in-law, Parker and Ogleby, are found sharing quarters. Sir Richard Cave stayed with his brother, an Oxford brewer, despite the latter's Parliamentarian sympathies. Two Frenchmen, Monsieur du Moulin and Sir William St Ravy, were placed under one roof, presumably because they were considered kindred spirits.

What is absolutely certain is that practically every house in St Aldate's was requisitioned and that the houses must generally have been full to bursting, literally crammed from cellar to attic. Even the tiniest, which we know had only one room up and one room down, were forced to hold several soldiers at need: they must have slept packed like sardines. The total number of 'strangers' is given at the end of the 'Accompt' as 408. Those of us who remember the congested conditions prevailing in Oxford during the Second World War, can sympathize with our predecessors of three centuries ago.

No indication of the Oxford landlords' point of view appears to have survived. It is otherwise with the evacuees, three of whose experiences it is worth recording. The first is enshrined in a well-known passage, but it applies so aptly to the St Aldate's scene that it is worth quoting in full. Ann, Lady Fanshawe (whose husband, Sir Richard, was a first cousin once removed of Edward Heath's future son-in-law) writes in her *Memoirs*: 'My father commanded my sister and myself to come to him to Oxford, where the Court then was; but we that had till that hour lived in great plenty and great order found ourselves like fishes out of water, and the scene so changed that we knew not at all how to act any part but obedience. For from as good house as any gentleman of England had we come to a baker's house in an obscure street, and from rooms well furnished to lie in a very bad bed in a garret; to one dish of meat, and that not the best ordered; no money, for we were as poor as Job; nor clothes more than a man or two brought in their cloak bags. We had the perpetual discourse of losing and gaining of towns and men; at the windows the sad spectacle of war, sometimes plague, sometimes sicknesses of other kinds by reason of so many people being packed together, as I believe there never was before of that quality; always want; yet I must needs say that most bore it with a martyr-like cheerfulness.'[76]

Captain John Windebank and Sir Robert Winde took their tribulations less philosophically. The former, in December 1643, had been having trouble over his billet, as appears from a letter preserved among the Manuscripts of the Earl of Bath: 'they made him a stalking horse to keep the house, and then turned him and his horse out of doors'.[77] Winde, 'an ancient man', privileged as an attendant of the House of Commons, was quartered in a house in Catte Street, whence he was ejected forcibly at night, about December 1644, by Dudley Ruse, brother of Scout Master Ruse. His unpublished petition for the restoration of his rights, addressed with success to the Lords of Parliament, is preserved among the Walker Papers in the British Museum.[78]

An interesting sequel to the parochial surveys is to be found in an unpublished Proclamation dated 2nd February 1643 [i.e. 1644], preserved among the Lindsay Manuscripts at Belvoir Castle, which speaks for itself:

'By the Kinge:

A Proclamation Commandinge all officers of the Army not members of eyther house or of the Garrison forthwith to depart this Citty

Whereas diuers officers of horse and foot of our Army that are not of this Garrison doe not only absent themselues from theire seuerall Comaunds but likewise possesse themselues of lodgeings and stable roome in seuerall Colledges and Halls in the Vniuesity [sic] and in other partes of this Citty whereby the Members of both houses by or proclamacon heere assembled want that fittinge accomodacon for themselues seruants and horses as is necessary and as wee assured them by or said proclamacon Wee doe therefore heereby strightly [sic] Charge and Comaund all and singular officers and souldiers of or Army (not beeinge officers Generall or of this Garrison) forthwith to depart this Citty & Vniuersity and to repaire to their respectiue Garrisons and Qrs and to leaue behind them listes of their respectiue Chambers and Stables and those who haue been lodged in Colledges and halls to leaue the keys of their Chambers with the heads or principalls of such Colledges and Halls and those lodged in the Citty to leaue theire Keys with the Gouernor Whereby the Members of both houses heere assemble[d] may be accomodated with lodgeings and Stables to their satisfacon, heereunto Wee Comaund all officers and others of or Army whome it may in any sorte Concerne to yeald all due obedience at their pills

Giuen &c 2 ffeb.

verso: 2 ffeb: 1643 A Proclamation for ye. departure of ye. officers of ye. Army out of Oxford.'[79]

In the task of identifying and recording the careers of the 'strangers' who figure in the St Aldate's 'Accompt' and Defaulters' List, we have made use of a variety of sources, beginning with the standard reference books — Peerages, Baronetages, Heraldic Visitations, family histories and papers — and such obvious quarries as the *Calendars* of State Papers, Committees for Compounding and the Advance of Money, and Treasury Books. For Members of Parliament, M. F. Keeler's study of the personnel of the Long Parliament, published in 1954, and *The Names of the Lords and Commons Assembled in the Pretended Parliament at Oxford, Ianuary 1643*, published in 1646, have proved invaluable. Extensive use has been made of manuscript Wills and Administrations and of Parish Registers both printed and unprinted. The Registers of St Margaret's, Westminster, which have been printed down to 1675 (burials to 1661 only), and those of St Martin's-in-the-Fields, which unfortunately have been published only as far as 1636, have been of great assistance, especially for the lesser Royal servants, many of whom were living in one or other of these parishes until the outbreak of the War. For the servants, too, official lists of the Households of the King, Queen, and Prince, preserved in the Public Record Office and the British Museum, have been extremely helpful, especially one of His Majesty's Servants in Ordinary of the Chamber drawn up in 1641 and actually altered and brought up to date while the Court was at Oxford. We have also been well served by a list of the Messengers of His Majesty's Chamber in Ordinary sworn before 1644, which includes certain men sworn at Oxford. Essential for the soldiers was *A List of [Indigent] Officers* (1663), of which there is a copy in the Public Record Office (S.P. 29/68): It is this which gives us the skeleton of Charles I's army. Another stand-by has been the Card Index of Royalist Soldiers who served in the armies of Charles I and Charles II compiled by one of us (Peter Young).

All the extant college Buttery Books and Bursars' Accounts for the War period have been examined for lists of 'strangers', and any migrations to or from St Aldate's have been noted.[80] The general subject of 'strangers' lodging in the colleges would require a separate study: to have attempted it here would have swelled this book to undue proportions. Taken together, these sources have yielded a quite surprising amount of information which has done much to bring to life even the humble folk whose names are included in the two surveys. It is gratifying how comparatively few names of any rank remain unidentified.

Although, as has been seen, the St Aldate's 'Accompt' is the only one to survive from the survey of January 1643/4, lists of Royalists lodging in the parishes of St Martin's and All Saints' about April 1644, in the handwriting of Edward Heath, exist among the 'Seige of Oxford' documents.[81] These we have printed, with biographical notes, in Appendix I. Further records of evacuees can be gleaned from the notes of Anthony Wood and also from the Registers of the Cathedral, parish churches, and college chapels. Memorial inscriptions are another useful source.

THE LANDLORDS

It is not only for the 'strangers' that the 'Accompt' is of importance. Equally valuable is the light which study of this document helps to throw upon an Oxford parish in the reign of Charles I, its inhabitants and its topography. We can learn something, too, of the effects of the War upon the parishioners and how certain of them reacted to it. For the student of local and social history here is a veritable mine of information.

At first sight, there was hardly a name among the householders which meant anything to us. Now, very few of the seventy-four men and women remain unidentified. Providentially, the St Aldate's Parish Chest is rich in documents, the most regrettable lacuna (and it is a serious one) being the earliest Register, which began in 1538:[82] the extant one only starts in 1678. This loss is in part atoned for by extracts made by Wood (who may have been guilty of not returning the original volume) from 1538 to 1676,[83] and by payments for burials in the church recorded in the Churchwardens' Accounts, which go back as far as the fifteenth century. Especially useful for the War period are the six parish taxation lists, five for 1645 and a double one for 1647, inscribed in the Churchwardens' Book: details of these are given later. St Aldate's owned a number of houses in the parish, and the splendid series of leases has proved extremely helpful both biographically and topographically.

The Oxford City Archives preserved in the Town Hall, especially the enrolments of apprentices and admissions of freemen, constitute another invaluable source.[84] As in the case of the evacuees, recourse has been had to Wills and Administrations: those of the landlords and landladies were often proved at Oxford, in the Archdeaconry and Consistory Courts and the Court of the Chancellor of the University, all preserved in the Bodleian Library. The special information derived from Inventories will be mentioned in connexion with the houses. Unpublished Parish Registers have been consulted more frequently in our research on the landlords than for the 'strangers'. There have been some unexpected finds in these. For instance, a friend's suggestion that the family of William Blay, one of the sacristans of Christ Church and an ex-stonemason, might be found at Iffley, was followed by a telephone conversation with the Rector, a hasty bicycle ride, and the rewarding discovery in the earliest Register of Blay's parents' names, his baptism, and his marriage. Finally, search in the college Buttery Books and Bursars' Account Books has disclosed the activities of some of the tradesman landlords, particularly the brewers and bakers.

Of the seventy-four landlords, fifty-eight were men and sixteen women. Of these we have traced the professions and trades of fifty-seven men and one woman (a widow), and the avocations of the husbands of seven other widows, making a total of sixty-five. The following table gives the figures:

Brewers	(8 + 2 widows of brewers)	10
Tailors		9
College Servants	(7, one an ex-stonemason + 2 widows of servants)	9
Bakers		4
Surgeons	(2 + 1 widow of a surgeon)	3
Coopers		3
Lawyers		2
Smiths		2
Tanners		2
Boatmen		2
Cordwainers	(2 widows of cordwainers)	2
Butchers	(one was a woman)	2
Innkeepers		2
Joiners		1
Carpenters		1
Barbers		1
Physicians	(also Master of Pembroke)	1
Chandlers		1
Glovers	(1 widow of a glover)	1
Cutlers		1
Basketmakers		1
Poulterers		1
Carriers		1
Parchmentmakers		1
Mercers		1
Slatters or Plasterers		1
		65

It will be noticed that the brewers, tailors, and college servants constitute much the largest groups. The last-named form an interesting section, which includes three manciples and two sacristans. Being among 'privileged persons' of the University, their names are usually entered in the Matriculation Register, and they and their widows were entitled to have their Wills proved in the Chancellor's Court. The widows of the 'privileged' are the earliest women to be described as 'of the University of Oxford'.

Of the forty-two landlords whose place of origin we have been able to recover, twenty-five were drawn from outside Oxford, while only seventeen were sons of her citizens. The majority of these 'foreigners', as they would have been termed in the seventeenth century, hailed from villages widely scattered over Oxfordshire. There would seem to have been a decided tendency in the reigns of Elizabeth I and James I for Oxfordshire yeomen and husbandmen to send at least one son to be apprenticed to a trade in the county town. But there were also natives of Berkshire, Wiltshire, and Northamptonshire, and even one of Yorkshire. The fathers of two others came to Oxford from a West Riding town, while those of three further

Oxford-born men originally belonged, two to Oxfordshire and one to Northamptonshire. Once established in Oxford as freemen, they had every inducement to stay there. John Keen, the solitary St Aldate's carpenter, removed to London, but he remembered his native city in his Will. The departure of Edward Carpenter, one of the brewers, to London, during the Commonwealth, was due to circumstances unconnected with trade.

The differences in wealth and status within the parish were considerable. Dr Clayton, the two lawyers, John Holloway and Unton Croke, John Earle, the mercer, and the brewers, especially the three brothers Thomas, Oliver, and John Smyth, Edward Carpenter, and Walter Cave, were all well-to-do. Thomas Lapworth, the carrier, John Richardson, one of the boatmen, John Dunte, the basketmaker, were poor men. The parish taxation lists and the Subsidy of 1648 afford a good indication of prosperity or the reverse: we have given the Subsidy assessment figures in every case.

The St Aldate's records confirm that town-life in the first half of the seventeenth century was singularly free from class feeling. Two tradesmen, Anthony Yates, the chandler, and John Wilmott, one of the bakers, were scions of Oxfordshire county families whose Arms they used. One of the brewers, Robert Wilson, married the daughter of an ancient family, the Doylys of Stadhampton. Naturally, marriages within the parish were not infrequent, but the ranks of bride and bridegroom sometimes differed. The son of one of the tailors, William Corpson, became M.A. of Christ Church, and the mother of Richard Miles, a servant of The House, could claim Dr John Bancroft, Master of University College, as her friend and appoint him the overseer of her Will. The church was a bond which drew together rich and poor. The absence of Puritan Christian names among the landlords and landladies is suggestive: of the few bearing Old Testament names, one, Abel Parne, was an ardent Royalist.[85] There was a single recusant among them, the brewer Carpenter.

For the student of seventeenth-century churchwardens' and overseers' books the popular myth (which owes much to Dickens) that the parish officials were almost always harsh and insensitive men is exasperating. Again, the St Aldate's Accounts underline the essential humanity of their outlook. When the wife of one of the smiths, Miles Godfrey, died leaving him with an infant, the parish paid for the nursing of his child. When the cutler, William Deverall, 'fell into his frenzy', two men were paid for watching him. Grants to the aged, poor, and needy were the accepted rule.

Such matters belonged to peacetime routine. What indications are there of how St Aldate's parish was affected by the War? On the one hand, it is touching to see how old customs were kept up. For instance, 'hollie and Ivie' were provided as usual for the church at Christmas 1644, and the traditional gifts to the brewers' draymen continued to be made by the colleges. The time-honoured 'drinking' when the churchwardens' annual accounts were presented was not foregone. On the other side of the picture, we find money expended by the parish on shrouds for soldiers who died in some of our landlords' houses. Disease — first 'the sickness' in 1643 and then the plague in 1644 — was, as Lady Fanshawe recorded, an ever-present shadow. John Lambe, one of our landlords, was 'shut up' with the latter disease, and several more (including householders named in the Defaulters' List) succumbed to one or other. From the papers of Edward Heath we learn of the appointment of three parishioners (all landlords in the 'Accompt') to 'take care of infected persons'. Almost as unpleasant must have been the local taxes occasioned by the War. In May 1645 the inhabitants of St Aldate's paid a tax for the mayor shutting up the gates; in June for a magazine for victuals for the poor and for the relief of 'visited' people; in July and December for the Governor of the Oxford garrison. In June 1647, a year after the surrender of the city, the parishioners were paying for the quartering of 142 soldiers (Parliamentarian ones now) by virtue of a warrant from the mayor and aldermen.[86] The Proclamation of April 1643 ordering all arms, above what was necessary for private use, to be handed over to the King's stores, with penalties for defaulters, must have been a considerable grievance, especially for those who were hostile to him at heart.[87] Debts from the 'wanting men' among the 'strangers' must have piled up alarmingly. Even to the well-disposed, the familiar sight of the King coming and going through the great gate of Christ Church for three and a half years during the winter months, can scarcely have compensated for these evils.

This brings us to the subject of the attitude of the parishioner-landlords of St Aldate's towards the War. It is commonly held that, by and large, the University was for the King and the town sided with Parliament. There were, however, many ardent Royalists among the citizens. A first-hand account by a citizen who favoured the Parliamentary party of the proceedings when Sir John Byron occupied Oxford on 28th August 1642, is of great value in this connexion.[88] Among the King's men living in St Aldate's, Thomas Smyth was particularly prominent: he became lieutenant-colonel of the City Regiment, and, as has been seen, housed the Lord General. Other St Aldate's supporters of King Charles named in the above-mentioned document are Edward Carpenter, Robert Wilson, David Woodfeild, and Abel Parne. The three latter were described as Delinquents in 1648,[89] and both Wilson and Parne (a baker) were turned out of the City Council in the 'purge' of that year. Woodfeild, as we know, became a provost-marshal in 1643, and he was active in training troops. Henry Vaughan, a tailor, was said to have been a sergeant (presumably in the City Regiment) when he was described as a Delinquent. Thomas Hawkes, another baker, was also listed as a Delinquent. As for the University element in the parish, Dr Clayton was strongly for the King and encouraged the enlistment of members of Pembroke College in the Royalist army. Pembroke is the only college for which we have a contemporary list of Cavalier soldiers:[90] the Master's labours, it seems, were not in vain. John Holloway was deprived of the stewardship of New College by the Parliamentary Visitors in 1648. Of the college servants who were still alive and not retired when the Visitation took place, Thomas Seymour, manciple of Corpus Christi College, refused to submit and was dismissed. The sons of boatman John Richardson were stout Royalists, so perhaps their father may have been one also.

The most influential men in St Aldate's to sympathize with the King's enemies were Unton Croke (a first cousin of Lucy Heath), John Smyth, and Walter Cave. It will be recalled that the two latter had Royalist brothers, yet further instances of the way in which families were divided over the War. John Smyth, one of the two M.P.s for Oxford in the Long Parliament, was strongly against the King in 1642, but he did sit in the Oxford Parliament and he lost his seat on the City Council in 1648. Cave's house was searched by the Royalists at the beginning of the War. George Dixon and William Blay, the two Christ Church sacristans, submitted to the Visitors, but this may simply have been due to the fear of small men of losing their livelihoods. Blay had had no scruple in ringing the Cathedral bells for Royalist victories. The later career of tailor John Lambe suggests that he was a Parliamentarian at heart. He, James Pinnell and Matthew Langley, the tanners, William Stephens, a well-to-do butcher, Cave, and Earle, all retained their seats on the Council after the 'purge'. Of the opinions of the many others we know nothing.

TOPOGRAPHY

Finally, we must consider the value of the 'Accompt' for the study of the topography of St Aldate's parish. Every student of Oxford topography lies under an immeasurable debt to the erudition and industry of the late Revd. Dr H.E. Salter. His *Survey of Oxford*,[91] which includes the South-East and South-West Wards (in which St Aldate's lay) has proved the indispensable starting-point for our investigations and has provided us with a wealth of information. The 'Accompt' however, appears to have been unknown to Dr Salter: he would have been the first to appreciate the significance of what virtually amounts to a parochial street directory for 1643/4.

It is essential to try to visualize the appearance of the parish as it then was. This we can readily do from the plan of Oxford city contained in Loggan's *Oxonia Illustrata* (1675): the relevant portion is published by us as Plate 10. From this we can see that St Aldate's was then, as now, a long and narrow parish, divided into eastern and western portions (lying respectively in the South-East and South-West Wards) by Fish Street and Grandpont, the 'kinges highe streete' as the phrasing of many contemporary leases has it. The parish then, as now, began a little way south of Carfax on either side and extended beyond the Thames at Folly Bridge. The street crossed two streams, Trill Mill, about half way down, and the Shire Brook near the southern end. Only on the western side of the thoroughfare were there side streets, Pennyfarthing Street and Sleying Lane. On the east side of Grandpont, the suburb which lay outside the South Gate, the houses backed on to Christ Church Meadow: on the west on to a complex of waterways.

The mid-seventeenth-century inhabitant of St Aldate's would find it hard to recognize his parish today. The church stands on the same site, but has been greatly restored, and the parish houses which masked the east end have gone. Christ Church and its one-time Almshouses still confront one another across the street, but Tom Tower is an innovation and the Almshouses are now part of Pembroke. The west side of the former Grandpont is cut by several streets, and there is a great gash on the east side where a number of old houses were demolished to make room for the Christ Church Memorial Garden in the mid-nineteen-twenties. The City Police Station has accounted for more. On the other hand, the squalid excrescences further south, which did not exist in the seventeenth century, and which formerly helped to give St Aldate's so bad a name, have also been cleared away. As late as 1923 Dr A.L. Rowse could write in his Diary: 'I walked down St Aldate's into the wretchedest poor quarter that there is in Oxford. From Christ Church to Folly Bridge is squalid enough; but turn into the courts and alleys that run out from the street and the place is worse than one would think possible; dismal shanties with roofs all askew and walls cracking; no drainage, no gardens, all the washing hung out on lines across the alleys.'[92] Comparatively few of the old houses remain. These include a group on the east side of the former Grandpont, not far from Folly Bridge, and another on the south side of Pembroke Street, as well as the houses of landlords Thomas Smyth, Unton Croke, Richard Miles, Thomas Seymour, and John Henslow. Fortunately, pictorial records exist of others: for example, the Church House (William Corpson) and the Blue Boar (John Mander).

Today St Aldate's is thronged with traffic, but, as the main road to the South, it must always have been an extremely noisy and busy thoroughfare. In Wartime, too, troops would have been constantly marching up and down: during the winter months the abiding presence of the red coats of the Lifeguard lent colour and bustle to the scene.

Turning to the subject of the individual houses, it has been possible to discover the exact site of nearly every one and to plot them on a sketch-map. This has been due in large measure to the fact that just over one-third (twenty-six, to be exact) were the property of Oxford colleges. Of these, fifteen belonged to Magdalen, which owned a solid block in north-west Fish Street, four to Christ Church, two to Oriel, two to New College, one to Merton, one to Balliol, and one to All Souls. These colleges have been most generous in allowing us to work through their Lease Ledgers and Account Books. In this matter, too, a great debt is owed to Dr Salter whose editions of the Cartularies of the Hospital of St John Baptist and Oseney Abbey (the town properties of which Magdalen and Christ Church respectively acquired) have proved invaluable guides.

After the colleges, the church was the largest landlord in the parish. No less than twelve properties were administered by the parochial feoffees: most of these clustered round the north and east sides of the churchyard. Here again, we are fortunate in the survival of a fine series of leases preserved in the Parish Chest. Two of the houses belonged to the city: for these Salter's *Oxford City Properties*[93] and the City Archives themselves have been of much assistance.

Several of our St Aldate's landlords, especially the wealthier ones, owned the houses in which they lived as well as another which they sub-let. Since 'in this period one of the few respectable ways of investment was the leasing and sub-letting of houses',[94] many were in fact sub-tenants of the colleges, the parish, and individuals. The ownership of fifteen houses has not been ascertained and we are unable to state whether in these cases the house belonged to, or was leased by, the particular landlord or landlady.

Just as the parishioners differed widely in wealth and status, so, too, did the size and amenities of their dwellings. Persons of contrasting social position, however, lived cheek by jowl in the seventeenth century, and while perhaps a larger percentage of the well-to-do inhabited the higher end of St Aldate's parish than the lower end, the exceptions are too numerous for any useful deduction to be made from this. For the number of rooms in the houses, the Inventories attached to Wills, already mentioned, are an excellent guide. It has been fascinating to be able in these cases to list the names of the rooms and thus to be in a position to visualize the kind of accommodation put at the disposal of individuals and families among the 'strangers'.

In conclusion, the method of presenting our material requires a few words of explanation. The 'Accompt' and Defaulters' List are followed by articles on each of the houses enumerated in the 'Accompt' in the order in which they appear there. In every case we begin with an account of the landlord (not always the same as in the Defaulters' List) succeeded by a history and description of his or her house wherever it is known. Then come biographies of the lodgers in each house; first those of January 1643/4 and then those of June 1643 where they differ: there are many cross-references between the two documents. Where a name in either list has not been identified, we have stated the fact.

NOTES

[1] Bulkeley Bandinel (1781-1861), Bodley's Librarian from 1813 to 1860.

[2] Philip Bliss (1787-1857), Under-Librarian from 1822 to 1828.

[3] Ed. Margaret Toynbee, Oxfordshire Record Society, Vol. XLII (1961), p. 13.

[4] Heath and Verney Papers: official and private papers of Sir Robert Heath and his two eldest sons Sir Edward and Sir John; and estate papers of the Greville and Verney families: Egerton MSS. 2978-3008. From these manuscripts it would be possible to construct a fully documented account of the career of Edward Heath.

[5] Heath accounts *c.* 1630-1682, Willoughby de Broke MS. 1651, and Heath Correspondence 1626-1685, Willoughby de Broke MS. 1652.

[6] See article in *D.N.B.* and his brief Autobiography, printed in *Philobiblon Society Miscellanies,* Vol. I (1854).

[7] *Liber Edwardi Heath Diarium Vitae Meae*, printed by J. Harvey Bloom in *Miscellanea Genealogica et Heraldica,* Series V, Vol. 4 (1920-22), pp. 156-64. Bloom prints a genealogy of the Heath family at pp. 156-7. The MS. of the complete *Diarium* is in the University of Illinois Library.

[8] MS. Egerton 2983, ff. 11-12.

[9] See article in *D.N.B.* Sir Robert Heath must have had a high opinion of Love as he sent his three younger sons to be under him at Corpus.

[10] MS. Egerton 2983, ff. 13-23.

[11] *Registers,* Harleian Society (1913), p. 107. 'Edward Heath son of Sr Robert Heath [of the temple in London] Knight Templer, & Lucy Crooke, daughter of Paule Ambrose Crooke of the Inner Temple. Lic.' The marriage licence is dated 17th May 1630.

[12] Both Sir Alexander Croke, *The Genealogical History of the Croke*

Family, Vol. II (1823), p. 629, and G. Lipscomb, *History of the County of Buckingham*, Vol. I (1847), p. 131, erroneously state that Lucy was the daughter of P.A. Croke's first wife, Frances, daughter and co-heir of Francis Wellesborne, of East Hanney, Berkshire, who died in 1605 aged twenty-two. For Susan Croke's family, the Coes, see J.G. Bartlett, *Robert Coe, Puritan, His Ancestors and Descendants* (Boston, Mass., 1911), pp. 542-3.
[13] *Registers*, Harleian Society (1904), p. 122.
[14] *Diarium*, p. 158.
[15] P.C.C. 87 Savile.
[16] P.C.C. 113 St John.
[17] MS. Egerton 2983, ff. 28 and 28v.
[18] *Diarium*, p. 161.
[19] P.C.C. 4 Sadler. The Will is undated but it must have been made before 29th December 1634 when the Heaths' second child, Susanna (died 2nd February 1634/5), was born at St Bartholomew's, where she was buried. Their eldest child, Mary, was also born at St Bartholomew's (2nd December 1632): she did not survive. Mrs Croke's Will was proved by Heath 31st January 1634/5.
[20] British Museum MS. Add. 37,232, f. I.
[21] *Diarium*, p. 161.
[22] Willoughby de Broke MS. 1652.
[23] An unbaptized son in 1635 and a son, Edward (who died the same day, 29th October, and was buried at Cottesmore), in 1639 (*Diarium*, p. 159).
[24] *Diarium*, p. 159. Verulam House, the predecessor of the present Gorhambury, was built by Francis Bacon.
[25] Ibid.
[26] Ibid.
[27] Ibid.
[28] He served as a captain of horse in Sir William Boteler's Regiment (a Kentish regiment). Accounts of money spent by him, including the sums laid out 'towards raysing of a Troope' and for 'Horsemeat at Oxford', will be found in MS. Egerton 2983, ff. 51-52v. He took part in the Second Civil War. After the Restoration he was made Attorney-General of the Duchy of Lancaster and he died in 1691.
[29] Born 7th September 1617. An account of him will be found in Venn's *Alumni Cantabrigienses.* For his presence at Oxford see A.G. Matthews, *Walker Revised* (1948), p. 357. He died in 1672.
[30] Robert and Francis were born 4th October 1620 and 29th October 1622 respectively. Brief accounts of them will be found in Appendix I, pp. 260-1.
[31] Bodleian MS. Add. D. 114, f. 59v.
[32] 'An account of charges about my wives funerall', Willoughby de Broke MS. 1651.
[33] See Ian Roy, 'The Royalist Council of War', *Bulletin of the Institute of Historical Research*, Vol. XXXV (1962), p. 160.
[34] Bodleian MS. Add. D. 114, f. 73.
[35] Ib., f. 15.
[36] Ib., f. 17.
[37] Ib., ff. 24, 24v, and 26. Additional evidence on this subject, of which we have made use, is to be found in a list of 'Seruants to the king, Prince and Duke of Yorke Charged wth payments towards the Workes their seuerall and determinate Answeres', contained in British Museum MS. Harleian 6804, f. 229: Walker Papers. We are indebted for this reference to Dr Ian Roy.
[38] Bodleian MS. Add. D. 114, ff. 31 and 41.
[39] Ib., ff. 32-6.
[40] Ib., ff. 40 and 41.

[41] Ib., f. 31.
[42] MS. Egerton 2978, f. 137.
[43] Willoughby de Broke MS. 1652. Katharine Wirdnam was the second of the three daughters of George Wirdnam, of Prior's Hold in Wantage (*Visitation of Berkshire* 1623, Harleian Society, Vol. LXVI (1907), p. 144). Paul Ambrose Croke had acquired through his first marriage the manor of East Hanney, near Wantage. It appears that he took his neighbour's daughter into his Rutland household.
[44] Willoughby de Broke MS. 1652.
[45] Lady Croke was the widow of Lucy Heath's uncle Sir George Croke (1560-1642), who was buried at Waterstock. She was Mary, daughter of Sir Thomas Benet, sometime Lord Mayor of London.
[46] Willoughby de Broke MS. 1652.
[47] *Diarium*, pp. 159-60. According to the *Rutland Magazine*, Vol. IV (1910), the child's coffin plate, found with others in the Croke and Heath family vault in 1860, bears the date 1646, but this must be an error.
[48] Willoughby de Broke MS. 1652.
[49] See *Visitation of Rutland* 1681, Harleian Society, Vol. LXXIII (1922), p. 34, and W.C. Metcalfe, *Visitation of Northamptonshire* 1618-19 (1887), p. 127.
[50] *The Letter Books of Sir Samuel Luke* 1644-5, ed. H.G. Tibbutt (1963), 834.
[51] Ib., 1118 (b).
[52] Willoughby de Broke MS. 1652.
[53] *Diarium*, p. 160. Great Milton and Waterstock villages lie near to each other, being both about 9½ miles east of Oxford.
[54] Willoughby de Broke MS. 1652.
[55] F. 20. See also MS. Wood F. 4, f. 74, and Wood, *L. and T.*, pp. 118-19. Wood states that the body was embalmed in lead and that the vault was under St Anne's chapel on the north side of the chancel. He gives a coloured shield with the Heath Arms impaling those of Croke.
[56] P. 160. For the *Diarium* see Note 7 above. 'An account of charges about my wives funerall' (see Note 32 above) gives exact details of the expenses incurred in May 1645; these amounted to £26 7s.
[57] See *Rutland Magazine*, Vol. IV, p. 200.
[58] *C.C.C.*, p. 1471. The fine was accepted by the Commons and an ordinance for granting his pardon was read 22nd April 1648 (*C.J.*, Vol. V, p. 540). The papers relating to the compositions of Edward and John Heath for their sequestered estates will be found in MS. Egerton 2978, ff. 180-288.
[59] 'The Account for Peggyes disbursements' was kept by her father from September 1646 to April 1647 (Willoughby de Broke MS. 1651).
[60] *V.C.H. Rutland*, Vol. I, p. 199.
[61] MS. Egerton 2978, f. 310.
[62] P.R.O. S.P. 29/44/139.
[63] *C.S.P.D.* 1650, p. 533.
[64] *V.C.H. Rutland*, Vol. I, pp. 200-1.
[65] British Museum MS. Add. 37,232, f. I. By a slip the year is given as 1649. Sir Robert Heath had died at Calais 30th August 1649 (N.S.), but 20th August (O.S.), as given by Edward Heath in his *Diarium*.
[66] We are indebted to the Rector of Cottesmore, the Revd. P.W. Cato, O.B.E., for this entry which reads: 'Sr Edw: Heath of Cotesmoor Kt of ye Bath was buryed Sept ye 5th at Cotesmoor'.
[67] P.C.C. 122 Penn.
[68] *Diarium*, p. 159. Her coffin plate was among those found in the Cottesmore church vault in 1860.
[69] *Diarium*, p. 161.
[70] Bodleian MS. Add. D. 114, f. 5.

[71] MS. Harleian 6804, f. 173. The lists are undated. We owe this reference to Dr Ian Roy.
[72] *A Bibliography of Royal Proclamations of the Tudor and Stuart Sovereigns*, ed. R. Steele, Vol. I (1910), No. 2517.
[73] Bodleian MS. Add. D. 114, f. 45.
[74] See British Museum Thomason Tract E. 693 (13): '*A Remonstrance, manifesting the lamentable miseries of the Creditors and Servants of the late King* . . . ', 13th May 1653.
[75] For this subject see W.L.F. Nuttall, 'King Charles I's Pictures and the Commonwealth Sale', *Apollo*, October 1965, pp. 302-9.
[76] *The Memoirs of Ann Lady Fanshawe* (1907), pp. 24-5.
[77] H.M.C., Appendix to IVth *Report*, p. 308.
[78] MS. Harleian 6802, ff. 344 and 346. We are indebted for this and the next reference to Dr Ian Roy.
[79] QZ 24, f. 5a. Printed by kind permission of His Grace the Duke of Rutland.
[80] The following colleges possess lists of 'strangers': University, Balliol, Oriel, Queen's, New College, Lincoln, Brasenose, St. John's, and Wadham. We are much indebted to the authorities of the above for allowing us to study their records. A few 'strangers' lodging in Corpus are recorded in Bodleian MS. Add. D. 114, f. 60. It is particularly to be regretted that the Christ Church Buttery Books for the War period are no longer extant. When James II visited The House in 1687, he told the Dean and Canons that 'he was senior to most of them, that he was entred into Ch. Ch. buttery-book after Edgehill-fight in 1642' (Wood, *L. and T.*, Vol. III, p. 231).
[81] F. 59v. The two youngest Heath brothers, Robert and Francis, were lodging in All Saints'.
[82] It was the oldest Register in the city.
[83] Printed in *C. of O.*, Vol. III, pp. 198-209.
[84] Much use has been made of the *Oxford Council Acts* 1583-1626 and 1626-1665 published by the Oxford Historical Society.
[85] For an analysis of the Christian names see Appendix II.
[86] This last taxation produced a double billeting list.
[87] See *R.O.P.*, Part I, p. 34, quoting MS. Harleian 6852, f. 67, and Bodleian MS. Twyne-Langbaine 2, f. 26.
[88] *The Manuscripts of the House of Lords*, Vol. XI, New Series, Addenda 1514-1714, ed. M.F. Bond (1962), No. 3592, pp. 322-33.
[89] Oxford City Archives F.5.9., f. 101.
[90] MS. Wood F. 28, f. 24: printed in Douglas Macleane, *A History of Pembroke College*, Oxford Historical Society, Vol. XXIII (1897), pp. 235-7.
[91] Printed respectively in Oxford Historical Society, New Series, Vol. XIV, *Survey* I, ed. W. A. Pantin (1960), pp. 163-264, and Vol. XX, *Survey* II, ed. W. A. Pantin and W. T. Mitchell (1969), pp. 1-132.
[92] A.L. Rowse, *A Cornishman at Oxford* (1964), pp. 62-3.
[93] Oxford Historical Society, Vol. LXXXIII (1926).
[94] *Oxoniensia*, Vol. XXVI/XXVII (1961/2), p. 323.

NOTE While this book was in the press Mr Paul Kopperman kindly drew our attention to the existence of further collections of MSS. relevant to the study of Edward Heath. The first (about 500 documents) belongs to the Society of Genealogists (Tweeddale Room and Tweeddale Annexe): the second (about 800 documents) is in the University of Illinois Library. A smaller collection of Heath letters is in the Kent Archives Office at Maidstone.
R. L. Hine's 'A Sidelight on the Civil War' (*The Cream of Curiosity* (1920), pp. 52-180) should also be consulted for Heath's career, but this ignores his Wartime activities at Oxford.

An Exact Accompt of all persons being strangers now resident within the parish of St. Aldates Oxon:

taken 23rd Jan: 1643

In Susan Smyths house a widdowe:
Monsieur de St. Pauls a French Lo: and his brother with two Men servants

Davids Woodfields his house
Mrs Moone a players wife
1 soldier of the life guarde

Mr John Holloways
The Earle of Bath and eight servants
Sr Francis Windebanke Kt
Tho: Windebanke Esqr
Mr John Windebanke Capt of the lifeguard his wife 2 men & 2 maidservants
5 of Sr Francis Windebanks servants

Mr William Days his house
The Earle of Carlisle and 5 men Attending him:
Mr Russell the Earle of Bedfords brother
Sr Robt Lee and their 2 men

Arthur Allin
Lieutent Leare
1 Soldier of the Life guarde

Mr Doctr Clayton
The Lady Cotterell & 1 mayde

Mrs Collier
Mr Andrewes his wife one childe & 1 maid
Mr Carnabie one of the kings servants

John Dixon
Colonell Hendersonde & 1 man

Anthony Yates
Mr Tapnorth the kings servant

John Leane
Lieutent Cotton of the life guarde & his wife and 1 childe aged three yeares

Widdow Willis
Captn Fisher of the life guarde

George Dixon
3 servants of the Duke of Richmond

Widdow Boyar
2 of the Lo: Arundells servants

Robert Saunders
The Lo: Arundell & 2 servants

Widdow Marcham
Sr Henry Radcliffe
Mr Batson the kings servant

Abell [illegible]
Mr Henderson [illegible] and his wife Lieutent Hall & 1 man: Mr Morris the kings taylor: Mr Bull and Mr Wilde the kings bakers
Mr Napper the princes barber
Mr Wood one of the Queenes servant
Mr Snow and Mr Horne yeomen of the guarde to his Matie

William Jewson
John Hewes servant to Mr Valentine Clarke
Peter Turnare } Baltero Colvon } 2 Corpor: of the Lifeguard

Tho: Floxe
Mr Hitchcock
Mr Littell & his wife and 2 Children aged 11 and 12

Andrewe Nicholls
Mr Ogleby } Mr Jarford } 2 of the Kings servants
2 of the Lifeguards soldiers

Thomas Wright
Mr Knowles } Mr Blunt } the Kings pastrymen
Mr Fielde servants to Prince Rupert
Mr Britwell one of the Kings Launder
2 soldiers of the life guarde

Thomas Marcham
Mr Hector belonging to the Kings [illegible]
Mr Mills the princes taylor
Mr Barnes yeoman of the guarde
Mr Heale a [illegible]
Mrs Sparkes a Tyrewoman

Richard Carter
Mr Applegarth and his wife & 2 Children aged about 9 & 12 & 1 man

William Corpson
Mr Dawes the Kings barber
Mr Littell a ~~barber~~ dancer

William Grey
George Mander } Rich Shepard } the Kings servants

William Deverall
John Bridges } Mathew Gallop } Edward Palmer: Barbers

Margarett Posse
Ensigne Hubbard of the Life guarde & 1 man. 2 servants to the Marques Hertford:

William Blow
Mr Cordall & his wife: Mr Bonnard Mr Harfbond Mr Edwards Mr Stones belonging to the Kings kitchin

John Harwood
Mr Wright Ensigne to the life guard
Samuell Nurse a [illegible]
Mr Tho: Smyth [illegible]
The Lo: Generall his Lady & his daughter 2 man & 3 mayd servants

Plate 1 An Exact Accompt . . . taken 23rd Jan. 1643. Page 1.

(Reproduced by courtesy of the Bodleian Library, Oxford)

Mr: Carpenter

1 Capt: Grindall

a: 1 Elizabeth Foster: Mr: Carpenters kinswoman

Richard Miles

Colonell Lee

Colonell Reade

4 Captain Starr

Mr Stanhope agent of the horse

to ye Marquesse Hertforde

Mrs Cantwells

3 Lieut: Colonell Tomson & his wife

2 small children 2 men & 2 maide servants

Mr Umpton Croke

3 Sergeant Major Laiton & 2 men 3

Mr John Smyth

The Lo: high Chamberlin 4 gent

attending him: 3 footmen 1

10 Cooke & 1 groome.

The Lady Lake her daughter &

a: 4 2 mayde servants

Widdow Nixon

ffrancis Lane wheelright to the 4

Artillery: the mason ye Lo: Dorchesters tayler

4 his wife 1 sucking child 1 mayd & 1 man

6 3 soldiers of ye Life guarde 8

Mr Seymor

Mr Elliotts mother & 2 of his

a: 4 sisters & 1 mayde 2

Mr Gaud

Sr Geo: Bynion his Lady his

5 6 Daughter 2 mayds & 1 man

Sr Rich: Gaud & his Lady 2 men 1 mayd

Jo: Dunte

4 4 of the Life guarde soldiers

James Bennett

4 Mr Lumley his wife & 3 maide servants

Widdow Mottley

Mr Cast yeoman of the kings bakehouse

5 5 soldiers of ye life guarde

Widdow Phillips

ffrancis Barnes a drummer & his wife

a: Jane warring a landresse.

2 Phillip Bourne a messenger: his

5 sonne & his sonnes wife & one of

his daughters. 3

2 2 of the Lo: Wentworths groomes

Widdow Ewin

William White a poulterer to the

3 6 king his wife & 2 men

5 soldiers of ye life guarde. 3

men – 39 women children & common soldiers 4450 men 39

1 Widdow Moore

3 Mr Thornell a Surgeon & his brother

& 1 man: 2 soldiers of ye life guarde

William Horne

William Lee a Taylor & servant to

secretary Nicholls his wife 1 small child

3 and 1 man.

1 servant of Sr ffred: Cornwallis 9

a: 2 women belonging to Sr Hen: Hunks

5 soldiers of the life guarde

Jo: Savery

Mr May a messenger belonging to ye

Lo: Tres: Mr Maylor belonging to

the Commissioners:

3 1 servant of Sr ffred: Cornwallis 2

2 of ye life guarde soldiers

Tho: Lappworth

4 soldiers of ye Life guarde 4

Rich: Horne

Mr Roymer

Mr Peachy } Messengers to ye

4 Nicholas Coxley } Councell of warr

Hen: Northorpe }

2 soldiers of ye life guarde 2

Mr Oliver Smyth

8 The Lo: Wentworth and 7 men

Robert Wilson

Capt: Beldon } of ye life guarde

2 Capt: fforster }

Robert Banting

5 soldiers of ye life guarde 5

Jo: Richardson

Mr Warde servant to ye duke of Burk.

3 of the dutches of Burks: maydes

3 soldiers of the life guarde 6

Widdow Burke

Ensigne Masterman & his wife 2

Widdow Treddwell

1 sarvant and } the life guarde 3

2 soldiers of }

Jo: Massey

1 Corporall of ye life guarde 1

Mrs Haukes

Collonell David Skringar and

his wife 2 men 1 maide servant 2

Miles Godfrey

Mr Pettiman & his wife & 1 man

Mr Dodson an officer in ye life guarde

2 soldiers of ye life guarde

Mr Stephens

Mr Jo: Cary & 5 men

Lieutent Webster & 1 man

women 40

Plate 2 An Exact Accompt . . . taken 23rd Jan. 1643. Page 2.

(Reproduced by courtesy of the Bodleian Library, Oxford)

Mr Langley
3 Major Legge & his wife 6 men & 2 mayd servants
Mr Tompson
2 Sr Fred: Cornwallis and 3 men
4 Serjant Benfeilde of ye Lifeguard & his wife
Thomas Hawkes
5 Sr Charles Dav[illegible] and 4 men
Widdow Hill
2 servants of the Lo: high Chamberline
2 1 of Collonell Russells servants
1 of ye princes servants
3 groomes and 1 footman of Mr Marrill
2 souldiers of ye life guarde
Widdow Wale
5 4 Sr Robert Lee & his Lady & 1 small childe
3 men 1 boy & 2 maid servants
Jo: Horne
3 Leivetent: Novids widdow & 2 small children.
Anthony Blunde
2 2 of Doctor Harvies men .
Mr Locksmyth
3 the Lord Wray & 2 men
Jo: Willmott
3 3 of ye Queenes servants .
Mr Carle
Sarjant Major Marckham
Monsieur Moleny = Reid
5 & there 2 servants
Mr Stone Quartermaster to ye Lifeguard
Francis West
3 Mr Miles of ye kings pantry & 1 man
1 of ye yeomen of ye mouth to ye king
John King:
1 Mr Doctor Hewitt Chaplen to ye Lifeguard
Robert Nixon
2 4 2 of ye kings pastryman
4 souldiers of ye life guarde
Jo: Bolte
3 Mr Rumley the kings Apothecary
his sonne & 1 servant
John Hinclos
the Lord: Jones & 1 man
11 Sr Jo [illegible] & 2 men
Serjant Major Lindsey & 2 men
Capt Lockett: & 2 yeomen of ye guarde: [illegible]
John Lambe
Leivetent: Edmondes:
Jo: Mander
3 of ye kings groomes of ye stable
4 of ye princes servants
The Lo: Traquaire & 2 servants
6 of ye Lo: Mowbrayes servants
78 women &c 18:

John: Mander
5 of ye Lo: Carnowlds servants
8 5r William Wallington &
2 of his servants:

In: parte of the house where
John Bolte liveth
5r William Howards & 4 men.
men 13

Of gent and theire servants — 267:
of women children & comon souldiers
of ye Lif guarde — 141
numerous total — 408

Of Gent & their men servants — 267
Of women — 66
Of Children under 16 yeares age — 13
Of souldiers of life guard — 62
Totall of this parish — 408.

Note in this number 62 of the souldiery are included all common souldiers serjeants & corporalls but quarter mrs auncients liftenants & Captaines are included in the number — 267.

note 16 officers of life guard are part of the 267 & if they must be excluded then the number of men is but — 251.

Plate 3 An Exact Accompt . . . taken 23rd Jan. 1643. Page 3.

(Reproduced by courtesy of the Bodleian Library, Oxford)

24 16

The names of the Defaulters in St Aldates parish
14th June 1643

In widdow Smiths house
1 Edward Whyte. The officers could not speak with him.

In Mr Holloways house
11 The Lord Newarke & 6 servants Sr Robert Stapleton & 2 servants &
Dr Hodges; removed to Trinity Colledge, & some gonne out of towne.

In Mr Day his house
2 Mr Clutterbuck & one man

In Mris Colliers house
2 Mr Ramsey & 1 man. Gonne out of towne before the 14th June.

1 In Richard Whittere his house a barbar; himselfe absent at London
Humphry Breath; The Mris answers, Her man cannot work nor can
she spare him till she be payd for what her husband did to the Kings souldiers.

In Edward Allens house
Mr Bartlett . noe answere. (for the father
3. Mr Stanhope & his sonne; The sonne gonne to his colledge; noe answere

In Mr Browns house
2 Mr Webb & his man. noe answere.

In John Browns house
2 The Lord Arundel & 1 servant gonne out of towne

In Mr Sanders his house
~~4~~ The Lord Cottington; above 60 yeares.
3 Barnard Sanders; Gonne to his Mr Mr Waldon in Magdalen parish.
William Hutchinson; a minister, curat of St Ebbs parish, his answere, that he must
attend the burings & Christnings

1 — In John Wilds house, John Woodfeild. under 16.

In Mr Flames his house. Leiftenant Godwin & 1 man. his answere that
when Collonels & other souldiers of his ranke payd he would also.
5 — Dr Frazer. noe answere. Mr Twine above 60 yeares.
Henry Wilmott. under 16.

In Thomas Fox his house ~~[illegible]~~, & Davy Little. noe answere.
12 Andrew Nichols above 60 yeares.

In Thomas Wrights house Mr Prickett, Mr Bridges, Mr Blunt, Mr Feild, all
4 of the Kings pastry; noe answere.

In Thomas Markhams house; Markhams man; Mr Forest. Noe answere.
3. Richard Carter above age.

2 — In Will Coopes his house, Mr Davies. Captaine Digby. Noe answere.

In widdow Voices house.
Mr Langly — they are the Kings servants about wax lights & refuse to pay.
3 — Mr Batty
Richard Shepheard

1 — In Will Wilsa his house. John Jones belongs to the court & refuseth.

In Will Harrolds house. Captaine Jise; gonne out of towne. Samuel Knott
2 belonging to the Kings kitchen & poore.

In Mr Thomas Smiths house
The Lord Generall
Sr Thomas Bysley
6 — Captaine Dingley — Noe answere but that they ought not to pay
Mr John Bysley
Mr Monroe
Mr Nicholas. above 60 yeares.

1 — In Mr Carpenters house. Mr Elston above 60 yeares.

67

Plate 4 The names of the Defaulters . . . 14th June 1643. Page 1.

(Reproduced by courtesy of the Bodleian Library, Oxford)

7 — In mr Miles his house. mr Miles himselfe; he will work double next weeke.
Lieftenant Cranfield & 1 man; he would pay when the king payd him.
Sr Matthew Carew & 1 man. not answere.
Captaine Waite & 1 man. not answere.

2 — In mris Cantwells house
Captaine Tomson } both out of towne.
mr Clarke

4 — In mr Wrington Grotes house; his sonne gonne away to the Temple at London.
serjeant major Leyton & 2 men. not answere.

5 — In mr John Smiths house
The Ld Spenser & 4 servants } he thought not fitt that Noblemen should pay, but when others did he would.

1 — Thomas Smith is the Constable.

2 — In mr Seamors house mr Elliot & his man. both out of towne.

1 — In Thomas Clutterbooks house
Ralph Marsh: one of the court, his wife answered, that when the king payd her husband, he should pay.

1 — In widdow Wottons house, Matthew Wotton. not answere.

5 — In James Dinnels house.
The Ld Wentworth & 4 servants } they refuse to pay, saying they are souldiers.

2 — In widdow Mores house. mr Wigford and another being Sr Fred. Cornwallis his servants. not answere.

9 — In Will Homes house.
William Lort, Henry Buffe
George Turner, Thomas Jokes, } not answere
Thomas Sad, William Lor
Christopher Lor, Robt Earney } these would not pay
Robt Warly, his answere that he would not pay.

1 — John Savery. above age.

1 — In Leyworths house. William Gyles; he belongs to the saltpeter house & sayth he cannot.

1 — In Homes house. John Home is a troop & went forth on service upon Munday last.

1 — In mr Olliver Smiths
mr Philip Nicholas. servant to Ld Wentworth & refuseth to pay.

6 — In mr Farmers house
three returned all his servants are foot souldiers
Captaine Nun & 1 man } not answere.
Lieftenant Forster

2 — Robt Panting & 1 man. they are bootmen & were then upon service for the king for wood for the canons running.

1 — Will Eggby. was then in prison.

3 — In widdow Burts house
mr Barnehalls
mr Wooddard } these are all out of towne.
Henry Burt

1 — John Masy his man. gonne into St Clements parish.

6 — In mris Hawkes his house
Serjeant Major Sugwood & 1 man } not answere.
Captaine Stringer & 3 men

12 — In Michael Godfries house.
[illegible] & } these are the kings farriers, & answere they would pay
Francis Windresse & } if others of their degree pay
Godfries man, sick in his bed, but he promiseth to send 2 next weeke.

6 — In mr Stephens house
mr Cary & 4 men } not answere
Lieftenant Webster

4 — In mr Langlyes house
Collonell Davison & 1 man } not answere.
mr Thanel surgion to the life guard
one of mr Langlies men under 16 yeares.

5 — In mr Thomsons house. he himselfe is above 60 yeares.
Sr Frederick Cornwallis & 2 men } not pay bicause their mr a Lieutenant & [illegible] ingaged his life & estate for him.
mr Godwin Clerke. not answere.

N 77

Plate 5 The names of the Defaulters . . . 14th June 1643. Page 2.

(Reproduced by courtesy of the Bodleian Library, Oxford)

26

6 — In Thomas Hankes house
Collonel Russell & 4 men, answere, not pay, because their mr spends life & estate here in kings service
mr Dudly smith . noe answere. 47

1 — In widdow Hills house
1 — William Jatterar. he sayth he hath noe mony.

5 — 2 of Ld Dungarvens men gonne out of towne on Saturday last.
1 of Sr John Stidmores men. his mr he sayth must pay for him
2 of Ld Mordents men . noe answere.

2 — In mr Hobortons house
will Giles . shewed a warrant whereby he was commanded with his boate to goe on the water on the kings service.
One of mr Grants men gonne away.

5 — In widdow Neales house
Sr Robt Lea & 1 man. The man answered noe reason his mr should pay haveing a troope of horse & ventured his life.
his 3 other men are troopers & abroad on service.

4 — In John Hornes house
Liftenant Awbry & 1 man. he would pay if other souldiers did.
Liftenant Rhadon. would not pay till the king payd him.
mr Martin. noe answere.

2 — In Slands house, 2 of mr Harris men . noe answere.

1 — mr Lordsmith refuseth to pay till he speake with the vicechancelor, being one of the Bedles

2 — In John Wilmotts house
2 of Sr Richard Hubbards men. they put them of to their mr in Coll. triall

2 — In mr Earles house
Captaine Markham . noe answere.
~~[struck out]~~
Beniamen Stone a quartermr. he not pay till the king pay him.

4 — John King is sick in his bed. there
2 of Coll: Herberts men sick. the 3d out of towne.

1 — In wyongs house . mr Del Hoy, of the party to the king & answeres because the king there.

5 — In John Wells house
mr Sumby & 2 men. answers that he is the kings Apothecary & must attend that
mr Gryffin & one man. answers that he is the princes surgeon & must attend that.

1 — In John Hunelose house. ~~[struck out]~~
mr Hines above 60 yeares.

1 — Reynolds in Constables
In widdow Wilsons house . mr Boulton at London a prisoner.

4 — mr Stanton
mr Browne
mr Woods } noe answere.

40

Plate 6 The names of the Defaulters . . . 14th June 1643. Page 3.

(Reproduced by courtesy of the Bodleian Library, Oxford)

Cr Ellis Hicks
Mr Thomas Newman
Sr John Strange
Mr Tho: Elington Esq
Mr Thom: Whitcome
Mr Ellis Crispe
Mr Richard Jennings
Mr Mitchell
Mr Colwell

the totall was ——— 394

bit: in mony ——— 128

those that paied ——— 68

196

returned ——— 204

400

43
58
53
48
204

In John Lambs house
one man returned, but since gonne into magdalen parish
4 of Ld Sturtons men . not answere.

In John Manders house the signe being blew bore.

4 of the kings servants
4 of the princes servants
3 of the Ld Mowbrays serv.
3 of Lord Jermyns servants
2 of Ld Herberts servants

answere that the Constables must goe to their mrs.

Mr Bacon . not answere.

17

22

48
56
53
43

202

Plate 7 The names of the Defaulters . . . 14th June 1643. Page 4.

(Reproduced by courtesy of the Bodleian Library, Oxford)

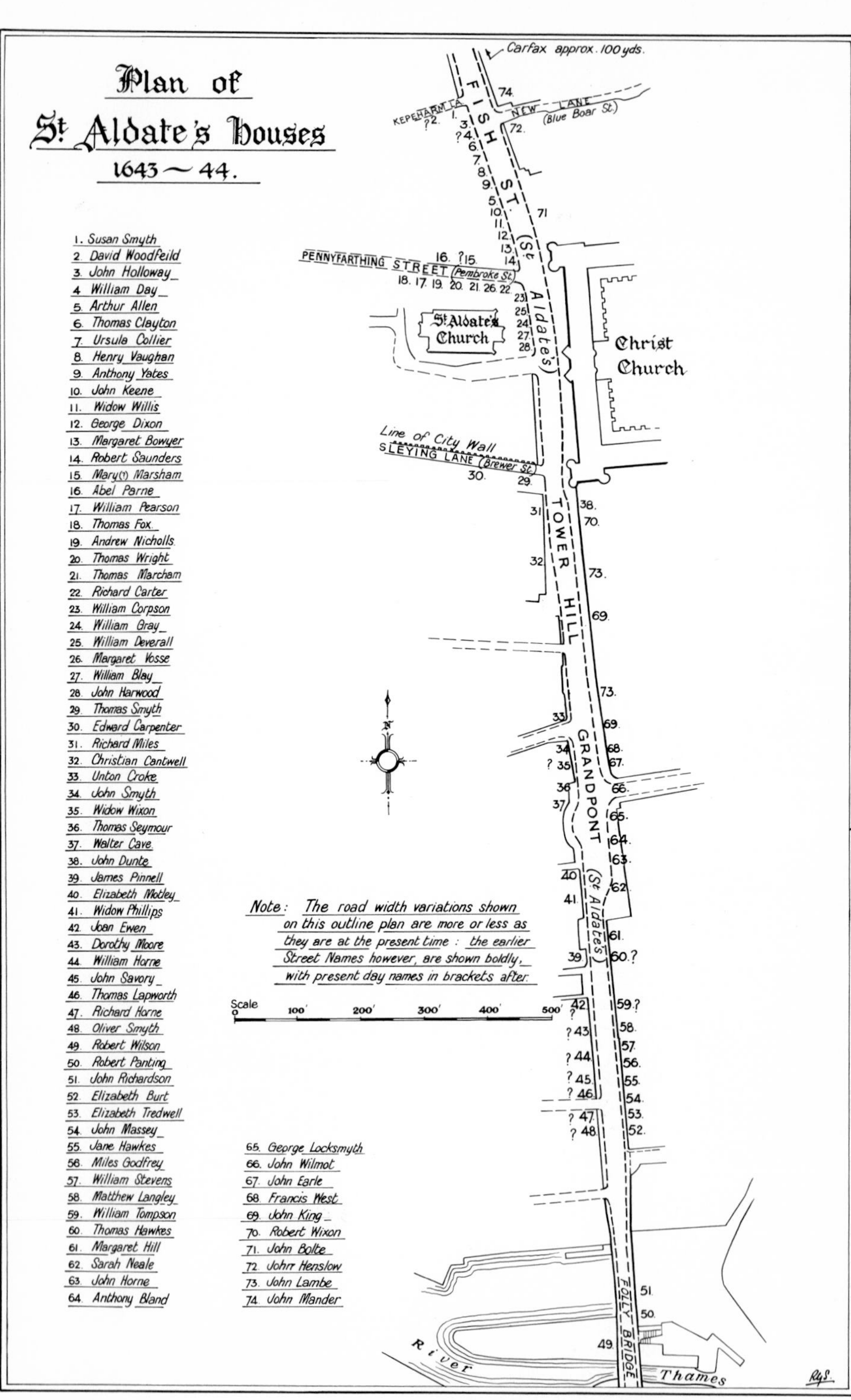

Plate 8 Plan of St. Aldate's, 1643-44, showing approximate locations of houses in the parish, as mentioned in the survey,

PART I

THE GARRISON OF OXFORD 1642-1646

CHRONOLOGY

1642	
23 October	Battle of Edgehill
9 December	Winter quarters settled. Four foot regiments at Oxford
1642/3	
10 January	Earl of Carbery's Regiment arrives
2 February	Storming of Cirencester. Detachment of the garrison present under Sir Lewis Kirke
1643	
25 April	Action at Caversham Bridge
Mid-May	Arrival of the Regiments of Lord Percy and Colonel Pinchbeck. Departure of Dutton's
Mid-July	Arrival of the Queen's Lifeguard
10 August-5 September	Siege of Gloucester
20 September	First Battle of Newbury
Autumn	Departure of Vaughan's and Pennyman's Regiments
December	The City of Oxford Regiment raised
1643/4	
By February	Raising of Sir Arthur Aston's Regiment
13 February	General Muster of garrison (6 regts.) in New Parks behind Wadham College
1644	
29 March	Battle of Cheriton
10 April	Rendezvous at Aldbourne Chase
28 April	Proclamation for raising Dover's and Littleton's Auxiliary Regiments
8 May	Departure of Gerard's Regiment
11 June	Surrender of Greenland House Hawkins' Regiment joins the garrison
12 June	Gage takes Boarstall House
29 June	Battle of Cropredy Bridge
August-September	The Cornish campaign
5 August	Gage's attempt on Abingdon
September	Gage relieves Basing
25 October	Relief of Banbury Castle
27 October	Second Battle of Newbury
1644/5	
January ?	Colonel Will. Legge's Regiment of Horse formed
1645	
14 June	Battle of Naseby
6 September	Raid on Thame
18 September	The Bristol Foot come to Oxford

1646	
25 April	Prince Rupert's troops disbanded
	The Exeter Foot come to Oxford
24 June	Surrender of Oxford.

THE ROYALIST GARRISON OF OXFORD 1642-1646

Oxford was the Royalist capital and headquarters during the greater part of the First Civil War. The King entered the city on 29th October 1642, a week after his hard-won victory at Edgehill, and the fortress, as it became, did not surrender until 24th June 1646 when all the serious fighting was over.

THE GOVERNORS

There may have been as many as six Royalist Governors of Oxford during the War. The first was Sir Jacob Astley (1579-1652), the Sergeant-Major-General of the Foot of the main Royalist army, the 'Oxford' army as it may be called. He was appointed, it seems, in December 1642. Astley was a veteran who had seen much service in the Dutch army, and in the Scots Wars. He was not Governor for very long presumably because his duties as a general officer were sufficiently arduous to occupy all his time.

There is evidence that Colonel Sir Lewis Kirke was Governor for a few days in April 1643, but the appointment was not confirmed.[1]

His successor was Sir William Pennyman, M.P. (1607-1643), a wealthy Yorkshire knight. He was M.P. for Richmond in the Long Parliament and was one of the fifty-nine members who voted against the attainder of Strafford. On the outbreak of war Pennyman raised a regiment of foot as well as a troop of horse, which on 25th December 1642 was serving in Prince Rupert's Regiment.[2] He was expanding his troop into a regiment when he died of the 'Morbus Epidemus' on 22nd August 1643 and was buried in Christ Church.

The next Governor was Sir Arthur Aston (*c.* 1590-1649), a testy and imperious person who was Sergeant-Major-General of Dragoons in the 'Oxford' army. He was a veteran soldier who had served as far afield as Muscovy and seems to have been a strict disciplinarian. He was detested for that as much as for his Roman Catholicism, and was actually assaulted on one occasion (22nd December 1643) while he was doing his rounds. Thereafter he was 'dayly attended by a guard consisting of 4 men in long redd coates and halberds'.[3] On 1st May 1644 he was made a Doctor of Medicine — a curious reward for military service. He was thrown while 'kerveting on horseback on Bullington Green before certain ladies' on 19th September, and amputation of his broken leg followed on 7th December. It was assumed that his soldiering days were done, and, much to the relief of the garrison and the country people who brought their produce to market in Oxford, he was relieved of his command. He lived, however, to be Governor of Drogheda, and when Cromwell stormed that town on 10th September 1649 the Parliamentarian soldiers dashed out his brains with his own wooden leg.

Aston was succeeded by another Catholic, Colonel Sir Henry Gage (1597-1645), who had been at Spinola's siege of Breda. He had commanded an English regiment in the Spanish service, but had given up that command and joined the King early in 1644. Gage, who was distinguished alike as scholar and soldier, was appointed (3rd June 1644) as one of the Council of War left to advise Aston during the absence of the King and the main field army. He recaptured Boarstall House (12th June), relieved Basing House in September,[4] a difficult operation conducted with great skill, and took part in the relief of Banbury Castle (25th October). On 1st November 1644 the King knighted him. In November he relieved Basing House a second time, and on the 23rd he was made Governor of Oxford, although the appointment did not become effective until Christmas Day, when Aston vacated office. Gage was a popular Governor but his tenure of the command was unhappily short: he was mortally wounded at Culham Bridge during Prince Rupert's unsuccessful attack on Abingdon (11th January 1644/5). Like Pennyman he was buried in Christ Church. There is a portrait of him perhaps after W. Dobson in the

National Portrait Gallery.

Rupert's friend Colonel William Legge (1609?-1670) succeeded Gage. As he lived in St Aldate's his career is given elsewhere in this volume (pp. 195-7). He was relieved of his command on 17th September 1645, as a direct consequence of Rupert's surrender of Bristol. There is a portrait after J. Huysmans in the National Portrait Gallery.

The last Royalist Governor was Sir Thomas Glemham (died 1649?). Glemham, who had been an undergraduate of Trinity College, Oxford (matriculated 1610), had served in the German Wars and had sat in the first two Parliaments of King Charles' reign. He was knighted in 1617. He had been colonel of a regiment of foot in the Scots Wars and colonel-general of Newcastle's army in the North. After Marston Moor he held York for a short time, and then Carlisle, where he taught the garrison to eat dogs before famine compelled him to capitulate. When he was eventually forced to surrender he joined the King at Cardiff before 6th August 1645.[5] He was made D.C.L. on 28th November. This excellent officer remained Governor until the surrender.[6]

THE REGIMENTS OF THE GARRISON

After Edgehill the Royalists marched on London, but not liking the look of the Parliamentarian array on Turnham Green, retired (13th November) and went into winter quarters. At this time the main army consisted of eleven regiments of horse, three of dragoons, and eighteen of foot, besides the Train of Artillery. In addition to the regiments of horse there were the two troops of the King's Lifeguard, the Gentlemen Pensioners, and the Lord General's troop.

Oxford now became the centre of a web of strongpoints as the list of quarters settled 9th December 1642,[7] shows:

	Horse	Dragoons	Foot
Reading	2	—	6
Wallingford	1	—	2
Abingdon	2	—	1
Faringdon	1	2	—
Oxford	3 troops[8]	—	4
Winchester[9]	1	—	—
Burford	1	1	—
Brill	—	—	2
Banbury	1	—	2
Woodstock	1 troop	—	1
Eynsham[10]	1	—	—
Islip	1	—	—

The garrison of Oxford itself consisted of the King's Lifeguard of Horse and four regiments of foot:

The King's Lifeguard
Colonel Charles Gerard's Regiment
Sir William Pennyman's Regiment
Sir Ralph Dutton's Regiment

Judging by the pay warrant of 16th November 1642[11] these were among the stronger regiments in the army, though their exact numbers are uncertain. On 1st January the King's Lifeguard had 400 private soldiers.[12] The Regiment probably had at least 10 companies and would therefore have about 110 officers, including sergeants and drummers, and so a total of over 500 may be assumed. In mid-November both Pennyman's and Dutton's had both been stronger than the Lifeguard, and it seems likely, therefore, that the garrison included between 2,000 and 2,500 foot.

The exact composition of the garrison throughout the War is uncertain, but the presence of certain regiments cannot be disputed.

FOOT

1. The King's Lifeguards. Redcoats.
Part II is devoted to the history of this Regiment, which was one of the four quartered in Oxford on 9th December 1642.
2. Colonel Charles Gerard's Regiment. Bluecoats.
The Regiment, probably raised in North Wales, was quartered at Oxford from 9th December 1642 until it marched with Gerard to South Wales when he went to take command there on 8th May 1644.[13] The Regiment was drawn out of Oxford to fight at First Newbury, where it suffered heavy casualties, and Cheriton. By 10th April 1644 it had shrunk to a strength of no more than 150.[14]
Among the senior officers were Lt. Colonel Ned Villiers, who was wounded at First Newbury, and Major Francis Windebank, who, after distinguishing himself at Cirencester and Cheriton, was shot in 1645 for surrendering Bletchingdon House.
3. Sir William Pennyman's Regiment.
This Yorkshire Regiment was the eldest in the army.[15] It was part of the original garrison and was at Oxford until after the death of its colonel (22nd August 1643), who was succeeded by his cousin, Sir James Pennyman. The Regiment was still at Oxford at the time of First Newbury, but seems to have moved to Reading when that town was reoccupied after the battle. It formed part of that garrison in April 1644, being then 479 strong.[16]
The Regiment fought at Cropredy Bridge, Lostwithiel, and Second Newbury, making part of the first tertia under Colonel Thomas Blagge. Sir James Pennyman was still colonel as late as 29th November.[17] He was succeeded by Lt. Colonel Richard Page. The latter and his major, William Bridges, were both knighted for their gallantry at the storming of Leicester (30th May 1645). The Regiment was destroyed at Naseby, where it fought in the tertia of Colonel Sir Bernard Astley.[18]
4. The Regiment of Sir Ralph Dutton and (Sir) Stephen Hawkins. Whitecoats.
This was the second regiment raised,[19] and was one of the four quartered at Oxford from 9th December 1642. It remained until mid-May 1643, when it joined the field army in 'the Leaguer' at Culham near Abingdon.[20] It was at the storming of Bristol (26th July) and at First Newbury. Hawkins succeeded to the command on 6th December.[21]
In March 1643/4 the Regiment, 275 strong, was in the Reading garrison,[22] and later held Greenland House near Henley. Here it was besieged for about a month by Major-General Richard Browne's forces. Relieved with two months' provisions by Colonel Sir Thomas Lunsford with a party from Oxford and Wallingford (8th June), it was attacked again next day. Browne 'by the continued Violence of his Canon, and the firing the Magazine within with a Granado shot, brought the stout Collonel three Days after to the Conditions to quit the place (almost levelled with the Earth) and to march away with all his Men, Arms, Horses, Baggage, Colours flying and Drums beating, safely to Oxford; . . . '[23]
The Regiment remained part of the garrison of Oxford until the surrender. Detachments were with Gage at the relief of Basing House (September) and of Banbury Castle (October 1644). The Earl of Dover got Hawkins knighted and made Lieutenant-Governor of Oxford (31st January 1644/5).[24]
The Regiment seems to have been a good one. At least five of its original ten company commanders had previous military experience in the Scots Wars.[25] They were:
Lt. Colonel Stephen Hawkins
Major Degory Collins
Captain John Palmer
Captain Charles Kirke

Captain Will. Atkins

Hawkins and Collins became colonels; Palmer rose to lieutenant-colonel and Kirke to major. Sir Ralph Dutton was a wealthy man and could, therefore, no doubt, attract experienced soldiers to his Regiment.

5. The Regiment of the Earl of Carbery and Sir Henry Vaughan.

This Welsh Regiment joined the garrison on 10th January 1642/3.[26] It seems to have been raised in Carmarthenshire for most of its officers came from that county.[27] Sir Henry Vaughan had assumed command, it seems, before 26th June 1643.[28]

By 11th September it had left Oxford, but there is no evidence that it fought at First Newbury. In April 1644, 258 strong, it was at Reading.[29] In the following autumn it served in the second tertia under Colonel (Sir) George Lisle. It was in Cornwall,[30] and must have been at Second Newbury, where Lisle's command greatly distinguished itself. Vaughan was captured by Cromwell at Bampton-in-the-Bush on 27th April 1645, and there is no mention of his Regiment thereafter.

6. Lord Percy. Whitecoats.

Percy's soldiers were 'commanded men' out of all the northern regiments which came to Oxford with a convoy of ammunition and were formed into two new units.[31] The Regiment was at Oxford by mid-May 1643. Although it seems to have been drawn out before First Newbury, it does not seem to have had any casualties there. As its colonel was General of the Artillery, it may have been guarding the train.

The Regiment was one of the six which were at the muster in New Parks behind Wadham College on 13th February 1643/4. It took part in the Cornish campaign of 1644.[32] Lord Percy was disgraced on 8th August,[33] and succeeded by Lord Hopton. Whether Hopton absorbed Percy's men in his own Regiment does not appear, but it seems not unlikely.

7. Colonel Thomas Pinchbeck. Greycoats.

The origin of this Regiment was the same as that of Lord Percy's.[34] Pinchbeck himself died of wounds received at First Newbury, which is strange as there is no evidence that the unit suffered any casualties. Pinchbeck was buried at Oxford on 23rd January 1643/4.[35] The Regiment, still called Pinchbeck's, was at the muster of the Oxford garrison on 13th February.[36] Command passed to (Sir) Henry Bard, who had been lieutenant-colonel of Percy's Regiment. Bard, whose impetuosity has been blamed for the defeat at Cheriton (29th March 1644), was wounded and taken at that fight with many of his men. On 7th April the Regiment was only 176 strong when it marched out of Oxford to go to the rendezvous at Aldbourne Chase.[37]

The Regiment was probably at Cropredy Bridge for it was certainly in the Cornish campaign, marching in the first tertia under Blague.[38] No doubt, therefore, it was also at Second Newbury.

Once more the Regiment's winter quarters were probably in Oxford. In the 1645 campaign it was part of the tertia commanded by its colonel, Sir Henry Bard, and was destroyed at Naseby.[39]

8. The Queen's Lifeguard. Redcoats.

The Regiment was raised in the North, and came to Oxford with the Queen on 14th July 1643. Her favourite, Lord Jermyn, was colonel of both her horse and her foot regiments, so it may be assumed that the actual commander was the lieutenant-colonel, Richard Gerard.

The Regiment formed part of the garrison of Oxford until the surrender, detachments taking part in many of its exploits. Its adventures can be deduced from those of certain of its officers. Captain Sturges, 'a gallant daring young man', was with Gage at the taking of Boarstall House (12th June 1644), in the attempt on Abingdon (5th August), and was killed at the relief of Basing House where he 'shewed exemplary courage' (September 1644).[40] Lt. Colonel Gerard was with

Gage at the relief of Banbury (25th October 1644).[41]

9. Sir Arthur Aston.

This Regiment, 'now raysing sans armes', was at the muster on 13th February 1643/4,[42] Aston being Governor at that time. The history of the Regiment is extremely obscure, but since 11 indigent officers survived the Restoration,[43] it looks as if its recruiting was fairly successful. What became of the Regiment after Aston lost both his leg and his Governorship is not known. His Major, Hanniball Bagnall, was at Oxford on 17th May 1646.[44]

10. The City of Oxford Regiment.

This Regiment, consisting of six companies, was raised in December 1643.[45] The first colonel was Sir Nicholas Selwyn, one of the Gentlemen Pensioners, and the other five company commanders were leading citizens of Oxford. Will. Legge became colonel soon after he was made Governor. Though the Regiment was raised and employed purely for the defence of the city, a detachment of 60 musketeers under Captain Burgh took part in the raid on Thame on 6th September 1645.[46]

11. The Earl of Dover.

This was one of the two auxiliary regiments raised at Oxford from among the numerous scholars and strangers there. It was raised by a Proclamation of 28th April 1644 and was exercised in Magdalen College Grove on 14th May and mustered on Bullingdon Green as early as 21st May. A further Proclamation of 24th May ordered all those strangers who had not enlisted to leave Oxford. The Regiment continued to do duty until the surrender.

12. Lord Keeper Littleton.

The other auxiliary regiment which, like Dover's, was brought into being by the Proclamation of 28th April 1644, included a number of gentlemen of the Inns of Court who had joined the King. It was exercised with Dover's in Magdalen Grove on 14th May.

Littleton died on 27th August 1645, but no doubt his Regiment survived him. It is not quite certain who was its second colonel. It *seems* to have been the young Duke of York for Captain John Brydall, a Bachelor of Law, faithfully served King Charles I as captain-lieutenant of the company commanded by Littleton and *afterwards* by the Duke of York.[47] The Duke had been colonel of a regiment which had been destroyed at Naseby *before* Littleton's death.

13. Prince Rupert's Firelocks. Redcoats.

Rupert had two regiments of foot, the Bluecoats, destroyed at Naseby, and the Firelocks. It is not certain when this last Regiment was raised, but it may have been as early as 1643.[48] It took part in the assault on Leicester (30th May 1645), where its major, Bunnington, a Gentleman Pensioner, was shot in the eye just as he was on the top of the ladder.[49] It escaped the débâcle at Naseby, perhaps because it had been left in garrison at Leicester. However that may be, when Prince Rupert surrendered Bristol (11th September 1645) 'his Life Guard of fire-locks came forth, all in red coats before him . . . ' The foot from Bristol marched to Oxford, where the Firelocks were presumably disbanded on 25th April 1646 with the rest of Prince Rupert's own units.[50]

In addition to these 13 regiments the garrison received other reinforcements. On 13th May 1644 about 120 Cornish foot soldiers, well armed with muskets, came to Oxford.[51] It may be that they were absorbed into the garrison regiments.

As we have seen, when on 11th September 1645 Prince Rupert surrendered Bristol to Sir Thomas Fairfax, his foot, some 2,000 strong,[52] marched to Oxford, arriving on 18th September.[53] They were probably commanded by Colonel Henry Tillier, who had been major-general of Rupert's foot at Marston Moor and was one of the Prince's commissioners for drawing up the articles upon which Bristol was yielded. He was one of the senior officers in Oxford on 17th May 1646.[54] At least four of the colonels in Bristol at the surrender had already lost their regiments at Naseby.[55] Among those who probably still had some men were:

Lord Hawley
Somerset Fox
Robert Slingsby
Walter Slingsby[56]

Fox's officers came from the Severn Valley and South Wales, while Lord Hawley's were mainly from Somersetshire.[57]

On 26th April 1646 Oxford received its last substantial reinforcement when about 700 of Sir John Berkeley's foot, which marched out of Exeter on the surrender, came into Oxford with their arms.[58] These must almost certainly have included some of Sir John's own men, most of whose officers were from Devonshire.[59]

The commissioners for the surrender of Exeter included two colonels of foot, William Ashburnham and William Godolphin.[60] It seems safe to assume that both their regiments were represented among the body that now reached Oxford. These two units were from Dorset and Cornwall respectively.

As the King's cause declined, the diehards from many small garrisons must have made their way to Oxford, armed or unarmed. It would be impossible to list them all. There is, however, a document[61] of 17th May 1646 in which 25 'officers of the Garrison of Oxford', declare upon their several reputations that it is absolutely against their wills and opinions to treat with Sir Thomas Fairfax. They declare that they have been forced to do so by the Privy Council and 'doe further declare to the world, that what inconvenience soever may arise to the King's cause or his freinds upon this Treaty, is not in or hands to prevent.'

The ranks and regiments of the gentlemen who signed this spirited document are not given, but most of them can be supplied from various sources. They show that by this time the garrison of Oxford was officered by commanders from all over the Kingdom.

They were:

	Signatures	Remarks
1.	T. Glemham	Sir Thomas Glemham. Governor of Oxford.
2.	S. Hawkins	Colonel Sir Stephen Hawkins. Lieutenant-Governor. F.
3.	R. Hamilton	Lt. Colonel R(obert?) Hamilton.
4.	R. Gosnold	Colonel Robert Gosnold. Had been a captain in Glemham's Regiment. F.
5.	T. Shirley	Lt. Colonel Sir Thomas Shirley of Sir Lewis Dyve's Regiment. F.
6.	H. Tillier	Colonel Henry Tillier. From the garrison of Bristol. F.
7.	R. Gerard (1613-1686)	Lt. Colonel Richard Gerard. The Queen's Regiment. F. (*D.N.B.*)
8.	W. Rose	Unidentified.
9.	R. Clayton	Unidentified.
10.	H. Crompton	Major Henry Crompton. Formerly in Lord Percy's Regiment. F.
11.	Cl. Martyn	Clement Martin. Captain and Adjutant-General. Formerly in Prince Rupert's Regiment of Horse. Probably came from Bristol with the Prince.
12.	R. Hall	Lt. Colonel Richard Hall. Lord Hopton's Regiment. Came perhaps from Bristol. F.
13.	W. Horwood	Major. H?. A relation of Lady Whorwood?.
14.	Rog. May	Major Roger May. John Buller's Regiment. From Exeter? F.
15.	W. Smyth	Captain and Provost-Marshal.
16.	Ro. Meade (1616-1653)	Captain Robert Meade. The Queen's Regiment (?) A minor poet. H. (*D.N.B.*)

17.	Jo. Sisson	Captain John Sisson. Sir Thomas Glemham's Regiment. H.
18.	Edw. Masters	Captain Edward Masters. David Walter's Regiment. H.
19.	M. Predeux	Captain Matthias Prideaux. From Exeter?
20.	Th. Graham	Major Thomas Graham. F.
21.	Fr. Hall	Lt. Colonel Francis Hall. City of Oxford Regiment. F.
22.	Jo. Cressey	Captain John Cressey. Henry Tillier's Regiment. F.
23.	Adam Roch	Major or Captain. Thomas Pigott's Foot or John Stuart's Horse.
24.	Hanniball Bagnall	Major. Formerly in Sir Arthur Aston's Regiment. F.
25.	Jo. Hughs	Major John Hughs. The Queen's Regiment. F.

HORSE

When the main army lay about Oxford there was little need for horse in the city itself, and most of it was in the out-quarters disposed so as to ensure against surprise. But when the main army marched far away, as in the Summer and Autumn of 1644, the garrison needed cavalry of its own. Units which were in the city at one time or another included the King's Lifeguard and the Gentlemen Pensioners. The first accompanied the sovereign wherever he went, doing escort duties. Although these had to be performed at Oxford when the King was in residence, the Lifeguard of Horse, unlike the Lifeguard of Foot, cannot be regarded as part of the garrison. Its commander, Lord Bernard Stuart (later Earl of Lichfield), who was Captain-General of all His Majesty's Horse Guards,[62] did not even take orders from Prince Rupert when the latter was Lord General,[63] let alone from the Governor of Oxford.

Although the Gentlemen Pensioners fought as a troop at Edgehill, they do not seem to have done so thereafter. Some of them, like Colonel Sir Nicholas Selwyn and Major Bunnington, became senior officers, and it may be that those who did not rode in the Lifeguard of Horse.

1. The Regiment of Sir Arthur Aston and Sir George Boncle.

This Regiment was formed in 1642, and was with the army by 22nd November.[64] On 9th December it was quartered at Reading, where its colonel was Governor, until compelled to surrender on 27th April 1643. The Regiment fought at the storming of Bristol (26th July) and at First Newbury. When Aston became Governor of Oxford, in place of Sir William Pennyman who had died on 22nd August 1643, he naturally wished to have his own Regiment with him. At the rendezvous at Aldbourne Chase on 10th April 1644 Symonds saw the Regiment in Lord Wilmot's Brigade. He noted four cornets and 120 men,[65] from which it may be assumed that only four troops were present, the implication being that the other two had been left at Oxford to carry out the normal mounted duties of the garrison, for the Regiment certainly had six troops as is clear from a document of July 1644 among the papers of Captain Henry Stevens, the Royalist Waggon-Master-General.[66] Calculating each troop as 30, the Regiment at this time would, therefore, have numbered about 180.

During the long absence of the main army from the end of June to November 1644, Aston's Regiment must have been the backbone of the Oxford Horse.

At the relief of Basing House, the lieutenant-colonel, George Boncle, led Gage's left wing. The Regiment must have contributed at least 100 of the 300[67] Royalist cavalry present.

When Aston was replaced as Governor the Regiment once more become part of the field army. Boncle, who had been Lieutenant-Governor of Oxford, was knighted on 30th January 1644/5, and replaced by Colonel Sir Stephen Hawkins.[68]

Boncle seems to have taken Aston's place as colonel of the Regiment. He was captured at Naseby,[69] and died in prison at Lambeth. Lloyd calls him 'an Ingenious Gentleman, and a good Commander' and attributes his end to 'hard usage'.[70]

Whether the Regiment survived under some other commander is uncertain.

2. The Lord Treasurer's Regiment.

This was a Regiment formed in 1644 from gentlemen-volunteers and the servants of the great men then living in Oxford. It was in effect an auxiliary regiment of horse. Its colonel, Lord Treasurer Cottington, the wily 'Volpone' to his friends, was not the man to lead a cavalry charge, and the actual commander, at least upon occasion, was Colonel William (?) Webb, 'an old German Souldier dear to Prince Rupert'.[71]

The Regiment, under Webb, made up part of Gage's 300 horse at the relief of Basing House.[72] It probably contributed a contingent about 100 strong. Webb led Gage's right wing and 'charged the Enemy so gallantly, that in a Moment' their opponents 'all turned Head and ran away'.[73] This was the occasion when Mr John Stanhope, Gentleman of the Horse to the Marquess of Hertford, was captured trying to take a Roundhead standard.[74]

Presumably the Regiment continued to operate in and around Oxford until the surrender, but its history is somewhat obscure.

3. Colonel Will. Legge's Regiment.

This Regiment was probably formed about January 1644/5. Legge was a great favourite of Rupert's and brought at least two troops from the Prince's Regiment, his own and that of Captain Sir Thomas Gardiner, who was killed near Oxford in July 1645.[75]

The greatest exploit in which the Regiment is known to have taken part was the raid on Thame on 6th September 1645. It was typical of much of the fighting round Oxford during the War. The colonel's brother and lieutenant-colonel, Robert Legge, commanded the Regiment on this occasion. The major, Scroope Medcalf, gallantly led the forlorn hope. Charging the rebels' guards, with the aid of seven troopers, he removed the carts which barricaded the end of the town. Charging into the market-place, the Cavaliers routed the Roundhead Colonel Greaves and compelled him to fly out of the town. Legge proceeded systematically to secure and search the houses and stables in the town. This done he withdrew with the captured horses and prisoners.

Some 200 Parliamentarians fell on his rear before he had gone two miles, but a counter-charge sent them back faster than they had come on. In a second successful counter-charge, Captain Henry Gardiner was unfortunately shot dead — 'a youth of such high imcomparable courage, mix'd with such abundance of modesty and sweetness, that wee cannot easily match him unless with his brave brother, young Sir Thomas Gardiner, which two are now buried both in one grave. . . . '[76]

Another casualty in this affair was Major Medcalf, who died of a shot in the arm. He was a Yorkshireman. Many arms were taken and 2 or 300 good horses besides three standards.[77]

Whether Legge's Regiment survived his own dismissal from the Governorship in October 1645 does not appear. Since the garrison can hardly have done without horse it seems likely that it continued in the service.

Towards the end of the War Sir John Cansfeild, who had commanded the Queen's Regiment of Horse, was Commander-in-Chief of the Oxford Horse under Glemham,[78] and Colonel Sir William Campion, the brave Governor of Boarstall House, was first warned to assist him upon occasion, and later praised for his punctuality in cooperating when others had proved less forward.[79] Campion had led 50 horse in Gage's relief of Basing,[80] and his major, George Aglionby, had distinguished himself at Thame. Another garrison that sometimes reinforced the Oxford Horse was Wallingford Castle. Captain Robert Walters had joined Gage with 50 men for the Basing Expedition.[81]

Additional strength was sometimes provided by Colonel David Walter, the High Sheriff of Oxfordshire. His Regiment was in the raid on Thame.[82]

Towards the end of the War Rupert's famous Regiment, whose remnants must have come from Bristol with the Prince, would have been available for operations in defence of the Royalist capital. Captain John Richardson, who was killed in a sally from the East Port during the final siege, had certainly belonged to this Regiment, though by the time he was buried (4th June) it had been disbanded (25th April).[83] The presence of Captain Clement Martin in the city at the surrender[84] is further evidence of the presence of Rupert's Regiment.

A hypothetical list of the regiments whose more determined survivors made their way to Oxford towards the end of the War would be as unrewarding to read as tedious to compile. Yet one cannot divorce the history of Oxford in the Civil War from the history of its garrison if only because the presence of so many soldiers, 'full of strange oaths, and bearded like the pard', was bound to have an effect alike upon city and University. If learning suffered, there was still a harvest to be reaped by the tradesmen. Acid old Wood recalls this piece of youthful observation:

'After his returne to the house of his nativity, he found Oxford empty as to scholars, but pretty well replenish'd with parliamentarian soldiers. Many of the inhabitants had gained great store of wealth from the Court and royalists that had for several yeares continued among them; but as for the yong men of the city and university he found many of them to have been debauch'd by bearing armes and doing the duties belonging to soldiers, as watching and warding, and sitting in tipling-houses for whole nights together.'[85]

They had been four dramatic years for Oxford. Dons, like John Nourse of Magdalen who fell at Edgehill,[86] had gone off to the wars. Students, too, like Wood's eldest brother, Thomas, who became a lieutenant of horse, found a buff coat more becoming than a gown.

The continual marching and drilling of Redcoats, Whitecoats, and Bluecoats had lent colour to the daily scene, breaking the mediaeval calm of the cloistered city. Strange scenes had been played, as when Prince Rupert, poleaxe in hand, came between two gentlemen who had quarelled over a horse and parted them.[87] Tall, hawk-nosed, and 'sparkish' in his dress, what must the peaceful citizens have made of this foreign Prince who rode so haughtily through their streets?

Grimmer scenes also met the gaze of the townsmen and the country people who came to market: delinquent soldiers riding the wooden horse over against the Guildhall,[88] or deserters swinging from the gibbet that stood at Carfax conduit.[89]

Unseen, if not unsuspected, gallants attempted to settle their differences 'at the further ende of Christchurch medowe'; though, as in the duel between Lord John Stuart and Mr. John Ashburnham (15th March 1642/3) — a future general and the Paymaster of the Army — where no hurt was done on either side,[90] these affairs were not always as fatal as the romantics would have us believe.

Endless labour on the defences, with felling of trees and casting up of earthworks, was the somewhat less picturesque side of Wartime life. There was a gloomier aspect as well. Time and again the ancient city witnessed a doleful cortège escort some great commander to his resting place in Christ Church or one of the many city churches. Thus it was on 13th January 1642/3 when Captain Lord d'Aubigny, one of the few Royalist cavalrymen slain at Edgehill, was brought from Magdalen College and interred in the Cathedral. 'The footmen soldiers came first with their muskets under their armes, the noses of the musketts being behind them; the pike men drayled [sic] their pikes on the ground; the horsemen followed with their pistolls in their handes, the handles beinge upwards; the topps of the auntients[91] allso was borne behind. A chariott covered with blacke velvett, where the body was drawen by 6 horses, . . . The man that drove the chariott strowed money about the streets as he passed. Three great voleys of shott at the enterringe of the body; and lastly, an herald of armes proclaymed his titles, . . . '[92]

All through the War the city had served not only as capital and headquarters but as supply base. The magazine of arms and gunpowder was in the little cloister of New

College — so easily guarded with its single entrance — and the magazine for victuals was in the Guildhall, that for corn in the Schools. In the Music School and the adjoining Astronomy School were the stores for soldiers' 'apparrell and coates' on which many tailors, 'forrainers' as well as townsmen, laboured constantly. Drawbridges were 'made & framed' in the Rhetoric School and in St Mary's College, now Frewin Hall, bells were melted and pieces of ordnance cast.[93] In Magdalen Grove was the Park of the Train of Artillery, where the great guns for field army and garrisons alike were parked.

Never in its long history could Oxford show so much to entrance the eye and intrigue the imagination: as witness Aubrey's irresistible picture of eccentric old Dr Kettle, forty years President of Trinity, being teased by Lady Thynne and Mistress Fanshawe, who, it seems, were quite unimpressed by his 'terrible gigantique aspect'. 'Our grove,' he writes, 'was the Daphne for the ladies and their gallants to walke in, and many times my lady Isabella Thynne (she lay at Balliol College) would make her entrey with a theorbo or lute played before her. I have heard her play on it in the grove myselfe, which she did rarely: for which Mr Edmund Waller hath in his Poems for ever made her famous . . . She was most beautiful, most humble, charitable, etc. but she could not subdue one thing. I remember one time this lady and fine Mistress Fenshawe,[94] her great and intimate friend who lay at our college (she was wont, and my lady Thynne, to come to our Chapell, mornings, halfe dressed, like angells) would have a frolick to make a visitt to the President. The old Doctor quickly perceived that they came to abuse him; he addressed his discourse to Mistress Fenshawe, saying "Madam, your husband and father I bred up here, and I knew your grandfather; I know you to be a gentlewoman, I will not say you are a whore; but gett you gonne for a very woman." '[95]

Others put a higher value on Ann Fanshawe's charms than the eighty-year-old President. On one occasion a company commander ordering a salute in her honour, nearly succeeded in blowing her pretty head off!

'We . . . heard drums beat in the highway, under the garden wall. My father asked me if I would go up upon the mount,[96] and see the soldiers march — for it was Sir Charles Lee's[97] company of foot, an acquaintance of ours — I . . . went up, leaning my back to a tree that grew on the mount. The commander seeing us there, in compliment gave us a volley of shot, and one of their muskets being loaded shot a brace of bullets not two inches above my head as I leaned to the tree . . . '[98]

One sometimes suspects that these Cavaliers were better warriors than soldiers! Be that as it may, they held Oxford for nearly four years and made a formidable if not impregnable fortress of it, which in the end Fairfax was glad to take by treaty rather than by storm.

APPENDIX

'A general muster in New Parkes behind Wadham College.'
13th February 1643/4.

'1 Regiment.	Kings life guard	— Red Coates
2 Reg:	Queens life guard	
3 R.	Lord Percyes Regiment	— White Coates
4 R.	Colonel Charles Gerards	— Blew Coates
5 R.	Colonel [Thomas] Pinchbecks	— Gray Coates
6 R.	Sr. Arthur Astons Reg: now raysing sans armes.'[99]	—

This force was estimated by Henry Connington, a Parliamentarian spy, to total 3,000 men. He reported a rumour that they were 'speedily to march forth but whither he knowes not.'[100] In fact, this was no more than a review or a training exercise.

NOTE: An illustrated article on De Gomme's plan of the defences of Oxford, entitled 'A Contemporary Map of the Defences of Oxford in 1644', by R.T. Lattey, E.J.S. Parsons, and I.G. Philip, was published in *Oxoniensia*, Vol. I (1936), pp. 161-74. This gives a comparison of the plan with other evidence and short accounts of the main fortification and the Fairfax lines. Chapters XIII and XIV of F.J. Varley's *The Siege of Oxford* deal respectively with the Garrison and the Governors. Detailed information about the Royalist Office of Ordnance will be found in the Introduction to Ian Roy's *The Royalist Ordnance Papers*, Part I, pp.7-58.

NOTES

[1] *R.O.P.*, Part I, p. 217.
[2] Belvoir Castle MSS.
[3] Luke, p. 237.
[4] See his interesting dispatch in Walker, pp. 90-5.
[5] Symonds, p. 219.
[6] All these Governors are in *D.N.B.* For further details of their careers see also Varley, Chapter XIV.
[7] MS. Harleian 6851.
[8] These three troops are not shown in the list of quarters. They are the Lifeguard and the Gentlemen Pensioners.
[9] Altered from Chipping Norton. Lord Grandison's Regiment of Horse and Grey's dragoons — from Faringdon — were destroyed there on 12th December 1642.
[10] 'Eynstone' in the MS.
[11] British Museum MS. Add. 34,713, f. l.
[12] *R.O.P.*, Part I, p. 195.
[13] Dugdale, p. 67.
[14] Symonds, MS. Harleian 986.
[15] Symonds, pp. 160-1.
[16] Symonds, MS. Harleian 986.
[17] Symonds, pp. 160-1.
[18] British Museum, Picture map of Naseby by Sir Bernard de Gomme.
[19] See undated petition (of c. December 1644) of Colonel Stephen Hawkins: MS. Harleian 6852, f. 253.
[20] R.O.P.
[21] See petition of Colonel Stephen Hawkins.
[22] Symonds, MS. Harleian 986.
[23] Walker, p. 38.
[24] Symonds, p. 162.
[25] For their service in the Scots Wars see Peacock.
[26] Dugdale, p. 46.
[27] *I.O.*
[28] He was a member of the court martial that tried Sir Richard Cave on that day. All the 12 military members appear to have been of the rank of colonel or above.
[29] Symonds, MS. Harleian 986.
[30] Symonds, p. 160.
[31] Symonds, MS. Harleian 986, f. 88.
[32] Symonds, p. 160.
[33] Walker, p. 60.
[34] Symonds, MS. Harleian 986, f. 88.
[35] Wood, *C. of O.*, Vol. III, p. 227.
[36] Symonds, MS. Harleian 986, f. 75.
[37] Ib., f. 88.
[38] Symonds, p. 159.
[39] British Museum, Picture map of Naseby by Sir Bernard de Gomme.

[40] *Mercurius Aulicus*, p. 1160.
[41] Sir William Sanderson, *A Compleat History of the Life and Raigne of King Charles* (1658), p. 730.
[42] Symonds, MS. Harleian 986.
[43] *I.O.* These officers were from L & W — 7; Berks — 1; Middlesex — 1; Bucks — 1; Surrey — 1.
[44] Dugdale, p. 88.
[45] Symonds, MS. Harleian 986, f. 76.
[46] Wood, *L. and T.*, Vol. I, p. 121.
[47] British Museum, MS. Add. 14,294, ff. 3 and 4. Grant of Arms, 13th August 1661.
[48] *C.S.P.D.* 1641-3, pp. 500 and 510.
[49] Symonds, p. 181.
[50] Warburton, Vol. III, p. 181.
[51] Dugdale, p. 67.
[52] Warburton, Vol. III, p. 181.
[53] Dugdale, p. 82.
[54] Ib., p. 88.
[55] Henry Tillier, Sir Matthew Appleyard, Will. Murray, and Lt. Colonel John Russell of Prince Rupert's Bluecoats.
[56] Warburton, Vol. III, p. 175.
[57] *I.O.*
[58] Dugdale, p. 85.
[59] *I.O.*
[60] Joshua Sprigge, *Anglia Rediviva* (1647), p. 236.
[61] Dugdale, p. 88.
[62] Symonds, p. 82: commission dated at Boconnoc 25th August 1644.
[63] See Symonds, p. 152: 15th November 1644.
[64] P.R.O. W.O. 55/423. Royalist Ordnance Papers.
[65] Symonds, MS. Harleian 986.
[66] Stevens, p. 32.
[67] Of these 100 were supplied by Boarstall House and Wallingford Castle.
[68] Symonds, p. 162.
[69] Peacock, p. 99.
[70] D. Lloyd, *State Worthies* (1665), p. 689.
[71] Ib., p. 680.
[72] Walker, p. 90.
[73] Ib., p. 92.
[74] *Mercurius Aulicus*, p. 1160.
[75] Buried in Christ Church Cathedral 29th July 1645: Wood, *L. and T.*, Vol. I, p. 120.
[76] Ib., Vol. I, p. 121. It seems likely that Henry had succeeded to the command of his brother's troop.
[77] Ib., p. 122.
[78] MS. Danny Papers, No. 74: 11th November 1645: East Sussex Record Office, Lewes.
[79] Ib., No. 78: Charles I to Campion, 3rd December 1645.
[80] Walker, p. 90.
[81] Ibid.
[82] Wood, *L. and T.*, Vol. I, p. 120.
[83] Wood, *C. of O.*, Vol. III, p. 246.
[84] Dugdale, p. 88.
[85] Wood, *L. and T.*, Vol. I, p. 129: September 1646.
[86] Ib., p. 59.
[87] Luke, p. 44.
[88] Wood, *L. and T.*, Vol. I, p. 83.

[89] Ib., pp. 91 and 93: set up on 13th January 1643 (p. 82).
[90] Ib., p. 91.
[91] Colours.
[92] Wood, *L. and T.*, Vol. I, p. 82.
[93] Ib., pp. 83 and 84.
[94] Ann Fanshawe.
[95] Anthony Powell, *John Aubrey and His Friends* (1948), pp. 47-8.
[96] In St. John's College garden.
[97] Knighted 25th December 1644: possibly in Charles Gerard's Regiment.
[98] Fanshawe, p. 33.
[99] MS. Harleian 986, f. 75.
[100] Luke, p. 254.

PART II

THE KING'S LIFEGUARD OF FOOT

CHRONOLOGY

1642	
July-September	Commissioned and raised
23 October	Battle of Edgehill
12 November	Storming of Brentford
9 December	Allotted winter quarters in Oxford
1642/3	
c. 1 February	Strength about 500
2 February	Storming of Cirencester. Detachment present
18 February	Strength about 600
1643	
c. 10 April	Escape of Sir William Vavasour from Windsor Castle
11 April	Little Dean. Detachment present
13 April	Ripple Field. Detachment present
23 April	Detachment surprised at Dorchester, Oxfordshire
25 April	Action at Caversham Bridge
10 August to 5 September	Siege of Gloucester
12 August	The Earl of Lindsey, colonel of the Regiment, arrives at Oxford
20 September	First Battle of Newbury
September	The Regiment returns to Oxford
1643/4	
13 February	Muster in the New Parks, Oxford
1644	
6 April	The Regiment marches from Oxford, about 350 strong
10 April	Rendezvous at Aldbourne Chase
29 June	Battle of Cropredy Bridge
21 August	Battle of Beacon Hill, Lostwithiel
31 August	Battle of Castle Dore, near Fowey
27 October	Second Battle of Newbury
November	The Regiment returns to Oxford
1645	
9 May	Strength about 200
14 June	Battle of Naseby
6 August	Glemham's Foot march as the Lifeguard
24 September	Battle of Rowton Heath
5 November	The King returns to Oxford
1646	
24 June	Surrender of Oxford.

THE KING'S LIFEGUARD OF FOOT

About a hundred of the 408 strangers living in St Aldate's parish in January 1643/4, were soldiers. Of these 81 belonged to the King's Lifeguard of Foot. The history of this regiment calls, therefore, for fuller treatment than those of the others in the garrison.

The Lifeguard was among the first regiments raised and its officers' commissions were probably signed in Yorkshire in July 1642.[1]

The colonel throughout the war was Montague Bertie, Lord Willoughby d'Eresby (1608?-1666), who became Earl of Lindsey in 1642 as well as Lord Great Chamberlain of England.

The senior officers were soldiers of some experience. Clarendon tells us that Lord Willoughby had been a captain in the Dutch service. His lieutenant-colonel, Sir William Vavasour (killed 1659), had been a colonel in the second Scots War (1640),[2] while the major, William Leighton, had served as a lieutenant in foreign parts before 1639.[3] No doubt, as Clarendon implies, some of the junior officers had also seen service on the Continent or in the Scots Wars, and since some of the soldiers had acquired Irish wives we may suppose that they were men who had fought in Ireland.[4] But veterans, of whatever ranks, were hard to come by in the England of 1642.

The men were raised for the most part in Lincolnshire and Derbyshire and to a lesser extent in Cheshire.[5] Clarendon tells us that when the Royal Standard was raised at Nottingham (22nd August 1642) Lord Willoughby 'brought up . . . from Lincolnshire another excellent regiment, near the same number [1000] under officers of good experience'.[5a] Though no doubt many of the men were from the estates of the Berties and their friends in Lincolnshire, a great number of the 'other ranks' were Derbyshire lead miners, raised through the good offices of Thomas Bushell. He claimed to have raised '1000 stout miners for a life-guard', but this seems to be an exaggeration.[6]

The soldiers of the Lifeguard wore red coats,[7] and as coats, breeches, and stockings were a general issue probably presented a fairly uniform appearance, though no doubt they would have struck horror into the hearts of the martinets of a century later. The soldiers of the Civil War knew nothing of regimental facings and lace and were spared the tyranny of powdered hair, queues, and stocks which afflicted their eighteenth-century descendants.

The Regiment distinguished itself in its first battle, Edgehill, where it fought in the tertia, or brigade, commanded by Sir Nicholas Byron.[8] Edmund Ludlow, who belonged to the Lifeguard of the Earl of Essex, describes the encounter. 'The enemy's body of foot, wherein the King's standard was, came on within musquet shot of us; upon which we observing no horse to encounter withal, charged them with some loss from their pikes, tho very little from their shot; but not being able to break them, we retreated to our former station . . . '[9]

The next Roundhead onslaught was better co-ordinated. 'The Earl of Essex order'd two regiments of foot to attack that body . . . where the King's standard was, which they did, but could not break them till Sir William Balfour at the head of a party of horse charging them in the rear, and we marching down to take them in flank, they brake and ran away towards the hill.'[10] Ludlow tells us that he saw 'about threescore lie within the compass of threescore yards upon the ground whereon that brigade fought in which the King's standard was'.[11] He does not say that all these casualties were from the Lifeguard, which probably did not suffer any more severely than the Lord General's Regiment.

Lord Willoughby was taken prisoner, 'piously endeavouring the rescue of his father', the Earl of Lindsey, who had been shot in the thigh and 'encompassed by the enemy'.[12] Sir William Vavasour and Captain Sir Henry Radley[13] were also captured while Major William Leighton was wounded. Sir Edmund Verney, the Knight Marshal, was killed but the great Banner Royal was gallantly rescued by Captain John Smith,[14] an exploit which, no doubt, did something to restore the *morale* of the men after their rude introduction to war. Though broken the Lifeguard was far from being destroyed. The total casualties do not seem to have been particularly heavy. Pay warrants exist for mid-November which show that the Regiment was still one of the strongest in the army.[15]

The Regiment evidently took part in the advance on London in November, but does not appear to have been seriously engaged. When on 9th December the Council of War allotted winter quarters, the Lifeguard was one of the four regiments chosen to garrison the Royalist capital, Oxford.

A good many men seem to have been lost through sickness or desertion during the winter and by 1st February 1642/3 the Regiment was only about 500[16] strong besides being badly armed. On that day Sir Jacob Astley wrote:

'Sir John Haydon Knt:[17] may be pleased to take notice that the regement of the Kings guards being very weakly Armed, as the last time his Maty saw this garrison in Armes, wher they appeared 190 armed and 210 vnarmed wherfor I pray as any Armes shalbe brought into the Magasine lett some espetiall care be taken first to furnish the Ks: guards before any other regements, with the nvmber of 110 Armes or some such suffitient suppley and for soe doeing this shalbe yor warrant. . . . '[18]

As we have seen, a contingent from the garrison of Oxford was with Prince Rupert at the storming of Cirencester (2nd February 1642/3), and Lt. Colonel (William) Layton (Leighton)[19] and Captain (Thomas) Min[20] are among those mentioned as present. The former's horse was shot through the neck. Lieutenant William St. John, who was killed leading the forlorn hope, may have belonged to the Lifeguard, but its losses on this occasion do not seem to have been heavy.

Recruits came in fast in early February — no doubt officers had been sent home in December to raise new men. On 18th February Astley wrote that the Regiment had had recruits and now had 512 men, though 322 were unarmed. With the officers, sergeants, corporals, and drummers of ten companies this would make a total strength of rather more than 600.

Despite Astley's urging, the officers of the ordnance were not able to arm the Regiment fully until the following April, an illustration of the shortage of arms at Oxford at this period.

The arms issued were:

	Muskets	Pikes	TOTAL
7 February	40	40	80
18 February	70	30	100
14 April	—	9	9
23 April	—	133	133
	110	212	322[21]

Since the Regiment had 512 private soldiers one would expect it to have about 170 pikemen and 340 musketeers, but it is evident that the proportion of pikemen in the Lifeguard was far higher than it should have been by mid-seventeenth-century standards. No doubt the explanation is that it was comparatively easy to make pikes locally, while muskets were 'in short supply'. For example on 18th January 1642/3 the officers of the ordnance had received from Thomas Hill 'Pikemaker for his Mats prsent service, by contract from the Commissioners' 202 'Longe pike staves'.[22] Thomas Hill, who is described as being 'of Cheeveley parish in North Heath neare Newbery', produced another 299 long pike staves on 21st February, and two days later 420 long pike heads arrived from Sir William Russell, the Governor of Worcester,[23] forwarded no doubt from the iron-working regions of Shropshire. It may well be that these very weapons found their way into the hands of the Lifeguards though one would hope that it took less than two months to fit the heads to the staves!

A detachment of the Regiment was evidently with Prince Maurice in his brief campaign against Waller in the Forest of Dean, for Major Leighton is mentioned by Captain Richard Atkyns in his account of Little Dean (11th April 1643).[24] Some Royalist cavalry were worsted but when the Parliamentarians pursued them into the town 'Major Leighton had made good a stone house, and so prepared for them with musketeers; that one volley of shot made them retreat: . . . '

Leighton and his men must also have been present when Prince Maurice worsted Waller at Ripple Field (13th April). The Regiment's next affair was less fortunate. On 23rd April it was one of those sent to attempt the relief of Reading.

Quartering that night at Dorchester, and 'not being so carefull of their watch as they ought to be,'[25] they were surprised and lost some 40 prisoners including the captain-lieutenant and another lieutenant.[26] It is not certain that all the casualties were suffered by the Lifeguard for other units from the Oxford garrison may have been represented. It is certain that the attempt to relieve Reading which ended in the abortive action at Caversham Bridge (25th April) denuded Oxford of its regular garrison. On the 24th and 25th 'the cuntry men of the trained bands of this county, beinge summoned, came in and appeared here at Oxford, to receive order about a garrison to be made of them, for the defence of the Universitie & cittie of Oxford duringe his majestie's absence, by the lords and the commissioners of the councell of warre which his majestie had left here.' On the 28th 'there was not so much as a drumme mo heard to beate, all the morninge (as usually they did) in Oxford, nor any tramplinge of horses &c; but every thinge hush and silent.'[27] But Reading had been yielded (27th April) and on the afternoon of the 29th all the horse and foot came trooping back.

It may be assumed that the lieutenant-colonel, William Vavasour, shortly to be created a baronet, commanded the Regiment at Caversham Bridge. Taken at Edgehill, he had been imprisoned for a time in Warwick Castle. He had then been transferred to Windsor whence he had succeeded in escaping about 10th April to Reading, 'where he was kindly entertained and welcomed.' He arrived at the Court in Oxford on 13th April.[28]

The Regiment remained quietly in its garrison for the next four months and apparently saw no action, though it took a share of the work on the defences of the city.[29] On 15th July 'all the common soldiers then at Oxford were new apparralled, some all in red, coates, breeches, & mounteers; & some all in blewe.'[30]

Vavasour did not remain long in command of the Regiment. He was still lodging in Oxford as late as 14th June,[31] and on that very day he was commissioned as Commander-in-Chief 'of all Forces in any of the Countyes of Hereford, Monmouth, Glamorgan, Brecon and Radnor.'[32] He was to command a brigade from those parts at Gloucester and at First Newbury. On 17th July he received a commission to raise a regiment of 500 horse.[33] The commissions of William Leighton to lieutenant-colonel and of Robert Markham to major should, therefore, have dated from 14th June 1643. Presumably one of the lieutenants became a captain at the same time, but who this was is not known.

We may assume that it was with Lt. Colonel Leighton at its head that the Regiment, not less than 600 strong, newly-clad and fully armed, marched off to take part in the siege of Gloucester.

The colonel, now the second Earl of Lindsey and Lord Great Chamberlain of England, probably rejoined before its walls, for he had arrived at Oxford from London on 12th August, presumably having been exchanged.[34] He had been treated with respect by his captors. In November 1642 while a prisoner in Warwick Castle he had asked to be sent to London as 'it would be more convenient for him to look to divers Occasions that concern his Estate.' The Lord General, Essex, was confident that Lindsey 'being a Person of Honour' could be trusted to render himself a Prisoner at London' and the House of Lords not only left the decision to Essex, but also ordered that the goods belonging to Lindsey's sister and remaining in the Earl of Rutland's house, should be exempted from any search 'being the House of a Peer'.[35] Such was their tenderness for one of their own House — regardless of party.

At the First Battle of Newbury (20th September) the Lifeguard fought in the first tertia under Sir Nicholas Byron, who made a determined advance against the so-called Round Hill, the key to the Parliamentarian centre. The Lifeguard suffered less severely than other regiments in the brigade, but even so had 29 common soldiers sufficiently badly hurt to require transport to convey them from the field.[36] The number of killed is unknown, nor do we know the names of any officer casualties. It may be that Lieutenants Cranfield and Godwin, whose names disappear from the records between June 1643 and January 1644, fell before Gloucester or at Newbury. It is even more likely that Lieutenant Abrie (Aubrey), whose widow and two small children were living in John Horne's house in January 1644, was a victim of this campaign. But on the whole the losses of the Regiment at First Newbury seem to have been lighter than those suffered at Edgehill.

Once more the Lifeguard returned to Oxford. A handful of the officers — Lt. Colonel Leighton; Major Markham and the Quartermaster, Benjamin Stone; and Lieutenant Webster — went back to their old billets, perhaps an indication that they were on good terms with their landlords, or that they were comparatively well-to-do. The majority had to look for new quarters. Perhaps the increasing number of strangers pouring into Oxford had made it impossible to keep their rooms vacant for them.

It is for this period that the 'Exact Accompt' is so valuable for the composition of the Regiment, listing well over half of the commissioned officers and giving some indication, by the number of their dependents, of their relative social status. The colonel, the Earl of Lindsey, was, as might be supposed, in an altogether different class from the rest. Four gentlemen attended him, not to mention three footmen, a cook and a groom, besides the two other servants who lodged with Widow Hill. Lt. Colonel Leighton could afford two servants, the equivalent perhaps of a bâtman and a groom in later days, and Captain Windebank, too, was evidently fairly affluent, since he and his wife were attended by two men and two maid servants. Major Markham had a servant, but the rest of the company commanders, even the Lincolnshire knight Sir Henry Radley, lacked any such attendants: perhaps their estates lay in the power of the enemy, perhaps they were soldiers of fortune who saw their pay too rarely to be able to support servants. Some of the subalterns, subsidized perhaps by fathers too old to take the field, were more fortunate. Lieutenants Webster, Abrie, Godwin, and Cranfield and Ensign Hubberstay each employed a man, though Abrie's widow could evidently afford no such luxury with two small children to support. Is it too far-fetched to suggest that to some extent the company commanders may have been chosen from among the class of professional 'swordsmen', and the subalterns from the landed gentry?

A few wives, besides the Irish ladies already mentioned, were with the Regiment. Captain Windebank, Lieutenants Cotton and Abrie, Ensign Masterman and Sergeant Benfield were among those whose wives were with them at Oxford. It was by no means uncommon even as late as the Crimean War for British soldiers to be accompanied on campaign by their wives. In the Civil Wars, with many districts infested or threatened by the Roundheads, it is quite understandable that a soldier's family would prefer the discomfort of cramped quarters in Wartime Oxford, to the uncertainties of life in Lincolnshire, Derbyshire, or Cheshire, all of which by January 1643/4 were partly overrun by the Parliamentarians.

As we have seen, 81 of the 100 or so soldiers lodging in St Aldate's belonged to the King's Lifeguard, including all three of its field officers and five of the captains. It is probable that there were ten if not eleven companies in the Regiment and so only two or three of the company commanders are left unaccounted for.

For some reason the majority of the rank and file were not billeted in St Aldate's. We may assume that 350 is a reasonable estimate of the strength of the Regiment in January 1643/4, for it seems to have had that number in April, yet no more than 62 of the 'other ranks' were living in St Aldate's. Perhaps this is some indication of the superior accommodation to be had in the parish! It may be that some of the 79 men housed in Pembroke College, were soldiers of the Lifeguard, for 79 seems a large number to cram into a small college.[37]

On 6th April 500 foot marched out of Oxford to join Lord Hopton. They were the

Lifeguard and Charles Gerard's Regiment.[38] We know that the last only had 150 men at the rendezvous at Aldbourne Chase four days later,[39] so we may safely assert that the Lifeguard was 350 strong.

Little is known of the part which the Lifeguard played in the campaigns of 1644. Its presence at Cropredy Bridge (29th June) may be assumed since it was not one of the regiments left to garrison Oxford, but its adventures on that day have found no chronicler.

When the King marched into Cornwall his Lifeguard went with him in the first tertia,[40] but the only record of its doings is a return of sick soldiers at Boconnoc and Liskeard. They are listed[41] by name under nine companies:—

	Boconnoc	Liskeard
My Lds Company	6	4
Leiut Coll: Comp.	2	1
Majors Comp.	4	3
Cap. Legg's Comp.	1	—
Capt. ffox	1	—
Capt. Levinz	4	—
Sr. Hen. Radly	1	3[42]
Capt. Stacy	2	—
Capt. Johnson	1[43]	2[44]

It seems that there were eleven companies in all, for Captains Beeton and Fisher, who were both with the Regiment both in January 1643/4 and June 1645, do not appear in the list — presumably because none of their men were sufficiently sick to be absent from the unit.

Captain Legg's [sic] company *may* be the firelocks who guarded the train. This company had been in the Scots War of 1640, under Captain Will. Legge, and his brother Lieutenant Richard Legge. Their company does not seem to have been disbanded in 1641, and was with the artillery at Edgehill. Its inclusion in the Lifeguard is possible since Will. Legge had the Court appointment of Master of the Armoury. If this is so, the Regiment consisted of ten normal companies and the firelocks. In the Royalist army most regiments had eight companies, and only a few of the strongest had so many as ten.

In Cornwall the Regiment had marched in the first tertia, under Colonel Thomas Blague.[45] No doubt it fought in the same formation at Second Newbury (27th October 1644) but nothing is known of its fortunes upon that day. The Earl of Lindsey was among those who accompanied the King on his forced march to Bath on the 'sad night' after the battle,[46] from which it looks as if the effective command of the Regiment was usually left to Leighton.

The Lifeguard must have spent the Winter 1644 to 1645 in quarters in Oxford. On 7th May 1645 Lindsey was once more in attendance upon the King when he set out upon the fatal campaign of Naseby.[47] The Lifeguard, which formed part of the marching army, had not apparently received many recruits during the Winter and on 9th May was only 200 strong,[48] though this figure may not include officers. At Naseby (14th June) the Regiment formed part of the reserve. Symonds, who gives some description of six of the ensigns borne in its ranks that day, notes in his very imperfect list of the Royalist units present:[49]

'The King's regiment of life-guards, commanded by the Earle of Lindsey their Generall.

Colonel, Layton: Major, Markham.'

These officers must have been well-mounted: at any rate they are not listed among the fourteen officer prisoners taken on that day of wrath. There are at least two versions of the list of those captured:

Lords' Journals, Vol. VII, p. 434.	Peacock, p. 95.	Remarks.
Captains		Captains
Fox	Cap. Fox	Charles Fox

Levins	Cap. Lewens	Rob Levinz
Fisher	Cap. Flyer	Fisher
Benton	Cap. Benton	John Beeton
Bartee	Cap. Barby	Nicholas Bertie
Captain Lieutenant	Cap. Lieut.	Captain-Lieutenant
Waller	Waller	Waller
Lieutenants		Lieutenants
Muese	Lieut. Mewsey	Mewsey ?
Browne	Lieut. Brown	Brown
Ensigns of the Guard		Ensigns
Chamberlain	Ensigne Chamberlain	Rob. Chamberlain
Porter	Ensigne Porter	Porter
Birkenhead	Ensigne Berkenhead	William Berkenhead
Ingoldsby	Ensigne Ingolsby	Ingoldsby
Moushall	Ensigne Mousehall	Peter Mowshall
Wildhall	(omitted)	Wildhall

Apparently the Regiment still had ten companies, and should, therefore, have had 30 officers. A few may have escaped besides the field officers, while a few were probably among the fallen. It seems unlikely that the Regiment still had its full complement of officers.

The prisoners were marched to London and marched through the City on 21st June 1645 escorted by the Green and Yellow Regiments of the London Trained Bands. On this occasion the captured colours of the Regiment were among the trophies displayed: [50]

'Six Standards of Foot Colours of the Foot Guard, all which have every of them a red Crosse in a white silver Field, next unto the Pole, and are severally distinguished thus, the Colours are all red.

1. The Kings Standard with a goulding lyon, and over the Lyon a goulden Crown, and over the Lyon and under the Crown this Motto, DIEV EST [sic] MON DROIT.
2. The Queens Standard, with a Dragon and a Crown, both in gould.
3. A Percullis [sic] and a Crown, both in gould.
4. A Rose and Crown, the Crown gould, the Rose white silver in the midle, and the outward leaves shadowed with silver.
5. Six Colours of the Standards of [the] Foot Guard, were every of them three Roses a piece, in the same manner that the Single Rose is described. All of those six Colours of [the] Foot Guard, the Colours are red, and have every of them a red Crossė in a white silver Field next the Pole.'

If Symonds is correct, the Regiment was not strong in its last campaign. Even so, it would appear from this description that it still carried ten colours in its last battle — hence the inference that it still had ten companies.

Some effort was made to replace the lost Regiment. There is a letter of 2nd July 1645 to Colonel Barnaby Scudamore, Governor of Hereford, from which it appears that the gentlemen of Herefordshire had failed to raise the men they had promised. However, 500 of those that had come in were to be handed over to the bearer of the letter (Leighton perhaps) to recruit the Lifeguard.[51] There is no evidence that this measure produced any good result. A week later an order was given for the exchange of 150 soldiers of the Life Guards for a similar number from among 400 prisoners taken by Sir William Vaughan at Bridgnorth.[52] Since the men taken at Naseby had been marched to London this measure, too, may have been difficult to perform.

Symonds records under 6th August 1645 that 'Sir Thomas Glemham's foot, that came from Carlisle to Cardiffe, marched as the King's life-guard.'[53] These northerners were not unworthy successors to the lost redcoats for their determined defence of Carlisle was a renowned episode of a war which was not lacking in soldierlike exploits.

Under 13th August Symonds, who belonged to the Lifeguard of Horse, writes that

'Sir Thomas Glemham's foot were made dragoons in Brecknockshire, and march too with us.'[54] The strength of the unit at this time does not appear. It was probably with the King at Chester at the time of the disaster at Rowton Heath (24th September) and no doubt returned with him to Oxford on 5th November 1645, remaining there until the surrender.

Presumably Lindsey continued as titular commander of the Lifeguard, but Leighton had remained at Hereford, and no doubt the junior officers were now men who had come south with Glemham. Colonel Robert Gosnold, who had once been a captain in Glemham's foot,[55] and who was certainly at Oxford on 17th May 1646,[56] may have been one of them.

There is apparently no direct connection as regards personnel between King Charles I's Lifeguard and the Regiment, now the Grenadier Guards, raised by his son in 1656. But it is interesting to see badges which have endured in the Brigade of Guards already in use, the Dragon, the Portcullis, and so on, and, of course, the red coat.

APPENDIX

A number of the officers of King Charles I's Lifeguard lived to see the Restoration and among those who claimed part of the £60,000 granted by King Charles II to his 'Truly-loyal and Indigent Party' were the following listed under 'Earl Lyndsy':[57]

L & W. Lt. Colonel Sir William Leighton.
Berks. Capt. John Beeton.
L & W. Capt. Nicholas Berty.
Gloucestershire. Lieut. William Fordred.
L & W. Capt. Charles Stevenson.
L & W. Capt. Charles Fox.
L & W. Ens. William Berkenhead.
L & W. Lieut. Rob Havercamp.
Warwick. Ens. Pet. Mowshall. (Capt. Rob Leven's[58] company).
L & W. Ens. Rob Hubberstay. (Capt. Johnson's company).
Somerset. Ens. John Ball. (Capt. Stuart's company).
L & W. Ens. Rob. Chamberlain.

Two Cheshire men and the widow of another, who had served under the Earl of Lindsey, claimed pensions after the Restoration as maimed soldiers. They were: Sergeant Randle Whittacker of Captain Richard Walthall's company, and William Pemberton and one Maykin of Captain Thomas Cholmondeley's company.

Whittacker served from Edgehill until Stow, though it is not clear why one of the Lifeguards should have been at Lord Astley's surrender at Stow-on-the-Wold on 21st March 1645/6.[59]

Joane Maykin, widow, claimed a pension in 1661, stating that Sergeant Whittaker and others under the same command could testify that her husband had been slain. He came from Hankelow, near Audlem.[60]

Pemberton had served from Edgehill to Naseby, and was among the prisoners taken to London after the latter battle. He had been ransomed, and had fought afterwards at Worcester in 1651.[61]

NOTES

[1] The commission of Lt. Colonel Stephen Hawkins of Sir Ralph Dutton's Regiment, the second raised, was signed at Beverley on 28th July 1642 (see MS. Harleian 6852, f. 253).

[2] Peacock, p. 83.

[3] 'A list of officers & gentlemen that have served in forraine parts wch have now elected for his Maties service' (National Library of Wales: Chirk Castle MS. F. 7442). Internal evidence shows that this list was compiled before July 1639.

[4] MS. Harleian 6851, f. 95. Minutes of the Council of War, 19th January 1643.
[5] The Post-Restoration Quarter Sessions Records include petitions from some who were maimed.
[5a] Bk. VI, § 62, note from the *Life*.
[6] *C.S.P.D.* 1668-9, p. 136.
[7] Symonds, MS. Harleian 986, f. 79.
[8] The brigade also included the regiment of the Lord General, of the Earl of Lindsey, and of Sir John Beaumont.
[9] *The Memoirs of Edmund Ludlow*, ed. C.H. Firth (1894), Vol. I, p. 42.
[10] Ib., pp. 42 and 43.
[11] Ib., p. 45.
[12] Clarendon, Bk. VI, §' 85.
[13] 'I.E.' assigns him to the Lord General's Regiment, but in 1644 Radley certainly belonged to the Lifeguard, and 'I.E.' is sufficiently inaccurate to be disbelieved on this point.
[14] An officer of Lord Grandison's Regiment of Horse.
[15] On 16th November they were to receive £238.16.0 for a week's pay. Only six of the nineteen regiments were stronger (B itish Museum MS. Add. 34,713, f. 1).
[16] About 100 officers, commissioned and otherwise, must be added to the 400 soldiers.
[17] Lt. General of the Ordnance.
[18] *R.O.P.*, Part I, p. 195.
[19] *Bibliotheca Gloucestrensis* (1823), Pt. I, pp. 159-74: 'A Particular Relation of the Action before Cyrencester'. At this date Leighton was still a major so the account may have been written a little later.
[20] Thomas Mynne (*R.O.P.*, Part I, p. 199).
[21] Ibid.
[22] They were 15½ feet long (*R.O.P.*, Part I, p. 66).
[23] Ib., p. 68.
[24] *The Vindication of Richard Atkyns.* See *Journal of the Society for Army Historical Research*, Vol. XXXV, No. 141 (1957), p. 7.
[25] *Mercurius Aulicus*, p. 210.
[26] The names of these officers are not given in Essex's letter to the Speaker: *L.J.*, Vol. VI, p. 17.
[27] Wood, *L. and T.*, Vol. I, p. 101.
[28] *Mercurius Aulicus*, p. 187.
[29] *R.O.P.*, Part I, p. 186.
[30] Wood, *L. and T.*, Vol. I, p. 103. Cf. letter of 11th October 1643, from Oxford, in which the Earl of Bath tells his Countess: 'Yo servant Tom Bold is now in a company of the Life Guards, in a red suit & montero which they wear.' A montero was a kind of cap, not unlike those once worn by fishermen.
[31] See p. 197.
[32] W.H. Black, *Docquets of Letters Patent . . . passed at Oxford* (printed 1838, but not published), p. 46.
[33] Ib., p. 57.
[34] *Mercurius Aulicus*, p. 435.
[35] *L.J.*, Vol. V, p. 463: 28th November 1642.
[36] 'Hurt Souldiers of Newbery' (MS. Harleian 6804, f. 92).
[37] Bodleian MS. Add. D. 114, f. 81.
[38] Dugdale, p. 64.
[39] Symonds, MS. Harleian 986.
[40] Symonds, p. 160.
[41] MS. Harleian 6804, f. 109.

[42] Including Sergeant Will. Parsons.
[43] 'The Drummer'.
[44] Ensign Hubberstat [sic] and Corporal Willyson.
[45] Symonds, p. 159.
[46] Ib., p. 146.
[47] Ib., p. 164.
[48] Ib., p. 166.
[49] P. 194.
[50] *The Manner how the Prisoners are to be brought into the City of London.* London, Printed by T.F. and J. Coe, 1645, p. 63.
[51] MS. Harleian 6852, f. 273.
[52] Ib., f. 277: 9th July 1645.
[53] Symonds, p. 219.
[54] Ib., p. 223.
[55] *I.O.*
[56] Dugdale, p. 88.
[57] We have omitted '(L & W) Cordwayne Tho Lieut to Cap. Tho. Draper', for the latter certainly belonged to the regiment raised by the 1st Earl of Lindsey — the Lord General's Regiment. Stuart and Stevenson, too, may have belonged to that unit.
[58] Levinz.
[59] Cheshire Quarter Sessions Records, 8th July 1662.
[60] Ib., 16th April 1661.
[61] Ib., Nantwich, 7th July 1663. His petition is attested by Captain Thomas Cholmondeley, who had presumably been his company commander in 1642 for he does not appear in any of the later lists

PART III

THE SURVEY

I ORIEL COLLEGE

SUSAN SMYTH, WIDOW

Probably a relative by marriage of Thomas Smith, second cook of Christ Church. His name first appears in the surviving Disbursement Books of the College for the academic year 1577-8 in the list of *Famuli* under the heading *Coqui.*[1] On 8 January 1578/9 as cook, and a servant of Christ Church for thirteen years, he was admitted to privilege by the University.[2] He received 10s. for each of the four academic terms and a livery allowance *(vestes liberatae)* of 10s. His name appears for the last time in the book for 1626-7, and he was buried at St Aldate's 29 June 1627.[3]

Smith's Will was made 13 June 1627 and proved in the P.C.C. 19 May 1628,[4] John Holloway [q.v.] being a witness. His executors were his son John (*c.* 1575-1654) and his unmarried daughter, Magdalen. John Smith was educated at Westminster and Christ Church and later lived at Kidlington, Oxfordshire, where he was buried. His only daughter, Anne, married Sir William Morton (died 1672), a Royalist, lieutenant-colonel to Lord Chandos in the Civil War: she received half her grandfather's moveable goods and £600 in money 'on my land in Oxford'.

There is no mention of Susan Smyth, who was probably of an inferior status, as in the St Aldate's Defaulters List of June 1643,[5] she is termed 'Widdow Smith', although she appears as 'Mrs Smith' in the St Aldate's parish taxation lists of 1645, where she was assessed at very small sums. Her name appears on one of the 1647 lists also, but not in the Subsidy of 1648, so that she may have been dead by then.

Thomas Smith's house, inhabited during the Civil War by Susan Smyth or Smith, was the first in the parish of St Aldate's on the west side of Fish Street (St Aldate's) coming south from Carfax.[6] It stood on the site now occupied by the Bulldog (formerly the New) Inn, No. 108 St Aldate's. Wood recalls that Smith 'built the faire freestone house against [i.e. opposite] the Blew bore in St Aldate's parish anno 1594'.[7] Wood also says that the house was 'called the Christopher tempore Elizabeth'.[8] It was still so called in the seventeenth century. In the 1630 Rental of Oriel College, from which it was held, the house is entered thus: 'Item de tenemento in parochia sancti Aldati vocato Christopher Parler quod tenet Thomas Smith' 4s.[9] It is strange that Thomas Smith's name is still given in this Rental and in that of 1631.[10] The Oriel Rentals 1647-1729[11] shew that John Smith was responsible for the rent of the Christopher Parlour during the War and had got into arrears, so that in 1647 he had to pay five years' rent ending at the Feast of St Thomas 1646. The Mortons inherited the house.

The house had a garden which reached towards the north side of Pennyfarthing (Pembroke) Street. In an indenture dated 10 April 1587 relating to a house there situated[12] the tenement is described as having Pennyfarthing Street to the south and 'the garden of one Thomas Smyth cooke belonginge to the Christopher on the north part.' From this it is clear that Thomas Smith executed a rebuilding in 1594.

The line of the one-time Kepeharme Lane, which was stopped up in Wood's day, is represented now by the courtyard of the Bulldog, as formerly by that of the Christopher. The City Chamberlains' Accounts for 1647-8 show that John Smith paid 14s. arrears of rent for the lane.[13] In the City Rental of 25 March 1658 the executors of Mr Thomas Smith are entered as owing 2s. 'for a passage through Kepeharme's Lane and the house over the gate', paid by Mr [John] Holloway [q.v.].[14]

[1] Ch. Ch. MS. xii. b. 20.
[2] *Register*, Vol. II, Pt. I, p. 289.
[3] Wood, *C. of O.*, Vol. III, p. 206.
[4] 48 Barrington.
[5] Bodleian MS. Add. D. 114, f. 24.
[6] See H.E. Salter, *Survey of the South-West Ward*, No. 125.
[7] *L. and T.*, Vol. II, pp. 149-50.
[8] *C. of O.*, Vol. I, p. 200, n. 11.
[9] *Oriel Records*, ed. C.L. Shadwell and H.E. Salter, Oxford Historical Society, Vol. LXXXV (1926), p. 411.
[10] Ib., p.413.
[11] Oriel College Muniments I E 1.
[12] Pembroke College Muniments A/35.
[13] *O.C.A.* 1626-1665, p. 431.
[14] *O.C.P.*, p. 11.

NICHOLAS, VICOMTE ST PAUL or ST POL

It has not been possible to discover his place of origin (although such evidence as exists points to Lorraine), his parentage, and the dates of his birth and death.

St Paul and his brother may well have come over to England in the train of Henri, de Lorraine, Comte d'Harcourt, who arrived in London 12 October 1643 and in Oxford 31 December 1643 (see under Monsieur du Moulin).

The Parish Constables' Account for Upton, a few miles west of Newark, shews that St Paul was at Newark in April 1644: 'Ale for one of my Lord St Poll soldiers — 2d.' He was present at the Battle of Marston Moor, where his brother was killed.[1] He was again at Newark about the beginning of December 1644, and probably back in Oxford before Christmas.[2]

St Paul served towards the end of the War as General of Horse to John, first Lord Byron, who was appointed Governor of Chester in January 1643/4, and was besieged 1645-6. On 9 October 1645 'my Lord St Paule (almost as naked as his sword) ran rageinge in his shirt up to the North Breach, where the enemy prest extreamely for an entrance, but were by him so bravely back't that sudden death denyes them tyme to call for quarter'.[3] In December, he was addressed as 'Thou French rogue' by the starving inhabitants of the city.[4] At the end of the month he escaped to Wales in order to try to bring relief to the city. On 2 January 1645/6 Archbishop Williams wrote from Conway to Lord Ormonde of Sir William Vaughan being 'expected by a French Lord, who serves the King, Mons. de Saint Pol, now in my house, to come down the end of this week'.[5] On 8 January an Intelligence reported that 'Lord St Paul came into Flint Castle privately without any forces — stayed not there but sent four men that night into Chester, and upon his going away a fire was made on ye top of Hawarden Castle to give them notice at Chester'.[6] On 25 January the Archbishop informed Lord Astley that 'the Lord of St Paul is in these parts at the head of 600 (as he saith), but I believe of 500 horse, good men and well-armed, to be directed and employed by your Lordship'.[7] On 2 February Sir William Brereton informed Speaker Lenthall that the intention of Vaughan and Astley was 'to have joined with the Welsh forces under Lord St Paul, with those Irish that came over in December last, and those other now lately landed at Beaumaris, which were part of Lord Digby's regiment, some whereof are English, and some Lorrainers'.[8] But this intended junction was prevented by Colonel Thomas Mytton, before whom St Paul and Colonel Gilbert Byron retreated at Rhuddlan on 25 January.[9]

St Paul was present at the last battle of the First Civil War. On 26 March 1646 Sir Edward Nicholas [q.v.] wrote to Lord Ormonde of 'lord Astley's defeat on saterday last at Stow on the Would, as he was coming from Worcester, with about 2000 foot and horse, to join with the forces hereabouts. Lord Astley is prisoner at Warwick, Sir Charles Lucas at Compton-house; about 400 horse escaped hither [Oxford] with the Lord St Paul, and some few foot'.[10]

St Paul subsequently returned to the Continent and was with Charles II in Scotland, being among proscribed 'Malignants'.[11] In July 1653 he wrote announcing the Duke of Lorraine's intention to seize the King if he should come into his neighbourhood: St Paul was evidently in the service of the Duke, to whom he may have been related.[12]

St Paul married Elizabeth, second daughter of Sir George Ayliffe, of Grettenham, Wiltshire, and younger sister of Sir Edward Hyde's first wife, Anna Ayliffe (died 1632). Elizabeth's first husband was her first cousin John St John, second son of Sir John St John, first baronet, of Lydiard Tregoze, Wiltshire. The date of John's birth (24 March 1615) and his kneeling effigy as a youth appear on the tomb of Sir John and his two wives (erected in his lifetime in 1634) in Lydiard church. The St John-Ayliffe marriage had taken place by 22 May 1640 when Sir George Ayliffe made his Will: 'my daughter *Debora* [our italics] Saint John' is there mentioned. John St John was a colonel in the Royal army, and was buried at Newark 15 December 1643. It seems not unlikely that it was at Newark that his widow met St Paul.

On 15 November 1648 Hyde wrote from The Hague to Lady St Paul (who was the executrix of her husband's Will, proved at York) about certain bonds.[13] On 20 April 1649 Elizabeth, wife of Nicholas, Lord St Paul, begged to compound for the discharge of the Delinquency of her first husband, Colonel John St John. On 29 April she was fined £75.[14]

[1] Warburton, Vol. II, p. 464.

[2] Sir Henry Slingsby, *Original Memoirs* (1806), p. 59.

[3] R.H. Morris, *The Siege of Chester* (1924), p. 228, quoting British Museum MS. Harleian 2155.

[4] Ib., p. 169.

[5] Ib., p. 189.

[6] Ib., p. 171.

[7] Ib., p. 190.

[8] Ib., p. 196.

[9] Ib., p. 188. Other references to St Paul will be found in Morris, pp. 146, 165, 170, 186, 231, and 232: see also J.R. Phillips, Vol. I, pp. 352-3 and H.M.C., Appendix to VIth *Report*, p. 96.

[10] Carte, Vol. VI, p. 359.

[11] Eva Scott, *The King in Exile* (1904), p. 188.

[12] *C.C.S.P.*, Vol. II, pp. 226 and 231.

[13] See Bodleian Library, Clarendon State Papers, Vol. 31, No. 2913: also *C.A.M.*, pp. 1010-11 for the Ayliffe-Hyde-St Paul-St John case. The Will cannot be traced.

[14] *C.C.C.*, p. 1980.

DAVID WOODFEILD
(c. 1597-1668)

Joiner. The son of Thomas Woodfeild, of Westwell, Oxfordshire, husbandman, he was apprenticed 30 May 1609 to Thomas Key, joiner, of Oxford.[1] On 26 October 1610, Key having died, he was apprenticed to John Frewen,[2] who had himself been apprenticed to Key. As Frewen's apprentice he was admitted a freeman 20 September 1619.[3] He was elected second serjeant at mace to the mayor 5 June 1635.[4] He did not resign this appointment until 9 September 1667, after having had a deputy since August 1662, when he was aged and lame.[5] His wages were £1.6s.8d. per annum.[6]

On 9 January 1638/9 Woodfeild was allowed £5 by the city for drilling the trained bands,[7] and on 19 September 1642 he received £5 for his great services therein.[8] This was shortly after the departure from Oxford of Sir John Byron and his troops, who had held the city for the King, with the connivance and assistance of the mayor and Vice-Chancellor, from 28 August to 10 September. In this dramatic episode Woodfeild played a prominent part, both as participant and witness of the events, as we learn from the graphic 'Breife of our Greivances at Oxford' written by the pro-Parliament bailiff George Heron on 17 September and dispatched by him to the House of Lords.[9] Heron declared that 'David Woodfeild (Mr Maiors second seriant and the then Captain or leader of our City soldiers If his Majesty had had any of our body) came before the said Sir John Byron and his companie immediatlie and the Vicechauncelor, and the said David entered them into the City and provided them lodgings'.[10] On 31 August, however, a fast day, when Royalist members of the University acted provocatively by 'striking up drum' during the evening sermon for the mayor, Woodfeild accompanied Heron to the church, where they unsuccessfully requested the taking of counter measures.[11] During the year Michaelmas 1641 to Michaelmas 1642 Woodfeild was paid 10s. by the Keykeepers, being described as a 'serviceable man to this City'.[12] On 25 August 1643 he received £5 'given him by the Cittie for his pains takeinge these troublesome tymes according to an act of Common Councell'.[13] Sir William Pennyman, Governor of Oxford (died August 1643), appointed him a provost-marshal.[14] On 13 March 1642/3 he supplied the King with a number of muskets, bandoleers, long pikes, short pikes, javelins, halberts, bills, horsemen's lances, cornets' staves, and calivers: the lances and staves were entered as 'rotten'.[15] He was serving with the City Regiment 5 July 1644.[16] His name occurs in a list of persons certified as Delinquents by the Sequestration Committee for Oxfordshire 3 August 1648.[17]

Woodfeild's name appears in three of the St Aldate's parish taxation lists for 1645 and in the list of 1647. He paid 1s. in the Subsidy of 1648 as of St Aldate's.[18] The Hearth Tax of 1665 shews him as living in the parish of All Saints.[19] In the Poll Tax of 1667 he and his wife, Sarah, each paid 1s.[20] Sarah Woodfeild was buried at All Saints 3 July 1668.[21] David was dead by 5 October 1668.[22]

[Administration: MS. Wills Oxon. 107, f. 145: Act Book B: 6 October 1668: grant made to his son John].

An Inventory of his goods was taken and was exhibited by John Woodfeild 9 December 1668.[23] The total value was £26.5s.

John Woodfeild was under sixteen on 14 June 1643, when he was living in the house of John Wild, joiner, in Pennyfarthing Street.[24] In October 1640 he had been apprenticed to Wild,[25] who, in his turn, had had David Woodfeild as his master.[26] John Woodfeild was admitted a freeman in 1647 and worked as a joiner in Oxford. For one year (1653-4) he filled his father's place as second serjeant at mace, David having been discharged from office by the Honourable Committee of Indemnity.[27]

Woodfeild's house may have stood in Kepeharme Lane: or possibly Pennyfarthing Street: it has not been possible to locate it. His Inventory enumerated the rooms of his small All Saints' house: 'the Streete chamber', 'the Shope', 'the little roome behind the Shope', and 'the kitching'.

[1] City of Oxford Archives L. 5. 1, f. 172: Hannisters 1590-1614.
[2] Ibid.
[3] *O.C.A.* 1583-1626, p. 284.
[4] Ib. 1626-1665, p. 61.
[5] Ib., p. 295 and 1666-1701, p. 12.
[6] City Archives P. 5. 2, f. 262 v: Audit Book 1592-1682, year 1646.
[7] *O.C.A.* 1626-1665, pp. 85 and 422.
[8] Ib., p. 107.
[9] *The Manuscripts of the House of Lords*, Vol. XI, New Series, *Addenda* 1514-1714, ed. M.F. Bond (1962), No. 3592, pp. 322-33.
[10] Ib., p. 324.
[11] Ib., p. 330.
[12] *O.C.A.* 1626-1665, p. 425.
[13] City Archives P. 5. 2, f. 250.
[14] Bodleian MS. Add. D. 114, f. 31.
[15] *R.O.P.*, Part I, p. 71.
[16] *O.C.A.* 1626-1665, p. 119.
[17] City Archives F. 5. 9, f. 101: Vellum Book II.
[18] *S. and T.*, p. 168.
[19] Ib., p. 203.
[20] Ib., p. 238.
[21] Bodleian Library, Parish Register Transcripts, MS. Top. Oxon. c. 172, f. 182.
[22] Bodleian Library, MS. Wills Oxon. 307, f. 114: Caveat Book.
[23] Ib., 88/2/27.
[24] St Aldate's Defaulters, Bodleian MS. Add. D. 114, f. 24. Wild made Lucy Heath's wooden coffin in May 1645 (Willoughby de Broke MS. 1651).
[25] City Archives L. 5. 3, no folio number: Hannisters 1639-1662.
[26] *O.C.A.* 1626-1665, pp. 38 and 41.
[27] Ib., p. 199.

MRS MICHAEL MOHUN

Wife of Michael Mohun, actor (c. 1616-1684).

In November 1682 Mohun addressed a petition to Charles II for the restoration of his theatrical rights denied him after the union of the King's and Duke's Companies, which is of much biographical value:

'To the kinges most Excellent Mate
The humble petition of Michaell Mohun,
One of yor Mates Actors at the Theatre Royall
Showeth

That yor petr hath faythfully served yor Mate & Father (of ever Blessed Memory) 48 yeares in ye quality of an Actor, and in all ye Warrs in England & Ireland & at ye seege of Dublin was desperately wounded & 13 Moneths a prisoner, and after that yor petr served yor Mate in ye Regimt of Dixmead [Dixmude] in Flaunders & came over with yor Mate into England when yor sacred pleasure was that he should Act againe, as he hath ever since vpon all Occasions continued. . . .'[1]

This petition shews that Mohun began his professional career in 1634. He was trained under Christopher Beeston (1570?-1638) at the Cockpit in Drury Lane, where he was a member of the company known as 'Beeston's Boys'. On 12 May

1637 the Privy Council issued a warrant to the messenger Jasper Heiley [q.v.] 'to fetch before the Lords Christopher Biston [sic], William Biston, Theophilus Burd, Ezekiel Fenn, and Michael Moone, with a clause to command the keepers of the playhouse called the Cockpit in Drury Lane . . . not to permit plays to be acted there till further order', on account of the Plague quarantine.[2] This could be taken to imply that Mohun was already of age, so that the date (1620) of birth suggested in *D.N.B.* would seem to be rather too late. The only recorded part played by Mohun before the Civil War is that of 'Bellamente' in Shirley's *Love's Cruelty* (licensed in 1631) which he is said to have resumed after the Restoration. Like other actors Mohun (as stated in his petition) joined the Royal army, and he was possibly among the prisoners taken to Lord Petre's house in Aldersgate Street after the surrender of Chichester, 29 December 1642,[3] and afterwards to Windsor Castle.[4] What simpler explanation of his absence from St Aldate's in 1643/4 than that of his being a prisoner of war?

It is uncertain in which of Charles II's five regiments of foot employed in the Spanish service in 1656 Mohun was a major, but as those of James, Duke of York, Lord Ormonde, and Lord Bristol 'were Irish, the relics of the loyal party that had been scattered by Cromwell', it may well have been in one of these. He does not seem to have been in the Royal Regiment of Guards (now the Grenadier Guards) which was quartered at 'Dixmeede' in December 1658. In February 1657/8 he was present at a ball given to Charles II by the Marquess of Newcastle at his house in Antwerp, when 'Major Mohun, that was the player, in a black satin robe and garland of bays, spake a speech in verse of his Lordship's own poetry'.[5]

After the Restoration Mohun had a notably successful career on the stage. Pepys wrote of him that he was 'said to be the best actor in the world'. He saw Mohun for the first time on 20 November 1660, at the King's House, in Beaumont and Fletcher's *The Beggar's Bush.* Mohun's name appears on the first Drury Lane playbill, for 8 April 1663, when the play was another piece by Beaumont and Fletcher, *The Humorous Lieutenant,* and he played 'Leontive'.

John Downes in his *Roscius Anglicanus* (1708)[6] notes: 'Major *Mohun,* he was Eminent for *Volpone; Face* in the Alchymist; *Melantius* in the Maids Tragedy; *Mardonius* in King and No King; *Cassius* in Julius Caesar; *Clytus* in Alexander; *Mithridates.* An Eminent Poet seeing him Act this last, vented suddenly this saying: *Oh Mohun, Mohun! Thou little Man of Mettle, if I should write a 100 Plays, I'd write a part for Thy Mouth*; in short, in all his Parts, He was most Accurate and Correct.'

Mohun was buried at St Giles-in-the-Fields, 11 October 1684.[7] Unfortunately, efforts to discover the Christian and maiden names of his wife and the dates of his marriage and her death have proved unsuccessful.

A portrait of Mohun as a young man, wearing his own hair and holding a sword, inscribed 'Majr Mohun', hangs in the Dining Room at Knole, where it is strangely ascribed to Kneller.[8]

(For full accounts see *D.N.B.* and works there cited: also Nicoll, *op.cit., passim.* We are much indebted to the Revd. Denis Shaw for help with this notice.)

[1] P.R.O., L.C. 5/191, ff. 102 v — 103: printed in full, together with Charles II's favourable answers of 23 November and 5 December 1682, by Allardyce Nicoll in *A History of the Restoration Drama* 1660-1700, 2nd edn. (1928), pp. 327-8.

[2] *C.S.P.D.* 1637, pp. 98-9.

[3] 'Captain Mohun', *C.J.,* Vol. II, p. 910: 2 January 1642/3.

[4] Sir Owen Morshead, *Royalist Prisoners at Windsor Castle* (1958), p. 24.

[5] *C.S.P.D.* 1657-8, pp. 296 and 311.

[6] P. 17.

[7] As of 'Brownlow Str.' We are indebted for this entry to the Rector of St Giles, the Revd. G.C. Taylor.

[8] C.J. Phillips, *History of the Sackville Family*, Vol. II, (1930), p. 441. It is reproduced in J. Doran's *Their Majesties Servants*, ed. R. Lowe, Vol. I (1888), opposite p. 100.

III MAGDALEN COLLEGE

MR JOHN HOLLOWAY
(1598-1675)

Notary, known as 'Notarie Holloway'. The second son of John Holloway, of Oxford, gentleman, by his wife, Alice Leigh. The elder John Holloway (died 1632) was a public notary and registrary of Berkshire. The younger John Holloway was baptized at St Michael's, Oxford, 17 July 1598.[1] He was a civilian and registrary of Berkshire and official to the Archdeacon. He was created B.C.L. 1 November 1642.[2]

Holloway, who was called by Wood a 'covetous civilian and public notary',[3] was much employed for his 'Counsell in Colledge Causes'.[4] Examination of college accounts for the War period has shewn that he was employed by University, Queen's, Magdalen, St John's, and (very extensively) by New College, of which h was steward.

On 22 and 24 April 1643 weapons were received from Holloway for the King's stores.[5] Together with Edward Carpenter and Matthew Langley [qq.v.] he was appointed to take care of infected persons in St Aldate's parish.[6] In October 1645 he was among those parishioners of St Aldate's who contributed towards the £500 borrowed from the City of Oxford by the Lords Commissioners: he lent £10, much the highest figure for the parish.[7] His name appears in all the St Aldate's parish taxation lists for 1645 and 1647. He was assessed at £10 and 16s. 'in lands' in the Subsidy Lists of 1641[8] and at 6s. 8d. in the Subsidy of 1648.[9] Although in the latter year he was expelled from his post of steward of New College for disaffection to the commonwealth and for having been in arms for the King,[10] he continued to live in his house in St Aldate's until his death there 1 February 1674/5: he was buried in the church.[11]

Holloway married Susanna Anyon (died 1685), sister of Dr Thomas Anyon, President of Corpus Christi College, Oxford, from 1614 to 1629, by whom he had four sons, Thomas, Richard (Sir Richard Holloway, the judge),[12] John, and William, and one daughter, Susan.

In his Will Holloway describes himself as aged and infirm. Everything was left to his widow and his son Richard, who were appointed executors. Presumably he left nothing to his daughter Susan Windebank [see under John Windebank] as she was well provided for.

[Will: P.C.C. 1675: 65 Dycer: made 30 December 1674: proved 22 June 1675].

Holloway's house was on the west side of Fish Street and occupied the site of Nos. 105/106 St Aldate's, the former Ministry of Pensions: it is not clear whether the site of No. 107 belonged to him or to the Christopher, to which his tenement adjoined. He rented his house of Magdalen College, and was already in occupation in 1624-5:[13] he is mentioned again as there 7 November 1640.[14] On 7 December 1640 the College granted him a lease of 'All that their Tente Backside & garden grounds wth all & singular Thappurtences theire vnto belonginge, sett & beeinge in the pish of St Aldath . . . Betweene a Tente or Inn late in the tenure of John Lante Mr of Arts, & comonly called and knowen by the name of the Christopher in the North parte And a Tenenement [sic] [of Magdalen] nowe or late in the tenure of Bartholomew Isacke, Baker, & on the backside of a garden of Thomas ffulsey and Elizabeth Adingesole widdowe on the South part & on the kings high streete on theaste part And a garden nowe or late in the tenure of Thomas Mawberley, Cooke, on the West part'. The lease was for forty years and the rent 20s. per annum.[15] The house must have been a large one.

(For the Holloway pedigree see *Visitation of Oxfordshire* 1574 and 1634, Harleian Society, Vol. V (1871), p. 290.)

[1] Wood, *C. of O.*, Vol. III, p. 249.

[2] Wood, *L. and T.*, Vol. II, pp. 220 and 308 and *Fasti*, ed. Bliss, Vol. II, p. 12.
[3] *L. and T.*, Vol. I, p. 391.
[4] St John's College 'Computus' for 1644-5.
[5] *R.O.P.*, Part I, pp. 77 and 86.
[6] Bodleian MS. Add. D. 114, f. 89.
[7] City Archives E. 4. 6, ff. 1-2: *O.C.A.* 1626-1665, p. 453.
[8] City Archives B. 1. 4. c.
[9] *S. and T.*, p. 168.
[10] *Register of Visitors*, p. 529.
[11] Wood, *L. and T.*, Vol. II, p. 308.
[12] See *D.N.B.*
[13] Bodleian Library, University Archives W.P. γ 28 (7), ff. 4 and 11: Assessment of Privileged Persons. He is described as John Holloway the younger and 'the Regis'r's son', and was assessed at 5s. for his house in St Aldate's.
[14] Magdalen College Lease Ledger M: lease to Thomas Clayton [q.v.], ff. 327v-328.
[15] Ib., ff. 337-337v. See also *Survey of South-West Ward*, No. 124.

HENRY BOURCHIER, fifth EARL OF BATH
(c. 1587-1654)

The fifth and youngest son of Sir George Bourchier, by his wife, Martha, daughter of William, Lord Howard of Effingham, he was educated at Trinity College, Dublin, and succeeded a cousin in 1637.

Bath was made a P.C. 8 August 1641. In August 1642 he was taken prisoner in Devon (where he had been sent with the Marquess of Hertford) and brought to London.[1] Clarendon says that he 'neither had or ever meant to do the King the least service, but only out of the morosity of his own nature had before in the House expressed himself not of their mind'.[2] But he was among the peers who subscribed in 1642 to pay for horses for the King's service.[3]

By November 1643 Bath had joined the King at Oxford for he was one of the peers who signed the letter to the Lords of the Scottish Privy Council that month. By 28 December, however, he was at Tavistock [Tawstock?] when Joseph Jackman addressed a letter to him there from Oxford apropos of the forthcoming Parliament summoned by the King.[4] He was still absent on 24 January 1643/4 when Jackman wrote to inform him of a number of appointments made by Charles to offices at Court, including the Earl's own appointment (on 22 January) to the post of Lord Privy Seal, 'a place of great honour and profit, being the second privy councillor in place in the kingdom'.[5] By 27 January Bath was again in Oxford as he signed the letter of that date from the Lords and Commons to the Earl of Essex.[6] Another reference to him as at Oxford occurs on 8 February.[7] Later in 1644 he was appointed a commissioner for the defence of Oxford. He was in Cornwall in 1644, and was living near Barnstaple when it surrendered in 1645. Having taken the Oath and Covenant, he begged to compound 1 January 1648/9, having been with the King at Oxford. He was fined £713 on 19 February 1648/9.[8]

In 1638 Bath married Rachel (died 1680), fifth daughter of Francis Fane, first Earl of Westmorland. He died 16 August 1654: there is a fine monument at Tawstock, Devon.

It should be noted that although absent from Oxford on 23 January 1643/4, Bath was accounted an inhabitant of Holloway's house on that day.

(For a full account see *C.P.)*

[1] *L.J.*, Vol. V, p. 318: Clarendon, Bk. VI, § 36.
[2] Ibid.
[3] Peacock, p. 8.
[4] H.M.C., Appendix to IVth *Report*, p. 308.
[5] Ibid.
[6] Rushworth, Vol. VII, p. 573.
[7] *C.S.P.D.* 1644, p. 13.
[8] *C.C.C.*, pp. 1885-6. See also *C.A.M.*, p. 636.

SIR FRANCIS WINDEBANK
(1582-1646)

This evidence for the presence of Charles I's former Secretary of State at Oxford in January 1643/4 is important. According to the *D.N.B.*, after his flight from England in December 1640, he paid a visit to this country in the autumn of 1642 and was refused access to the King at Oxford. On the strength of a copy and translation in his handwriting of an edict of the French King concerning belligerent ships, dated Paris 10 July 1643, Windebank is stated by the *D.N.B.* to have been back in France by that date. He was at Exeter with the Queen 26 May 1644.[1] It is unfortunate that a large hole follows the entry 'came back to Oxford 16' in 'Memorials of Sir Francis Windebank' in the handwriting of William Fulman (1632-1688).[2]
For Windebank's sons Thomas and John see below.
(For a full account see *D.N.B.*)

[1] *C.S.P.D.* 1644, p. 171.
[2] Bodleian, MS. Rawlinson B. 224, f. 40.

THOMAS WINDEBANK, Esq., afterwards SIR THOMAS WINDEBANK, first BARONET
(c. 1612-before 1669)

The eldest son and heir of Sir Francis Windebank [q.v.], by his wife, Edith Jackson, of Essex. He was born c. 1612, and matriculated from St John's College, Oxford, aged seventeen, 13 November 1629. He was admitted to Lincoln's Inn 19 March 1632/3. From 1633 to 1637 he travelled in France, Spain, and Italy: numerous letters from him are among the S.P.D. By 1637 he was a Gentleman of the Privy Chamber[1] and was still holding the post in 1641.[2] About 1637 he was made a Clerk of the Signet. Thomas accompanied the King north in 1638/9,[3] and was sent on a mission to Paris in 1639/40.[4] He was M.P. for Wootton Bassett in the Short Parliament.
Thomas Windebank may have been the Windebank who was arrested by the Sheriff of Berkshire for taking up arms in Oxford for the King 12 September 1642, but this may have been his brother John [q.v.]. Thomas was at Exeter 26 May 1644.[5] He was created a baronet 25 November 1645. He compounded on the Oxford Articles 27 August 1646, having been present at the surrender in June: on 4 April 1647 he was fined £810.[6]
Windebank married c. 1646 Anne, daughter of John Grymes, of Bury St Edmunds. He was living in 1655, but was dead by July 1669.
(For a full account see *C.B.*)

[1] *C.S.P.D.* 1637-8, p. 123.
[2] L.C. 3/1.
[3] *C.S.P.D.* 1638-9, pp. 549, 615; 1639, passim.

[4] Ib. 1639-40, pp. 147, 320: 1640, pp. 21, 80.
[5] *C.S.P.D.* 1644, p. 167.
[6] *C.C.C.*, pp. 1465-6. See also *C.A.M.*, p. 614.

CAPTAIN JOHN WINDEBANK
(1618-1704)

The fifth (fourth surviving) son of Sir Francis Windebank [q.v.], by his wife, Edith Jackson, he was baptized at St Margaret's, Westminster, 11 June 1618.[1] He was educated at Winchester and New College, Oxford, from which he matriculated 23 September 1634. Many of his early letters are in S.P.D. He became a Fellow of New College, and graduated M.A. 21 January 1641/2.

Windebank shewed his Royalist sympathies when Sir John Byron arrived in Oxford 28 August 1642.[2] Bailiff Heron included him in his list of persons accused of aiding Byron,[3] and recorded in his 'Breife of our Greivances' that 'one of the schollers which watched the first Monday night vist 29 Aug. at Bailiff Herons dore by Mr Windebankes appointment wished there was as much powder under the parliament house as ever'.[4]

By 1643/4 Windebank was a captain in the Lifeguard of Foot. Unfortunately we do not know when he joined the Regiment or whether he began his military career as an ensign or a lieutenant. In December 1643 he had been having trouble over his billet in Oxford. In Jackman's letter of the 28th to Lord Bath [q.v.]. already quoted, he writes: 'Capt. Windebanke courts your honour to part with your quarter, as by his enclosed appears; — they made him a stalking horse to keep the house, and then turned him and his horse out of doors'.[5] Windebank's letter to Lord Bath is not calendared, and may therefore be missing. But it would appear that he appealed for Bath's accommodation in Holloway's house, where his father and brother were lodging, and obtained it. Whether he had to move again on the Earl's return, we do not know, but as he married his landlord's daughter, this seems highly improbable.

Windebank's military career may have ended in 1644. We have a list, probably complete, of the captains of the Lifeguard when the army was in Cornwall in August,[6] so he had almost certainly left by then. If he was already married (which seems unlikely since his second child was not born until c. 1649), his young wife may have persuaded him to lay the sword aside, although it may be that he continued to serve in one of the auxiliary regiments at Oxford.

John Windebank compounded, as of Oxford, 30 July 1649 and was fined 10s. on 9 August.[7] On 26 April he received a licence in pursuit of the medical profession which he had adopted, to exceed the limits of travel imposed on Delinquents by the recent Act.[8] He was created D. Med. by Cromwell 5 April 1654.[9] At some previous period he had studied medicine abroad, and later he practised at Guildford, of which he was mayor in 1663. He was made an honorary Fellow of the Royal College of Physicians 30 September 1680.

Windebank married Susan, only daughter of John Holloway [q.v.], and he had four sons and five daughters. Many years afterwards, the second daughter, Frances, was living with her Holloway grandparents, and married in 1666 Matthew Loveday, of Oxford,[10] the son, by her second marriage, of Dorothy Mander (see under John Mander), who was buried at St Aldate's 25 February 1681/2. The Holloways' house was immediately opposite to Loveday's home, the Blue Boar. Mrs Windebank was buried in the cloisters of Westminster Abbey 11 January 1681/2,[11] and her husband joined her on 16 August 1704.[12]

[Will: P.C.C. 1704: 171 Ash: made 17 February 1703/4: proved 15 August 1704, as of St Margaret's, Westminster, by Frances Loveday].

(For Windebank and his family see *Visitation of Surrey* 1662-8, Harleian Society, Vol. LX (1910), p. 122. The fifth daughter, Anne, buried in Westminster Abbey cloisters in 1681, is not entered).

[1] *Registers* 1539-1660, ed. A.M. Burke (1914), p. 98.
[2] See under David Woodfeild.
[3] *The Manuscripts of the House of Lords*, Vol. XI, New Series, p. 326.
[4] Ib., p. 331.
[5] H.M.C., Appendix to IVth *Report*, p. 308.
[6] MS. Harleian 6804, f. 109.
[7] *C.C.C.*, p. 2119.
[8] *C.S.P.D.* 1650, pp. 125, 537.
[9] *Fasti*, Vol. II, p. 185.
[10] *Marriage Allegations of the Vicar-General of the Archbishop of Canterbury*, Harleian Society, Vol. XXIII (1886), p. 128, where she is stated to be 'of Oxford'. Her age is given as about seventeen on 24 November 1666, which tallies with the entry of her burial in Westminster Abbey in January 1736/7 where she is described as eighty-seven.
[11] *Registers*, ed. J.L. Chester, Harleian Society, Vol. X (1876), p. 204.
[12] Ib., p. 254.

In June 1643 Holloway had lodging with him 'The Lord Newark & 6 servants, Sr Robt Stapleton & 2 servants & Dr Hodges, removed to Trinity Colledge, & some gonne out of town.'[1]

HENRY PIERREPONT, VISCOUNT NEWARK, afterwards second EARL OF KINGSTON AND MARQUESS OF DORCHESTER (1607-1680)

The eldest son of Robert Pierrepont, first Earl of Kingston-upon-Hull, by his wife, Gertrude, eldest daughter and co-heir of the Hon. Henry Talbot. He was born in March 1606/7, and matriculated as a Fellow Commoner from Emmanuel College, Cambridge, in 1624. He was M.P. for Nottinghamshire as Viscount Newark 1628-9 and was called to the Upper House in his father's lifetime as Baron Pierrepont in 1641. In 1642 he was Lord Lieutenant of Nottinghamshire. On 15 June he was a signatory to Charles I's declaration at York that he had no intention of war.[2] Later in the summer he tried unsuccessfully to obtain the powder of Nottinghamshire.[3] He was among the peers who subscribed in 1642 to pay for horses for the King's service.[4] In September he was excepted by Parliament from peace at any price. According to some authorities, he was created M.A. of Oxford University in November 1642, but there seems no evidence for this. On 14 December 1642 he was present at a Council of War at Oxford.[5] He succeeded his father as second Earl of Kingston in July 1643. He sat in the Oxford Parliament in January 1643/4. On 1 March 1644/5 he was made a P.C. and on 25 March 1645 was created Marquess of Dorchester. He was one of the commissioners for the King at the Treaty of Uxbridge. On 4 September 1646 he begged to compound on the Oxford Articles for his Delinquency in sitting in the Assembly there: he does not appear to have been in arms for the King. On 18 March 1646/7 he was fined at 1/10, £7,467.[6]

He was admitted to Gray's Inn in 1651, becoming a Bencher in 1658 and an honorary F.R.C.P. the same year. He was again a P.C. from 1660 to 1679.

He married first, c. 1630, Cecilia (died 1639), eldest daughter of Paul Bayning, first Viscount Bayning of Sudbury, and sister-in-law of Henry Murray [q.v.]; secondly, in 1652, Catherine, third daughter of James Stanley, seventh Earl of Derby. He died 8 December 1680.

(For full accounts see *C.P.*; *D.N.B.*; W. Munk, *Roll of the Royal College of*

Physicians, Vol. I (1878), pp. 282-92: *Memoirs of Colonel Hutchinson*)

[1] St Aldate's Defaulters, Bodleian MS. Add. D. 114, f. 24.
[2] Clarendon, Bk. V, § 346.
[3] *C.S.P.D.* 1641-3, p. 368.
[4] Peacock, p. 9.
[5] *R.O.P.*, Part I, p. 179. This shews that the statement that he was appointed to the Council in January 1643/4 is incorrect.
[6] *C.C.C.*, pp. 1472-4.

SIR ROBERT STAPLETON
(c. 1603-1669)

Dramatic poet and translator. The third son of Robert Stapleton, of Carlton by Snaith, Yorkshire, by his wife, Elizabeth, daughter of Sir Henry Pierrepont, of Holme Pierrepont, and sister of Robert Pierrepont, first Earl of Kingston. He was a first cousin of Lord Newark [q.v.]. Educated at the Benedictine monastery of St Gregory at Douay, he was professed as a monk there in 1625. He turned Protestant, however, and became a Gentleman in Ordinary to Prince Charles.
Stapleton was with the King at Nottingham, where he was knighted 13 September 1642. It seems likely that he took part in the Edgehill campaign, for he was one of those honoured in the so-called 'Caroline Creation', being created a D.C.L. of Oxford University 1 November 1642. A man of his standing may well have been one of the King's Lifeguard of Horse, the 'Troop of Show' as it was called by the rest of the army. Stapleton remained at Oxford until its surrender. The Oriel College Buttery Books shew that he was lodging there from 1643 to 1644.
After the Restoration he was Gentleman Usher of the Privy Chamber until his death, which occurred 10 or 11 July 1669. He married a Mrs Hammond, née Mainwaring.
[Will: P.C.C. 1669: 90 Coke: made 11 June 1669: proved 29 July 1669].
(For a full account see *D.N.B.*)

DR HODGES

A man of this name was created D.D. at Oxford 20 December 1642 from Christ Church.[1]
Venn in his *Alumni Cantabrigienses* thought that the Doctor might be identified with the Thomas Hodges who was admitted a pensioner at Jesus College, Cambridge, 17 June 1620, matriculated in 1620, and graduated B.A. in 1623/4, M.A. in 1627, and D.D. in 1660. He was vicar of Kensington from 1641 to 1672, Dean of Hereford from 1661 to 1672, and rector of St Peter's, Cornhill, from 1662 to 1672. His Will was proved in the P.C.C. in 1672.[2] But this divine was a preacher at St Margaret's, Westminster, before the Long Parliament on 28 September 1642,[3] and on 23 August 1643 was assessed as of Throckmorton Street. Wood, who was puzzled by Dr Hodges, considered this identification and was highly sceptical. So are we.

[1] *Fasti*, Vol. II, pp. 52-3.
[2] 121 Eure.
[3] *C.J.*, Vol. II, p. 747.

Holloway continued to lodge Royalists for, on 4 August 1645, Sir Henry Poole, of Sapperton, Gloucestershire, died in his house.[1]

[1] Wood, *L. and T.*, Vol. I, p. 120.

MR WILLIAM DAY
(c. 1604-1665)

Surgeon. He was born c. 1604, the son of Richard Day, *generosus*, of Abbots Langley, Hertfordshire.[1] He was licensed by Oxford University as a privileged person to practise surgery 4 December 1635.[2] In the Subsidy List of 6 December 1641 his name occurs among inhabitants of the South-West Ward as paying 20s. and 8s. 'in lands'.[3] In May 1645 he was paid £9 by Edward Heath for encasing Lucy Heath's body in 'seare-cloathes with spices & odors'.[4] In October 1645 he contributed £2.10s. towards the loan to the Lords Commissioners.[5] His name appears in four of the St Aldate's taxation lists of 1645 and in the lists of 1647. He paid 4s. 6d. in the Subsidy of 1648, as of St Aldate's.[6] His name appears in the list of those who lent money for the King's service in the Oxford Engagement December (?) 1648 as having subscribed £54.[7]
Later, Day moved to the parish of St Peter-in-the-East, where, in 1662, he rebuilt the Angel Inn,[8] which he had first leased from Magdalen in 1637. He also built a house on Brasenose College ground to the west of the South Bridge.[9] This was Swinsell Farm, which was sub-let to him by Margaret, widow of Thomas Smyth [q.v.], 22 July 1647, Smyth's lease being dated 3 March 1643/4.[10]
Day died in the parish of St Peter-in-the-East 29 September 1665 and was buried in the church on 3 October. An M.I., with his Arms, is on the south wall.[11] He married Ann . . . , who died in 1667 and was buried beside him. They had no children.
[Will: P.C.C. 1666: Mico 23, 38: made 6 July 1665: proved 15 March 1665/6].
It is not possible to locate Day's house with absolute precision, but it must have been one of the Magdalen College tenements on the west side of Fish Street, which extended from the house of John Holloway [q.v.] on the north to that of Robert Saunders [q.v.] on the south. In all probability Dr Thomas Clayton [q.v.] sub-let to him the northern of the two tenements which he leased from Magdalen, as Day was not himself a tenant of the College for his St Aldate's house.

[1] According to his M.I. in the church of St Peter-in-the-East, he was aged sixty-one at the time of his death in 1665 and his father was of Abbots Langley. But according to the entry in the Oxford University Matriculation Register 1615-1647, he was aged thirty-eight in 1635 and his father was of Kings Langley. For a pedigree of the Days of Micklefield Green see J.E. Cussans, *History of Hertfordshire*, Vol. III, Pt. 2 (1881), p. 142.
[2] University Archives S.P.2, f. 338v: Matriculation Register 1615-1647: 'Guliel Day: Hartford: Chyrurgus: fil. Rich. Day de Kings Langley in Com p'd: Gen: an: nat' 38.'
[3] City Archives B.1. 4. d.
[4] Willoughby de Broke MS. 1651.
[5] City Archives E. 4. 6, ff. 1-2: *O.C.A.* 1626-1665, p. 453.
[6] *S. and T.*, p. 168.
[7] *C.A.M.*, p. 999.
[8] Wood.
[9] Wood, *C. of O.*, Vol. I, p. 463.
[10] City Archives A. 5.4, ff. 48-49v. For leases to Day of Swinsell and adjoining properties, dated 10 December 1651 and 16 March 1658/9, see Brasenose College Muniments, Swinsell 69 and 70.
[11] Printed in Wood, *C. of O.*, Vol. III, p. 174.

JAMES HAY, second EARL OF CARLISLE
(c. 1612-1660)

The second (but only surviving) son of James Hay, first Earl of Carlisle, by his first wife, Honora, daughter of Edward Denny, Earl of Norwich. He succeeded his father in 1636. In 1631/2 he married Margaret (died 1676), third daughter of Francis Russell, fourth Earl of Bedford, and sister of Colonel John Russell and Mr Edward Russell [qq.v.]. He left no children.

Carlisle joined the King at Oxford and sat in the Parliament. He signed the letter to the Earl of Essex of 27 January 1643/4. In August 1644, after he had deserted Charles I, he asserted that he had had a commission from the King to raise a regiment of horse, but never did so, although he attended him with sixty followers.[1] Royalist colonels often underrated their services when dealing with the Committee for Compounding.

In October 1643 the regiment was allotted quarters in Buckinghamshire.[2] Carlisle's Regiment under a Captain Russell was being sent to Prince Rupert in November 1643. This must have been Edward Russell [q.v.]. 'H.M. intends to Prince Rupert Sir Jo [?] Lucas's regiment and the Earl of Carlile [sic]'s regiment now commanded by Captain [Edward] Russell'.[3] In addition a Captain Tobias Wood of Essex is listed under Carlisle in the 1663 List of Indigent Officers.[4]

Carlisle further stated in August 1644 that, disliking the King's proceedings, he came in on the Declaration. This was the Declaration of Both Kingdoms, dated 30 January 1643/4, in which a pardon was offered to all those who would desert the King before 1 March ensuing.

On 5 December 1644 Carlisle was fined £1,000, but this was reduced to £500 on 3 March 1644/5. He died 30 October 1660.

[Will: P.C.C. 1661: 171 May].

(For a full account see *C.P.*)

[1] *C.C.C.*, p. 853.

[2] Contemporary list of Royalist horse in the possession of Brigadier P. Young. This was one of Sir Edward Walker's papers.

[3] Sir Edward Nicholas to Prince Rupert, 16 November 1643: British Museum Add. MS. 18,980, f. 152.

[4] S.P. 29/68.

MR EDWARD RUSSELL
(1625-1665)

The sixth (fourth surviving) and youngest son of Francis Russell, fourth Earl of Bedford, by his wife, Katherine Brydges, daughter and co-heir of Grey Brydges, third Baron Chandos. He was the younger brother of William Russell, fifth Earl of Bedford and Colonel John Russell [q.v.], and brother-in-law of James Hay, second Earl of Carlisle [q.v.]. In February 1639/40 he had a licence to travel for three years.[1]

According to Russell's statement in the petition which he presented to Parliament on 3 June 1644, he was liable to severe censure and claimed no excuse by the friends or pretences that drew him to Oxford. His repentance prevented [i.e. forestalled] the Declaration [of 30 January 1643/4] he having obtained a pass from the Lord General on 6 January, yet opportunity failed till near the end of February.[2] On 15 December 1655 Russell stated that he was seventeen when the War broke out and that in 1643 he went to Oxford to visit relatives [obviously the Carlisles or his brother John], but returned seven or eight months later and had lived peaceably since.[3]

Russell's eldest brother, the fifth Earl of Bedford, lodged for a short time in

Wadham College, when he was entered as a Fellow Commoner 15 October 1643.[4] But he had left Oxford on 26 December 1643.

Carlisle's Regiment was commanded by a Captain Russell in November 1643.[5] It may be assumed with confidence that this was Edward.

Edward Russell compounded, as of Woburn, 27 July 1644 and was ordered to pay £1,000. His fine was reduced to £500 on 7 March 1644/5, and his sequestration was discharged 19 March 1644/5.[6]

He married Penelope, daughter of Moyses Hill, of Hillsborough Castle, Ireland, and widow of Sir William Brooke. He died 21 September 1665, and was buried at Chenies 19 October 1665.

[1] *C.S.P.D.* 1639-40, p. 493.
[2] *C.C.C.*, p. 846.
[3] Ibid.
[4] R. B. Gardiner, *Registers of Wadham College*, Vol. I (1897), pp. 158-9.
[5] British Museum MS. Add. 18,980, f. 152.
[6] *C.C.C.*, ib. and *C.J.*, Vol. III, p. 573 and Vol. IV, pp. 67 and 84.

SIR RICHARD LEE, second BARONET, M.P.
(1600-1660)

Sir Robert must be a mistake for Sir Richard Lee. The only Sir Robert Lee alive at this time was of Billesley, and he was lodging with his wife and infant daughter at the house of Sara Neale in St Aldate's (see later).

Sir Richard Lee, second baronet of Langley and Acton Burnell, Shropshire, was born 6 September 1600, the son and heir of Sir Humfrey Lee, first baronet, by his wife, Margaret, daughter of Reginald Corbett, of Stoke, Shropshire. He was educated at Shrewsbury and matriculated from Queen's College, Oxford, 10 May 1616. He succeeded his father in 1631, and was High Sheriff of Shropshire in 1639. He was elected M.P. for the county in the Long Parliament of 1640, was a strong supporter of Strafford, and was disabled from sitting 6 September 1642 for his Royalism.[1] He sat in the Oxford Parliament and signed the letter to Essex of 27 January 1643/4. He was captured at the taking of Shrewsbury 22 February 1644/5 and on the 27th was ordered to be sent up to Parliament in safe custody. He remained a prisoner at Nantwich from 1645 until 1648. He compounded 11 February 1650/1, and was fined £2,966.[3]

Lee married Elizabeth, daughter of Alderman Edward Allen; all his sons predeceased him, but he was survived by two daughters. He died shortly before the Restoration, and was buried at Acton Burnell 3 April 1660.

(Keeler, p. 246; *Shropshire Archaeological Transactions*, IVth Series, Vol. II (1927-8), pp. 171-2)

[1] *C.J.*, Vol. II, p. 755.
[2] Ib., Vol. IV, p. 64.
[3] *C.C.C.*, pp. 1005-8.

In June 1643 Day had lodging with him 'Mr Clutterbuck & one man'.[1] This must be

JOHN CLUTTERBUCK or CLOTTERBOCK
(c. 1602-c. 1669)

He was born in London, and was a King's Scholar of Westminster, elected to Christ Church in 1616, matriculated 10 June 1618, aged sixteen, B.A. 1620, M.A. 1623.

On 10 February 1635/6 John Clotterbocke, gent, of St Martin-in-the-Fields, bachelor, aged twenty-four [sic], had a licence to marry Catherine Finch, of Stepney, spinster, aged twenty-one.[2]

Clutterbuck was a member of the Royal Household for, in a petition addressed to Charles II in November 1660, he stated that he had spent his youth in the service of the late King.[3] He was created B.D. at Oxford 1 or 2 November 1642, which implies participation in the Edgehill campaign.

Clutterbuck went abroad after the end of the First Civil War and was at Rouen by 1 February 1646/7.[4] There are numerous references to him in the Clarendon State Papers. He was back in England by 7 August 1656.[5]

After the Restoration Clutterbuck was employed successively as receiver of the Voluntary Present to the King, of subsidies for the nobility, and of Poll Money for the House of Peers.[6] There appears to be no reference to him after 1669.

[1] St Aldate's Defaulters, Bodleian MS. Add. D. 114, f. 24.
[2] Harleian Society, Vol. XXVI (1887), p. 225.
[3] *C.S.P.D.* 1660-1, p. 356.
[4] *C.C.S.P.*, Vol. I, p. 360.
[5] MS. Rawlinson A. 41, f. 212.
[6] *C.T.B.*, passim.

ARTHUR ALLEN
(c. 1603/10-1655)

Barber. He was the son of Thomas Allen, yeoman, of Water Eaton, in the parish of Kidlington, Oxfordshire.[1] His name appears in all the St Aldate's parish taxation lists of 1645 and 1647. On 28 January 1647/8 he had a licence for a sign: 'Arthur Allen, barber, St Aldate's to hang out figures drawing teeth'.[2] In the Subsidy of 1648 he was assessed at 9d.[3] On 15 September 1651 he was admitted a freeman.[4] The churchwardens of St Aldate's paid him £1 16s. 6d. 'for the drinking' in 1648/9. He was a churchwarden himself in 1652-3.

Allen died between 12 May and 16 June 1655. In his Will he mentions his small portion of worldly goods. All his children were under age, the two daughters, Elizabeth and Anne, being under eighteen. The son, Charles, was appointed executor. To his apprentice, Edward Stroud, who during Allen's illness had been 'very carefull of mee in my shoppe', he bequeathed 'all my Instruments that I did vse in drawing teeth'.

[Will: P.C.C. 1655: 272 Aylett: made 13 April 1655, with codicil dated 12 May 1655: proved 16 June 1655].

In June 1643 the householder was Edward Allen, tailor, clearly Arthur's eldest brother.[5] The Kidlington Parish Registers contain entries of the baptisms of three children of a Thomas Allen in 1599, 1603, and 1610, but unfortunately there is a gap between 1603 and 1610, the period in which Edward and Arthur are likely to have been born. Edward was apprenticed to Ralph Nickles, tailor, of Oxford, 27 December 1623.[6] He was constable of the South-West Ward 19 September 1636,[7] and was a churchwarden of St Aldate's in 1637-8. He died between 14 June and 16 October 1643 when an Inventory of his goods was taken.[8] On 20 March 1643/4 administration of his goods was granted to his father, Thomas Allen,[9] who, on 15 November 1644, presented his account.[10] From this it appears that Edward Allen's wife had died shortly before him and that they were both buried in St Aldate's. It is probable that the Allens were victims of 'the sicknesse' raging in Oxford in August 1643: one of Sir Samuel Luke's scouts reported that 'they dye 20 a day' of it.[11]

The Allens' house was on the west side of Fish Street and occupied part of the site of Nos. 99-100 St Aldate's. It was Magdalen College property and had been leased to Alderman John Sare and Timothy Carter on 7 December 1637: Edward (and later Arthur) Allen must have been their sub-tenant. The lease of the house (£30) was included among the items listed in Edward's Inventory. On 30 August 1645 the College granted a lease to Thomas Allen 'the elder', of Water Eaton, for forty years at a rent of 16s. per annum: Edward Allen's children, Thomas 'the younger', Anne, Jane, and Sarah, were originally associated with him, but their names have been crossed through.[12] On 16 January 1657/8 a grant of the lease was made by the College to Thomas Hudson, but Thomas Allen was not buried until 16 August 1659.[13]

In Allen's lease the house is described as 'extending eastward vppon the kings high streete called ffishstreete, and westward vppon another Tenement [of the College] late in ye tenure of John Bentley . . . on ye south part, & vppon ye foresaid Tenement wch was late in ye tenure of ye sd John Bancks on ye North part'. Edward Allen's Inventory shews that the rooms were 'the litill chamber over the barbers shope', 'the greate Chamber', 'the garret', 'a inner roome there', 'cichin', and 'the shope and the littill roome within the shope'.

The house is placed out of order in the 'Accompt'.

[1] This information is derived from the apprenticeship enrolment of his brother Edward: see below.

[2] *O.C.P.*, p. 340.
[3] *S. and T.*, p. 169.
[4] *O.C.A.* 1626-1665, p. 184.
[5] St Aldate's Defaulters, Bodleian MS. Add. D. 114, f. 24.
[6] City Archives L. 5. 2. f. 122: Hannisters 1613-1640.
[7] *O.C.A.* 1626-1665, p. 69.
[8] MS. Wills Oxon. 295/1/76.
[9] Ib., 107, f. 76: Act Book B.
[10] Ib., 295/1/76.
[11] Luke, p. 130: 7 August 1643.
[12] Magdalen College Lease Ledger N, ff. 58-58v.
[13] Kidlington Parish Registers deposited in the Bodleian Library, MS. D.D. Par. Kidlington c. 2. He died intestate.

LIEUTENANT HUGH (?) LEA or LEIGH

Apparently of the Lifeguard of Foot. Ashburnham's *Accompt* records a payment of £5 'To Lieut Lee by Mr Nevill'.[1] The latter is presumably Thomas Nevill, brother-in-law of Sir Edward Nicholas, who, with Sir George Benyon [q.v.], was charged with overseeing provisions in the parish of St Aldate.[2] This payment shews that Lea was with the main Royalist army before 26 October 1643, and may have been a gratuity for a wound received at, say, Gloucester or Newbury.
Lee, Legh, and Leigh are very common surnames in the Royalist army. Even so we suspect that an officer who was in the Second Scots War is our man. He is given in 1640 as Ensign Hugh Leigh, apparently in the Company of Captain Edward Drury, in Sir William Ogle's Regiment of Foot.[3] On 25 March 1641 he again appears as Lieutenant Hugo Leigh in Captain Griffith's (i.e. Conyer Griffen's) Company in the same regiment.[4] Thus he had the sort of military background which would justify his being commissioned as a lieutenant when the Lifeguard was raised in 1642. If this is the same man he must have been a fairly senior lieutenant in January 1643/4, but he never attained the rank of captain, perhaps because he had been disabled.

[1] P. xxxiv.
[2] See Introduction.
[3] Rushworth, Vol. III, p. 1249.
[4] Sir Jacob Astley's Muster Roll: MS. in the possession of Lord Cottesloe.

In June 1643 there were lodging in Edward Allen's house a Mr BARTLETT (unidentified) and 'Mr Studhopp & his sonne: The sonne gonne to his colledge: noe answere for the father'.[1]

WILLIAM STIDOLPHE or STIDOLFE
(c. 1590-1659)

The son and heir of William Stydolfe (the name is variously spelt), of St Giles-in-the-Fields (who came of a Surrey family), by his wife, Elizabeth, daughter of John Fox, of St John's near London, son of Auditor Fox.
At the Visitation of Surrey in 1623 he is described as being thirty-three years of age, so he must have been born c. 1590. He is also described as 'Armiger pro corpore Regis Jacobi'.[2] On 5 February 1624/5 a marriage licence was granted by the Biship of London for 'William Stydolffe Gent of St Martins [sic] in the Fields and Mary Lupie of the same, spinster, aged 21, parents dead, and she living the last

3 years with one Mr Stydolf, of the same parish, who consents'.[3] William Stidolphe was later of Headley, Surrey.
He subscribed £20, as of Headley, to the Loan to Charles I in 1625.[4] He is entered as the third of the Esquires of the Body to Charles I in 1641.[5]
His son is his heir WILLIAM, who was admitted to Brasenose College as *armiger* 10 May 1643, aged fifteen.[6] He matriculated 26 June 1643, his age being given as seventeen.[7] His name appears throughout the Brasenose Junior Treasurer's Book for 1644.[8]
On 16 September 1646 William Stydolph, Esquire of the Body Guard, of Headley, begged to compound for delinquency in going into the King's quarters in attendance on him. He returned to his house in July 1645, and had never been in arms against Parliament. In 1646 he took the Covenant and Negative Oath. On 18 June 1649 he was admitted to compound on the Oxford Articles, and on 28 June was fined £1,746. This was paid on 12 February 1649/50 and the estate discharged.[9] On 29 August 1651 he was assessed at £800, but on 31 January 1651/2 he was discharged because he had paid his fine.[10] He was buried 18 November 1659 in the church of St Giles-in-the-Fields,[11] where an M.I. and effigy (no longer extant) were erected to him.[12]
When Stidolphe made his Will he described himself as of Headley. He left everything to the discretion of his residuary legatee and executor, his wife, Mary.[13]
[Will: P.C.C. 1660: 147 Nabbs: made 13 November 1659: proved 19 July 1660].

[1] St Aldate's Defaulters, Bodleian MS. Add. D. 114, f. 24.
[2] Harleian Society, Vol. XLIII (1894), p. 42 and *Surrey Archaeological Collections*, Vol. XII (1895). The Assessment of 1623 shews that Stidolphe was living in Princes Street in St Giles' parish (John Parton, *Some Account of the Hospital and Parish of St Giles in the Fields* (1822), p. 358.)
[3] *Marriage Licences issued by the Bishop of London*, Harleian Society, Vol. XXVI (1887), p. 150.
[4] *Surrey Archaeological Collections*, Vol. XVIII (1903), p. 81.
[5] L.C. 3/1.
[6] *B.N.C. Register* 1509-1909, Oxford Historical Society, Vol. LV (1909), p. 180.
[7] Foster's *Alumni* wrongly calls *him* Esquire of the Body.
[8] A 8 11*.
[9] *C.C.C.*, p. 1493.
[10] *C.A.M.*, p. 1378.
[11] We are indebted for this entry to the Revd. G.C. Taylor.
[12] Parton, op.cit., p. 220. Stydolphe was living in Drury Lane in 1652, when his house was described as being worth £21 per annum (ib., p. 358).
[13] Her Will was made 17 December 1667 and proved in the P.C.C. 9 March 1667/8 (35 Herne). She desired to be buried near her husband. William Stidolphe, junior, was presumably dead by then as Mary mentions only her sons John and Sigismund.

DR THOMAS CLAYTON
(c. 1575-1647)

Physician and Master of Pembroke College. Thomas Clayton the elder (c. 1575-1647) was the most important parishioner in St Aldate's. He matriculated from Balliol College, as of London, *generosus*, in 1591, graduated B.A. from there in 1594 and M.A. from Gloucester Hall in 1599. In 1610 he was licensed to practise medicine, and he graduated B. and D. Med. in 1611. He was appointed Regius Professor of Medicine in 1612, and held the post until his death. He was Principal of Broadgates Hall from 1620 until 1624 and Master of Pembroke College (its successor) until his death. He was an adherent of Laud and a strong Royalist: many members of Pembroke served as officers in the King's army.

On 17 May 1645 Clayton sent Bernard Rawlins, the plumber who had made Lucy Heath's leaden coffin, to Edward Heath with a note beginning 'healthe and comfort to you and yours' in which he vouched for the accuracy of the amount charged for the worke.[1]

Clayton married Alice, daughter of Bartholomew Warner (1558-1619), his predecessor as Regius Professor, and had three sons, Thomas (who succeeded him in his Chair, was knighted, and became Warden of Merton), William, and James, and four daughters, Bridget, Jane, Susanna, and Elizabeth. He died 10 July 1647, and was buried on the 13th in St Aldate's.

In his Will Clayton mentions his land in Yorkshire and some Oxford college leases, but not the lease of his St Aldate's house (see below). He left £5 to the poor of St Aldate's, and his bequests include anatomical and medical works to his sons Thomas and William. His wife was appointed executrix.

[Will: P.C.C. 1648: 76 Essex: made 3 March 1643/4: proved 17 May 1648].

Clayton's house was on the west side of Fish Street and occupied the site of the former No. 104 St Aldate's, the northern part of the present General Post Office. It was rented from Magdalen, and was the house belonging to the College which had a remarkable crypt.[2] At one time it was known as Dokelinton's Inn, later the Old Swan, and comprised two tenements.[3] Clayton had been in occupation of the property since at least as early as 17 December 1623.[4] The College tenant, who sub-let to him, was Jane, widow of Thomas Fulzey.[5] On 7 November 1640 the College granted to Thomas Clayton 'yelder' . . . 'All that their Tenemt & Garden sometimes called the old Swan scituat . . . in ye parrish of St Aldathes . . . And also one other Tente adioyning to ye foresaid Tenemt on ye north part yeareof, which two Tenemts doe lie and adioyne togeither, And are now in ye occupacoñ of the said Thomas Clayton and of Sibell Swifte Widdowe, And the Said Tenemts & garden doe abutt vpon a Tenement and garden belonging to ye said Colledge, nowe in ye tenure of John Holloway gent [q.v.] on ye north side, And on another Tenemt and garden belonging to the said Colledge hearetofore in ye tenure and occupacon of John Bancks Blacksmith [sic] deceased, And nowe in ye occupacon of Vrsula Collyer widdowe Henry Vaughan Taylor, and Anthony Yates Chaundler [qq.v.] . . . The west head or end of the said Tenemts abutteth vpon a garden ground of the said John Holloway in ye occupacoñ of John Clarck Cutler, And theast heade or end yeareof abutteth vpon ye kings high way or Streete called ffishstreete leadinge from Southbridge to Carfax.'[6] The lease was for forty years and the rent was £20 per annum.

On 28 July 1641 the lease was renewed to Clayton for forty years, but the rent was to be only £3 per annum.[7] The lease was evidently inherited by Clayton's eldest son, Thomas, who, on 15 January 1657/8, was granted a lease on the same terms as those accorded his father in 1641.[8] Dr Salter in his edition of the *Cartulary* already cited[9] failed to distinguish between the two Claytons.

[1] Willoughby de Broke MS. 1651.
[2] Wood, *C. of O.*, Vol. I, Appendix F, p. 617.
[3] See Salter, *Cart. H. St. J.B.*, Vol. II, pp. 170-2 and *Survey of the South-West Ward*, No. 123.
[4] Magdalen College Lease Ledger L: lease to William Booden of the house later rented by John Savory [q.v.], ff. 60v-61: he is there described as 'William Cleydon [sic], Doctor of Phisick'.
[5] *Cart. H. St. J.B.*, Vol. III, p. 324.
[6] Lease Ledger M, ff. 327v-328.
[7] Ib., ff. 361-2. He paid £10 and 16s. in the Subsidy Lists of 1641 (City Archives B. 1. 4. c.).
[8] Ledger P, ff. 54v-55.
[9] Vol. II, pp. 185-6.

ANNE, LADY COTTERELL
(died 1660)

The widow of Sir Clement Cotterell, of Wilsford, Lincolnshire (1585-1631), whom she married in 1606. Cotterell was Groom Porter to James I for twenty years and was knighted in 1620. He was buried at St Martin-in-the-Fields 12 November 1631.[1]
Anne was the daughter of Henry Allen or Alleyne, of Wilsford, by his wife, Bridget Bussey.[2] She was the mother of Sir Charles Cotterell, Master of the Ceremonies (1615-1702), and of a number of daughters, several of whom died young.[3] Her daughter Bridget (c. 1611-1687) was the wife of Dr Thomas Clayton the younger (afterwards Sir Thomas Clayton), in whose father's house Lady Cotterell was lodging. Lady Clayton's 'ugly face' is mentioned by Wood.[4]
Lady Cotterell's portrait, painted in 1641 and attributed to Gilbert Jackson, hangs at Rousham House, Oxfordshire, where her Will is preserved. She died in 1659/60 and was buried at St Martin-in-the-Fields on 5 January.[5]

[1] *Registers*, Part II, 1619-1636, ed. J.V. Kitto, p. 264: Harleian Society (1936).
[2] *Lincolnshire Pedigrees*, Vol. I, p. 10: Harleian Society, Vol. L (1902).
[3] See the *Registers* of St. Martin-in-the-Fields.
[4] *L. and T.*, Vol. I, p. 398.
[5] MS. Registers. We are indebted to Mr Cottrell-Dormer for the information about her Will (which was not proved in the P.C.C.) and for the fact that she was buried at St Martin's which enabled the exact date to be found. We also owe to him the correct date of Sir Charles Cotterell's birth.

MRS URSULA COLLIER
(died 1666)

Widow. She must be the Ursula Collier who was buried at St Aldate's 20 February 1665/6 as 'wife of William Collier the elder'.[1] Her name occurs in all the St Aldate's taxation lists of 1645 (in all but one she is described as 'widow Collier') and in the lists of 1647 (in one of these her Christian name is given). In the Subsidy of 1648 she was assessed at 1s.[2] The churchwardens received 6s. 8d. for Mr Collier's grave in 1640-1 and for her grave in 1665-6.

Mrs Collier's house was on the west side of Fish Street and probably occupied the site of the former No. 103 St Aldate's, the middle part of the present General Post Office. It was Magdalen College property, and had been leased on 1 December 1626 and again on 2 December 1636 to John Savory [q.v.].[3] In the reign of Queen Elisabeth I it had been rented to John Bancks, tailor. In the lease to 'John Saverie . . . Pulterer' of 1 December 1626 the College granted 'all that theire tenemt & backside situate . . . in the pish of St Aldate' described as lying 'betweene an other tenemt [of the College] nowe in the occupacion of William Clayden [sic] doctor of Phisicke vppon ye north & another tenement [of the College] nowe in the occupacion of Edward Britten vppon the South & Abutteh vppon the highe streete leading from the South bridge to the Carfox vppon the East & vppon a tenemt of Merton College vppon the west And the vse of an Entry standing betweene the said before demised tenemt & another tenemt of the said College nowe in the occupacion of the said william Clayden wch Entry standing betwene the said towe tenents doth indifferentlye belonge to both of them, for all mannr of Carriages in to the backsides of the said two tenemts indiffrentlye, and also a well belonging to the said demised tenemt lieing on the south side with thappurtenancies'.[4]

It is interesting to note that this entry was still in existence more than two centuries later. When Magdalen leased to the Postmaster-General on 29 March 1879 the Old Swan and the adjoining tenement to the north, there was reserved 'the free right of way for themselves and the occupiers of Nos. 102 and 103 St Aldate's . . . along the passage from St Aldate's Street to the doors of Nos. 102 and 103 St Aldate's.'[5] Nos. 102 and 103 were subsequently leased to the Post Office, pulled down, and rebuilt.

[1] Wood. *C. of O.*, Vol. III, p. 209.
[2] *S. and T.*, p. 168.
[3] Magdalen College Lease Ledger L, ff. 150v-151 and M, ff. 186v-187.
[4] M, ff. 186-7.
[5] *Cart. H. St. J.B.*, Vol. II, p. 187.

MR MICHAEL ANDREWES
(c. 1600?-1646)

Surgeon to King Charles. On 25 August 1625 Sir James Fullerton wrote to Secretary Conway that it was His Majesty's pleasure to grant Michael Andrewes a pension of £150 per annum, for life, in continuation of a similar grant made to him when the King was Prince of Wales:[1] the pension was granted by letters patent on the succeeding 9 October.[2] On 25 March 1630 Andrewes petitioned the King for £1,000 granted him by James I out of arrears of a subsidy detained in Wales, or in lieu of this a grant of lands of the Duchy of Lancaster of £40 per annum for forty-one years in reversion of the present estates.[3] On 27 January 1635/6 a grant was made to him of the benefit of a bond of £200 forfeited to the Crown in James I's reign.[4]

In 1641 Andrewes was the second of the King's chirurgeons, coming immediately after the serjeant, William Clowes.[5] In an undated list of Royal servants charged with payments towards the Oxford city works, probably belonging to the summer of 1643, 'Mr Andrews the kings Chirurgion' is entered as owing 7s. 6d. for three weeks. The answer which he gave to Richard Poole, the official deputed to extract the money, was that he 'sayth he will pay but cannot presently'.[6]

Andrewes married Mary . . . *The Registers of St Martin-in-the-Fields* 1619-1636 shew that Michael and Mary had a daughter, Katharine, baptized 16 November 1627,[7] a son, Thomas, baptized 25 August 1632,[8] and a daughter, Mary, baptized 8 April 1635.[9] The two elder children must have been dead by 1643/4, and it is Mary, alone mentioned in her father's Will, who is the child entered in the 'Accompt' as lodging with her parents at Mrs Collier's house. Andrewes was dead by 9 October 1646.

In his Will, which is undated, but which was probably made in the late summer or early autumn of 1646, Andrewes is described as of St Martin-in-the-Fields, esquire. It is likely that he returned to his London house (the lease of which he left to his wife) after the fall of Oxford on 24 June 1646, or possibly after the departure of the King from the city on 27 April. He states that 'there is in my Cabinett att Oxford seavenscore and odd poundes in Debentures which was for my diett'.

It is little wonder that Andrewes was unable to pay his share towards the city works. He says: 'Nowe I must make manifest the debts which his Maiestie is oweing to mee. Item there is due to mee by his Matie at this tyme my Pension, and my wifes being six yeares due, the Pension being one hundred and fiftie poundes a yeare, which Arreares for six yeares att one hundred and fiftie pound a yeare cometh to nyne hundred poundes. Item more there is due to mee from his Matie six yeares ffee being fortie pound per Annum, which cometh vnto two hundred and fortie poundes. Item more there is due to mee vpon Debenture I knowe not how much, onelie there is in my Cabinett att Oxford seavenscore and odd poundes in Debentures which was for my diett.'[10] Andrewes left these Royal debts to his 'deare and loveinge wife' and to his daughter Mary 'if ever itt shall please God it may be paid'. The elder Mary Andrewes survived the Restoration, and on 10 April 1661 a money warrant for £37.10s.0d was issued to her for the last Lady Day quarter on her late husband's pension,[11] presumably all that Charles II could afford to make up for the immense arrears.

Andrewes left his daughter £300 for her maintenance and, if she proved dutiful to her mother, 'that lease of the demeanes of Tedbury'. His wife, who was appointed his sole executor, was to receive £1,000.

[Will: P.C.C. 1648: 148 Duke: undated: proved 9 October 1646].

[1] *C.S.P.D.* 1625-6, p. 89.
[2] *C.T.B.*, Vol. I, p. 234.
[3] *C.S.P.D.* 1629-31, p. 220.
[4] Ib. 1635-6, p. 191.
[5] L.C. 3/1.
[6] MS. Harleian 6804, f. 229.
[7] P. 51.
[8] P. 87.
[9] P. 114.
[10] Debentures were vouchers given in the Royal Household certifying to the recipient the sum due to him for salary, etc., and serving as his authority for claiming payment.
[11] *C.T.B.*, Vol. I, p. 234.

MR CARNABY

Unidentified. His name does not occur in L.C. 3/1. He may be the Walter Carnabie who, with his wife and maid, had a pass to go to Holland 7 August 1650.[1] In June 1655 a Mr Carnaby was included in a list of persons working for the exiled King Charles II to whom payment was made.[2]
Mary, daughter of Walter and Mary Carnaby, was baptized at St Margaret's, Westminster, 6 May 1649, and Walter, son of the same, 6 April 1651.
There were many Carnabys in the Royalist army.

[1] *C.S.P.D.* 1650, p. 554.
[2] *C.C.S.P.*, Vol. III, p. 41.

In June 1643 Mrs Collier had lodging with her 'Mr Rumsey & 1 man'.[1]
Rumsey is not a very common name, and in the seventeenth century was most frequently found in Monmouth and Brecon. It is possible that the individual intended is EDWARD RUMSEY, son of the Royalist judge Walter Rumsey, of Monmouthshire (died 1660), by his wife, Barbara, daughter and heiress of Matthew Prichard, of Llanover, Monmouthshire. Edward Rumsey matriculated from Broadgates Hall, Oxford, 6 February 1623/4, aged thirteen, and graduated B.A. of Pembroke College 26 October 1626. He was admitted to Gray's Inn 6 June 1627, and was called to the bar in 1635. He married Janet, daughter of Morgan Awbrey, of Ynyssedwyn, Breconshire.[2]
It is unlikely that the Mr Rumsey of Pembroke College, Oxford, who was absent from Oxford when the Protestation Returns were made in 1641/2 and who is to be equated with the 'George Rumsey, Lievt' who is listed among the Royalist officers of Pembroke,[3] would have been lodging outside the College. This George Rumsey is not recorded in Foster's *Alumni.*

[1] St Aldate's Defaulters, Bodleian MS. Add. D. 114, f. 24.
[2] For the Rumsey pedigree see Sir J. A. Bradney, *History of Monmouthshire*, Pt. II (1904), p. 384.
[3] D. Macleane, *A History of Pembroke College*, p. 236.

HENRY VAUGHAN
(c. 1606-1652)

Tailor. The son of George Vaughan, cutler, of St Aldate's, by his wife, Mary . . . , and grandson of William Vaughan, yeoman, of Cropredy, Oxfordshire.[1] George Vaughan, as late apprentice of John Poole, cutler, of Oxford, obtained his freedom 22 January 1601/2.[2] On 21 March 1634/5 he was matriculated as a *serviens*, he then being a servant of a Fellow of Corpus Christi College, when his age was given as fifty-nine.[3] In January 1613/4 he was committed to Bocardo Prison for 'abuseing A Constable of this Cittie being about the execucoñ of his Office.'[4] Administration of his goods was granted to his son Henry 27 July 1643.[5]

Henry Vaughan was enrolled apprentice to Edward Carter, tailor, of Oxford, 17 October 1620.[6] He transferred in 1623 to Henry Clarke[7] and in 1626 to John Harries.[8] His name appears in the Journeymen Taylors' Accounts for the first time in 1629.[9] He obtained his freedom 23 April 1630.[10] On 19 January 1638, having been a chief constable, he was allowed (with three others) £25 of the £200 given by the Recorder, for five years.[11]

Vaughan was a churchwarden of St Aldate's in 1645-6. His name does not occur in the St Aldate's parish taxation lists of 1645, but it does figure in both lists of 1647. He was assessed at 8d. in the Subsidy of 1648.[12] He seems to have inherited his father's quick temper, for in April 1646 he was fined 1s. 8d. for 'calling Mr Cave [Walter Cave, q.v.] a member of the Councell House knave'.[13] He was certified as a Delinquent in two lists of the Oxfordshire Sequestration Committee: in the first it is recorded that 'Vaughan was a Sargt'.[14]

Vaughan's name is linked with that of the well-known instructor in dancing and vaulting, William Stokes, whose school was just outside the North Gate of Oxford. Letters of administration were granted to Vaughan, a creditor, 2 October 1643, Stokes' children being minors.[15] The rent for the school was paid by him. (See Note 18).

In December 1651 Vaughan was in receipt of £10 of Wilkinson money.[16] He was living on 20 July 1652[17] but dead by 9 December 1652.[18] It may have been his widow, or that of John Vaughan, who, in 1654, occupied a room in the house of Robert Saunders [q.v.].

Vaughan's house was part of the Magdalen College tenement also occupied by Ursula Collier and Anthony Yate [qq.v.]: for particulars see under the former. It probably stood on the site of the former No. 102 St Aldate's, the southern end of the present General Post Office.

[1] William Vaughan's Will was proved in the Peculiar Court of Banbury 10 March 1599/1600: the value of his chattels as listed in his Inventory was £31. 10s. 5d. (Bodleian Library, MS. Wills Peculiars 53/5/1). His wife, Anne, who was to have 'my black Cow wch I call Rose', and his son George were appointed residuary legatees and executors.

[2] City Archives L. 5. 1, f. 261.

[3] University Archives S P 2, f. 348v: his father's name is here given. In 1617 George and Mary Vaughan had been granted a piece of ground near Jews Mount (City Archives D. 5. 5, f. 341).

[4] City Archives O. 5. 9, f. 46: Quarter Sessions Roll 1614-1638.

[5] MS. Wills Oxon. 107, f. 73: Act Book B. His widow died, also intestate, in March 1643/4. George Vaughan occupied the St Aldate's parish house subsequently inhabited by William Deverall [q.v.].

[6] City Archives L. 5. 2, f. 76v.

[7] Ib., f. 122.

[8] Ib., f. 76v.
[9] City Archives F. 4. 2.
[10] City Archives L. 5. 2, no folio number.
[11] *O.C.A.* 1626-1665, p. 78.
[12] *S. and T.*, p. 169.
[13] City Archives P. 4. 2, f. 6: Audit 1644-1685.
[14] Ib. F. 5. 9, f. 101: Vellum Book II. He was probably a sergeant in the Oxford City Regiment.
[15] MS. Wills Oxon. 173/4/33. For an account of Stokes see *S. and T.*, pp. 119-20. Prince Charles attended his school while in Oxford.
[16] *O.C.A.* 1626-1665, p. 180.
[17] Ib., p. 190.
[18] On that date the city received 'of the executors of Henry Vaughan ffor ye Dauncing Schoole' £1. 6s. 8d. (P.5.2, f. 285v). Payments of varying amounts continued to be made until 1655. Unfortunately, no Will has been traced. It is interesting that the Dancing School continued to function during the Commonwealth.

COLONEL SIR JOHN HENDERSON

This is clearly a mistranscription as there is no such name as Henderforde, which is evidently a mistranscription of 'Hendêrfônne'.
John Henderson was knighted before 1640, when he was appointed Governor of Dumbarton.[1] He arrived at York 29 September 1640 together with Patrick, Lord Ruthven, afterwards successively Earl of Forth and Brentford [q.v.].[2] Henderson's sister Jane or Joanna was Ruthven's second wife.
In 1642 Henderson was probably one of the twenty-two Scots officers who came over with Ruthven to join the Cavaliers.[3] In December of that year he was appointed Governor of Newark, when it was first garrisoned. On 5 January 1642/3 he wrote to Guilford Slingsby about the local military situation.[4] He was in command of the Royalists at Winceby Fight on 11 October 1643, but was probably still Governor of Newark. However, he was superseded soon after by Sir Richard Byron, perhaps as a result of the defeat at Winceby.
Henderson was certainly at Oxford by the beginning of 1643/4, for on 3 January letters written by him from there and sent by a trumpeter, were read in the House of Commons. He asked Lord Maitland, Mr Alexander Henderson, and Sir Henry Vane senior for their favour to purchase a pass for himself, his wife, and children to go into Holland, and settle there. The request was refused.[5]
Later in 1644 Henderson was dispatched by the King as ambassador to Denmark.[6] After his return to England he was taken prisoner and committed to the Tower for levying war against Parliament and the Kingdom.[7] On 6 June 1645 he was released on the proviso that he went beyond seas immediately and returned to England no more.[8] He again went to Denmark, but returned to England in October with a letter from Christian IV to Charles I, offering mediation.[9] On 18 October Henderson petitioned Lenthall for a safe conduct from the Commons to go to the King and deliver the letter.[10] But on 31 October he was ordered to return to Denmark with it.[11] The Commons refused to recognize Henderson as an intermediary.
Henderson thereafter remained abroad, and for a time took service with the Emperor.[12] On 31 January 1654/5 he wrote from Cologne to Hyde (who already distrusted him) that he had quitted the Imperial service, in which he had lost his father and two brothers, for that of the King (Charles II) and had ruined himself, his wife, and eleven children, never having been noticed by the King for the good services done to the King's father and the miseries suffered for himself.[13] Immediately afterwards he was acting as a spy for Thurloe,[14] a fact of which

Charles II was aware. In 1657 he was commanding infantry in the Island of Fünen.[15] He probably died abroad.

[1] *C.S.P.D.* 1640-1, p. 84 and 1625-49, pp. 629-30; also H.M.C., Appendix to VIth *Report*, p. 621.
[2] *C.S.P.D.* 1640-1, p. 111.
[3] Sir Henry Slingsby, *Original Memoirs* (1806), p. 38.
[4] H.M.C., Appendix to VIth *Report*, p. 1, where the letter is wrongly calendared as 1643/4.
[5] *C.J.*, Vol. III, p. 356.
[6] Rawlinson MS. A. 148, f. 74: see also the account of Lord Forth later.
[7] *C.J.*, Vol. IV, p. 89.
[8] Ib., p. 162.
[9] *C.S.P.D.* 1645-7, p. 181.
[10] H.M.C., *Portland*, Vol. I, p. 291.
[11] *C.J.*, Vol. IV, p. 328: see also *C.S.P.D.* 1645-7, *passim.*
[12] *C.C.S.P.*, Vol. II, p. 102.
[13] Ib., Vol. III, pp. 10-11.
[14] Ib., p. 13 etc.
[15] *Nicholas Papers*, Vol. IV, p. 24.

ANTHONY YATE
(c. 1609-1672)

Chandler. The son of John Yate, brewer, of St Aldate's, fifth son of James Yate, of Standlake, Oxfordshire, by his wife, Mallyn, daughter of Andrew Hulse, of Sutton Courtenay, Berkshire.[1] Anthony's mother was Alice, sister of Oliver Smyth or Smith, of St Aldate's, alderman and brewer, the father of Thomas, Oliver, and John Smyth [qq.v.]. Anthony's parents were married at St Aldate's 2 November 1601; as the bride was entered as 'Ales Jennings' she must have been a widow.[2] John Yate was admitted by the University to brew 17 February 1618/9.[3] In his Will[4] Alderman Smyth [Smith] devised to his eldest son, Thomas 'All that my messuage or tenement and brewhowse . . . in the pishe of Saint Aldate . . . nowe in the tenure or occupacoñ of my brother in lawe John Yate'. He gave to 'my sister Alice yate fforty pounds in monyes And to Mary yate my servant [probably his niece] Tenn pounds in moneys'. He further gave to 'my godchildren Antonie yate and Oliver yate five pounds a peece'. Administration of Alice Yate's estate was granted to her husband 11 April 1638[5] and an Inventory made on the 10th was presented the next day: this comprised her brother's legacy.[6] According to Wood,[7] Alice Yate's M.I. in St Aldate's church stated that she died 10 April 1637, but this must be a mistake for 1638. John Yate was buried at St Aldate's 5 July 1642.[8]

Anthony Yate was apprenticed 16 April 1621, as the son of John Yates [sic], of the University of Oxford, *generosus*, to William Goode, chandler, of Oxford.[9] He obtained his freedom 4 August 1628,[10] and was practising his trade in September 1633.[11] He was admitted by the University to brew 9 October 1638.[12] In 1639-40 and in 1640-1 he was a churchwarden of St Aldate's. He was constable of the South-West Ward in September 1641.[13] In October 1643 arms were delivered to him.[14] His name occurs in one of the St Aldate's parish taxation lists of 1645, but not in the lists of 1647. On 18 January 1654/5 he was sued for the repayment of £25 of Sir Thomas White's money which he owed upon bond to the city.[15]

In 1641-2, 1642-3, 1643-4, and 1644-5, payments were made to Yate by the St Aldate's churchwardens for candles for the church. He died in 1672 and was buried in St Aldate's, the churchwardens receiving 6s. 8d. for his grave in the year 1672-3. In his Will[16] he desired to be buried by his wife (name unknown) and children in St Aldate's. His legatees included his brothers Thomas and Paul Yate and his sister-in-law Susanna Bolt, which suggests that his wife's maiden name may have been Bolt: she could have been a daughter or granddaughter of John Bolte [q.v.]. His residuary legatee and executor was his brother Oliver, who had been apprenticed to his uncle James Yate, mercer, in 1631-2.[17] The value of Anthony Yate's goods as listed in the accompanying Inventory was £53. 19s. 2d.

[Will: MS. Wills Oxon. 75/4/91: made 20 May 1672: proved 24 August 1672].

Yate's house was part of the Magdalen College tenement also occupied by Ursula Collier and Henry Vaughan [qq.v.]: for particulars see under the former. It probably stood on the site of No. 101 St Aldate's, The old Tom. No rooms are listed in the Inventory.

[1] *Visitation of Oxfordshire* 1574 and 1634, Harleian Society, Vol. V (1871), pp. 158 and 257.
[2] Wood, *C. of O.*, Vol. III, p. 201.
[3] *Register*, Vol. II, Pt. II, p. 329.
[4] P.C.C. 82 Goare.
[5] MS. Wills Oxon. 107, f. 47v: Act Book B.
[6] Ib. 88/6/2.
[7] *C. of O.*, Vol. III, p. 130.

[8] Ib., p. 207.
[9] City Archives L. 5. 2, f. 80v.
[10] Ib., no folio number.
[11] *S. and T.*, p. 431.
[12] *Register*, Vol. II, Pt. I, p. 330.
[13] *O.C.A.* 1626-1665, p. 103.
[14] City Archives E. 4. 5, f. 55.
[15] *O.C.A.* 1626-1665, p. 208.
[16] The seal displays the 'three gates' contained in the Arms of Yate of Standlake.
[17] City Archives L. 5. 2, f. 219.

MR TAPWORTH

Unidentified.

JOHN KEENE
(died 1669)

Carpenter. The son of Thomas Keene, weaver, of Oxford, by his wife, Bridget . . . Thomas Keene was admitted a freeman 23 September 1604.[1] In his Will, which was proved at Oxford 27 January 1620/1,[2] he gave 'vnto my two children John Keene and Jane Keene all my moveable goods & Chattells wch weare not my wifes before I married her'. These included 'my Loomes & all the rest of my tooles'.

Jane Keene married Richard Bettris, barber, of Oxford. In June 1643 he was the owner of Keene's house, but absent in London: his wife was at home, and declared that her man could not be spared until she 'bee payd for what her husband did to the kings sould:'[3] By January 1643/4 Keene had become the householder. His name occurs in four of the St Aldate's taxation lists of 1645, but not in those of 1647, by which time he had probably followed the Bettrises to London.

When Keene made his Will in 1669 he was established as a carpenter in the parish of St Martin-in-the-Fields. He must have prospered in London, since he leased not only his own house but also another tenement, both situated in 'Bedfordberry'. These he left to his sister Jane Bettris and her son Edward:[4] his brother-in-law, Richard Bettris, now described as 'Chirurgeon', was then living in the parish of St Peter le Bailey, Oxford. Keene was not unmindful of his native city, and the most important of his bequests was a benefaction. 'Item I give and bequeath vnto the Citty of Oxford for euer the sume of Tenn pounds to be disposed of and lent by the Major of the said Citty to Two poore ffreemen of the said Citty And they to have the vse of it for ffiue yeares gratis'.[5] His 'working Tooles' he left to his 'loveing ffreind Mr Robert Little Carpenter'. As there is no mention of wife or children, Keene was either a bachelor or a childless widower: he made his sister one of his executors.

[Will: P.C.C. 1669: 56 Coke: made 18 May 1669: proved 25 May 1669].

Keene's house was on the west side of Fish Street, and presumably occupied a portion of Nos. 99-100 St Aldate's (see under Arthur Allen).

[1] *O.C.A.* 1583-1626, p. 169.
[2] MS. Wills Oxon. 39/2/31.
[3] St Aldate's Defaulters, Bodleian MS. Add. D. 114, f. 24.
[4] Edward Bettris, chirurgeon, of Oxford, had his Will proved in the P.C.C. in 1685 (15 Cann).
[5] Keene's bequest is recorded in the Oxford City Benefactions Book 1630-1824 (E.4.2, f. 25): 'John Keene late of this Citty Carpenter who gave vnto the Citty ffive [sic] pounds to be lent out for five yeares'. The bequest is correctly copied from his Will in Vellum Book II (F. 5.9, f. 64).

LIEUTENANT COTTON

Unidentified. Lodging in St Aldate's, he was probably an officer in the Lifeguard of Foot. This makes it likely that he is either Charles or John Cotton, two Gentlemen of the Privy Chamber Extraordinary in 1641.[1] A Charles Cotton was a captain in the Earl of Chesterfield's Regiment of Foot in 1667.[2]

[1] L.C. 3/1.
[2] Dalton, Vol. I, p. 79.

WIDOW WILLIS

Almost certainly the widow of William Willis, brewer, of St Aldate's. William was the second of the three sons of John Willis, brewer, also of St Aldate's, by his wife, Elizabeth . . . John Willis was admitted by the University to brew in 1588, became a servant to the Warden of New College and rent-gatherer for the College in 1592, and was bailiff of New College from 1603 to 1608. He became a freeman and bailiff in 1601. In his Will, proved in the Court of the Chancellor of Oxford University 24 February 1619/20, he left William 10s. to buy a ring.[1] The latter, who was born c. 1581, was apprenticed to Richard Bartholomew, tailor, of Oxford, 25 January 1596/7.[2] He was admitted a freeman and given a bailiff's place 4 March 1614/15[3] and was senior bailiff in 1618.[4] He was admitted to brew 11 July 1619.[5] On 10 June 1621, at the age of forty, he was matriculated as a privileged person of the University, being collector of rents for New College.[6] Willis was a churchwarden of St Aldate's in 1616-17. He was dead by 3 April 1637 when his son William was apprenticed.[7] The churchwardens paid Mrs Willis' rent (£1) for the year 1638-9. Widow Willis' name does not occur in the St Aldate's parish taxation lists of 1645 and 1647.

Mrs Willis' house was on the west side of Fish Street, and presumably occupied a portion of the site of Nos. 99-100 St Aldate's (see under Arthur Allen).

[1] Oxford University Archives Hyp. B. 35.
[2] City Archives L. 5. 1, f. 58v.
[3] *O.C.A.* 1583-1626, p. 242.
[4] Ib., p. 276.
[5] *Register*, Vol. II, Pt. I, pp. 319 and 344.
[6] S P 2, f. 335v: 'Gulielmus Willis, Oxo: Generos: Collector redituum pro Collegio Nouo, an: nat: 40'. His elder brother, Martin, was collector for Exeter College.
[7] *Register*, Vol. II, Pt. I, p. 344.

CAPTAIN FERDINANDO (?) FISHER

A ffardinando ffisher was ensign to Captain Kirten's (i.e. Posthumus Kirten's) Company in the Earl of Newport's Regiment of Foot at 25 March 1641.[1] He had joined the regiment since 1640, but even so would be sufficiently senior to have attained the rank of captain in the Lifeguard by January 1643/4.

Captain Fisher of the Lifeguard of Foot was taken prisoner at Naseby (1645).[2]

[1] Sir Jacob Astley's Muster Roll.
[2] Rushworth, Vol. VII, p. 46.

GEORGE DIXON
(c. 1592-c. 1652)

Sacristan of Christ Church. He was of Wiltshire origin. His name first appears in the Christ Church Disbursement Books, in the list of *Famuli*, for 1619-20,[1] but as the books for 1617-18 and 1618-19 are missing, he may have been appointed slightly earlier. On 31 March 1620 he was matriculated as a servant of the University, in his capacity of servant to Dr William Goodwin, Dean of Christ Church from 1611 to 1620. Dixon's age is given as twenty-eight.[2]

Dixon (who signs his name Dicson) was the senior sacristan, Henry Cope and later William Blay [q.v.] being the junior ones under him. He received 10s. for each of the four academic terms and an annual livery allowance (*vestes liberatae*) of 13s. 4d. In the academic year 1644-5 (which is the last Disbursement Book[3] extant in Dixon's lifetime) he was also *Virgifajulus* (verger) for the last three terms, receiving 10s. a term in this capacity and livery money also of 10s. The Disbursement Books also contain references to bills paid to Dixon: and there are occasionally payments for separate items such as candles.

Dixon is entered in two of the St Aldate's parish taxation lists of 1645. On 14 July 1648 he submitted to the Parliamentary Visitors of Oxford University.[4] He married Amy . . . , probably an Oxford woman. (See below). He died between 9 December 1652 and 14 February 1652/3.

In his Will, where he is described as Verger and Sexton of Christ Church, Dixon desired to be 'decently buried in the Cathedrall Church of Christ at Oxford'.[5] He mentions his son George and his daughter Juliana Dicson, his brother Thomas Dicson, of Ogbourne St George (Wiltshire), his brother's wife, and his own wife, Amy Dicson, whom he appointed his executrix.

[Will: preserved, but not apparently proved, in the Court of the Chancellor of Oxford University: Hyp. B. 24: made 1 December 1652, with a codicil dated 9 December 1652].

Amy Dixon (Dicson) died between 14 February and 18 March 1652/3. In her Will she desired to be buried 'neare my Deare Husband in the Cathedrall Church of Xt in Oxford'. She mentions her son George, her daughter Juliana, her brother Thomas Dicson and his wife, and her kinsman Robert Harper, of Oxford.[6] Juliana Dixon was appointed residuary legatee and executrix and Harper and Matthew Loveday (of St Aldate's) overseers. An Inventory of Amy Dixon's goods was taken 18 March 1652/3 by Thomas Langley, yeoman bedle of Law, and Richard Davis, verger. The total value of the goods was £187. 19s. 10d.

[Will: preserved, but not apparently proved, in the Court of the Chancellor of Oxford University: Hyp. B. 24: made 14 February 1652/3].

Dixon's house was on the west side of Fish Street and occupied the site of No. 98 St Aldate's. It was Magdalen College property and had been leased to John Hawkes, butcher (see Mrs [Jane] Hawkes) for forty years at a rent of 18s. per annum on 7 December 1637.[7] In his Will, dated 23 April 1642, Hawkes bequeathed to his wife 'my howse in the psh of Snt Aldats now in the Occupacon of George Dixon wch I hold by lease from the P'sident and Schollers of Magdalen Colledge in Oxon'.[8] In the lease the house is described as 'All that their Tenement scituat . . . in the parrish of St Aldath . . . Betweene a Tenement of the said Colledge nowe or late in the tenure of Isaack Bartellmewe on the south and west parts, And another Tenement of the said Colledge nowe or late in the tenure of George Crewe on the North, and abutteth on the high streete on the east. Latelie demised to Thomas Hills of Hyegate in the Countie Midd gent & Ann his wife'. Amy Dixon's Inventory mentions 'ye upper Chamber', 'ye Litle Chamber', 'ye Lowe Chamber', 'ye Milk-house', and 'ye Woodhouse'.

[1] Ch. Ch. MS. xii. b. 64.
[2] S P 2, f. 345: 'Georgius Dixsone, Wilton: pleb: famulus Doris Goodwin, an: nat. 28'.
[3] Ch. Ch. MS. xii. b. 88.
[4] *Register of the Visitors*, p. 153.
[5] As there are no entries in the Cathedral Burial Registers between 13 February 1649/50 and 3 April 1660, his burial is not recorded there.
[6] He was of Holywell in 1648.
[7] Lease Ledger M, ff. 228-228v.
[8] MS. Wills Oxon. 32/2/16.

THREE SERVANTS OF JAMES STUART, first DUKE OF RICHMOND (1612-1655)

He was a favourite cousin and close personal friend of Charles I, with whom he doubtless lodged in Christ Church. He was made a P.C. in 1633, and in 1641 was a Gentleman of the Bedchamber and Lord Steward.[1] He sat in the Oxford Parliament and was a Commissioner for the defence of the city 1644-6. He surrendered on the Oxford Articles, and compounded 1 October 1646. On 15 December 1646 he was fined £9,810.[2]
(For full accounts see *C.P.* and *Archaeologia Cantiana*, Vol. XII (1878), pp. 49-105).

[1] L.C. 3/1.
[2] *C.C.C.*, p. 1526.

In June 1643 Dixon had lodging with him a MR WEBB and his man from whom no answer was received.[1] He is unidentified.

[1] St Aldate's Defaulters, Bodleian MS. Add. D. 114, f. 24.

MARGARET BOWYER, WIDOW
(died 1682)

The widow of John Bowyer, glover, who was the householder on 14 June 1643.[1] John Bowyer was the son of Richard Bowyer, husbandman, of Stanton Harcourt, Oxfordshire, and was apprenticed to John Wythers, glover, 3 December 1621.[2] He obtained his freedom 27 January 1630/1.[3] He was one of those who took the Inventory of the goods of John Henslow senior 22 January 1635/6, and was a witness to his Will.[4] He was appointed constable of the South-West Ward in 1639.[5] It is probable that, like Edward Allen and his wife (see under Arthur Allen), he fell a victim to 'the sicknesse' which was raging in Oxford in the summer of 1643.
Widow Bowyer's name does not appear in the St Aldate's parish taxation lists of 1645 and 1647, but in 1673 she was occupying a tenement on the south side of Pennyfarthing Street which was part of a messuage belonging to St Aldate's parish.[6] She was buried at St Aldate's 7 July 1682.[7]
Mrs Bowyer's house was on the west side of Fish Street, apparently on the site of No. 97 St Aldate's, which must have been a tenement of the house rented by Robert Saunders [q.v.] from Magdalen, since the house of George Dixon [q.v.] was bounded on the south by that of Saunders.

[1] St. Aldate's Defaulters, Bodleian MS. Add. D. 114, f. 24.
[2] City Archives L.5.2, f. 87v.
[3] L. 5. 2, no folio number.
[4] MS. Wills Oxon 132/1/22.
[5] *O.C.A.* 1626-1665, p. 88.
[6] Indenture between St Aldate's feoffees and John and Anne Wild 14 April 1673 (Parish Chest).
[7] Parish Registers.

TWO SERVANTS OF HENRY ARUNDELL, third BARON ARUNDELL OF WARDOUR
(1606?-1694)

For Lord Arundell see under Robert Saunders' house. In June 1643 he and one servant were lodging with John Bowyer.[1]

[1] St Aldate's Defaulters, Bodleian MS. Add. D. 114, f. 24.

ROBERT SAUNDERS
(c. 1598-1654)

Physician. One of the seven children (and a younger son) of Thomas Saunders, yeoman, of Cokethorpe, Oxfordshire, by his wife, Edith . . . Thomas Saunders was buried at Ducklington 6 May 1613.[1] In his Will, which was proved in the P.C.C. 27 May 1614,[2] he left each of his children £30. One of his overseers was Francis Yate, of Standlake, uncle of Anthony Yate [q.v.]. His widow was buried at Ducklington 23 September 1619.

On 15 June 1632, aged thirty-four, Robert Saunders was matriculated as a privileged person of the University, in his capacity of servant to Dr Henry Ashworth,[3] D. Med. of Oriel College, under whom he would have acquired his medical knowledge.

In the Subsidy List of 1641, under the South-West Ward, Saunders paid 20s. and 8s. 'in lands'.[4] In October 1645 he contributed £3. 6s. towards the loan to the Lords Commissioners.[5] His name occurs in four of the St Aldate's parish taxation lists of 1645 and in the lists of 1647. He was assessed at 3s. 3d. in the Subsidy of 1648.[6] He married Avis . . . He died between 20 April and 10 June 1654, and was buried in St Aldate's, the churchwardens receiving 6s. 8d. for his grave in the year 1654-5.

In his Will he states that he was born at Cockthropp [Cokethorpe]. He appointed his wife his executrix. There is a very full account of his house. (See below).

[Will: P.C.C. 1654: 74 Alchin: made 20 April 1654: proved 10 June 1654].

Mrs Saunders paid 20s. and 8s. in the Subsidy of 1664.[7] She died between 22 April and 13 June 1671. In her Will she mentions her two sons, Bernard as dead and Ralph as living. Both her daughters were dead: one of these was Elizabeth, first wife of John Earle [q.v.], to whom his mother-in-law left 10s. Her granddaughter, Elizabeth Earle, 'who hath ever been dutifull to mee,' received a number of bequests: she had been remembered also in Saunders' Will.

[Will: MS. Wills Oxon. 149/3/4: made 22 April 1671: proved 16 June 1671].

Saunders' house was on the west side of Fish Street, on the site of Nos. 95-97 St Aldate's, being the corner tenement between Fish Street and Pennyfarthing Street. He rented it from Magdalen College, who granted him a lease for forty years at a rent of 45s. 4d. per annum on 4 August 1645.[8] The house had previously been leased to Isack Bartholomew and his widow, Marie Bartholomew: the latter's lease is dated 27 November 1621 and must have been taken over by Saunders. Unfortunately, no bounds are given for this property in any of the leases: that to Saunders (described as 'of the vniversitye of Oxford gentl') merely states that the College had let to him 'All that yeir Tenement wth Thappurteñces scituate . . . in the pish of St Aldates . . . and all Edifices and gardens therevnto belonging, In as large and ample manner as Mary Bartholomewe widdowe or Isaack Bartholmewe [sic] her husband . . . held vsed occupied and enioyed'. A lease on similar conditions was granted to Avis Saunders on 22 December 1662:[9] her name appears in the Magdalen Rental of 1659.[10] In his Will Saunders gives directions about the disposal of the remainder of his lease, the profits of which his trustees were to allow his widow to enjoy for her life.

The house consisted of north and south portions (which could be divided off) and some tenements. After his wife's death, the north part of 'the said Messuage from the Streete Doore with the Garden and the house of office to the Pales' was to be made over to Saunders' son Bernard, who in June 1643 was living with his father,[11] and who in 1654 had a room in the house in his tenure. He was described as 'chirurgion' when he was buried at St Aldate's 8 February 1658/9.[12] In connexion with the south part of the messuage, which was eventually to be held by his daughter Mary Coles, there is mention of 'the Bakehouse', 'ffewell house', 'the Roome over the Oven', 'the Chamber where the Presse is', and other rooms, including that in the tenure of Bernard Saunders and those in the tenure of 'ye Widd' Vahon.'[13] Wood[14] rightly identified Bernard Saunders' house with the former 'Blewbore' [Blue Boar] Inn, as the tenement was called in the reign of Henry VIII.

There were five hearths in 1665.[15] Avis Saunders left elaborate directions about the house in her Will. She mentions her lease and directs her executors to let it for the benefit of her orphan grandsons, two Saunders and three Coles. When these boys were of age, the house was to be divided between them on the lines laid down in her husband's Will. Mrs Saunders' Will alludes to the 'Chirurgery house'. In the Inventory of her goods taken on 13 June 1671 the following rooms are listed: 'the Dining Roome', 'the Aple Room', 'the great Chamber', 'the Garrett', 'the Roome over ye Entry', 'the Cockloft', 'the Buttery', 'the Kitching', 'the Parlor', 'the Hall', and 'the Backside'. The total value of her possessions was £40. 14s. 5d.

[1] Parish Registers.
[2] 48 Lawes.
[3] University Archives S P 2, f. 338: 'Robtus Saunders, Oxo, famulus Doris Ashworth fil: Thomas Saunders de Cockthorpe in Com p'd: pleb: an: nat' 34'. Ashworth's Will was proved in the P.C.C. 8 November 1633 (109 Russell): Saunders is not mentioned in it.
[4] City Archives B. 1. 4. e.
[5] Ib., E. 4. 6, ff. 1-2: *O.C.A.* 1626-1665, p. 453.
[6] *S. and T.*, p. 169.
[7] City Archives B. 1. 4. f.
[8] Lease Ledger N, f. 65.
[9] Lease Ledger P, ff. 358-9.
[10] *Cart. H. St J.B.*, Vol. III, p. 359.
[11] St Aldate's Defaulters, Bodleian MS. Add. D. 114, f. 24.
[12] Wood, *C. of O.*, Vol. III, p. 208.
[13] Possibly the widow of Henry Vaughan [q.v.] or of John Vaughan.
[14] *C. of O.*, Vol. I, p. 198 and note 2.
[15] *S. and T.*, p. 192.

HENRY ARUNDELL, third BARON ARUNDELL OF WARDOUR (1606?-1694)

The son and heir of Thomas, second Baron, a devoted Royalist, who raised a regiment for the King and died at Oxford 16 May 1643. His mother was Blanche, sixth daughter of Edward Somerset, fourth Earl of Worcester, who defended Wardour Castle against the rebels in 1643. He was Master of the Horse to the Queen.

In June 1643 Lord Arundell and one man were lodging with John Bowyer [q.v.], but it was reported that they had gone out of town by the 14th.[1] Arundell was with Prince Maurice's force which had left Oxford for the West on 15 May, and he took part on 10 June in Chewton Fight, where he captured a dragoon's colours.[2] Arundell sat in the Oxford Parliament. He retook Wardour in March 1644, but destroyed the castle in order to prevent it from being used as a fortress.

He married Cicely (died 1675/6), widow of Sir John Fermor, of Somerton, Oxfordshire, and daughter of Sir Henry Compton, of Brambletye, Sussex. Lady Arundell's half-sister, Mary, was wife of John Lumley [q.v.]: her first husband was a first cousin of Anne, Lady Lake [q.v.]. Arundell died 28 December 1694.
[Will: P.C.C. 1695: 195 Irby: proved 12 August 1695].
(For full accounts see *C.P.* and *D.N.B.*)

[1] St Aldate's Defaulters, Bodleian MS. Add. D. 114, f. 24.

[2] *The Vindication of Richard Atkyns Esq.*

In June 1643 Saunders had lodging with him 'The Lord Cottington; above 60 yeares'.[1]

FRANCIS COTTINGTON, BARON COTTINGTON (1579?-1652), had been appointed a P.C. in 1628 and was Chancellor of the Exchequer from 1629 to 1642. He did not join the King at York but followed him to Oxford in 1643. On 3 October the King appointed him Lord Treasurer, and he was one of the junto set up by Charles I that autumn. Cottington sat in the Oxford Parliament of January 1643/4, by which time he had moved to Oriel College, where his name occurs in the Buttery Book for 1643-4, for one term only. He signed the letter of 27 January 1643/4 to the Earl of Essex, and the Articles of the capitulation of Oxford in 1646, and then went abroad, dying in Spain.
(For full accounts see *C.P.* and *D.N.B.*)

[1] St Aldate's Defaulters, Bodleian MS. Add. D. 114, f. 24.

MARY (?) MARCHAM, WIDOW

Probably to be identified with Mary Marcham, widow of Robert Marcham, of St Aldate's, whose Will was proved 3 February 1620/1 by his relict, who was also his residuary legatee. In that case she cannot be the mother of Thomas Marcham [q.v.], whose father's name was Thomas also.

Widow Marcham's name occurs in all the St Aldate's taxation lists of 1645. Payments to Goodwife Marcham (probably the same person) occur in the Churchwardens' Accounts for 1646-7 and 1647-8.

Mrs Marcham's house must have been on the north side of Pennyfarthing Street, perhaps on the site of No. 45 Pembroke Street, the next tenement to the corner house of Robert Saunders [q.v.]. This is probably the house which in 1659 was in the tenure of Thomas Jackson and is described in a deed belonging to Pembroke College as 'scituate . . . in the parish of St Aldats . . . in a Street there called . . . penny farthing Streete . . . abutting on a garden ground of John Holloway [q.v.] on the north and vpon a house and Garden of Thomas Clayton Doct of Physicks [q.v.] and vpon a Coach house and Garden of George Low Esq. on the East vpon a house and Garden ground now in the occupacon of Thomas Moore on the West and the streete aforesaid on the South'.[2] Mrs Marcham's house could alternatively have been on the site of Nos. 43 and 44 Pembroke Street.

[1] MS. Wills Oxon. 44/1/6.
[2] Pembroke College Muniments A/35.

SIR HENRY RADLEY
(1590-1653)

There was no individual of the name of Sir Henry Radcliffe, so that this is almost certainly a mistranscription of Sir Henry Radley. The eldest son of William Radley, of Yarborough, Lincolnshire, by his wife, Anne, daughter of William Simcotts, of Louth, he was baptized at Yarborough 6 August 1590, and matriculated as a Fellow Commoner from Magdalene College, Cambridge, at Easter 1607. He was knighted at Newmarket 6 December 1616.

Radley was a captain of the Lifeguard of Foot: he was captured at Edgehill.[1] His name occurs in Ashburnham's *Accompt*: 'To Sr Henry Radley' £60.[2] The Lincoln College Computus Books for 1643, 1644, and 1645 shew him lodging in the Old Quadrangle in the 'Chamb: next ye hall dore'. He paid for the fourth quarter of 1643 only (that is Christmas 1643 to Lady Day 1644) so that it would seem that, if our identification is right, he left Widow Marcham's house soon after the St Aldate's 'Accompt' was taken. On 17 April 1644 Charles I ordered Lord Percy, General of the Ordnance, to supply thirty muskets and bandoleers and twelve pikes for arming Sir Henry Radley's Company 'in our Lifeguard'. These were received on 20 April. The company was therefore fifty-three strong, including officers.[3] On 22 May 1644 a number of muskets and pikes were received into the King's stores from Radley.[4] He took part in the campaign in Cornwall in the summer of 1644.[5] He begged to compound on the Newark Articles 13 June 1646, and on 18 September 1646 was fined £450. This was reduced to £180 on 17 July 1649.

Radley married Mary, eldest daughter of (Sir) Robert Payne, of Medloe, Huntingdonshire: she was living 18 November 1668. He was buried at Yarborough 26 July 1653.

[Administration: P.C.C. 1653/4, f. 102].

(See *Lincolnshire Pedigrees*, Vol. III, p. 808: Harleian Society, Vol. LII (1904)).

The possibility that the knight referred to is Sir George Radcliffe (1593-1657),

cannot be ruled out. He was in Oxford from October 1643 to June 1644, and was created D.C.L. 31 October 1643.
(See *D.N.B.* and Carte, op. cit., Vols. V and VI)

[1] *A Remonstrance of the Present State of His Majesties Army* (1642).
[2] P. xxiii.
[3] P.R.O., W.O. 55/423/215.
[4] *R.O.P.*, Part I, p. 135.
[5] MS. Harleian 6804, f. 187.
[6] *C.C.C.*, pp. 1325-6.

MR BELSON

Unidentified. A John Belson and his wife, Mary, had a son (John) baptized at St Margaret's, Westminster, 17 November 1639.

ABEL PARNE
(c. 1610-1650)

Whitebaker. Son of Richard Parne, yeoman, of Marston, Oxfordshire, he was apprenticed to William Bailie or Baylie, whitebaker, of Oxford, 15 January 1621/2,[1] and obtained his freedom 31 January 1628/9.[2] He was admitted by the University to bake 21 March 1633/4.[3]

Three of Abel Parne's brothers were privileged persons or servants of the University in consequence of their holding college posts. Richard was cook of Exeter College;[4] Francis was senior butler of New College;[5] and John was butler of Corpus Christi College.[6] The last-named, like his 'fellowe Servant' Thomas Seymour, the manciple [q.v.], whom John remembered in his Will and appointed one of his executors, refused to submit to the Parliamentary Visitors.

Abel Parne was among the several bakers who supplied New College with bread and flour:[7] he was also one of those employed by Magdalen.[8]

Parne was elected to the Common Council 3 October 1639.[9] He was mayor's chamberlain in 1639[10] and remained a chamberlain until 1647.[11] The reason why his name does not appear in the Council list of 1648 is probably because, as a certified Delinquent,[12] he was a victim of the 'purge' which took place at this time. In September 1642 'Abel pawne Baker' had been included in Bailiff Heron's list of persons accused of aiding Sir John Byron.[13] Arms were delivered to him in October 1643.[14] He was a churchwarden of St Aldate's in 1638-9. He paid 20s. and 8s. 'in lands' in the Subsidy Lists of 1641.[15] His name occurs in all the St Aldate's parish taxation lists of 1645 and 1647, but not in the St Aldate's Subsidy List of 1648: the 'Mr Parne' of St Peter's-in-the-East who was assessed at 1s.[16] could be either Abel or his brother John. Abel must have died between 24 June and 28 September 1650, as in the New College 'Long Books' payment is made in the fourth academic term of 1649-50 to 'Mris Parne', who thereafter appears in the books as 'Widdow Parne'. John Parne in his Will gave 'my Sister Parne Late Wife of Abell Parne deceased fforty shillings'.[17] Abel was not buried at St Peter's-in-the-East, so probably the entry of his burial would have been found in the lost St Aldate's Register.

The Thomas Parne who was a churchwarden of St Aldate's in 1651-2 was perhaps Abel's son, and is likely to have been the same person as the Parne who was supplying Magdalen with bread in the 'fifties.

Parne's house was in Pennyfarthing Street, where he enjoyed the distinction of being the landlord of Brian Twyne, the Oxford antiquary and Keeper of the University Archives. Twyne is mentioned as being over sixty when living there in June 1643.[18] He died in Parne's house 4 July 1644, having made his Will the same day. In it he states: 'I doe give to Abell Parne my landlord forty shillings'. The house was burnt in the great fire of 6 October 1644.[19]

Hitherto unpublished evidence derived from the Liber Rationarius Bursarium of Merton College[20] has proved conclusively that Parne's house was, as Wood believed,[21] the former Bull Hall, which had been granted to Merton in 1271.[22] This large building, which was capable of lodging so considerable a number of persons in January 1643/4, stood on the north side of Pennyfarthing Street and probably occupied the site of Nos. 41-2 Pembroke Street. In mediaeval deeds relating to the house (No. 12) occupied by Andrew Nicholls [q.v.] this tenement is described as being opposite to Bull Hall, and Wood[23] stated that Bull Hall was 'almost opposite to the place where now stands a fair house built of freestone and brick' (Nos. 13 and 14). The property ran back to the north and the messuage rented by John Savory [q.v.] and occupied by Ursula Collier, Henry Vaughan, and Anthony Yate [qq.v.] is described in the Magdalen leases as being bounded by a 'Tenemt of Merton Colledge' [i.e. Bull Hall] vpon the west'.

In October 1632 Merton leased its tenement in Pennyfarthing Street to John Price, cook of Pembroke College, with power to alienate.[24] His name first appears in the Liber Rationarius Bursarium under the heading *De ffirmariis* for 1634.[25] When Price died in 1637 he bequeathed all his leases to his son Henry, a cook in London. Parne first appears as paying the rent to Merton for the period March to August 1638,[26] and he continued to pay his annual rent of £2 in two instalments until August 1646,[27] but he did not receive a lease from Merton. In October 1648 the tenement was leased by the College to Arthur Dimmock, of St Thomas's parish.[28] It seems probable that Twyne had long been a lodger in the house, for John Price appointed as one of his overseers 'my good frend mr Brian Twyne Batchellor of divinitie'.

Fortunately, the rooms of the former Bull Hall are listed in Price's Inventory, which was taken 28 September 1637,[29] and gives us an idea of the size of Parne's house. This enumerates 'the hall', 'the Chamber ouer the hall', 'the little Roome ouer the parlour', 'the Buttry', 'the Milkhouse' 'the Roome ouer the bran loft', and 'the Chamber ouer the Candleloft'. In addition the Inventory speaks of 'A parcell of goods let with certaine Roomes wt a lease a table whereof is annexed to the Lease, whose names followe'. These are given as 'the parlor', 'the darke Roome', 'the kitchin', 'the Bakehouse', 'the backside', 'the Chamber ouer the Wheete Loft', 'the candleloft', 'the pastry', 'the wheatloft', and 'the chamber ouer the entry'. The lease is valued at £206.

[1] City Archives L. 5. 2, f. 99v.
[2] Ib., no folio number.
[3] *Register*, Vol. II, Pt. I, p. 339.
[4] University Archives S P 2, f. 337 v.
[5] Ib., f. 348, and New College 'Long Books' (Bursars' Accounts) *passim*. In his Will (P.C.C. 56 Fines 1646/7) he describes himself as of the University of Oxford, 'gentleman'.
[6] Bodleian Library MS. Add. D. 114, f. 60. In his Will (P.C.C. 131 Berkeley 1656) he adds 'maltster' to his University status.
[7] 'Long Books' under the heading of 'Emptio Panis'.
[8] Bursars' Boks under the heading 'Impensae Panis'.
[9] *O.C.A.* 1626-1665, p. 83.
[10] Ib. 1626-1665, p. 88.
[11] City Archives A. 5. 7, f. 162: Council Book C.
[12] Ib. F. 5. 9, f. 101.
[13] *The Manuscripts of the House of Lords*, Vol. XI, New Series, p. 326.
[14] City Archives E. 4. 5, ff. 55-55v.
[15] Ib. B. 1. 4. d.
[16] *S. and T.*, p. 176.
[17] She was apparently a recusant. In the Subsidy Lists for 1641, under the South-West Ward, occurs the entry '— Parne for her Pole' 8d. and 16d. (City Archives B. 1. 4. d.).
[18] St Aldate's Defaulters, Bodleian MS. Add. D. 114, f. 24. On 24 April 1643 he had supplied two weapons to the King (*R.O.P.*, Part I, p. 88).
[19] *Oxoniensia*, Vol. V (1940), p. 110, quoting MS. Wood E. 4.
[20] II 1633-1652: Merton College Muniments 3.2.
[21] *C. of O.*, Vol. I, p. 195, n. 7.
[22] See *Survey of South-West Ward*, Nos. 114 and 115; and for some topographical information see *Cart. H. St. J.B.*, Vol. II, p. 171.
[23] *Op. cit.*, Vol. I, p. 196.
[24] Merton College Muniments Lease Book 6. 2, f. 174.
[25] Ib. 3. 2, f. 8.
[26] Ib. 3. 2, f. 28v: 'De Parne pro domo in Paraecia Sti Aldati' £1.

[27] Ib. 3. 2., f. 79v. His Christian name is entered on this occasion only.
[28] Ib. Lease Book 6. 2., f. 486.
[29] University Archives Hyp. B. 17.

MR HENDERSON

A Scots cleric. It has not been possible to identify him, but he is certainly the man mentioned by Gerard Langbaine the elder, who succeeded Brian Twyne as Keeper of the University Archives. 'A note of such books, papers, or other muniments as were received by me Gerard Langbaine, Custos Archivorum, from Richard Twine executor of Mr Brian Twyne my predecessor at New Coll, in Mr Vice-chancellor's lodgings[1] in the presence of one Mr Henderson, a Scottish man, July 13th 1644'.[2] Henderson and Twyne were fellow lodgers in the house of Abel Parne [q.v.]. Andrew Clark wrongly identified him with Alexander Henderson (1583?-1646), the well-known divine, but he was in London in 1643/4 and was unmarried.

[1] The Vice-Chancellor was Robert Pinck, the Royalist Warden of New College.
[2] Wood, *L. and T.*, Vol. IV, p. 219.

LIEUTENANT WILLIAM HULL

He belonged to the Lifeguard of Foot. He signed for ammunition in January 1642/3,[1] and on 1 May 1643 there were received for the King from 'Willm Hull Ensigne to Colonell Vavasor to be fixed' three muskets.[2] William Vavasour was lieutenant-colonel of the Lifeguard of Foot.
It may be assumed that Hull was in the attempt to relieve Reading (April 1643), the siege of Gloucester, and the First Battle of Newbury (20 September 1643).

[1] P.R.O., W.O. 55/457.
[2] *R.O.P.*, Part I, p. 96.

MR ANDREW MORRISON
(died c. 1646)

He was clearly a Scot. He is mentioned twice under 'Taylors' in 1641, the second time as 'for his Mats Person'.[1] The senior tailor was David Murray. The reversion of the post of King's tailor, after Murray and Morrison, was granted to John Waite on 28 April 1645.[2]
In an undated list of Royal servants charged with payment towards the Oxford city works, probably belonging to the summer of 1643, there appear the names of 'Mr Hector [q.v.], David Forest and Andrew Morrison inferior Officers in ye kings Robes'. Between them they owed £3 for eight weeks, and described themselves in their answer to Richard Poole, the official deputed to try to extract the money, as 'very wanting men & therefore excused by the king himselfe'.[3]
On 12 September 1645 the address of Andrew Morrison, tailor to the King and Prince, was given as the Strand. Information was supplied that he was with the King at Oxford and the Prince in Cornwall and that Lord Howard of Escrick owed him £300.[4] He married Lilias . . . , who was dead by 8 June 1661, and he had a son, William.[5] He himself was dead by 31 December 1646.
In his Will, made in 1639, Morrison was stated to be of the parish of St Clement Danes. The occasion of the making of his Will was 'beinge suddainely to travel out

of the Realm of England into Scotland to attend the Cort'. Charles I had left for the North on 27 March 1639. Morrison made bequests to some fellow Royal servants: Clement Kynnersley, yeoman of the Wardrobe; David Mallocke, shoemaker to the King; and David Murray, the senior Royal tailor.
[Will: P.C.C. 1646: 189 Twisse: made 27 May 1639: proved 31 December 1646, by his widow].

[1] L.C. 3/1.
[2] *C.S.P.D.* 1660-1, p. 25: 25 May 1660.
[3] MS. Harleian 6804, f. 229.
[4] *C.A.M.*, p. 597.
[5] See P.C.C. *Calendar.*

MR LAWRENCE BALL
(died 1679)

Bull is clearly a mistranscription of Ball. The person intended is Lawrence Ball, who appears as a conduct of His Majesty's Bakehouse in 1635/6.[1] He appears as 'groome of the Backhouse' in March 1638.[2] Upon the second list of Charles I's necessitous servants and creditors, allowed by Parliament on 13 August 1651, Ball received a warrant for £10, receipted by him 11 May 1653.[3] He subsequently received another warrant for £30 through his assignee Edward Basse.[4] In January 1655/6 he is entered under 'The Bakehouse' in a 'Breife perticular' of warrant-holders upon this list as being paid £40 and 4d. in goods.[5] In 1662, as Lawrence Ball senior, he was groom of the Bakehouse, his son Lawrence Ball junior being a yeoman and his son Edward a conduct.[6] He married Joan . . . He died between 25 May and 17 September 1679.
In his Will Ball is described as yeoman of Eastshire [Esher], Surrey. He mentions his sons Edward and William and his daughters Elizabeth, Mary, and Anne. The last-named was to have the 'Beare at Eastshire'. Each of his grandchildren was to have 20s. 'if they live untill the Receipt of the money due to me from his Majestie paid by his Maties Cofferer'. His son Lawrence was appointed overseer and his 'Loving wife' residuary legatee and executrix.
[Will: P.C.C. 1679: 66 King: made 25 May 1679: proved 17 September 1679].

[1] *C.S.P.D.* 1635-6, p. 161.
[2] S.P. 16/386/97, f. 184.
[3] S.P. 28/350/9, f. 33: No. 816.
[4] Ib., f. 46: No. 1143: no date of receipt. The actual warrants appear to be missing.
[5] S.P. 18/123/19, f. 121v.
[6] S.P. 29/60/65, f. 117v.

MR GEORGE WILDE

George Wyld was a conduct of His Majesty's Bakehouse in 1635/6.[1] He was the first of five conducts of the Bakehouse in March 1638.[2]

[1] *C.S.P.D.* 1635-6, p. 161.
[2] S.P. 16/386/97, f. 184.

MR PATRICK (?) NAPIER

Almost certainly Patrick Napier or Napper, like Morrison obviously a Scot. He was

a member of the Barber-Surgeons Company. An apprentice of William Hann, he was admitted by servitude in January 1629/30.[1] His name appears in the list of members of the City Companies in the return of the Poll Tax in 1641,[2] being described as of St Martin-in-the-Fields.
Archibald Napper 'filius Patricii et Elizabethae' was baptized at St Martin's 29 October 1633.[3]

[1] Barbers Freedoms Admissions MS. 5265/1, f. 78v.
[2] P.R.O. E 179/251/22 and E 179/272/36 and 49. We owe these references to the kindness of Dr A. H. Hall, the late Guildhall Librarian.
[3] *Registers* 1619-1636, p. 98.

(SIR) HENRY WOOD
(1597-1671)

He was Treasurer of Queen Henrietta Maria's Household from 1644 until 1671 (two years after her death).
The son of Thomas Wood, of Hackney, Sergeant of the Pastry (died 1649), and brother of Dr Thomas Wood, Dean (1664-1671) and Bishop (1671-1692) of Lichfield, Henry was baptized at Hackney 17 October 1597. According to the statement in his composition (1649), he had been 'from childhood in the household of the late King and for twenty-six years a sworn servant, which put an extraordinary obligation on him to attend his Majesty, his wife, and children'.[1] He became Clerk of the Spicery.
Wood accompanied the Queen to Holland in 1641/2, as overseer of provisions of her diet, and attended her to the Court at Oxford in July 1643. Ashburnham's *Accompt* records that he received £800. 6s. 6d. 'for payment of the Northern Regiments that came along with her Majestie out of the North One week's pay'.[2] He was knighted at Oxford 16 April 1644 as Clerk Comptroller. Next day Wood accompanied Henrietta to Abingdon, and thence to Exeter, and finally to France, as Treasurer of her Household. There is a letter written by him from Paris to Thomas Webb at Oxford 30 March/9 April 1645.[3] Wood compounded 31 May 1649, and was fined £273 upon his own discovery.[4] He is mentioned by Evelyn as being in Paris on 17 November 1651. He was created a baronet c. 1657.
After the Restoration Wood was appointed a Clerk of the Green Cloth. There are many references to him in the *Calendars of Treasury Books.* He was responsible for paying Queen Henrietta's legacies. He also became a member of the Council of Queen Catherine.
He married first, c. 1630, Anne Webb (died 1648), and secondly, in 1651, Mary (died 1665), fourth daughter of Sir Thomas Gardiner, of Cuddesdon, Oxfordshire, Solicitor-General in 1643. She was a maid of honour to Queen Henrietta. He died 25 May 1671.
In his Will he is described as of Loudham, Suffolk. The Will shews that his young daughter and sole heiress, Mary (aged about seven), was betrothed to Charles Palmer, Earl of Southampton, eldest natural son of Charles II and Barbara Villiers, Duchess of Cleveland, and that she had a pension from the King of £100 per annum for her life. She married Southampton soon after her father's death. Wood appointed his brother the Dean his executor.
[Will: P.C.C. 1671: 54 Duke: made 24 May 1671: proved 29 May 1671].
(For a full account see *C.B.* and R.E.C. Waters, *Family of Chester* (1878), with a pedigree)

[1] *C.C.C.*, p. 2072.
[2] P. xxviii.
[3] *C.S.P.D.* 1644-5, p. 376.

[4] *C.C.C.*, loc. cit. See also *C.A.M.*, p. 472.

MR NICHOLAS SNOW

Snow received a warrant for £10 on 11 November 1651[1] and another on 8 March 1652/3 for £6. 18s. 7d,[2] both upon the second list of Charles I's necessitous servants and creditors, allowed by Parliament on 13 August 1651. In January 1655/6 he is entered under 'The Guard' in a 'Breife perticular' of warrant-holders upon this list as being paid £16. 18s. 7d.[3] His receipts for the two warrants are dated 30 May 1656.

A Michael Snowe, perhaps the son of Nicholas, appears in a list of Charles II's Yeomen of the Guard dated 20 August 1667.[4]

[1] S.P. 28/284.
[2] Ibid.
[3] S.P. 18/123/39, f. 120v.
[4] Sir Reginald Hennell, *The History of the King's Bodyguard of the Yeomen of the Guard* (1904), Appendix VII.

MR NICHOLAS HORNE
(died 1647)

A brother of Robert Horne, one of the ordinary Yeomen of His Majesty's Chamber, who, on 27 December 1623, was paid 60s. for wages in September of that year, for which he signed.[1]

Robert Horne's Will, as of the parish of St Martin-in-the-Fields, in which he is described as Yeoman Usher in Ordinary to His Majesty, was made 9 October 1635 and proved in the P.C.C. 6 November 1639 by his relict, Anne.[2] In this Robert's brother Nicholas is termed 'one of the wardoures of the tower of London in Ordinary'. He received an annuity of £10 and the reversion (after Anne Horne's death) of property in St Martin's parish (the Strand), 'the three goates heades' and 'the swan with twoe necks'. Robert also left his brother 'my best gowne and my furr Coate'. Nicholas' son, Robert, his uncle's godson, was left 40s.

On 3 April 1643 Nicholas Horne signed a petition of ten Yeomen of the Guard from Oxford on behalf of a fellow Yeoman, Edward Midwinter, addressed to Lord Capel and Sir Francis Wortley [sic].[3] On 13 November 1645, as of Westminster, he begged to compound for a small estate fallen to him on the death of his sister-in-law. He stated that he gave £310 for his place, which obliged him to attend the King, having no other maintenance for himself and five children. On 20 December 1645 he was fined £93, and this was accepted by the House of Commons on 9 March 1646. In December 1646 Horne was complaining that, although he only attended the King as his servant, and never took up arms, and although it was four months since he got his composition passed by the Commons, he could not get it passed by the Lords, although he hoped long since to have his pardon under seal. He declared that he was not disaffected but aged and infirm, with a wife and many children, and therefore begged a licence to remain within the lines of communication.[4] He married Elizabeth ... He was buried at St Giles-in-the-Fields 20 September 1647.[5]

In his Will he is described as gentleman, of St Giles-in-the-Fields. He mentions the property left to him by his brother in reversion. He had four children living: Robert, Anne, Elizabeth, and Barbara. His wife and son were appointed executors. To them Nicholas left 'all such sume and sumes of money as is or shalbe due and oweing vnto me at ye tyme of my decease from ye kings matie.' Barbara was to have 'my East India Cabinet' after his wife's decease.

On 10 October 1648 a warrant was issued by Charles I from 'Our Court at Newport' to Robert Reeves, Clerk of the Check to the Guard: 'You are to sweare in Henry Chaplaine, yeoman of our Great Chamber in ordinary, *vice* Nicholas Horne deceased'.[6]
[Will: P.C.C. 1647: 199 Fines: made 1 September 1647: proved 14 October 1647].
Robert Horne appears in a list of Charles II's Yeomen of the Guard dated 20 August 1667.[7]

[1] MS. Rawlinson A. 215, f. 3v. See also *C.S.P.D.* 1637, p. 23. As Royal service ran in families, it is probable that Robert and Nicholas were relatives (possibly brothers) of Thomas Horne, a page of the Chamber, who was granted a lease in the parish of St Giles-in-the-Fields in 1598 and died in 1612.
[2] 175 Harvey.
[3] 'Ottley Papers', *Transactions* of the Shropshire Record Society, 2nd Series, Vol. VII, Pt. III, p. 241, et seq.
[4] *C.C.C.*, p. 959.
[5] We are indebted for this entry to the Revd. G. C. Taylor.
[6] *C.S.P.D.* 1648-9, p. 30.
[7] Sir R. Hennell, op. cit., loc. cit.

In June 1643 Parne had lodging with him LIEUTENANT GODWIN and one man. He must be the Lieutenant Godwyn who was in the Lifeguard of Foot 3 June 1643.[1] He said that 'when Collonels & other souldiers of his rank payd he would also'. There were besides in the house Dr Frazer (from whom no answer was received) and HENRY WILMOT, a boy under sixteen (not identified).[2]

(SIR) ALEXANDER FRAIZER
(c. 1606-1681)

Physician, the only son of Adam Fraizer, of Dores, Kincardineshire, was born c. 1606. He was educated at Aberdeen University and graduated D. Med. at Montpellier 1 October 1635. He was incorporated at Cambridge 9 March 1636/7, and became F.R.C.P. 23 November 1641.
His name occurs in 1641 in L.C. 3/1 in the list of Physicians: 'Dr Alexander ffrazier next in reversion', and also at the bottom of the list of Physicians Extraordinary, again 'in reversion'. He is said to have been made Physician in Ordinary to Charles I in 1645. By 1644 he had moved to a house in All Saints' parish, Oxford.[3] On 8 August of that year, as of Philpott Lane, London, he was assessed at £300 and styled a Delinquent.[4]
Fraizer followed the fortunes of Charles II as Prince and King, and attended the Royal Family in exile and after the Restoration, becoming Principal Physician in Ordinary in 1664. He was knighted between 19 September 1664 and 7 June 1666, and was created a baronet 2 August 1673. He was a founder F.R.S. in 1663.
He married twice: first, Elizabeth Dowchly, from near Bristol, and secondly, after 1659, Mary, fourth daughter of Sir Ferdinando Carey, and relict of Dudley Wylde, of Canterbury (died 1653). He died at Whitehall in his seventy-fifth year 28 April (3 May?) 1681, and was buried at Dores 20 July 1681.
[Will: P.C.C. 1681: 106 North: made 9 October 1679: proved 7 July 1681].
(*C.B.: D.N.B.:* J. Venn, *Alumni Cantabrigienses;* W. Munk, op. cit., Vol. I, pp. 23-4)

[1] P.R.O., W.O. 55/1661.
[2] St Aldate's Defaulters, Bodleian MS. Add. D. 114, f. 24.
[3] Ib., f. 59v.
[4] *C.A.M.*, p. 407.

WILLIAM PEARSON
(c. 1607-1667)

Tailor. The son of Silvester Pearson, plasterer, of Oxford,[1] he was apprenticed to Andrew Nicholls, tailor [q.v.], 31 May 1619.[2] The record of his freedom has not been found, but his name occurs in the Journeymen Taylors' Accounts 1613-1699 for the first time in 1630.[3] His name does not appear in the St Aldate's taxation lists of 1645 and 1647, but he was assessed as of St Aldate's at 1s. 8d. in the Subsidy of 1648,[4] in which year he was appointed constable of the South-West Ward.[5] In 1661-2 he was paid £7 by the churchwardens of St Aldate's 'being the remainder of the 14li for the keeping of Elizabeth Joyners children'. In March 1662/3 he was one of the recipients of Mr Wilson's money.[6] He had moved to St Martin's parish by 1665 when his name is entered in the Hearth Tax returns,[7] and, with that of his wife, Anne, appears there in the Poll Tax returns of 1667.[8] [Administration: MS. Wills Oxon. 107, f. 138: Act Book B].

Pearson's house was on the south side of Pennyfarthing Street and was Nos. 13 and 14 Pembroke Street. Once a tenement of Abingdon Abbey, the site passed to the Crown after the Dissolution, and when leased in 1553 contained two cottages and a garden.[9] In 1621 the tenement is described as 'of our Sowaigne Lord the kings Matie that now is in the tenure of Sylvester Person', who was still holding it in 1635.[10] The date of William's father's death is unknown, but in 1641, when Richard Hannes, a brewer, of Holywell, was building a messuage on the site, he called it his own inheritance.[11] It looks as if William Pearson was installed by Hannes [q.v. under Walter Cave] as his tenant. 'Mr Hans his house' is entered in some of the St Aldate's taxation lists of 1645 and 1647, which would account for the absence of Pearson's name. Nos. 13 and 14 (originally one) form the 'fair house built of freestone and brick' mentioned by Wood and alluded to under Abel Parne [q.v.]. It was much altered c. 1800.[12]

[1] As Silvester Pearson, slatter, 'servant or feed man' to Exeter College, he was the occasion of a dispute in 1609 between the city and the University, when the latter attempted to privilege him. (*O.C.A.* 1583-1626, pp. 190-1).
[2] City Archives L. 5. 2, f. 56.
[3] Ib. F. 4. 2.
[4] *S. and T.*, p. 169.
[5] *O.C.A.* 1626-1665, p. 158.
[6] Ib., p. 306. For Mr Wilson's money see under Robert Wilson.
[7] *S. and T.*, p. 185.
[8] Ib., p. 224. For his widow see p. 427.
[9] *Survey of South-West Ward*, No. 110.
[10] Leases of Moses Hall at Oriel College: see under Thomas Fox.
[11] *O.C.P.*, p. 112.
[12] For a full description see R.C.H.M. *City of Oxford* (1939), p. 173.

JOHN HEWES, SERVANT TO MR VALENTINE CLERKE

Unidentified.

VALENTINE CLERKE was Groom of the Privy Chamber to Queen Henrietta Maria. He had a brother, Edward, who was Groom of the Bedchamber to King Charles: Edward was in service by 1626, but dead by 1637. Valentine was probably in service by 9 October 1633, when Dorington [sic], son of Valentine and Elizabeth Clark, was baptized at St Martin-in-the-Fields.[1] Valentine is mentioned as the Queen's servant in 1637.[2] On 14 February 1643/4 Henry Clarke (almost certainly a relative) was sworn a Groom of the Chamber in Ordinary to the Queen at Oxford.[3]

On 15 October 1660 (?) a warrant was issued to Valentine as Groom of the Privy Chamber to the Queen Mother for remission of £320, being one year's arrear of rent for the rectory of Outbourne (Ogbourne), Wilts, due to the late usurping powers and now forfeit to the King.[4] On 6 February 1670/1 Clerke received a legacy of £175 from the Queen Mother.[5] He married first, Elizabeth . . . , and secondly, Luce . . . He died between 28 December 1678 and 22 January 1678/9.

In his Will he mentions his wife, Luce, his sons Valentine (whom he appointed his executor), St John, Doddington [sic], and Charles, and his daughters Lucy, Elizabeth, Frances, and Mary. He also mentions a lease of lands in Cumberland granted to him by 'my Mistris the late Queene Henrietta Maria', and marshlands and other lands in Lincolnshire leased to him by the same Queen.

[Will: P.C.C. 1679: 2 King: made 28 December 1678: proved 22 January 1678/9].

[1] *Registers* 1619-1636, p. 97.
[2] *C.S.P.D.* 1637, p. 525.
[3] Ib. 1644, pp. 14-15.
[4] Ib. 1660-1, p. 39. also pp. 115 and 134: see also *C.T.B.*, Vol. I, p. 277.
[5] *C.T.B.*, Vol. III, p. 779.

CORPORAL PETER FURNACE

Unidentified, but almost certainly of the Lifeguard of Foot.

CORPORAL BALFOUR COLDRON

Unidentified, but almost certainly of the Lifeguard of Foot.

THOMAS FOX
(died 1645)

Whitebaker. The younger son of Anthony Fox, whitebaker, of St Aldate's, by his wife, Katherine... Anthony Fox, son of Anthony Fox, of Kings Sutton, Northamptonshire, yeoman, was apprenticed to Andrew Burnett, whitebaker, of Oxford, in 1575,[1] and obtained his freedom in 1584.[2] In his Will, made on 1 May and proved at Oxford 17 December 1624,[3] he is described as 'gent', and as 'Mr Antony Foxe' in the entry of his burial at St Aldate's 3 May 1624.[4] In his Will he states: 'I give to ffrancis ffox my eldest son and to Thomas ffox my youngest son each of them a silver spoone'. His residuary legatee and executrix was his wife. The value of his goods listed in his Inventory (taken by John Wilmott [q.v.] and another) was £36. 15s. Katherine Fox made her Will on 4 March 1629/30: it was proved at Oxford 17 October 1632.[5] She was of St Thomas's parish, but desired to be buried in St Aldate's churchyard, 'as neere vnto my husband as conveniently may bee'. Her son Thomas was her residuary legatee and executor. The Inventory of her goods (which Wilmott helped to take) gives their value as £81. 5s. 4d.

On 24 November 1632 Thomas Fox was admitted by the University to bake.[6] On 2 November 1634 he obtained his freedom.[7] Fox is found supplying various colleges with bread during the Civil War years. His name, with that of other bakers, occurs under the heading 'Impensae Panis' in the Magdalen Bursar's Books for 1641 to 1644. 'Foxes skores' and 'Widow Foxes skores' appear at the end of the University College Bursar's Journal for 1643, which also has later jottings. The Brasenose College Junior Bursar's Book for 1644,[8] the only volume to survive for the War years, shews that Fox was one of several bakers supplying the College with bread. On 18 July 1644 he signs a receipt at the back of the book for the first quarter, but although the name 'ffox' appears until the end of the year, his relict Elizabeth (who makes her mark), was only paid on 5 May 1645 for 'bread brought in by her husband the Qrter ending at Midsomer 1644'. Fox died between 18 January 1644/5 and 6 May 1645. Widow Fox appears in the St Aldate's parish taxation list of 6 May 1645.

In his Will Fox expressed the wish to be buried in St Aldate's churchyard, near his mother. Except for one trifling bequest, everything was left to his wife, who was appointed executrix.

[Will: MS. Wills Oxon. 127/1/31: made 18 January 1644/5: proved 1 July 1645].

Fox's house was on the south side of Pennyfarthing Street and occupied the site of No. 15 Pembroke Street. This was the former Moses or Moyses Hall, which had been granted to Oriel College in 1362.[9] On 15 October 1621 Oriel granted a lease of the property for forty years at a rent of 18s. per annum to Thomas Forward, manciple of the College. In this it is demised 'as all that their messuage and tenement sett... in Pennyfarthinge lane within the parish of St Aldats in Oxon and a garden ground therevnto apperteyninge Betweene a tenement of our Souaigne Lord the kings Matie that now is in the tenure of Sylvester Person on the East side and a garden now in the tenure or occupacon of John Price Coocke on the West side ['tenement now in the tenure of (blank) Edwards' written above] and are bounded betweene penny ffarthinge street on the North and Beef Hall on the South.' A similar lease was granted on 20 December 1635 to Forward's son, Robert Forward, B.D., his executors, administrators or assigns. Forward, who had just resigned his Fellowship at Oriel, was a chaplain to Lord Wentworth in Ireland, precentor of St Patrick's, Dublin, in 1635, and Dean of Dromore in 1639: he died in 1641. It is obvious that he did not occupy the St Aldate's house himself and that he must have sub-let it. This appears to be equally true of Thomas Forward, for there can be little doubt that Anthony Fox had been the sub-tenant of this house before his son Thomas, who was almost certainly the sub-tenant at the time of Robert Forward's death. In the College Rental for 1631 after the entry 'In Pennyfarthinge Lane Item of a tenement Thomas Forwarde holdeth' there has been added in a later hand 'Fox, Amand'[10] which seems to imply that first Thomas Fox, and, after his death, another whitebaker, Richard Almond, were allowed to pay the rent to Oriel as occupants of the house from 1641 onwards. Almond obtained a lease from the College in 1655 when the house is described as in his 'tenure or occupacon'. The house is given out of order in the 'Accompt'.

In Anthony Fox's Inventory, taken on 16 December 1624, the following rooms are mentioned: 'the Hale', 'the kitchin', 'the Chamber', 'the vpper Chambr', 'the loft ouer ye kitchin', and 'the Buttry'.

[1] City Archives A. 5. 3, f. 273: Enrolment of Apprentices 1514-1591.
[2] Ib., f. 19.
[3] MS. Wills Oxon. 22/2/37.
[4] Wood, *C. of O.*, Vol. III, p. 206.
[5] MS. Wills Oxon. 22/3/37.
[6] *Register*, Vol. II, Pt. I, p. 339.
[7] City Archives L. 5. 2, no folio number.
[8] A 8 11.*
[9] See *Survey of South-West Ward*, No. 111 and Wood, *C. of O.*, Vol. I, p. 196, where it is wrongly stated to lie west of Bull Hall.
[10] *Oriel College Records*, p. 413.

MR THOMAS HITCHCOCK
(1605-1673) ?

Almost certainly Thomas Hitchcock or Hitchcox, barber-chirurgeon, of Stratford-on-Avon, concerning whom information was given on 25 November 1651 that in the years 1643 to 1645 he left his own house and stayed in the King's garrisons in Worcester and Oxford; was familiar with the soldiers and commanders, and rode armed; and that in 1642 he raised the town of Stratford against Colonel Needham, the Parliamentary officer.[1] On 10 February 1651/2 an order was made that Hitchcock should have leave to examine witnesses in his defence.

Thomas Hitchcox was the son of Isaac Hickcoks or Hitchcocks, innholder or alehousekeeper of Stratford, by his wife, Joan Hannis: Isaac and Joan were married at Stratford 1 May 1586. Thomas was baptized there 5 January 1604/5. The father seems never to have joined the corporation, but he must have been of some standing to be named one of the collectors authorized by a Royal patent of 5 December 1614 to solicit alms for the sufferers by the fire of that year. He was buried 3 July 1646.

Nothing is known of Thomas Hitchcox's activities before 4 September 1639, when he appears as a member of the Borough Council. He was elected aletaster in 1639 and served until 1640. He served as constable for 1641 and 1642. He was absent from meetings with or without licence from March to June 1642, September to December 1642, May 1643 to January 1643/4, May to July 1644, October to December 1644, and April to July 1645 inclusive. He was junior chamberlain in 1648, and chamberlain in 1650 and 1651. On 1 October 1651 he was chosen alderman. On 30 November 1653 he obtained his release from continuing any longer a member of council.

A mortgage of 25 April 1657 and a settlement of 10 December 1668 describe him as a barber-chirurgeon.

Hitchcox died in 1672/3, and was buried at Stratford 4 February 1672/3. He had no children or at any rate no surviving ones.[2]

[1] *C.A.M.*, pp. 1413-14.
[2] We are greatly indebted to Mr Levi Fox for the above particulars of Hitchcox's career.

MR DAVID LITTLE
(died 1682)

His Christian name (as Davy) is given in the St Aldate's Defaulters List of 14 June 1643, when he was already lodging with Thomas Fox and no answer could be obtained from him.[1]
In 1641 David Little was in the service of Prince Charles as third of the three 'Groomes of the Hunting Stable'.[2] In December 1660 David Little, His Majesty's padman, petitioned for the place of King's Waiter in the Custom House, the Customs Commissioners having denied him the place which His Majesty had formerly granted him.[3] According to *Angliae Notitia*,[4] there were thirty-four grooms of the Hunting and Pad Stable. He died between 8 March 1681/2 and 29 March 1682.
In his Will he is described as of St Martin-in-the-Fields, gentleman. His residuary legatee and executrix was his only (surviving) child, Mary Ewry, who must have been one of the two children lodging in Thomas Fox's house in 1643/4.
[Will: P.C.C. 1682: 35 Cottle: made 8 March 1681/2: proved 29 March 1682].

[1] Bodleian MS. Add. D. 114, f. 24.
[2] MS. Harleian 3791, f. 113.
[3] *C.S.P.D.* 1660-1, p. 449.
[4] Edition of 1670, p. 282.

ANDREW NICHOLLS
(c. 1579-before 1656)

Tailor. The son of Thomas Nicholls, slatter, of Oxford, by his wife, Joane, he was apprenticed to Simon Dobson, tailor, of Oxford, 1 November 1591, his father then being dead.[1] On 2 August 1605 he was admitted a freeman.[2] He is described as being over sixty years of age on 14 June 1643.[3] In November 1604 he was of Headington, but by December 1611 was of the city of Oxford (see leases below). On 29 September 1612 he was chosen a constable.[4] He married Magdalen . . . His name does not occur in the St Aldate's parish taxation lists of 1645 and 1647, nor in the Subsidy of 1648, but he was alive at Michaelmas 1649[5] and dead before 30 July 1656, when he is described as 'Andrew Nicholls Taylor since deceased'.[6] Nicholls' house stood on the south side of Pennyfarthing Street, on the west of the pathway leading from that street to St Aldate's churchyard and Pembroke College: it is No. 12 Pembroke Street. The house was the property of Magdalen College, which, on 27 November 1604, granted him a lease of 'All that their tente situate . . . in the parish of St Aldath . . . wth appurtences' for twenty years at a rent of 5s. per annum.[7] The lease was renewed on 2 December 1611 on the same terms.[8] On 14 December 1631 a lease to Andrew and his wife, Magdalen, was granted by the College for forty years at the same rent.[9] The house had previously been rented from Magdalen College by Andrew's parents, Thomas Nicholls (1574) and Joane Nicholls (1590).[10] Unfortunately, no bounds are stated in any of the leases before the year 1703, but in a lease then granted (6 December) by Magdalen, the house is described as 'between a tenement now in the tenure of Joshua Lasher, doctor of physick, on the west, and the turnstile leading to Pembroke College on the east, the said cottage south, the street north'.[11] The turnstile has gone, but the passage remains. The house was a small tenement, described in the lease of 1703 as measuring thirty-two feet from east to west and twenty-four feet from north to south. Salter commented that 'the original small stone house is easily seen: a more modern upper storey was added' probably in 1772.[12] The single storey house can be seen in Loggan's plan of the city.[13]

[1] City Archives L. 5. 1, f. 16.
[2] *O.C.A.* 1583-1626, p. 168.
[3] St Aldate's Defaulters, Bodleian MS. Add. D. 114, f. 24.
[4] *O.C.A.* 1583-1626, p. 224.
[5] *Cart. H. St J.B.*, Vol. III, p. 324.
[6] Magdalen College Lease Ledger O, f. 717.
[7] Lease Ledger J, f. 130v.
[8] Ib., f. 442.
[9] Lease Ledger M, ff. 2v-3.
[10] *Cart. H. St J.B.*, Vol. II, p. 144.
[11] Op. cit., loc. cit., quoting Ledger T, f. 841.
[12] *Survey of South-West Ward*, No. 109.
[13] *Oxonia Illustrata* (1675).

MR GILBERT OGLEBY

His name is entered amongst the Serjeants at Arms in L.C. 3/1: it has been substituted. He married Anne, daughter of Bartholomew Parker senior, a brewer of Westminster. Her baptism is recorded in the Registers of St Margaret's 13 March 1607/8, and entries relating to the children of Gilbert and Anne Ogleby are also to be found there between 1627 and 1642, and again in 1647.

Ogleby was the brother-in-law of Bartholomew Parker junior [q.v.], his fellow lodger, and William Parker (see below). The Will of Bartholomew Parker senior, made 23 July 1652, and proved in the P.C.C. 12 September 1653,[1] mentions his 'daughter Ogleby' and his grandchildren James and Mary Ogleby, who, together with their Parker grandmother, were named residuary legatees and executors. Gilbert Ogleby was presumably dead by this date.

[1] 162 Brent.

MR BARTHOLOMEW PARKER

He is entered among the Gentlemen Usher Quarter Waiters in L.C. 3/1: his name has been substituted. He was the youngest son of Bartholomew Parker, a brewer of Westminster, by his wife, Katherine . . . , and was baptized at St Margaret's 10 March 1615/16.[1] His elder brother, William, also a brewer, compounded on the Oxford Articles 5 December 1646.[2] Bartholomew was brother-in-law of Gilbert Ogleby [q.v.].

[1] *Registers*, p. 92.
[2] *C.C.C.*, p. 1592: see also *C.A.M.*, p. 1152.

Plate 9 Patrick Ruthven, Earl of Forth, later of Brentford (1573-1651), Lieutenant-General of the Royal Army. By an unknown artist. He lodged in the house of Thomas Smyth, Slaying Lane (now Brewer Street), St. Aldate's. *(Reproduced by courtesy of the Nationalmuseum, Stockholm)*

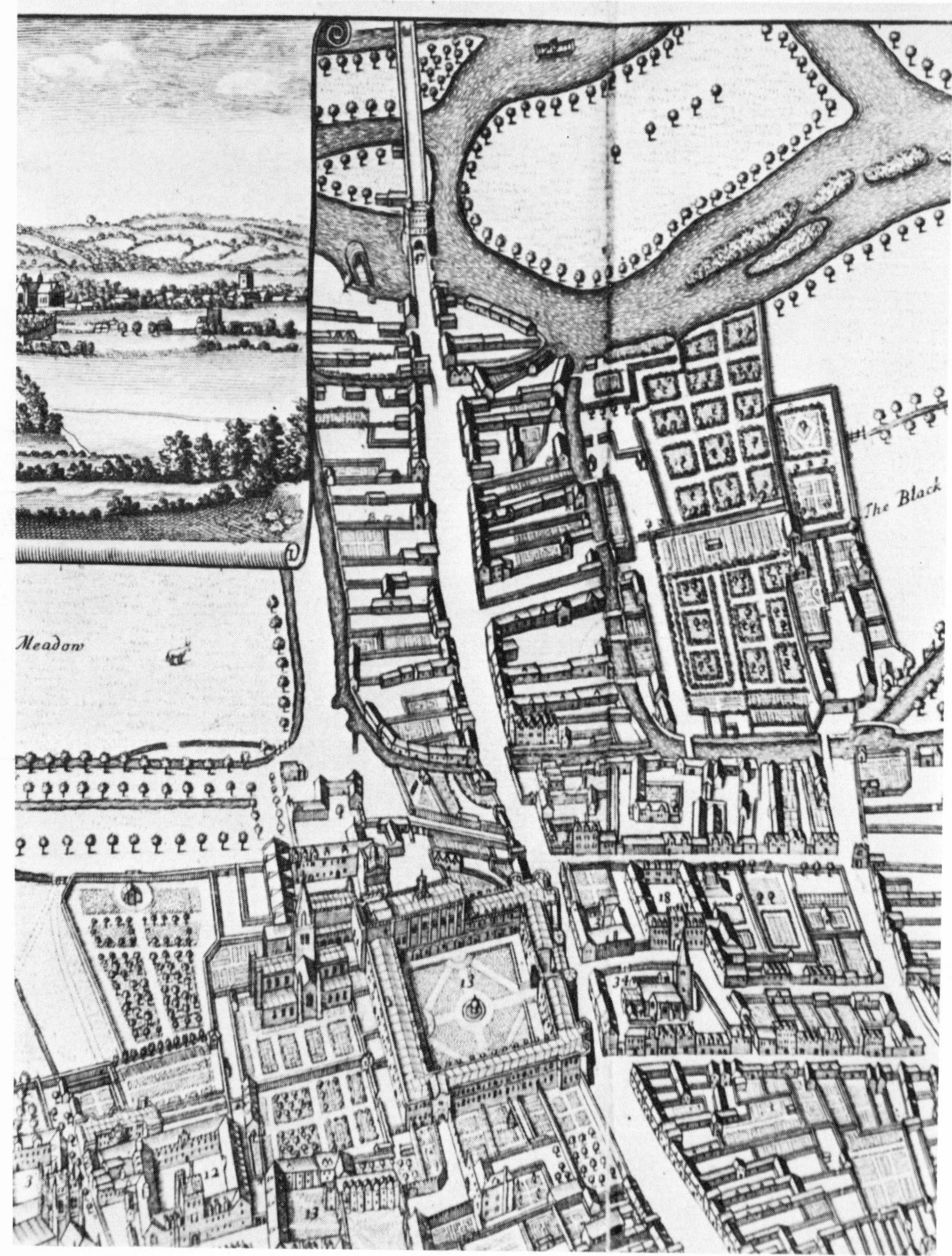

Plate 10 The Parish of St. Aldate's. From Loggan's plan of the City of Oxford, 1675.

Plate 11 St. Aldate's Church and Pembroke Street, between 1865 and 1870. From a watercolour by J. Pyne.

(Reproduced by courtesy of the Bodleian Library, Oxford)

Plate 12 The house of Thomas Seymour, Manciple of Corpus Christi College. Now No. 84 St. Aldate's. By J. C. Buckler, 1811.

(Reproduced by courtesy of the Bodleian Library, Oxford)

THOMAS WRIGHT
(died c. 1645)

Occupation unknown. On 24 April 1643 a pike was received from him into the King's stores 'wch was leaft with him by a souldier'.[1] He was, together with John King [q.v.], a constable of St Aldate's in October 1643.[2] He was dead by 1645 since his widow appears in the parish taxation lists of that year. One of the two soldiers of the Lifeguard entered as lodging with Wright appears in the St Aldate's Churchwardens' Accounts: 'Paid for a shrowde for a Souldier that died at Thomas Wrights on the 30th of June 1644' 4s.

Wright's house was on the south side of Pennyfarthing Street and must have been on the site of 11 Pembroke Street. His house and the rest of those on this side of the street going east had been the property of St Aldate's parish since 24 Henry VIII (1532-3).[3] The ground on which they stood had originally been a single messuage on which stood a malthouse, and was described in 1614 as 'abuttinge eastwards vppon the waye or passage leading into the Churchyard of St Aldates . . . and Westward vppon a little lane or passage leading from pennye farthinge streete towards Broadgates[4] and next betweene the Churchyard . . . on the South and pennye farthinge streete on the North'.[5] By 1628 the messuage had been divided into two adjoining portions, an east and a west messuage, of which the western one, immediately east of the little passage leading to Pembroke, was Wright's house. It was then in the occupation of Judith Fowler and Rowland Barber.[6] In 1631 the St Aldate's feoffees leased the property to the widowed Judith in whose occupation and Barber's it still was.[7] By the year 1633-4 Mrs Fowler had married John Savory [q.v.], but although now living elsewhere in the parish, she continued to lease her house, for which she paid £1 per annum, from the parish feoffees.[8] Thomas Wright would have been their sub-tenant.

The present house was built late in the seventeenth century and altered in the eighteenth century.[9] The earlier house contained 'in breadth at the west end Eleaven yards and a halfe'.[10]

[1] *R.O.P.*, Part I, p. 82.
[2] City Archives E. 4. 5, f. 67v.
[3] *Survey of the South-West Ward*, No. 117.
[4] The passage east of the house of Andrew Nicholls [q.v.]. Broadgates Hall became Pembroke College in 1624.
[5] Indenture between the feoffees of St Aldate's and William Furness, yeoman, 2 February 1613/14 (Parish Chest).
[6] Indenture between the feoffees and William Furness, tailor, 20 April 1628 (Parish Chest).
[7] Indenture dated 25 April 1631 (Parish Chest).
[8] It is possible that Judith's first husband, Walter Fowler, had occupied the house: his house is described in his Inventory (University Archives Hyp. B. 12) as having a hall, a parlour, three chambers, and a buttery.
[9] See R.C.H.M. *City of Oxford*, p. 173.
[10] A Particular of the St Aldate's parish messuages in 1670 (Parish Chest).

MR JOHN KNOWLES

John Knowllis was second of the three 'Children of the Pastry' in 1638.[1] On 24 January 1650/1 John Blakiston, assignee of John Knowles, signed a receipt for a warrant for £10 upon the first list of Charles I's necessitous servants, allowed by

Parliament 14 March 1649/50.[2]

[1] S.P. 16/386/97, f. 190.
[2] S.P. 28/390/9, f. 18: No. 539.

MR ANDREW BLUNT

He was servant to William Booreman, Clerk of the Pastry in 1638.[1] He was already lodging in Wright's house in June 1643.[2]

[1] S.P. 16/386/97, f. 190.
[2] St Aldate's Defaulters, Bodleian MS. Add. D. 114, f. 24.

MR JOHN (?) FIELD

He is possibly identical with the John Field of London and Westminster who was quartermaster to the troop of Colonel William Legge [q.v.] in Prince Rupert's Regiment (Horse).[1] Rupert was in Oxford from 20 January to 6 February 1643/4, and sat in the Oxford Parliament as Earl of Holderness and Duke of Cumberland.[2]
Possibly also he is the John Field who received a grant of the office of Falconer in Ordinary with a fee of £50 per annum and £30 for keeping four (later six) couple of spaniels in March 1660/1.[3] He received a legacy of £30 from the Queen Mother 6 February 1670/1.[4] This John Field died between 10 October 1673 and 14 August 1674.[5] In June 1643 Field was already lodging in Wright's house, when he was described as 'of the kings pastry', but this is almost certainly a mistake.

[1] *I.O.*, col. 111.
[2] Prince Rupert's 'Journal', *English Historical Review*, Vol. XIII (1898).
[3] *C.S.P.D.* 1660-1, p. 557. See also *C.T.B.*, Vol. I, p. 391.
[4] Ib., Vol. III, p. 780.
[5] Ib., Vol. IV, pp. 407 and 568.
[6] St Aldate's Defaulters, Bodleian MS. Add. D. 114, f. 24.

MR WILLIAM PRICHARD

He appears as Yeoman of the Larder in 1662.[1] He was already lodging in Wright's house in June 1643.[2]
An unidentified MR BRIDGES, also described as of the King's Pastry, was lodging with Wright in June 1643.

[1] S.P. 29/60/65, f. 121.
[2] St Aldate's Defaulters, Bodleian MS. Add. D. 114, f. 24.

THOMAS MARCHAM
(c. 1605-1646)

Tailor. The son of Thomas Marcham, tailor, of Oxford, he was apprenticed to Roger Stevens, tailor, of Oxford, 1 September 1617, his father then being dead.[1] He obtained his freedom 2 March 1626/7.[2] He was a churchwarden of St Aldate's in 1641-2, 1642-3, and 1643-4. He became a common councillor 29 September 1644[3] and junior chamberlain 30 September 1645.[4] Arms were delivered to him in October 1643.[5] In October 1645 he contributed £2. 10s. to the loan to the Lords Commissioners.[6] His name appears in all the St Aldate's parish taxation lists of 1645. He married Edith . . . He died between 2 and 14 February 1645/6.

In his Will his surname appears as Marchant. He desired his wife, whom he named executrix, to 'allow my Mother during her life sufficient and competent dyett and lodging fitt for her degree in my now dwelling house' (plus £4 a year). If Mrs Marcham senior disliked the arrangement and removed, other provision was to be made for her. Thomas also mentions his eldest son and namesake and his daughters Anne, Elizabeth, and Dorothy. John Savory [q.v.] was appointed an overseer and was to receive 'my cloath cloake'. One of the witnesses was William Corpson (Corpes) [q.v.].

[Will: MS. Wills Oxon. 89/4/10: made 2 February 1645/6: proved 14 February 1645/6].

Marcham's house was on the south side of Pennyfarthing Street and was leased from the feoffees of St Aldate's parish. On 20 April 1628 they leased to him 'All that their East part of a Messuage or Tenemt wth a backside thereto adioyninge heretofore vsed for a Maltehowse[7] but nowe converted into two dwelling howses and these howses being in the seuerall occupacons of Edward Carter Taylor William Redborne Taylor and of the said Thomas Marchem situate in a certen streete or lane called Penny farthing streete And allsoe one other Tenemt newly erected upon the east . . . lately belonging to the said Messuage now in the occupacon of Richard Carter Smyth [q.v.] scituate and being at theast end of the sayd streete All wch demised p'ses are scituate between a way or passage leading to the churchyard of St Aldates on theast and the other parte of the sayd Messuage lately devided from the sayd demised East parte of the sayd Messuage on the west abutting north upon the sayd streete and southward uppon the churchyarde'.[8] Thus Marcham's leased premises extended as far as the former passage west of the house on the site of No. 94 St Aldate's, at the corner of Pembroke Street. These two tenements together contained 'in length ffive and ffifty yards and one foot and the breadth at the East end of the churchyard dore seaven yards'.[9] He paid £1 per annum and the lease was for thirty-one years. He left 'the howse wherein I now dwell wth the Celleridge vnderneath the same' to his son Thomas, with the proviso that his wife should enjoy it during her lifetime.

[1] City Archives L. 5. 2, f. 33v.
[2] Ib., no folio number.
[3] *O.C.A.* 1626-1665, p. 122.
[4] Ib., p. 131.
[5] City Archives E. 4. 5, ff. 55-55v.
[6] Ib. E. 4. 6, ff. 1-2: *O.C.A.* 1626-1665, p. 453.
[7] See under Thomas Wright.
[8] Parish Chest.
[9] A Particular of the St Aldate's parish messuages in 1670 (Parish Chest).

MR THOMAS HECTOR

A Scotsman. He appears in 1641 in L.C. 3/1 under 'Roabes'. He is first entered as a 'Groome': this is struck out, and he is then entered as yeoman in place of Robert Jocey. The Registers of Christ Church Cathedral, Oxford, contain the entry under date 18 December 1644 of the burial of Robert Josse, 'Yeoman of the robes', who was said to be eighty years old at the time of his death.[1]
In an undated list of Royal servants charged with payments towards the Oxford city works, probably belonging to the summer of 1643, there appear the names of 'Mr Hector, David Forest and Andrew Morrison [q.v.] inferior Officers in ye kings Robes'. Between them they owed £3 for eight weeks; and described themselves in their answer to Richard Poole, the official deputed to try to extract the money, as 'very wanting men & therefore excused by the king himselfe'.[2] 'Mr Jocey of ye kings Roabes' is entered as owing for four weeks and 'hath payd willingly'.
Mrs Bridget Hector, not described as a widow, so probably Thomas Hector's daughter, received two warrants upon the first list of Charles I's necessitous servants, allowed by Parliament 14 March 1649/50. One, dated 24 May 1650 and receipted 29 May 1650, was for £30. 4s.:[3] the other, dated 23 September 1650 and receipted 8 July 1651, was for £17.[4]

[1] *C.A.M.*, p. 1012.
[2] MS. Harleian 6804, f. 229.
[3] S.P. 28/282 and S.P. 28/350/9, f. 2: No. 35.
[4] Ib. and S.P. 28/350/9, f. 5: No. 112.

MR JOHN MILLER ?

Probably the John Miller who in 1641 is entered in L.C. 3/1 under 'Taylors' as 'in reversion Taylor for ye Guard'. In May (?) 1660 Miller petitioned for readmission to the office of tailor to the King (Charles II), the Duke of York, and the Duke of Gloucester.[1]

[1] *C.S.P.D.* 1660-1, p. 25.

MR RICHARD BARNES
(c. 1613-c. 1672)

His name appears in a list of Charles II's Yeomen of the Guard dated 20 August 1667.[1] On 10 April 1661 a money warrant was issued to Richard Barnes, gent., for supply of his necessary occasions known to His Majesty.[2] It is possible that the Yeoman is also to be identified with the Richard Barnes, gent., of St Peter ad Vincula in the Tower of London, widower, aged twenty-seven, who had a licence to marry Margaret Jones, widow, of St Botolph Aldgate, aged twenty-eight, at St Faith's, London, 21 October 1640.[3]
In his Will, in which he is described as of St Margaret's, Westminster, the only relatives mentioned by Barnes are five kinsfolk of the name of Marsham. He appointed as his executors two fellow Yeomen, Peter Hickman and Nathaniel Williamson, whose names occur in the list of 1667.[4]
[Will: P.C.C. 1672: II Eure: made 7 November 1670: proved 15 February 1671/2].

[1] Sir R. Hennell, op. cit., Appendix VII.
[2] *C.T.B.*, Vol. I, p. 234.
[3] *Marriage Licences of the Bishop of London*, p. 254.
[4] Peter Hickman's own Will was proved in the P.C.C. (23 Foot) in 1687. Nathaniel Williamson's name appears in the 1667 list as Williams.

MR JASPER HEILY or HELYE

He had been a Messenger at least as early as 25 July 1631.[1] On 29 April 1635 there was recorded the bond of Jasper Heily, of St Martin-in-the-Fields, gentleman, with two others, in £5,000 for his appearance before Secretary Windebank [q.v.] whenever commanded.[2] He seems to have been a somewhat difficult character. In December 1635 he was committed to the Fleet for high-handed behaviour and had to apologize for his offence and pay £10.[3] He was in trouble again in 1638[4] and in 1639.[5]

Heily is entered in the list of forty Messengers in ffee (Messengers of the Chamber in Ordinary) in 1641.[6] On 11 November 1651, upon the second list of Charles I's necessitous servants and creditors, allowed by Parliament on 13 August 1651, he was granted a warrant for £15, which he receipted (as Jasper Heily) on 28 November 1651.[7] On 8 March 1652/3 he was granted a warrant for a further £15. 3s. 9d.[8] In January 1655/6 he is entered under 'Messengers' in a 'Briefe perticular' of warrant-holders upon this list as being paid £30. 3s. 9d.[9] He probably died before the Restoration, as his name does not appear in the list of the Messengers of the Chamber drawn up in May 1660.[10]

Heily married Mary . . . John, son of Jasper and Mary Helye, was baptized at St Martin-in-the-Fields 15 October 1635.[11]

[1] *C.S.P.D.* 1631-3, pp. 305, 345-6, and 362: these references incidentally illustrate the hazards run by Royal Messengers on their travels.
[2] Ib. 1635, p. 48. There are numerous references to his activities in ib. 1635, 1636, 1636-7, 1637, 1637-8, 1638-9, and 1639.
[3] Ib. 1635, pp. 546-7, 555, 557, and 611.
[4] Ib. 1637-8, pp. 556-7.
[5] Ib. 1639, pp. 531-2.
[6] L.C. 3/1.
[7] S.P. 28/284 and S.P. 350/9/f. 23: No. 557.
[8] S.P. 28/285: unreceipted.
[9] S.P. 18/123/39, f. 122v.
[10] S.P. 29/1/63.
[11] *Registers* 1619-1636, p. 119.

MRS SPARKES

Unidentified. The *Oxford English Dictionary* gives two quotations of 1611 relating to the occupation of tire-maker: (1) a perruquiere is defined in a *Dictionary* published in that year as equivalent to a tyre-maker, 'a woman that makes Perriwigs or Attires': (2) 'She holdeth on her way to the Tyre makers shoppe'. Shakespeare lodged in the early sixteen hundreds with a male tire-maker, Christopher Mountjoy, of Silver Street in the City of London.

In June 1643 Marcham had lodging with him a MR FOREST (unidentified) from whom no answer was received.[1]

[1] St Aldate's Defaulters, Bodleian MS. Add. D. 114, f. 24.

RICHARD CARTER
(c. 1592-1644)

Blacksmith. One of the three younger sons of John Carter, blacksmith, of Adderbury, Oxfordshire, by his wife, Margaret . . . , he was apprenticed 31 May 1606 to Thomas Ranckell, smith, of Oxford,[1] and obtained his freedom 12 July 1613.[2] In his father's Will, proved in 1616,[3] he received £4 and 'one Cow, & halfe of the sawed boards wch are abowt my howse, wth the halfe of the transomes'. He was over sixty in June 1643,[4] but arms were delivered to him in the following October.[5] He married Joane . . . He died between 23 January and 10 February 1643/4.
[Administration: MS. Wills Oxon. 107, f. 74v: Act Book B: 10 February 1643/4: grant made to his widow].
An Inventory of Carter's goods was exhibited the same day, the value being £3. 3s. 10d.[6]
Carter's house was on the south side of Pennyfarthing Street, near the east end of the present Pembroke Street. It was already occupied by him in April 1629 when the feoffees of St Aldate's leased this parish tenement to Thomas Marcham [q.v.], whose tenant Carter became.[7] In Marcham's Will, proved 14 February 1645/6,[8] he left to his daughter Anne 'Marchant', after her mother's death, 'the tenemt and howse in St Aldates pish wherein Richard Carter Smith latelie deceased in his lief tyme inhabited wth all the backside wch was leased to Richard Carter'. The house is not mentioned in Carter's Inventory.

[1] City Archives L. 5. 1, f. 137v.
[2] Ib., f. 302.
[3] MS. Wills Oxon. 11/5/33.
[4] St Aldate's Defaulters, Bodleian MS. Add. D. 114, f. 24.
[5] City Archives E. 4. 5, ff. 55-55v.
[6] MS. Wills Oxon 296/3/27.
[7] Parish Chest.
[8] MS. Wills Oxon. 89/4/10.

MR THOMAS APPLEGARTH (?)

Perhaps the Thomas Applegarth, of the parish of St Margaret's, Westminster, six children of whom were baptized and three buried there between 1624 and 1636. Dorothy was baptized 16 February 1630/1 and George 6 May 1636, so that their ages would be right for the children of twelve and seven.
Mr Thomas Applegarth was buried at St Margaret's 4 January 1652/3. A widowed Dorothy Aplegarth [sic], who may have been Thomas' wife, married Danyell Terry at St Margaret's 1 January 1656/7.

WILLIAM CORPSON
(c. 1610-c. 1667)

Tailor. The son of Richard Corpson, baker, of Oxford, he was apprenticed to Alfred Rance, tailor, of Oxford, 3 September 1622.[1] The record of his freedom has not been found, but his name (as 'Corpes')[2] appears for the first time in the Journeymen Taylors' Accounts 1613-1699 in 1630.[3] As 'Corps, malster', he contributed £2. 10s. to the loan to the Lords Commissioners in 1645.[4] His name appears in all the St Aldate's parish taxation lists of 1645 and 1647. In 1644 he was paid 5s. by the churchwardens for 'hollie & Ivie by him provided for thuse of the church at Christmas', and on 3 February 1644/5, together with John Earle [q.v.], he received 4s. 'for severall warnings of the pshioners to meete to make Taxes by them laid forth during the tyme that John Lambe [q.v.] was shutt vp of the plague'. John Lambe was a churchwarden for 1644-5. In 1646-7 and 1647-8 Corpson was himself a churchwarden.

The date of Corpson's death is unknown: he signed the Churchwardens' Nomination Book for the last time on 5 April 1662, but he and his wife were entered in the Poll Tax of 1667.[5] He married Blanche . . . who, in her widowhood, occupied one of the parish tenements in Pennyfarthing Street.[6] On 13 November 1679 Wood noted: 'The Oxford natives their feast. Mr Richard Corpson of Xt. Ch. [preached] a taylor's son of St Aldate's parish'.[7] Richard matriculated as the son of William of Oxford city 17 May 1667, aged sixteen. There were also a son William and a daughter Blanche.[8]

Corpson's house was situated at the corner of Fish Street and Pennyfarthing Street, and occupied the site in front of, and partly of, No. 94 St Aldate's, now the St Aldate's Church Bookshop and Coffee House. Known as Church House, it was, as its name implies, the property of the parishioners of St Aldate's. The house was leased to Corpson at a rent of £5 per annum at least as early as 1640-1.[9] By an indenture of 12 May 1664[10] it was leased to Arthur Dimocke, but was inhabited by Corpson and a chandler called Edward Prince, who were both still living there 18 May 1666.[11] A lease to Corpson dated 3 April 1646 describes its position as a 'corner Messuage or Tenment commonly called the Church howse . . . betweene a certain tenement belonging to the parishioners . . . now in the occupacon of William Deverall cutler [q.v.] on the south and the streete leading into the lane called Penniefarthing streete towards St Ebbes church on the North and the Churchyard of the parish church of St Aldats on the west and the high streete leading towards Christ church College on theast part'. It was a double tenement which looked north up the street[12] and measured twenty-seven feet eight inches from north to south and twenty feet from east to west.[13] There was a shop with a cellar under it and two chambers and three garrets above.[14] The passage on the west of the house, leading to the churchyard, has been mentioned under Thomas Marcham [q.v.]: the opening to it is shewn in Loggan's plan of the city.[15] For the appearance of the Church House see Plate 11. It was sold under the Oxford Paving Act of 1831.

[1] City Archives L. 5. 2, f. 105.
[2] It is sometimes rendered 'Corps' or 'Corpes'.
[3] City Archives F. 4. 2.
[4] Ib. E. 4. 6, ff. 1-2: *O.C.A.* 1626-1665, p. 453.
[5] *S. and T.*, p. 260.
[6] Indenture of 4 August 1753 in Parish Chest.
[7] *L. and T.*, Vol. I, p. 467.
[8] *S. and T.*, pp. 260 and 281.
[9] Churchwardens' Accounts.
[10] Parish Chest.

[11] Lease to Mary Deverall of the neighbouring parish house (Parish Chest).
[12] *Survey of South-West Ward*, No. 96.
[13] Lease of 5 January 1759 in Parish Chest.
[14] Ibid.
[15] *Oxonia Illustrata* (1675).

MR THOMAS DAVIES
(died 1671)

This Welsh Royal servant was already lodging with Corpson in June 1643.[1] On 26 May 1626 order was given to the Attorney-General to draw a bill for the King's signature for Thomas Davies to be Barber in Extraordinary.[2] On 10 October 1636 a warrant was issued to him for £91, the sum allowed him annually for barbing linen, such payment being for the year ended the previous Lady Day.[3] On 12 May 1637 the Treasurer of the Chamber was ordered to pay him £67 for the necessary provisions for His Majesty's trimming for the half year ended at the previous Lady Day.[4] On 17 February 1638/9 Davies addressed the Commissioners of the Household about his claim that previous Royal barbers had been sergeants of the Ewry and had the sole disposal of the barbers' tents that attended the Household.[5]

In 1641 Davies was the first of two Royal barbers.[6] On 3 February 1641/2 Captain Robert Fox wrote to Sir John Penington: 'Almost all his Majesty's servants are declared to be enemies of the State, and not to be permitted to come near his Majesty; nay they have shaved him so close that poor Tom Davies must not trim him'.[7]

Davies was Master of the Barber-Surgeons Company in 1639-40,[8] although he had not served the office of warden. In 1640-1 the Barber-Surgeons' Accounts contain the entry: 'Paid and given to Mr Davies men and the watermen and Porters to bring King Charles figure in Brasse to the hall', 4s. 6d.[9] He is described as of Whitehall in the Poll Tax return of 1641.[10]

In an undated list of Royal servants charged with payments towards the Oxford city works, probably belonging to the summer of 1643, 'Mr Tho: Davis ye kings Barber' is entered as owing 15s. for six weeks. The answer which he gave to Richard Poole, the official deputed to exact the money, was that he 'hath pd 5s at first & now 5s more & sayeth that he ought to pay no more'.[11]

On 28 February 1660/1 a warrant was issued to pay £100 per annum to Thomas Davies as the King's Barber in Extraordinary as by Letters Patent of 19 June 1626.[12] On 13 June 1661 a warrant was issued to pay him £637, being arrears of his allowance of £91 per annum from Lady Day 1641 until the death of Charles I.[13] Also in 1661 (?) a warrant was issued to pay £640 to Thomas Davies, barber to the late King, for moneys disbursed for his trimming linen, washing, etc. from Michaelmas 1642 to Ladyday 1646.[14] This last entry shews that Davies remained with the King throughout the Civil War. On 11 July 1661 an annuity of £160 (granted the previous June) was ordered to be paid to him.[15] Many later payments to him are recorded in the *C.T.B.*, the last being dated 17 July 1671.[16] Davies had been a Groom of the Privy Chamber as well as barber to Charles I. In 1671 (?) his son, James Davies, petitioned Charles II for an order for his admission as a Groom when James Progers should die, having been sworn a Groom (supernumerary) in 1661 in the room of his father, Thomas Davies.[17]

On 16 December 1664 Thomas Davies received a grant of Arms from Sir Edward Walker, Garter King of Arms. 'Wheras Thomas Davies Esquire Barber to his late Maty King Charles ye First . . . , & one of the Groomes of his Matys privy Chamber did very many yeares wth all diligence, & Fidelity serue ye King his Master in these Capacityes, & during all ye unhappy tymes neuer deserted his Service, & hath synce wth ye losse of his Fortune & hazard of his person endeauoured his Matys

Restauration, Wherefore, & for that he derives himselfe from a Family of Good respect & antiquity in ye principality of Wales, hee justly deserves, to have such Armes, &c.'[18]

Davies married Ann . . . She was buried at Christ Church, Oxford, 22 June 1645.[19] Thomas and Ann Davies evidently had a house at Barnes. A silver paten belonging to St Mary's parish church there is inscribed: 'Ex dono lectissimae feminae Annae Davis, uxoris Thomae Davis Ar: 1639'.[20] It will be noted that Davies was described as *armiger* before the grant of Arms in 1664. In his Will, made on 6 June 1658,[21] the sequestered rector of Barnes, John Cutts (who had been with the King at Oxford and compounded on the Oxford Articles in 1649), left £10 to his 'old friend and neighbour Mr Thomas Davis' and forgave him all that he owed him.[22] Davies desired in his Will to be buried in Barnes churchyard. The Barnes Parish Registers record: '1671 October ye 14 bureed Mr Thomas davis'.

Davies' Will was drawn up 'being in Winsor Castle'. He mentions his two sons, James and George. James, in addition to being a Groom of the Privy Chamber, had been since 1661/2 'Keeper of His Majesty's Wardrobe of Beds within the Castle of Windsor', and had been granted the reversion of the post by letters patent on 29 August 1642.[23] James continued to hold the post until his death in 1681. His father, who had doubtless taken refuge with him from the Plague in 1665, named him his executor.

Davies' only bequest other than those to his sons was £5 for a ring to 'my deare and lovinge freind Mr Humphray Painter'. Painter was Principal Surgeon to Charles II and had been appointed a Chirurgeon in Ordinary 21 February 1644/5.[24] In 1649 he compounded for Delinquency in adhering to the forces raised against Parliament, though never in arms.[25] The friendship of Davies and Painter must thus have gone back to the days of the Civil War in Oxford.

Davies added to his Will a memorandum dated 21 September 1671. A witness to this was Hartgill Baron, of Windsor, Clerk of the Privy Seal, who had been in exile with Charles II, and had brought him the first news of the Restoration.[26] Baron made James Davies an overseer of his Will (1673).

[Will: P.C.C. 1671: 130 Duke: made 31 August 1665: proved 3 November 1671].

[1] St Aldate's Defaulters, Bodleian MS. Add. D. 114, f. 24.
[2] *C.S.P.D.* 1625-6, p. 339.
[3] Ib. 1636-7, p. 160.
[4] Ib. 1637, p. 99.
[5] Ib. 1637-8, p. 283. See also the answer to his claim, p. 468.
[6] L.C. 3/1.
[7] *C.S.P.D.* 1641-3, p. 274.
[8] S. Young, *Annals of the Barber-Surgeons* (1890), p. 8.
[9] Ib., p. 404.
[10] P.R.O. E. 179/251/22 and E. 179/272/36 and 49.
[11] MS. Harleian 6804, f. 229.
[12] *C.T.B.*, Vol. I, p. 216.
[13] Ib., p. 257.
[14] *C.S.P.D.* 1661-2, p. 203.
[15] Ib., p. 24 and *C.T.B.*, Vol. I, p. 261.
[16] Ib., Vol. III, p. 912.
[17] *C.S.P.D. Addenda* 1660-85, p. 344 and ib. 1661-2, p. 201.
[18] British Museum MS. Add. 14,294, f. 16.
[19] Wood, *C. of O.*, Vol. II, p. 550.
[20] *Surrey Archaeological Collections*, Vol. XIII (1896-7), p. 166.
[21] P.C.C. 558 Wootton.
[22] *S.A.C.*, Vol. IX (1885-8), p. 310.
[23] *C.T.B.*, Vol. I, p. 366.
[24] *C.S.P.D.* 1660-1, p. 556 and *C.T.B.*, Vol. I, p. 618.

[25] *C.C.C.*, p. 965.
[26] *C.S.P.D.* 1661-2, p. 153.

MR WILLIAM LITHELL (?)

The individual intended may be William Lithell, a member of the Barber-Surgeons Company. He was an apprentice of Henry Edwards. He obtained his freedom by servitude 15 January 1632/3.[1]

[1] Barbers Freedom Admissions MS. 5265/1, f. 81v.

In June 1643 Corpson had lodging with him a CAPTAIN DIGBY (unidentified) from whom no answer was received.[1]

[1] St Aldate's Defaulters, Bodleian MS. Add. D. 114, f. 24.

WILLIAM GRAY
(c. 1596-c. 1649)

Cooper. The son of William Gray, labourer, of Yarnton, Oxfordshire, he was apprenticed to Jedeon Turner, cooper, of Oxford, 19 November 1608.[1] The record of his freedom has not been found. On 4 October 1633, as of St Aldate's parish, he was recommended by Mrs Brookes to receive £10 of the £100 given by her.[2] On 21 August 1634 he received £10 a year for three years from the Fulsey bequest.[3]

There is no documentary evidence for the position of Gray's house, but from its place in the 'Accompt' the natural conclusion is that it was the second of the two tenements which composed the Church House. In 1647-8 and again in 1648-9 the churchwardens of St Aldate's parish paid Goodman Gray's rent (20s.).

[1] City of Oxford Archives L. 5. 1, f. 165v.
[2] *O.C.A.* 1626-1665, p. 50.
[3] Ibid.

GEORGE MANDER

His position in the Royal Household has not been discovered, but it is certain that he was with Charles II in Jersey in 1649-50. In a small book of payments by the King running from 10 January 1649/50 to 29 March 1650, there occurs the entry: '26 Jan pd to George Maunder for providing wax for the Broad Seale 0033 livers'.[1]

Charles II had a new Great Seal made while in exile in 1649 and a few perfect impressions are known.[2]

[1] MS. Harleian 6804, f. 257.
[2] See Hilary Jenkinson, 'The Great Seal of England: some notes and suggestions' in *The Antiquaries Journal*, January 1936, pp. 16-17.

RICHARD SHEPPARD

He is entered in 1662 under Chandry as Richard Sheppard groom.[1] He was lodging with Margaret Vosse [q.v.] in June 1643, when he was noted as one of 'the kings servants about waxlights' and as refusing to pay.[2]

[1] S.P. 29/60/65, f. 119.
[2] St Aldate's Defaulters, Bodleian MS. Add. D. 114, f. 24.

WILLIAM DEVERALL
(c. 1618-c. 1666)

Cutler. The son of Anthony Deverall, maltster, of New Woodstock, he was apprenticed to John Slatford, cutler, of Oxford, 1 July 1630,[1] and obtained his freedom 26 October 1639.[2] His name occurs in all the St Aldate's parish taxation lists of 1645 and 1647. He was assessed at 8d. in the Subsidy of 1648.[3] On 29 January 1659/60 his son was chosen to be placed out as an apprentice with 20 marks of Mrs Lloyd's money.[4] In 1661-2 the churchwardens of St Aldate's paid 5s. to 'John Carter and Paul Garrett for watching wth William Deverell when he fell into his frenzy'.[5] He married Mary . . . He died before 10 January 1665/6. She was living in 1667.[6]

[Administration: MS. Wills Oxon 107, f. 130: Act Book B: grant made to his widow 18 January 1665/6].

An Inventory of Deverall's goods was taken 10 January 1665/6, the value (including his lease) being £12. 12s. 0d.[7]

Deverall's house was the most northerly of four small houses which had belonged to St Aldate's parish at least as early as 24 Henry VIII (1532-3) and which lay to the east of the churchyard and faced on to Fish Street: the church was thus enclosed both on its north and east sides by parish property. These four houses lay in 'one pcell of grounde' which, 'as it is now mounded and walled abowts, conteyninge in length North, and sowth fowre and Twentye yards, and in breadth East and West sixe yards or thereabowts', stretched from the Church House on the north to the way leading to Pembroke College (formerly Broadgates Hall) next to the Christ Church Almshouses,[8] on the south: in September 1597 the St Aldate's feoffees leased the land, together with the two houses then standing on it, one of which was occupied by John Harwood [q.v.], to William Maycock, of London.[9] On 3 February 1613/14 the feoffees leased the ground, now containing four houses, to Harwood for forty-four years, at a rent of 10s. per annum, from the previous Michaelmas.[10]

In Harwood's Will, made on 21 September and proved 24 October 1645,[11] he directed: 'Item I give and bequeath vnto my sonne Ralphe Harwood if he be living my howse in the said parish of St Aldate in wch howse mr [blank] Deverell now liveth'. In a grant of the house to Ralph Harrud (Harwood) by the feoffees on 9 July 1646 it is described as 'their Messuage or Tenement consisting of a Sellar a Shoppe and lowe roome Three Chambers and a little Cockloft wth thapurtenances . . . now in the occupacon of William Deverell Cutler betweene a Tenemt there belonging to ye parishioners . . . now in ye occupacon of William Corpson Taylor [q.v.] on ye Northside and another Tenement there belonging likewise to the parishioners . . . now in ye occupacon of Sibell Carter Widow on ye Southside. Theast head or end of ye said messuage or tenement abutting vpon ye Kings high streate leading from Carfax towards Southbridge ye west heade or end thereof abutting vpon ye church yard of St Aldats and latelie was in ye Tenure or occupacon of George Vaughan Cutler deceased'.[12] As George Vaughan was dead by July 1643 (see under Henry Vaughan) Deverall probably went to live in the house in that year. The churchwardens received 10s. for his rent in 1647-8. 'The Chamber', 'the Shop' and his lease (£10) are mentioned in his Inventory. On 18 May 1666 the feoffees leased the house, which was then occupied by Thomas Robinson, a cordwainer, to the widowed Mary Deverall for thirty-one years at a rent of 5s. per annum.[13]

Deverall's house, together with the other three on this site, are shewn in Loggan's plan of the city.[14] In 1834 the land was sold to the Commissioners of the Oxford Paving Act in accordance with the scheme for removing the houses and widening the road.[15]

[1] City Archives L. 5. 2, f. 196v.
[2] Ib., no folio number.
[3] *S. and T.*, p. 169.
[4] *O.C.A.* 1626-1665, p. 252.
[5] Accounts.
[6] *S. and T.*, p. 260.
[7] MS. Wills Oxon 79/1/24.
[8] Now the Lodgings of the Master of Pembroke.
[9] Indenture in Parish Chest.
[10] Indenture in Parish Chest.
[11] MS. Wills Oxon 132/1/32.
[12] Parish Chest.
[13] Lease in Parish Chest.
[14] *Oxonia Illustrata* (1675).
[15] *O.C.P.*, p. 111. See also *Survey of South-West Ward*, No. 95.

JOHN BRIDGES, MATTHEW CALSEY, EDWARD PALMES

All unidentified. In one of the St Aldate's parish taxation lists of 1645 'The barber at Deueralls' is entered.

MARGARET VOSSE, WIDOW

Widow. In June 1643[1] she was styled 'widdow voice'. Her name does not occur in any of the St Aldate's parish taxation lists of 1645 and 1647, but she is mentioned twice in the Will, made 2 and proved 14 February 1645/6, of Thomas Marcham [q.v.]: 'I doe give vnto . . . Edith my daughter [to be enjoyed after her mother's death] the Tenemts in St Aldats parish wherein Richard ffrogley and Margaret Wasse now dwell'.[2]
Mrs Vosse's house was one of the tenements in Pennyfarthing Lane belonging to St Aldate's parish and leased by the feoffees to Thomas Marcham, whose tenant she was. Her house is placed out of order in the 'Accompt'.

[1] St Aldate's Defaulters, Bodleian MS. Add. D. 114, f. 24.
[2] MS. Wills Oxon. 89/4/10.

ENSIGN ROBERT HUBBERSTAY

He belonged to the Lifeguard of Foot. His name, as of London and Westminster, appears under 'Earl Lyndsy' in *I.O.*[1] He was in Captain Johnson's Company in Cornwall in 1644, when, as Ensign Hubberstat, he figures in a list of sick soldiers of the Lifeguard.[2] He is probably the Robert Hubbersley [sic] of St Giles-in-the-Fields who, in July 1660, together with Randolph Armstrong of the same parish, gave evidence against Major Brent for concealing arms in his house and requested a warrant for his apprehension.[3]
Hubberstey appears to be a North Lancashire name.

[1] Col. 90.
[2] MS. Harleian 6804, f. 187.
[3] *C.S.P.D.* 1660-1, p. 127.

TWO SERVANTS OF WILLIAM SEYMOUR, first MARQUESS OF HERTFORD (1588-1660)

He was made a P.C. in 1640/1 and was a Gentleman of the Bedchamber in 1641.[1] He was Governor to Charles, Prince of Wales from 1641 to 1643. In 1642 he was appointed commissioner of array for the western counties, and after seeing much active service in 1643, joined the King at Oxford in July of that year. He was Chancellor of the University from 31 October 1643 to 3 August 1647. On 21 January 1643/4 he was appointed Groom of the Stole, and he sat in the Oxford Parliament. He signed the Articles for the surrender of Oxford 20 June 1646 and compounded on them on 22 September following. On 21 November 1646 his fine was assessed at £12,603 6s. 9d.; but on 12 January 1647/8 it was reduced to £8,345.[2]
(For full accounts see *C.P.* and *D.N.B.*)

[1] L.C. 3/1.
[2] *C.C.C.*, pp. 1329-30.

In June 1643 there was lodging in 'widdow voices house' 'Mr Langly Mr Balding (?),

Richard Shepheard. They are the kings servants about waxlights & refuse to pay'.[1]

WILLIAM LANGLEY

In 1638 as Geo: [sic] Langley he is entered under Chandry as yeoman, with Matthew Sheppard as his servant.[2] In the same year Guliame Langeley was yeoman of the Chandry to Prince Charles with wages of £5 per annum and diet,[3] and was holding the same position in 1641.[4] In Ashburnham's *Accompt* occurs the entry: 'To Langley for Wax-lights' £10.[5]

In May (?) 1660 Guillem Langley petitioned for the place of Serjeant and Purveyor of the Chandry which he claimed belonged to him as eldest yeoman in that office.[6] He also petitioned for restoration to his place of yeoman of the Chandry, which he had discharged with care, and for provision for him as for others his fellow servants.[7] He further petitioned to be owned as His Majesty's servant: a stranger now supplies his place which he had bought twenty-three years ago [i.e. in 1637]. Being a prisoner when his Majesty [Charles II when Prince] marched to the West, he could not attend him there, but followed him to The Hague, and, though kept out of his place, served three years under Prince Rupert.[8]

It is possible that Langley was among the Royalist prisoners, who included Prince Charles' falconer, taken when the enemy fell on the quarters of the King's own troop at the beginning of March 1644/5.[9]

In May (?) 1662 Langley petitioned to be employed to make the King's waxlights, and for allowance as his fellow servants. He had waited two years to obtain his right as yeoman of the Chandry, but was answered that the list could not be increased and now he finds that there are two vacancies.[10]

In 1662 Langley appears under Chandry as yeoman, Matthew Sheppard following him as yeoman, and Richard Sheppard as groom.[11]

[1] St Aldate's Defaulters, Bodleian MS. Add. D. 114, f. 24.
[2] S.P. 16/386/97, f. 186.
[3] MS. Harleian 7623, f. 10. 'The Booke (assigned by his Maiestie) of Dietts Wages etc. for Prince Charles his Highnes and the rest of his Mats Royall Children Anno xiiijto Rs Caroli.'
[4] MS. Harleian 3791, f. 111v. 'The Names of all the Servants that attend the Prince his highnes, and the rest of his Mats Royall Children in Chamber household and Stable 1641.'
[5] P. xxiii.
[6] *C.S.P.D.* 1660-1, p. 30.
[7] Ibid.
[8] Ibid.
[9] See *The Letter Books of Sir Samuel Luke* 1644-5, 1572: 3 March 1644-5.
[10] *C.S.P.D.* 1661-2, p. 395.
[11] S.P. 29/60/65, f. 119. For Richard Sheppard see under William Gray's house.

MR BALDING (?)

He may be the Stephen Boulton who was page of the Chandry in 1638.[1] Fortune, daughter of Thomas Balden, was baptized at St Margaret's, Westminster, 14 November 1637.

[1] S.P. 16/386/97, f. 186.

WILLIAM BLAY
(1591-before 1663)

Freemason, and sacristan of Christ Church. The eldest of the three sons of Leonard Bleye or Blay, weaver, of Littlemore, Oxfordshire, by his wife, Anne, daughter of Oliver Wetherall, rough mason, of Iffley,[1] he was baptized at Iffley 24 February 1590/1. The record of his apprenticeship to his uncle Thomas Wetherall,[2] freemason, of Oxford, and a privileged person of Oxford University, has not been found, but as Wetherall's apprentice he was admitted a freeman 2 October 1618.[3] Blay worked with Wetherall on repairs at Woodstock Palace in 1623-4[4] and was one of the seven masons who made the pinnacles of the Schools quadrangle at Oxford in 1624.[5] The taxation Assessment of Privileged Persons for 1624-5 shews him as living in the parish of St Ebbe's, his position being unspecified:[6] he was assessed at 4d.[7]

Blay married at Iffley 6 December 1615 Edith Clements: both bride and bridegroom were of Oxford. Mrs Blay may have been the aunt of Tristram Clements or Clement, mason. William and Edith Blay had two sons, William and Nicholas,[8] who, together with their father, are mentioned in the Will of Leonard Bleaye [sic] the elder, made 14 July 1634 and proved 18 June 1636, as of Iffley.[9] In this he says: 'I give vnto William Bleay my eldest sonne tenne shillinges . . . I give vnto William Bleay and vnto Nicolas Bleay the two sonnes of William my sonn to either of them twentie shillinges a peice . . .'.

As Blay (which he always signs) William first appears in the Christ Church Disbursement Books for the academic year 1641-2 in the list of *Famuli* as junior sacristan.[10] But as there is a gap in the books between 1630-1 (when Henry Cope was junior sacristan under George Dixon [q.v.]) and 1640-1, he may have been appointed considerably earlier. He received 6s. 8d. for each of the four academic terms and an annual livery allowance (*vestes liberatae*) of 10s. Blay was also *custos horologij*, in which capacity he received 5s. a term: this post appears to have gone with that of junior sacristan. The Disbursement Books contain several references to bills paid to him and payments for specific items: e.g. on '19 Septemb die Triumph' 1644 he received 5s.,[11] and in 1644-5, 'pro pulsandis campanis mandatu Gubernatoris', another 5s.[12]

Blay's name appears in all the St Aldate's parish taxation lists of 1645 and 1647. He was assessed at 8d. in the Subsidy of 1648.[13] On 14 July 1648 he submitted to the Parliamentary Visitors.[14] On 26 October 1654 a man of his name was elected an almsman of St Bartholomew's Hospital.[15]

Blay's house was the third of the four parish houses lying between the Church House on the north and the way to Pembroke on the south: it was immediately north of the house of John Harwood [q.v.] who leased it to Blay. The second house appears to have been unoccupied in 1643/4.[16] In his Will, made 21 September and proved 24 October 1645, Harwood directs: 'Item I give and bequeath vnto my sonne John Harwood All that part of my howse or Tenemt in the parish of St Aldats . . . wherein William Bley Sexton of Christchurch now inhabiteth'.[17] By an indenture dated 9 May 1649 a grant was made by the feoffees of St Aldate's to John Harrud (Harwood), son of the deceased John Harwood, of 'All that their Messuage or Tenemt now in the tenure or occupacon of William Bley one of the Sextons of the Cathedrall Church of Christ Church Oxford consisting of a Sellar Two lowe roomes Two Chambers and one Cockloft wth thappurtences . . . between a Tenemt there belonging to the parishioners now in the tenure or occupacon of John Norman Butcher on the Northside and one other Tenemt there belonging to the parishioners now in the tenure or occupacon of Margaret Harwood widow on the Southside'.[18] The position of the house between the 'kings high streete' and the churchyard is rehearsed. An indenture dated 1 April 1663 mentions the tenement 'late in the tenure or occupacon of Widow Bley'.[19]

[1] Iffley Parish Registers, I, 1572-1639, consulted by kind permission of the Rector, the Revd. R.J. Hills. '1585 Leonard Bleye of Littlemoore wthin the pish of St Maryes in Oxford, and Anne Wytherall, of the pish of yefteley, were married the Xth daye of maye.' The Blays were a well-known Iffley family, whose gravestones may be studied in the churchyard.
[2] The Will of Oliver Wetherall, made and proved in 1581 (MS. Wills Oxon. 69/1/23), mentions his son Thomas. The relationship between Thomas Wetherall and William Blay has not previously been known, and is of considerable interest.
[3] *O.C.A.* 1583-1626, p. 277.
[4] P.R.O.: Declared Accounts. We owe this reference to Mrs J.C. Cole, who suggested that Blay was an Iffley man, thus leading us to a rewarding examination of the Registers.
[5] *V.C.H. Oxfordshire*, Vol. III, p. 47, n. 74.
[6] University Archives W.P. γ 28 (7), f. 4.
[7] Ib., f. 7.
[8] Bound apprentice in 1630/1, when his father is still described as freemason: City Archives L. 5. 2, f. 204.
[9] MS. Wills Oxon, 5/4/18.
[10] Ch. Ch. MS. xii. b.85.
[11] Ch. Ch. MS. xii. b.87.
[12] Ch. Ch. MS. xii. b.88.
[13] *S. and T.*, p. 169.
[14] *Register of the Visitors*, p. 158.
[15] *O.C.A.* 1626-1665, p. 207.
[16] In 1645 Harwood bequeathed 'vnto my daughter Sibill Carter [see under William Deverall] my messuage or Tenemt . . . late in the tenure of Joane Paradise widowe and now in the tenure or occupacon of her the said Sibill'. John Paradise, blacksmith, had occupied the second house in 1613/14 when John Harwood senior received his grant.
[17] MS. Wills Oxon. 132/1/32.
[18] Parish Chest.
[19] Ibid.

MR CORDALL

This is possibly George Cordwell, Sergeant of the Ewry in 1638.[1]
An Edward Cordell or Cordall, who signed as Cordwell, received three warrants under the lists of necessitous servants of Charles I: for £29 in 1650,[2] £100 in 1651,[3] and £20 in 1656.[4]

[1] S.P. 16/386/97, f. 186v.
[2] S.P. 28/282.
[3] S.P. 28/283.
[4] S.P. 28/350/9, f. 22, No. 543.

MR BONNAR, MR HARSBONE, MR EDWARDS

Unidentified.

MR STONES

Possibly Thomas Stone, yeoman of the 'Scullary' in 1638.[1]
In June 1643 JOHN JONES, who 'belongs to the court & refuseth' to pay, was lodging with Blay.[2] He is probably the John Joanes [sic] who, in 1638, was a page of the 'Picher house'.[3]

[1] S.P. 16/386/97, f. 190v.
[2] St Aldate's Defaulters, Bodleian MS. Add. D. 114, f. 24.
[3] S.P. 16/386/97, f. 186.

JOHN HARWOOD
(c. 1571-1645)

Tailor. The son of Richard Harrod [sic], husbandman, of Dorchester, Oxfordshire, he was apprenticed to John Clifton, tailor, of Oxford, 9 December 1583, his father being then dead.[1] In 1586 he transferred to John Wardell and in 1590 to Robert Holby. As late apprentice to Clifton he obtained his freedom 18 January 1591.[2] Harwood was appointed a member of the Common Council 5 October 1607[3] and was a chamberlain from 1609 to 1614[4] when, on 24 September, he became a bailiff.[5] He served continuously almost until his death: his name does not appear in the Council List of 1645. He also held the offices of surveyor of nuisances and fair-master at various dates. He was Master of the Company of Journeymen Taylors in 1626.[6] In one Subsidy of 1600 he paid 20s. and 4s. 'in lands',[7] in that of 1608-9 £3. 3s. 'in goods',[8] and in that of 1628 20s. and 8s. 'in lands'.[9]
Arms were delivered to Harwood in October 1643.[10] His name appears in all the St Aldate's parish taxation lists of 1645, but in the last 'Mr Harwood' is probably his son William. He was a churchwarden in 1609-10, 1610-11, 1619-20, 1620-1, 1635-6, and 1636-7. He was buried in St Aldate's churchyard 16 October 1645,[11] according to the wish expressed in his Will to be buried there near his wife's grave.
In his Will Harwood mentions his sons John, William, and Ralph, his daughter, Sibill Carter, and William's wife, Margaret.
[Will: MS. Wills Oxon. 132/1/32: made 21 September 1645: proved 24 October 1645].
An Inventory of his goods was taken 22 October 1645.
Harwood's house was the southernmost of the four parish houses lying between the Church House on the north and the way to Pembroke on the south. He had been in occupation of it at least as early as 1597.[12] On 3 February 1613/14 he obtained a lease of the messuage on which the houses stood for forty-four years at a rent of 10s. per annum dating from the previous Michaelmas.[13] In his Will he directs: 'Item I give and bequeath vnto my sonne William Harwood and Margaret his wife the Messuage wherein I now dwell'. In a surrender to the feoffees of his father's remaining term of the lease by William, dated 2 April 1646, the house is described as 'One Corner Messuage or Tenemt consisting of one lowe roome Three Chambers Two Cocklofts One butterie and One Shoppe'.[14] John Harwood's Inventory lists 'the upper chamber', 'the upper Cockloft', 'the second Chamber', 'one great Chamber', 'the Butterie', 'the Lower Roome'. William Harwood also surrendered 'one other Messuage or Tenemt consisting of a Sellar Two lowe roomes Three chambers and Two Cocklofts' which was in the tenure of his sister Sibill Carter.[15]
On 14 December 1614 John Harwood received permission from the city authorities to make an encroachment on the south side of his house.[16] It was declared that a grant had been made to him of 'all that pte of their plotte or peice of wast grounde lying . . . in the pishe of St Aldats . . . next adioyninge vnto the Sowthend of the nowe dwellinge howse of the said John Harwoode vppon which plott or piece of wast grounde the said John Harwoode hath newlie builte and erected a pte of a shoppe or Owtset which Conteyneth in length east and west sixteene foote or thereabouts and in breadth Sowthward from the wall of the said dwellinge howse, the quantitie of one yarde or thereaboute And jutteth out in length north and sowth into the streete right over against Christ Church seaven footes [sic] and a half, or thereabouts, and in breadth from the East pte of the said dwellinge howse the quantitie of one yard To have and to hould the said demysed plotte or peice of grounde wth thappurtenences vnto the said John Harwoode' for forty-one years from the following Michaelmas. The rent was 2s. per annum, and Harwood was to keep

the shop in repair.

[1] City Archives A. 5. 3, f. 322v.
[2] Ib., f. 409.
[3] *O.C.A.* 1583-1626, p. 184.
[4] Ib., pp. 195, 207, 230.
[5] Ib., p. 238.
[6] City Archives F. 4. 2: Accounts of the Company 1613-1699.
[7] Ib. B. 1. 2. f.
[8] Ib. B. 1. 2. h.
[9] Ib. B. 1. 3. e.
[10] Ib. E. 4. 5, ff. 55-55v.
[11] Wood, *C. of O.*, Vol. III, p. 208.
[12] Indenture between the feoffees of St Aldate's and William Maycock, of London, 27 September 1597 (Parish Chest). The Churchwardens' Accounts contain receipts for the payment of his lease of 10s.
[13] Parish Chest.
[14] Ibid.
[15] Bequeathed to her by her father (see under William Blay, Note 16).
[16] City Archives D. 5. 5, ff. 201v-202: Leases 1578-1636. See also *O.C.P.*, pp. 111-12.

MR ENSIGN WRIGHT

Unidentified, but probably Lifeguard of Foot.

SAMUEL NURSE

Samuell Nurse's marriage to Elizabeth Morris is entered in the *Registers* of St Margaret's, Westminster, on 6 May 1634. A daughter, Annis, was baptized there 24 November 1637 and a son, Samuell, on 23 December 1640. Elizabeth Nurse was buried there 20 March 1643/4. The son Samuell was living in the parish after the Restoration.
In June 1643 Nurse described himself as 'belonging to the kings kitchen & poore'.[1] The house was then entered as 'will Harrolds'.

[1] St Aldate's Defaulters, Bodleian MS. Add. 114, f. 24.

In June 1643 'Captaine Ivie: gonne out of towne' had also been lodging there.[1]

This is pretty certainly CAPTAIN WILLIAM IVIE or IVYE, who as an Indigent Officer in 1663 is described as living in Dorset and having served in the Marquess of Hertford's Foot.[2] Ivy is a West Country name, and the Captain is probably to be identified with the William Ivye who was in prison for debt at Dorchester in 1641/2.[3] Although Hertford's army was still in the West in June 1643, and he did not join the King at Oxford until July, Ivie may have been employed on some mission to the Court. On 24 July 1660 he was appointed Comptroller of the Port of Poole,[4] and there are numerous references to the Captain as Comptroller thereafter. He died not long before 14 September 1680.[5]

[1] St Aldate's Defaulters, Bodleian MS. Add. D. 114, f. 24.
[2] *I.O.*, col. 88.
[3] *C.S.P.D.* 1640-1, p. 432.

[4] Ib. 1660-1, p. 129; *C.T.B.*, Vol. I, p. 7.
[5] *C.T.B.*, Vol. VI, p. 692.

MR THOMAS SMYTH, MAYOR
(1604-1646)

Brewer. The eldest of the three sons of Alderman Oliver Smyth or Smith, brewer (1584-1637), an important figure in Oxford civic life and the largest individual property holder in the parish.[1] Thomas' mother was his father's first wife, Anne (died 1609), daughter of John Bussey. He was baptized at St Aldate's 11 December 1604.[2] He was admitted by the University to brew 18 January 1622/3.[3] He was elected a bailiff in 1626 and was senior bailiff in 1631 when his father was mayor and his youngest brother, John Smyth [q.v.], was junior bailiff.[4] He was chosen mayor in 1638 and again in 1643.[5] He became a member of the mayor's council in 1640,[6] and an alderman 14 September 1643 in place of the disloyal John Nixon, who had been removed.[7]

Smyth shewed his Royalist sympathies on the occasion of the entry into Oxford of Sir John Byron 28 August 1642. Not only did Bailiff Heron include him in the list of those accused of aiding Sir John,[8] but as a J.P. he joined with the mayor, Leonard Bowman, according to Heron, in committing to prison two citizens who tried to stop the destruction by Byron's soldiers of the 'great Arched ston bridge between Oxford and Botley'.[9] He further united with the mayor and others in wishing for 'an act of Councell that the City should ioyne with the University and Sir John and his company, make one Body and lay out powder Match and Bullet together'.[10] Smyth also used bitter words against Heron in the Council House. He did, however, wish to help the mayor to suppress force used against a citizen's house in High Street.[11]

Arms were delivered to Smyth in October 1643.[12] He was lieutenant-colonel of the City Regiment. It is probable that he is the Colonel Smyth who delivered on 29 August 1644 into the King's stores at New College a quantity of powder and musket shot.[13]

Smyth was one of the brewers (the other two being Edward Carpenter and Walter Cave, qq.v.) who supplied Brasenose College with beer throughout the year 1644.[14] There are entries of payments to his drawmen, including their reward at Christmas 1643. On 3 March 1643/4 the College granted Smyth a lease of Swinsell Farm and adjoining property west of South Bridge.[15] Payments to him also occur in the University College Bursar's Journals for the Civil War period. His name appears in all the St Aldate's parish taxation lists of 1645.

Smyth married 14 October 1622 Margaret, daughter and heiress of John Wilmott, baker, of St Aldate's parish [q.v.].[16] He died 20 April and was buried 22 April 1646 at St Aldate's.[17]

[Will: MS. Wills Oxon. 307, f. 91, 22 April 1646: Caveat Book].

Smyth's house was on the south side of Slaying or Slaughter Lane, Nos. 1 and 2 of what is now known as Brewer Street. The main block was built c. 1600, and a separate house was erected on the west side by Oliver Smyth at a slightly later date. Five properties are enumerated in a grant of them, dated 4 October 1622, by Oliver Smyth to John Wilmott and others for the eventual use of his son Thomas shortly to be married to Margaret Wilmott.[18] Included in these properties were three messuages, one of which was the tenement called Slaughter House, which had been converted by Oliver Smyth into a single capital messuage. In a grant of Slaughter House, dated 31 May 1663, by Thomas' eldest son, Oliver, to Thomas Rowney and others, it is confirmed that the new capital house had been settled by the first Oliver on Thomas.[19] This document fully describes Slaughter House, with all its appurtenences — brewhouse, malthouse, stables, garden ground, etc., 'and the bridge covered with slatt and beinge made for a Passage over the water leadinge out of the backside into a certaine peece of ground called the hither fryers and [the messuage] extendinge in length from the lane called Sleying lane on the North pte to a water called Trill Mill Bow on the South pte . . . situate without the Southgate of the Citty of Oxon.'[20] On the death of Oliver I in 1637, Thomas Smyth must have moved from the house which he had built at the entrance to Grandpont (see under Unton Croke) to Slaughterhouse, where his brewery was established, his step-mother, Mrs Christian Smyth, being established in the tenement next door.[21]

The Slaughter House was of two storeys with cellars and attics. There is an early seventeenth-century plaster ceiling.[22] Oliver I rented a parish tenement 'lyeinge in Slatter Lane' which also stretched from Slaying Lane to the Trill Mill Bow stream and which also passed to his son Thomas,[23] and to his grandson Oliver.[24] It lay to the east of a tenement in Slaying Lane leased from Balliol College by the Smyths since 1589.[25]

[1] For his Will see P.C.C. 82 Goare, made 26 February 1632/3, proved 13 May 1637.
[2] Wood, *C. of O.*, Vol. III, p. 199.
[3] *Register*, Vol. II, Pt. I, p. 329.
[4] *O.C.A.* 1626-1665, pp. 2 and 36.
[5] Ib., pp. 81 and 115.
[6] Ib., p. 94.
[7] Ib., p. 115.
[8] *The Manuscripts of the House of Lords*, Vol. XI, New Series, p. 326.
[9] Ib., p. 327.
[10] Ib., loc. cit.
[11] Ib., p. 331.
[12] City Archives E. 4. 5, ff. 55-55v.
[13] *R.O.P.*, Part I, p. 141.
[14] Brasenose College Muniments A 8 11*: Junior Bursar's Book 1644: the only volume to survive for the Civil War period.
[15] Ib. Swinsell 68: see also under William Day.
[16] Wood, *C. of O.*, Vol. III, p. 202.
[17] Ib., pp. 32 and 208.
[18] City Archives K. 8. 2.
[19] Ib. K. 16. 2.
[20] See also ib. A. 5. 4, the settlement made 11 September 1648 by Oliver Smyth previous to his marriage to Anne Bourne.
[21] St Aldate's parish taxation lists of 1645.
[22] For a full description see R.C.H.M. *City of Oxford*, pp. 175-6: the ceiling is illustrated on Plate 38. See also *Survey of South-West Ward*, No. 37.
[23] See lease of 14 February 1591/2 in Parish Chest, and Churchwardens' Accounts for 1637-8 for Thomas Smyth's rent.
[24] Balliol College Leases B. 15. 5 and 6.
[25] Ib. B. 15. 3, B. 15. 4, and B. 15. 5 and 6.

PATRICK RUTHVEN, EARL OF FORTH, later EARL OF BRENTFORD (c. 1573-1651)

In his younger days Ruthven had been in the Swedish service and was a captain of horse in 1612, becoming colonel of the Kalmar Regiment in 1623. He took part in Gustavus Adolphus' Prussian campaign in 1626 and in the German campaign in 1631, leaving the Swedish service in 1637. He is described as 'Sir Patricke Ruthven, Governour of Vlma and since Generall' in Colonel Robert Monro's *Monro his Expedition* (1637).[1] In 1638 he was Muster-Master-General of the forces in Scotland, was created Baron Ruthven of Ettrick in 1639, and was Governor of Edinburgh Castle. He was created Earl of Forth 27 March 1642, joined the King at

Shrewsbury, fought at Edgehill, and was appointed Lord Lieutenant-General of Charles I's army. He was already lodging with Smyth in June 1643, when he declared that he ought not to pay.[2] He was created Earl of Brentford 27 May 1644. He signed the letter of the Royalist commanders to the Earl of Essex 8 August 1644.[3] He was superseded by Prince Rupert in November 1644.

Brentford followed the fortunes of Charles II, both as Prince and King. He died at Dundee 2 February 1650/1. His Will, made at St Germain-en-Laye 8 August 1649, is printed in *Ruthven Correspondence.*[4]

By 'his Lady' is meant Forth's third wife, Clara Berner, daughter of John Berner, of Sackendorff and Ventzim in Mecklenburg, whom he married in 1633. She received various bequests in Brentford's Will. She was later (c. 1651-3), a servant to Queen Christina of Sweden.[5] She died in August 1679.

In her Will she left Jane Urrie, widow of Colonel William Urrie, her heir to prevent 'the pretensions that some that are Allyed to me may make to what I shall leaue behind me, but have dealt vnkindly by me'.

[Will: P.C.C. 1679: 138 King: made 21 August 1678: proved 26 November 1679].

Forth's daughter mentioned here was probably his third daughter, Jean or Janet, most likely his only daughter by his second wife, Jane or Joanna, sister of Colonel Sir John Henderson [q.v.].[6] Her father made provision for her in 1642, and she is mentioned in his Will.[7] Jean was at Stockholm with her stepmother, as a servant to Queen Christina. She married between March 1660 and July 1661, as his second wife, James, second Lord Forrester, of Corstorphine (1629-1679). She was living in October 1668.

(See *C.P.; Scots Peerage; D.N.B.;* and Jonas Berg and Bo Lagercrantz, *Scots in Sweden* (1962))

[1] Part II 'The list of the Scottish Officers in Chiefe . . . that served his Majesty of Sweden, Anno 1632.'
[2] St Aldate's Defaulters, Bodleian MS. Add. D. 114, f. 24.
[3] Walker, p. 61.
[4] Ed. W.D. Macray (1868), pp. 104-9.
[5] Ibid.
[6] See the letter of Christian IV of Denmark to Brentford accrediting his agent, 27 November 1644: *Ruthven Correspondence*, p. 89.
[7] Ib., pp. 75-7, and 108.

In June 1643 there were also lodging in Thomas Smyth's house 'Sr Thomas Ogleby, Captain Pringle, mr John Ogleby, mr Morris, mr Nicholas aboue 60 yeares'. The first four said that they ought not to pay.[1]

SIR THOMAS OGLEBY (OGILVY) (1616-1645), was the second son of James Ogilvy, first Earl of Airlie, by his wife, Lady Isabel Hamilton, second daughter of Thomas Hamilton, first Earl of Haddington. He was born 23 August 1616. He was a Gentleman Usher of the Privy Chamber.[2]

Ogilvy married in 1640 Christian Ruthven, Lady of Fernilee, second daughter of Patrick Ruthven, Earl of Forth (later Earl of Brentford) [q.v.], by his first wife, and relict of Thomas Kerr, of Fernilee (died 1637): they had two daughters.

Ogilvy was killed fighting for the King at the Battle of Inverlochy 2 February 1644/5.

[1] St Aldate's Defaulters, Bodleian MS. Add. D. 114, f. 24.
[2] L.C. 3/1: his name has been added after an erasure.

For CAPTAIN PRINGLE see Edward Carpenter's house.

Mr John Ogleby is probably JOHN OGLEBY, the author and printer (1600-1676), whose present-day collateral relatives claim a distant kinship with the House of Airlie. He was born in Scotland, and was employed by Strafford as Master of the Revels in Ireland. After Strafford's execution he came over to England and is known to have been at Cambridge.
(For a full account see *D.N.B.*)

Mr Morrice is possibly the THOMAS MORRYS, gent, who was created D.C.L. at Oxford 21 February 1642/3. He in turn may perhaps be identified with the Thomas Morris, Esq. who was taken prisoner of war at Shrewsbury 22 February 1644/5.[1] This is likely to be Thomas Morris, of Whittington, Shropshire, a recusant.[2]

[1] Phillips, Vol. II, p. 237.
[2] *C.C.C.*, p. 2936.

Mr Nicholas is perhaps JOHN NICHOLAS (1566-1644), the father of Sir Edward Nicholas [q.v.], Principal Secretary of State, who was lodging close by in Pembroke College. John Nicholas was born 21 July 1566 and was thus nearly seventy-seven in June 1643. He was living at his home at Winterbourne Earls in Wiltshire on 26 May 1644, when he wrote to tell his grandson, who was then in Paris, of the plundering of his house. He died at Winterbourne 9 December 1644 and was buried there on the 11th: there is a M.I. in the church. But there is no extant evidence to shew that he did not make a stay in Oxford, to visit his son, in 1643. His Will was proved at Oxford in 1644.

MR EDWARD CARPENTER
(c. 1597-1658)

Barrister-at-law and brewer. The son and heir of Edward Carpenter, gentleman, of Oxford, possibly the individual of that name who was admitted to New College 30 October 1601 aged forty-three. The barrister's father is certainly to be identified with the Edward Carpenter of the parish of St Aldate's (see his widow's Will) who was admitted by the University to brew 23 January 1595/6,[1] was buried at St Peter's-in-the-East 24 July 1618,[2] and whose Will, made 17 July 1618, was proved in the Court of the Chancellor of Oxford University 17 August 1618.[3] In this he mentions his 'welbeloved wife', Thomasine Carpenter, and appoints his son Edward residuary legatee and executor. His Inventory, presented 23 November 1618, shews that he was a well-to-do citizen, as the value of his effects was £1,648 9s. 6d.

Thomasine Carpenter, his widow (also of St Aldate's), and possibly a daughter of Thomas Heath, blacksmith, of St Michael's (died c. 1587), was admitted to brew 14 January 1619/20.[4] She was buried at St Peter's 25 February 1628/9.[5]

Her Will, made 20 November 1628, was proved in the Chancellor's Court 3 March 1628/9.[6] In it she mentions her brother, Mr Thomas Heath, and appoints her son Edward residuary legatee and executor. A clause in this document states: 'I desire Mr Provost & the Fellowes of Quenes Colleadge in Oxford to accept of me as a poore memoriall of my great thankfullnes vnto them for ther longe continued kindnes vnto me & my deceased husband a peece of plate of seventie Nobles to be bestowed at the discretion of my Executor'. A number of members of the Carpenter family were buried at St Peter's between 1579 and 1637.

The younger Edward Carpenter matriculated from St John's College, Oxford, 13 October 1615, aged eighteen, and graduated B.A. 29 October 1616. He was admitted to Lincoln's Inn 6 December 1619, his father being then dead,[7] and was called to the bar 5 June 1627.[8] On 6 September he stood godfather to Edward Wood, an elder brother of Anthony, who described him as 'sometime fellow of Merton College [an error] and then counsellour of Lyncolne's Ynne'.[9] Carpenter inherited his parents' brewery in Oxford and was probably in business there some years previous to the Civil War. Evidence of his carrying on the brewery during the War is furnished by the records of several colleges. Carpenter was one of three brewers (the other two being Thomas Smyth and Walter Cave qq.v.) who supplied Brasenose with beer during 1644:[10] it is possible to follow the number of barrels provided each week for the four terms together with the prices and the total sums received. The receipts at the end of the Bursar's Book are normally signed by Carpenter's man, Christopher Garrie, but one bears Carpenter's own signature. There are entries of payments to his drawmen, including their reward at Christmas 1643. He also supplied New College,[11] Queen's,[12] and St John's[13] with beer during the War period.

The Subsidy assessments of 1641 reveal that both Carpenter and his wife were recusants: he paid 20s. and 16s. 'in lands', and she 8d. and 16d. for her pole.[14] 'Mr Carpenter the Brewer' appears in the list of those accused by Bailiff Heron of siding with Sir John Byron when he entered Oxford 28 August 1642.[15] Together with John Holloway and Matthew Langley [qq.v.] he was appointed to take care of infected persons in St Aldate's parish.[16] He contributed £3 towards the loan to the Lords Commissioners in October 1645.[17] His name appears in all the St Aldate's parish taxation lists of 1645 and 1647. He was assessed at 7s. in the Subsidy of 1648.[18] On 22 December 1652 he is described as 'late of Oxford, now of London'. The Oxford Committee having seized and secured part of his estate, he begged discharge on the Act of Pardon, no part of his estate in Oxford or London being sequestered on 1 December 1651.[19]

Edward Carpenter married before 1634 Elizabeth, daughter of Edmond Colles, of Leigh, Worcestershire, by his wife, Martha, daughter of William Tyrrwhitt, of Kettleby, Lincolnshire.[20] Her sister Anne Colles was buried at St Aldate's 28 March 1640.[21] He died between 12 April and 2 November 1658.

In his Will he mentions his 'deare wife', Elizabeth, and his daughters Elizabeth and ffredisweede: the two former were appointed executors together with a William Brent. Among other legatees he mentions his 'deare ffather' (his father-in-law, Edmond Colles) and his 'deare sister Mistris Ursula Parker', whom he remembers in gratitude 'for her great Care and true love which shee hath shown vnto mee in my long sicknes'. This was his wife's sister, née Ursula Colles.

[Will: P.C.C. 1658: 630 Wootton: made 12 April 1658: proved 2 November 1658, as of Cursitors Alley in the parish of St Dunstan's-in-the-West].

Carpenter's house was on the south side of Slaying or Slaughter Lane, and occupied the site of Micklem Hall, now Campion Hall. It stood to the west of the tenement rented from Balliol by Thomas Smyth [q.v.],[22] and was considerably west of Smyth's dwelling house. The house was Carpenter's own property. In his Will he says: 'I give and devise simple and inheritance of my dwelling house and Brewhouse in Oxford with the Appurtenences and the standing stocke thereof and the present rent I receave in the name of my trustie ffreind Mr Roche from Master White the present tennant thereof for certaine yeares therein yet to come to my deare wife Elizabeth Carpenter and her heires'. The rooms are listed in the Inventory of Edward Carpenter the elder which enumerates 'the hall', 'the Chamber over the hall', 'the Chamber over the Larder', 'the Chamber over the entrye', 'the Chamber over the kitchen', 'the Studdye', 'the Lardyer', 'the Boulting house', 'the Mens Chamber', 'the kitchen', 'the Stables', 'the Inner backside', 'the backside nexte the streete', 'the Brewhouse', 'maultlofte', 'firehouse & stillinghouse', 'the hoppehouse'. There were five hearths in 1665.[23] On 18 September 1618, Mrs Carpenter, Edward's mother, had permission to set out two chimneys in Slaying Lane, paying 12d. for a langable.[24]

Some of the seventeenth-century structure of this commodious house is preserved in the present Campion Hall.[25]

The situation of the brewhouse is given in the City Rental of 25 March 1658: 'The heirs of Mr Thomas Smith for a bank at the Friers on the south side of Trillmillbow between Littlegate Bridge and Mr Carpenter's brewhouse'.[26]

[1] *Register*, Vol. II, Pt. I, p. 228.
[2] Wood, *C. of O.*, Vol. III, p. 263.
[3] Hyp. B. 23.
[4] *Register*, Vol. II, Pt. I, p. 329. She paid 2s. in the Assessment of Privileged Persons in 1624-5 (University Archives W.P. γ 28 (7), ff. 6 and 11).
[5] Wood, op. cit., Vol. III, p. 263: wrongly printed as 1629/30.
[6] Hyp. B. 23.
[7] *Admissions Register*, Vol. I, p. 183.
[8] *Black Books*, Vol. II, p. 270.
[9] *L. and T.*, Vol. I, p. 27 and Vol. V, p. 8.
[10] Brasenose Muniments A 8 11*: Junior Bursar's Book of 1644.
[11] 'Long Books', passim.
[12] Bursar's Books 1641-2, 1642-3, 1643-4.
[13] Buttery Book 1642-3.
[14] City Archives B. 1. 4. c.
[15] *The Manuscripts of the House of Lords*, Vol. XI, New Series, p. 326.
[16] Bodleian MS. Add. D. 114, f. 89.
[17] City Archives E. 4. 6, ff. 1-2: *O.C.A.* 1626-1665, p. 453.
[18] *S. and T.*, p. 169.
[19] *C.C.C.*, p. 3068.
[20] *Visitation of Worcestershire* 1634, Harleian Society, Vol. XC (1938), p.

25. The Colles family was Roman Catholic: see *The Responsa Scholarum of the English College, Rome,* Part I, 1598-1621, Catholic Record Society, Vol. LIV (1962), pp. 263-4.
[21] Wood, *C. of O.*, Vol. III, p. 207. She is called Coles and described as 'sister to Mr Carpenter'.
[22] See Balliol College Leases B. 15. 5 and 6.
[23] *S. and T.*, p. 192.
[24] *O.C.A.* 1583-1626, p. 275.
[25] See *Survey of South-West Ward,* No. 40 and R.C.H.M. *City of Oxford,* p. 176a.
[26] *O.C.P.*, p. 12.

ELIZABETH COLLES

She must have been a relative of Mrs Carpenter, possibly her second cousin of the half-blood, Elizabeth, daughter of John Colles, of Grimley, Worcestershire, by his wife, Mary Coningsby, of Hopton Wafer, Herefordshire. It is not unlikely that the cousin Elizabeth Scurlock to whom Edward Carpenter left 20s. in his Will, is the same person, then married to a member of a Carmarthenshire family.

CAPTAIN GEORGE PRINGLE

Prindell is an error for Pringle. George Pringle or Pringill, of Balmungo, Fife, was the second son of James Pringle or Pringill, by his first wife, Christian Lundie. James predeceased his father, James Hoppringill the second, of Whytbank, Selkirkshire (died 1625). George Pringle married Elspeth Ruthven, eldest daughter of Patrick Ruthven, Earl of Forth, later Earl of Brentford [q.v.], by his first wife: Elspeth was relict of William Lundie, of that Ilk (died 1623).
In June 1643 Pringle had been lodging, together with his father-in-law, his wife's brother-in-law, Sir Thomas Ogilvy (Ogleby) [q.v.], and others in the house of Thomas Smyth [q.v.], and said that he ought not to pay.[1]
George Pringle died between Balmungo and St Andrews 23 August 1655 and was buried at St Andrews 25 August.[2] George's elder brother, James Pringle, of Whytbank, was one of Lord Forth's most trusted friends.

[1] St Aldate's Defaulters, Bodleian MS. Add. D. 114, f. 24.
[2] Alexander Pringle, *The Records of the Pringles or Hoppringills* (1933), pp. 237-8, where it is stated that George is alleged to have served under his father-in-law.

In June 1643 Carpenter had lodging with him a MR ELSTON, unidentified, over sixty years of age.

RICHARD MILES
(died c. 1644)

Yeoman, and *auriga* (waggoner) of Christ Church. He was the son of Richard Miles, of St Aldate's, yeoman, by his wife, Bridget . . . The elder Richard Miles was entered as a privileged person of the University, belonging to University College, on 1 December 1581.[1] His name first appears in the Christ Church Disbursement Books for the academic year 1588-9:[2] the book for 1587-8 is missing. He received 10s. for each of the four terms, and an annual payment of 10s. as livery money (*vestae liberatae*). In the early books he is described as *baiulus* (carrier) or *operax* (worker), but in the book for 1598-9 he is given the title of *auriga*, which thenceforth always follows his name. In the Assessments of Privileged Persons he is listed under bailiffs.[3] It is clear from the numerous entries concerning him that the elder Miles' duties were various and that he was a true handyman. He was concerned with timber and various kinds of repairs; he bought oxen for the College; he undertook carriage of materials; and he was in charge of the 'colledge' horse, for which he purchased a saddle and collar, and he replaced it by another when it died. Miles' unmistakable mark appears throughout the books up till the first term of the academic year 1614-15. He made his Will on 24 September 1615, and it was proved in the Court of the Chancellor of Oxford University 15 November 1615.[4] Among other small bequests he left 'Briget Myles the daughter of my sonne Richard Myles two silver spoones'. He made his wife, Bridget, residuary legatee and executrix, 'knowinge that hir motherly Love & affection towards my sonne & hirs Richard Myles is such that if he doe well shee will gladdly doe all the good shee can both for him & his'. One of the overseers was Oliver Smyth I.

Bridget Miles, who was also a privileged person of the University, and was taxed as such (2s. 6d.) in 1624-5, made her Will 2 November 1626: it was proved in the Chancellor's Court 10 October 1627.[5] She expressed the wish to be buried in St Aldate's. She left to 'my sonnes two children John and Thomas Xli apeece, and to my goddaughter Bridgett Myles Xli and the peece of plate with my name vppon it'. Her residuary legatee was 'my Nephew [i.e. grandson] Richard Myles my sonne Richards sonne', and she appointed him executor, although he was under age. In the interests of this boy she directed her friend and overseer, Dr John Bancroft, Master of University College, 'to provide & appoynte a sufficiente tenant for my howse', and to use the rent for the young Richard's benefit. If the latter died before he was twenty-one, Bridget requested Dr Bancroft to divide her belongings among her 'other legataries or theire father, if he proove a good & thrifty husband, soe that his wife never come to dwell in my howse, as I haue ofte vowed heretofore'. The administration bond of Bridget Miles is signed by Bancroft, who was to administer during her grandson's minority, and her son, who signs his name and uses a seal.[6]

Richard Miles II, who was born about 1589,[6a] succeeded his father immediately as *auriga* of Christ Church. The payment for Miles in the second term of 1614-5 is receipted 'Rich: Miles' in place of his father's mark. There are numerous references to payments of bills to him, and for separate items under repairs in the Disbursement Books. In the Assessment of Privileged Persons 1624-5 Miles is described as 'Bayly and Rentgatherer of Christchurch': he was assessed at 18d.[7] He held his post at the College until his death: the last entry of his name is in the first term of the academic year 1643-4.

An entry in the Oxford City Quarter Sessions Rolls for 8 April 1624 records that 'Richard Myles of the Cittie of Oxon yeoman beinge formly convicted for killinge of Richard Reynolds for wch he had his trial the last Gaole deliuie and prayed the benefitt of his Clergie and was reprieved for his burneing in the hand vntill this Sessions in the interim to prcure his Maties pdon wch he nowe brought in and soe is discharged'.[8]

In June 1643 Miles was a defaulter, but declared that 'he will work double next week'.[9] He was dead by Easter 1644, as the accounts of the churchwardens of St Aldate's for 1643-4 record the payment of 13s. 4d. for the graves of 'Mr Richard Miles and his wief' in the body of the church. Probably they were yet further victims of the 'sicknesse' of 1643.

Miles left no Will. His wife's christian name was Mercy.[9a] There was a surviving son, John, and the daughter, Bridget, mentioned in both her grandparents' Wills. This John Miles, a carpenter, made his Will 20 September 1644 'being very sick of the plague': one of the witnesses was Thomas Marcham [q.v.]. The Will was proved at Oxford 28 November 1644, and the Inventory is dated 4 February 1644/5.[10]

Richard Miles' house was at Tower Hill, on the west side of Grandpont, and was Nos. 92-93 St Aldate's. 'At the place where this gate [South Gate] stood is now a descent knowne in dimissions of houses thereabouts by the name of Tower Hill, and parts Fish Street and Grandpont'.[11] The house was the property of St Aldate's parish, and is described in the Churchwardens' Accounts of 1635-6 as 'lyeinge att the end of Slater [Slaughter] Lane'. The Assessments of Privileged Persons show that Richard Miles I had originally been of St Thomas' parish, but in 1592 he moved to St Aldate's. On 6 April of that year the feoffees granted him a lease of 'All that theire messuage or tente & garden grounde thereunto belonginge wth thapptences sett . . . at Tower Hill in grauntpont'.[12] The lease was for forty-one years and the rent 18s. per annum. After the death of Richard Miles I the house was rented by his widow, Bridget, to whom the feoffees granted a fresh lease 25 January 1623/4: the term named was thirty-one years and the rent was raised to £1.[13] In spite of his mother's testamentary provisions, Richard Miles II and his wife went to live in the house after her death, from which time onwards he paid the rent. The feoffees granted him a fresh lease for thirty-one years 22 November 1636, when he is described as in occupation.[14] John Miles, who had been associated with his father in this indenture, gave 'his lease of his house wherein he lived and all his goods' to his sister, Bridget, his executrix. The lease is mentioned in his Inventory. On 20 May 1652 Bridget and her husband, John Cule, a tailor, received a lease of the house from the feoffees.[15]

The house was built in the seventeenth century.[16] 'The garden ground thereof conteyneth in breadth Eleaven yards or thereabouts and in length Nine yards And the said Tenemt, conteyneth in length Seaven and Twenty yards and a foot from the hither part of the garden to the streete dore and the breadth of the outside of the streete from the one side to the other is Ten yards or thereabouts'.[17]

[1] *Register*, Vol. II, Pt. I, p. 392.
[2] Ch. Ch. MS. xii. b. 31.
[3] University Archives W.P. γ 25 (5) and 28 (6), passim.
[4] Ib. Hyp. B. 30.
[5] Ib. G.G.5, f. 133v.
[6] Ib. Hyp. B. 41.
[6a] He was aged about 40 on 7 December 1629: see University Archives Hyp. B. 6, Depositions 1627-1644: case of John Donne the Younger against Robert Bedingfield.
[7] Ib. W.P. γ 28 (7), f. 11.
[8] City Archives O. 5. 9, f. 184: Quarter Sessions Roll 1614-1638.
[9] Bodleian MS. Add. D. 114, f. 24v.
[9a] University Archives Hyp. B. 6: case cited above. Her age on 7 December 1629 was given as about 36, and she was described as a native of St Aldate's parish.
[10] MS. Wills Oxon. 44/3/18.
[11] Wood, *C. of O.*, Vol. I, p. 251.
[12] Indenture in Parish Chest.
[13] Indenture in Parish Chest.

[14] Indenture in Parish Chest.
[15] Indenture in Parish Chest.
[16] For a description see R.C.H.M. *City of Oxford*, p. 175. See also *Survey of South-West Ward*, No. 30.
[17] A Particular of the St Aldate's parish messuages in 1670 (Parish Chest).

COLONEL (SIR) GEORGE LISLE
(shot 1648)

The son of Lawrence Lisle, who obtained a monopoly in viewing and repairing arms in England from James I and was therefore probably a soldier: he was later concerned with the import of tobacco into Ireland. George's mother was a near kinswoman of George Villiers, first Duke of Buckingham. Lisle is said to have had his military education in the Netherlands,[1] and may be the Mr Lyle who fought at the siege of Breda in 1637. In 1640 and 1641 he was a captain of foot in Lord Grandison's Regiment.[2] He was serving as a captain in Colonel William Cromwell's Regiment in Ireland in 1641-2, and his company was still over there on 18 January 1642/3.[3]

As lieutenant-colonel of a regiment of dragoons, Lisle fought at Edgehill.[4] He commanded fifty dragoons at Chalgrove (17/18 June 1643) and fought at the First Battle of Newbury (20 September 1643), after leading a thousand musketeers towards Aldbourne Chase in support of Prince Rupert.[5] He became colonel of foot *vice* Richard Bolle who was killed at Alton in December 1643.[6] On 2 February 1643/4 a Parliamentarian scout incorrectly reported that 'Leiftenant Collonel Lisle is made governour of Redding';[7] he probably meant Deputy-Governor. His Regiment served in the garrison there.[8] He fought at Cheriton (29 March 1644) and probably at Cropredy Bridge (29 June), as a tertia commander. Lisle was with the King in Cornwall in August 1644, commanding the second tertia of foot.[9] He signed the letter of 8 August to the Earl of Essex.[10] He particularly distinguished himself by his defence of Shaw House at the Second Battle of Newbury (27 October 1644). On this occasion Lisle, stripped to his shirt, was said to be mistaken by the enemy for a witch. He was Governor of Faringdon from 1644 to 1645. A letter from Lisle to Rupert, dated from Faringdon 13 December 1644, is printed in H.M.C., Appendix to IIIrd *Report*.[11]

On 16 April 1645 Lisle was created D.C.L. of Oxford University, perhaps the equivalent of a D.S.O.[12] A Mistress Margaret Lisle, who was probably George's wife, was buried at St Mary's, Oxford, 1 May 1645.[13] He was a tertia commander at the siege of Leicester, and was made Lieutenant-General of Leicestershire under Lord Loughborough (a short-lived command!) in 1645.[14] At Naseby he also commanded a tertia, which was lost, but he escaped, presumably because he was on horseback. He was knighted at Oxford 21 December 1645, when he was described as Master of the King's Household.

Lisle's petition to compound was received 26 January 1646/7, and he was ordered to have a licence to come to London.[15] He was prominent in the Kent insurrection of 1648, and took part in the defence of Colchester, where, after the surrender, he was shot, with Sir Charles Lucas, 28 August 1648, an unforgettable outrage.

(For a full account see *D.N.B.*)

George's brother Francis was an ensign of foot in George Goring's Regiment in 1640 and 1641.[16] He was killed at Marston Moor (1644) as major or lieutenant-colonel, so that it is practically impossible that he could be the Colonel Lyle in question.

[1] *D.N.B.*
[2] Rushworth, Vol. III, p. 1245.

[3] H.M.C., *Ormonde*, Vol. I, pp. 124, 128, and 143.
[4] Sir R. Bulstrode, *Memoirs* (1721), p. 81: he is here erroneously described as 'Collonel'.
[5] MS. Prince Rupert's Diary.
[6] MS. Harleian 986.
[7] Luke, p. 243.
[8] Symonds, MS. Harleian 986.
[9] Symonds, p. 160.
[10] Walker, p. 61.
[11] P. 258.
[12] Wood, *Fasti*, Vol. II, p. 88.
[13] Wood, *C. of O.*, Vol. III, p. 246.
[14] Symonds, p. 184.
[15] *C.C.C.*, p. 1654.
[16] Rushworth, Vol. III, p. 1245.

COLONEL (SIR) JOHN READE

Colonel (Sir) John Reade was a 'Scottish man borne and bred in England and always serving in his majestie's armies'.[1] He was a nephew of Sir Henry Bruce.[2] Bruce had been in the King's secret service, perhaps in 1625, but at least as early as 1627;[3] had commanded a regiment which was present at Cadiz, Rhé, and Rochelle:[4] was appointed a member of the Council of War in 1627/8;[5] and was a Gentleman of the Privy Chamber to the King in 1641.[6] He was in Ireland by 1639.[7]

In a letter to Charles I, dated 27 January 1639/40, Reade speaks of himself as 'Your Majesty's servant' and reminds the King of a promise made to him at York when Charles had commanded him to go for his service to Ireland. Reade also mentions his fifteen years' service and command abroad.[8] Together with Endymion Porter and Edward Reade he successfully petitioned the King 27 May 1640 for the monopoly of making white writing paper.[9] In 1641 he was an Esquire of His Majesty's Body Extraordinary.[10]

On 5 January 1641/2 he is described as having been in the last expedition to the north of Ireland lieutenant-colonel to [his uncle] Sir Henry Bruce,[11] who wrote to Reade 2 November from London;[12] and on 6 November 1641 Reade is said to have been living in Tredagh [Drogheda?] and to be a great Papist.[13]

On 16 March 1643/4 the Irish Lords Justices and Council wrote to the King that although Reade claimed to have been employed by the rebellious noblemen and gentry of the Pale in December 1641 to present a petition to Charles, he had waited until March 1641/2, after the raising of the siege of Drogheda, and had then surrendered to Ormonde and was no messenger from them.[14] The Catholic nobles and gentry, on the other hand, claimed that, as the bearer of their assurances of loyalty, Reade had fallen into the hands of the Puritan government at Dublin, where he was examined and tortured on the rack.[15] In June 1642 he and two other prisoners were brought over to England and imprisoned in the Tower.[16] The prisoners presented various petitions for clothes, etc., and when the news came in December 1642 of the death of Reade's wife, he was allowed a mourning suit.[17] On 3 May 1643 the prisoners were ordered to be removed from the Tower to Newgate.[18] On 18 May they protested.[19] Reade subsequently escaped to Oxford and engaged in Sir Basil Brooke's abortive plot to win over the City of London to the King in December to January 1643-4.[20]

Reade was knighted at Oxford 5 February 1643/4. On 8 February Lord Digby wrote to Ormonde: 'This bearer, Sir John Reade, is thought very faithfull to the king and capable of negotiating with good effect in soem things: the particulars [of which] he is commanded to shew your lordship'.[21] On 8 March 1643/4

Ormonde wrote to Digby: 'Sir John Read is not yet com'.[22] He then disappears from view. Sir Henry Bruce was also imprisoned in the Tower, but had a pass to go to Scotland 6 December 1645.[23]
Reade is pretty certainly identical with the Captain John Read who was serving in Ireland in 1626,[24] who is mentioned in 1627,[25] and who was a recusant for whom the penal laws were relaxed in the 1630s.[26] A Captain Read was serving in the Dutch army at the siege of Breda in 1637, but, as our man was a Catholic, this is, perhaps, not likely to be him.

[1] Carte, Vol. V, p. 371.
[2] H.M.C., Appendix to VIth *Report*, p. 351: although the surname is missing, the reference is obviously to Reade.
[3] *C.S.P.D.* 1627-8, p. 431.
[4] Ib. 1628-9, p. 489.
[5] Ib. 1627-8, p. 563.
[6] L.C. 3/1.
[7] H.M.C., *Cowper*, Vol. II, p. 230.
[8] *C.S.P.D.* 1639-40, p. 380.
[9] Ib. 1640, p. 226.
[10] L.C. 3/1.
[11] H.M.C., *Ormonde*, N. S., Vol. II, p. 61.
[12] H.M.C., Appendix to Vth *Report*, loc. cit.
[13] Ibid.
[14] H.M.C., *Ormonde*, N.S., Vol. II, pp. 247-8.
[15] Carte, Vol. V, pp. 297, 309, and 371 and *C.C.S.P.*, Vol. I, p. 234.
[16] *Ormonde*, N.S., Vol. II, pp. 115, 145, 151-2, 155.
[17] H.M.C., Appendix to Vth *Report*, pp. 30 and 60: see also *L.J.*, Vol. V, p. 487.
[18] Ib., p. 83 and *L.J.*, Vol. VI, p. 29.
[19] Op. cit., pp. 86 and 51.
[20] S.R. Gardiner, *History of the Civil War*, Vol. I (new impression (1914)), pp. 269-70; *C.J.*, Vol. III, p. 358; and *L.J.*, Vol. VI, p. 369 etc.
[21] Carte, Vol. VI, p. 34.
[22] Ib., p. 53.
[23] *C.J.*, Vol. IV, p. 367.
[24] *C.S.P.I.* 1625-32, pp. 82, 73, and 195.
[25] *C.S.P.D.* 1627-8, p. 380.
[26] E.g. ib. 1634-5, p. 145.

CAPTAIN STACE

Probably the Captain Stacy who was in the King's Lifeguard of Foot in Cornwall in 1644.[1]
A Captain-Lieutenant Henry Stacy, who came from Glamorgan, had served in the foot regiment of Sir Charles Kemys.[2] Kemys, of Keven Mabley, Glamorgan, was knighted at Oxford 13 June 1643, but there is no reason why he should have been quartered at Oxford.

[1] MS. Harleian 6804, f. 109.
[2] *I.O.*, col. 77.

MR JOHN STANHOPE

He was created M.A. of Oxford University 16 January 1642/3.[1] On 9 September

1644 he took part in (Sir) Henry Gage's expedition for the relief of Basing House and was captured. 'Of His Majesties Forces . . . foure taken prisoners, whereof one was Master Stanhope, Gentleman of the Horse to the Lord Marquesse of Hertford, who engaging himselfe to gaine a Standard of the Rebels, for want of Seconds, was hemm'd in, after he had runne a Captaine Lieutenant of theirs through the body'.[2] On 8 July 1648 the Committee of Both Houses resolved that 'Mr Stanhope, servant to the Marquess of Hertford, be sent up in custody to this Committee'.[3]

John Stanhope may possibly be identified with John Posthumus Stanhope, fifth son of Sir John Stanhope, of Shelford, Nottinghamshire, by his second wife, Catherine Trentham. Sir John died in 1611, his Will being proved in the P.C.C. on 4 May.[4] John Posthumus was therefore born in 1611. He was a half-brother of Philip Stanhope, first Earl of Chesterfield, and a whole brother of Sir John Stanhope, of Elvaston, Derbyshire (died 1638). He was a third cousin of Lord Hertford.

[Administration, as of Shelford, 'esq and batch', is dated 1653/4: P.C.C., Vol. II, f. 265].

[1] Wood, *Fasti*, Vol. II, p. 33: Wood calls him Master of Horse to the Marquess of Hertford [q.v.].
[2] *Mercurius Aulicus*, 12 September 1644.
[3] *C.S.P.D.* 1648-9, p. 175.
[4] 45 Wood.

In June 1643 there were lodging in Miles' house Lieutenant Cranfield and one man, Sir Matthew Carew and one man, and Captain Waite and one man.[1]

LIEUTENANT JOHN CRANFIELD

On 25 March 1641 Lieutenant Cranefeld was serving in Captain Hearon's troop of horse belonging to the regiment of the General of the Horse, Viscount Conway.[2] On 11 May 1643 Sir Edward Nicholas [q.v.] wrote from Oxford to Prince Rupert: 'Sir James Mills was lately shot by an officer upon a private quarrel: and the last night Lieutenant Cranefeild was wounded by one Captain Hastings upon the like occasion. There is here no punishment, and therefore nothing but disorder can be expected'.[3] When Cranfield was lodging in St Aldate's he said that 'he would pay when the king payd him'. His departure from Oxford was probably due to the fact of his obtaining a company of foot in the regiment of Colonel (Sir) Edward Seymour, Governor of Dartmouth. Sergeant-Major Cranfield was present at a Council of War held at Dartmouth 15 July 1644:[4] he is referred to as Major Cranfield nine days later.[5] This rapid promotion can be accounted for by his being a soldier of some experience before the Civil War. He is likely to be the John Cranfield who in 1660 figures in the list of Gentlemen Pensioners.

[1] St Aldate's Defaulters, Bodleian MS. Add. D. 114, f. 24v.
[2] Sir Jacob Astley's Muster Roll.
[3] Warburton, Vol. II, p. 189. It is impossible to identify Captain Hastings with certainty: there were several Royalist officers of this name.
[4] H.M.C., *Somerset*, p. 75.
[5] Ib., p. 77.

SIR MATTHEW CAREW
(c. 1590-after 1648)

The eldest son of Sir Matthew Carew, LL.D., Master in Chancery, by his wife, Alice,

eldest daughter of Sir John Rivers, lord mayor of London, and widow of one Ingpenny. The family was of the Carews of Antony, Cornwall. The younger Matthew matriculated from Balliol College, 7 November 1606, aged sixteen. He was knighted at Dublin Castle by Sir Arthur Chichester 6 October 1611. In 1624, as Captain Carey, he was serving under Count Mansfeld, his colonel being the Earl of Lincoln and his Company two hundred strong.[2] His name occurs in the List of Soldiers returned from foreign parts (1639?).[3] In 1640 he was lieutenant-colonel of Sir John Douglas' Regiment of Foot (XIX).[4] On 11 January 1642/3 two muskets and two bandoleers were received into the King's stores from Carew,[5] who returned no answer in June 1643. He was sequestered at Westminster in March 1648,[6] after which he disappears from view.
Carew married Elizabeth (? Frances) daughter of Sir James Cromer, of Tunstall, Kent. A son, Edward, matriculated from University College, 4 July 1634, aged seventeen, his father then being of Cokethorpe, Oxfordshire (see Robert Saunders). Carew's younger brother Thomas (1595-1639) was the poet. He was Gentleman of the Privy Chamber to Charles I and Sewer in Ordinary.

[1] *D.N.B.*
[2] Marshall Business, 5 MSO/1531, f. 81: Winchester County Record Office.
[3] National Library of Wales, Chirk Castle MS. F 7442.
[4] Rushworth, Vol. III, p. 1250.
[5] *R.O.P.*, Part I, p. 65.
[6] *C.C.C.*, p. 91.

It has not been possible to identify CAPTAIN WAITE, but he may have been the Thomas Wayte junior, of Stillington, Yorkshire, who, on 24 May 1650, compounded on his own discovery for Delinquency in adhering to the King against Parliament in the First War, and was subsequently fined at 1/6th, £3. 6s. 8d.[1]

[1] *C.C.C.*, p. 2309. See also *Yorkshire Royalist Composition Papers*, Vol. III, p. 31, where he is stated to have adhered to the forces raised against Parliament.

MRS CHRISTIAN CANTWELL
(died 1644)

Christian Cantwell was the widow of John Cantwell, surgeon. He petitioned 2 May, and was licensed 5 May, 1620 to practise surgery by the University of Oxford. Dr Thomas Clayton [q.v.], Regius Professor of Medicine, testified that he was a 'well-experienced chirurgian, of good practice here, at London, and in other countries beyond the seas'. He had practised some thirty years.[1] He subscribed 16 October 1620.[2] His name appears in the Assessment of Privileged Persons in 1624-5, when, as of St Aldate's, he was assessed at 2s. 6d.[3] He was buried at St Aldate's 6 March 1632/3.[4] The Churchwardens' Accounts shew that they received 6s. 8d. for his grave in the year 1632-3.

Cantwell's Will was made 2 September 1628 and proved in the Court of the Chancellor of Oxford University 16 March 1632/3.[5] In this he describes himself as 'well stricken in yeares'. He made his 'welbeloved wief X'ian Cantwell' his residuary legatee and executrix. The overseers named were 'my welbeloved frend Oliver Smyth Alderman and Thomas Smyth [q.v.] his sonne'.

Christian Cantwell had previously been married to a man of the surname of Smyth, by whom she had a son, Richard Smyth. Richard had a son, John Smyth, and a daughter, Hanna Smyth, afterwards married to Cresswell Bowell, mercer, a member of the Common Council in 1643:[6] she died of the plague and was buried at St Aldate's after 6 July 1644.[7] Cantwell left Hanna £10 and John £5.

Christian Cantwell was assessed at 20s. and 8s. 'in lands' in the Subsidy Lists of 1641.[8] Although her Will was not proved until 8 August 1646, she was dead by the summer of 1644. This is shewn by the graphic nuncupative Will of her granddaughter, Hanna Bowell, made between Midsummer and St James's tide 1644, in which she speaks of 'my Grandmother maistris Christian Cantwell deceased'.[9] In Christian's Will she describes herself as 'somewhat weake aged and well stricken in yeares'. She expressed the wish to be buried in St Aldate's 'neare my late husband'. She left her son, Richard, £5 and her grandchild, Hanna (still unmarried), property in Barnet and South Minns [sic], as well as making her her residuary legatee and executrix. Hanna left two silver bowls bequeathed to her by her grandmother to her stepson, William Bowell, dividing the rest of her inheritance between him and his sister, Ann. As Hanna was dead by the time that Christian's Will was proved, administration was granted to her grandson, John Smyth. Two of her overseers were Unton Croke and Thomas Smyth [qq.v.], who were left 20s. each to buy a ring, as was also Croke's wife.

Mrs Cantwell left her brother Reighnold Bryan 40s. If, as seems probable, Bryan was her blood brother (not brother-in-law), she must have been an Oxford woman. For Reginald Bryan of Oxon., pleb., matriculated from Corpus Christi College, Oxford, 28 November 1581, aged fifteen. It is possible that Reginald and Christian were the children of Edmund Bryan, of St Nicholas' parish, Oxford, administration of whose goods was granted to his widow, Agnes, 29 July 1584.[10]

[Will: P.C.C. 1646: 122 Twisse: made 6 April 1642: proved 8 August 1646]

Mrs Cantwell's house was on the west side of Grandpont, and occupied the site of No. 89 St Aldate's. It was leased from Thomas Smyth [q.v.] whom, in her Will, she terms 'my Landlord'. On 11 September 1648 Oliver Smyth, Thomas' son and heir, being about to marry Anne, daughter of Robert Bourne, settled on her inter alia 'All that Messuage or Tenement wth thapptences late in the Occupacon of one John Cantwell or of his Assigne or Assignes & being in the said pish of St Aldates . . . wthout the Southgate of the said Cittye [of Oxon] on the West side of the waye leading from the said gate vnto Trillmill Bowe betweene a house or tenement some tyme in the tenure or occupation of John ffurnivell & lately in the tenure or occupation of John [Howson] heertofore Bishopp of Oxon on the South and a garden or Orchard of the said Oliver Smyth on the North side', together with all appurtenances, 'sometyme being the Inheritance of John Singleton of the Cittye of Oxon Chandler deceased'.[11] As Howson's house (Waterhall) was by Trill Mill Bow,[12] this places the Cantwell house as lying just north of the stream.

[1] *Register*, Vol. II, Pt. I, p. 124.
[2] Ib., Vol. II, Pt. II, p. 384.
[3] University Archives W.P. γ 28 (7), f. 6.
[4] Wood, *C. of O.*, Vol. III, p. 207.
[5] Hyp. B. 23.
[6] On 22 April 1643 one half pike was received from him for the king's use (*R.O.P.*, Part I, p. 76).
[7] Wood, op. cit., Vol. III, p. 208, where her name is printed 'Crossbowell').
[8] City Archives B. 1. 4. c.
[9] P.C.C. 1646: 95 Twisse.
[10] MS. Wills Oxon. Series I, 9, f. 312.
[11] City Archives A. 5. 4, f. 54.
[12] Wood, *C. of O.*, Vol. I, pp. 299 and 415.

LIEUTENANT-COLONEL JAMES (?) TOMPSON

He is almost certainly the Captain James Thomson who was in Sir Arthur Aston's Regiment of Foot in 1640.[1] In June 1643 Captain Tompson was already lodging at Mrs Cantwell's, but was out of town by the 14th.[2] In January 1643/4 he was still at the same address, but had become a lieutenant-colonel. A captain of 1640 would have been sufficiently senior to receive such rapid promotion and may have done so in the new regiment of his old colonel, Sir Arthur Aston, which was raised at Oxford during this very period. It is worth noting that his wife and two young children, with the not inconsiderable entourage of four servants, had joined Tompson in the interim. If he was now second-in-command of a regiment belonging to the Governor of Oxford, nothing could be more natural.
One of the twelve members of the Lottery of the Royall Oake in 1674 was Colonel James Thompson.[3] His career in the meanwhile remains obscure.

[1] Peacock, p. 79.
[2] St Aldate's Defaulters, Bodleian MS. Add. D. 114, f. 24v.
[3] Original Will of Paul Smith preserved at Somerset House, made in 1678 and proved in the P.C.C. in 1685: 37 Cann.

A MR CLERKE (unidentified) was also lodging in the house in June 1643.[1]

[1] Bodleian MS. Add, D. 114, f. 24v.

MR UNTON CROKE, M.P.
(c. 1595-1671)

(Serjeant) Unton Croke, the fourth son of judge Sir John Croke, of Chilton, Buckinghamshire, by his wife, Catherine, daughter of Sir Michael Blount, of Mapledurham, Oxfordshire. He was a first cousin of Lucy, wife of Edward Heath. (See Introduction). He matriculated from Christ Church (as Umpton) in 1609/10, being called to the bar in 1616 and the bench in 1635.[1] He was appointed Deputy-Steward of Oxford University in 1619/20.[2] In 1624-5 he was assessed, under Stewards etc., as a privileged person of the University, living in St Aldate's, at 3s. 4d.[3] He was M.P. for Wallingford in 1626 and 1640. He married Anne, daughter of Richard Hore, of Marston, Oxfordshire, who brought him a messuage there. The house was rebuilt by Croke, who made it his principal residence. In 1645 the house was requisitioned as Fairfax's headquarters during the siege of Oxford, and in 1646 it accommodated the commissioners who treated about the surrender of the city.

Croke and his wife must, however, have made use of their St Aldate's house before the outbreak of the Civil War (see Mrs Christian Cartwell above). He was assessed at £10 and 16s. 'in lands', as of the South-West Ward, in the Subsidy Lists of 1641.[4] His sympathies were with the Parliamentarian party, with some of whose most prominent leaders (including Cromwell) he was connected. He would have disliked having to hand over three muskets to the King in 1642/3 and 1643.[5] He doubtless lived quietly at Marston during the War, the members of his family also absenting themselves from Oxford, and the house being perhaps first requisitioned by the Royalists and afterwards let. Croke's name does not occur in any of the St Aldate's parish taxation lists, nor does it appear in the Subsidy of 1648. Moreover, on 8 February 1648/9 'Bridgett, wife of Mr Unton Croke' was buried, not at St Aldate's, but at St Mary Magdalen's.[6] She was Serjeant Croke's daughter-in-law, the first wife of his second surviving son and namesake, who served as an officer in the Parliamentarian horse. The younger Unton's son and namesake, by his second wife, was, however, baptized at St Aldate's 17 March 1658/9.[7]

Croke was in high favour with Cromwell. He became a serjeant-at-law in 1654 and a commissioner for treason trials in 1656. He died 28 January 1670/1, and was buried at Marston, where there are memorial inscriptions to himself and his wife.

In June 1643 one of the defaulters was Croke's 'sonne gonne away to the Temple in London'.[8] This refers to Croke's eldest surviving son (Sir) RICHARD CROKE, who had been admitted to the Inner Temple in 1635 and was called to the bar in 1646 and the bench in 1662: he became a serjeant in 1675.[9] He was M.P. for the City of Oxford in 1654, 1656, 1659 (possibly with his father), and 1661-1679, and was Recorder of Oxford from 1660 until his death 15 September 1683. He was knighted in March 1680/1. He married Elizabeth (died 1683), daughter of Martin Wright, goldsmith and alderman of Oxford. There is a M.I. to him in Marston church.

Unton Croke's house was on the west side of Grandpont, being an entity of the Old Palace, Nos. 86 and 87 St Aldate's, at the south corner of Rose Place. On 21 January 1620/1 Thomas Barksdale and Joan his wife sold to Oliver and Thomas Smyth [q.v.] a tenement in St Aldate's for £100.[10] This tenement, on the west side of the main house, was a separate entity, and the dwelling was probably built by Edward Barksdale, Thomas' father (died 1595), who had acquired it between 1580 and 1595.[11] It would seem to have been let to Croke by the Smyths. The main house, with its east end abutting on Grandpont and its north front of five gabled bays, was built by Thomas Smyth between c. 1622 and 1628, but seems to have incorporated portions of an earlier building. The cost of erection was said to have been more than £1,300.[12] The date 1628 is on the corbels supporting the middle window on the first floor. The east room on the first floor has an oval cartouche displaying the Arms of Smyth impaling those of Wilmott.[13] This main house was doubtless occupied by the Thomas Smyths until 1637 when, on the death of his father, Thomas inherited the capital messuage in Slaying Lane.

Between 1637 and 1642 Thomas Smyth must have sold the main house to Croke, the smaller (Croke's previous home) being taken over by John Smyth [q.v.]. After the death of Thomas in 1646, his widow, Margaret, was installed in the smaller entity. This is clear from the settlement made by her eldest son, Oliver, on 11 September 1648 on his intended bride, Anne Bourne, in which he specifies 'All that Mansion or Dwelling house in Grampoole wherein Ales Perye sometymes wife of John Perrye doctor of divinetye & Eleanor Barksdale widd did lately inhabit & now in the tenure or occupation of Margaret Smyth Widd . . . heretofore parcell of the possessions of the late dissolved howse or Priorye of the Blackfryars . . . since the inheritance of Will ffryer esq.'[14]

In 1665 the larger portion (thirteen hearths) was let, presumably by Croke, to Abraham Davis, whose wife kept a girls' school.[15] Serjeant Croke left no Will, but it is clear that, while his son Richard inherited the Marston property, and owned a town house in All Saints' parish, his son Unton received the St Aldate's house as his portion, by which time the separate entities seem to have been united. The younger Unton was living there in 1672.[16] A letter from Thomas Gilbert to Lord Anglesey, dated 19 November 1679, describes Croke's house as 'standing in the Entrance to Grampole, over against the lower end of Christ Church'. He adds that, 'the house is no College Lease . . . but good freehold.'[17] According to Bliss,[18] Unton Croke devised 'all that mansion house and garden in St Aldates [bounded by] the street east, part of the river Thames west and north and a garden south' to three of his daughters, but in his Will, proved in the P.C.C. 4 May 1694,[19] he left all the remainder of his estate real and personal to them, without specific mention of the St Aldate's house. When a fourth daughter sold it in 1733, its measurements were given as 228 feet long, 32 feet at the east end, and 45 feet at the west.[20] On 4 January 1729/30 Hearne recorded that 'the Garden plot is not large & the Hall but small: all the other rooms (wch are many) very good'.[21]

(For the Crokes see Sir Alexander Croke, *The Genealogical History of the Croke Family*, Vol. II (1823), pp. 511-14 (Unton senior) and 514-23 (Richard): for the latter see also *Oxoniensia*, Vol. XXV (1960), pp. 74-5)

[1] *Members of the Inner Temple*, 1547-1660 (1877), p. 191.
[2] *Register*, Vol. II, Pt. I, p. 242. 'Two servants of Mrj Vmpton Croke Vniusit Oxon Subsenescallj' were matriculated as privileged persons in 1631 and 1635 respectively (University Archives S P 2, ff. 348 and 349).
[3] Ib. W.P. γ 28 (7), f. 7.
[4] City Archives B. 1. 4. c.
[5] *R.O.P.*, Part I, pp. 70, 76, and 79: 12 March 1642/3, as of All Saints: 21 and 24 April, as of St Aldate's.
[6] Wood, *C. of O.*, Vol. III, p. 227.
[7] Ib., p. 200.
[8] Bodleian MS. Add. D. 114, f. 24v.
[9] *Members of the Inner Temple*, p. 286.
[10] Feet of Fines, quoted in *Survey of South-West Ward*, Nos. 24 and 23 (a).
[11] Op. cit. and R.C.H.M. *City of Oxford*, p. 175.
[12] Hearne *Collections*, ed. H.E. Salter (Oxford Historical Society), Vol. X (1915), p. 224.
[13] For a full description see R.C.H.M. and Plates 38 and 39 therein. There is a drawing by J.C. Buckler (1821) in the Bodleian (MS. Don. a. 2 (10)).
[14] City Archives A. 5. 4, f. 53v. See also St Aldate's parish taxation lists for 1647 and *S. and T.*, p. 169.
[15] *S. and T.*, p. 192 and Wood, *Life and Times*, Vol. I, pp. 386-7.

[16] *Journal of James Yonge* (1963), p. 142.
[17] Quoted in *Collections*, loc. cit.
[18] Wood, *L. and T.*, Vol. I, p. 368.
[19] 96 Box.
[20] Wood, *L. and T.*, p. 368 and *Survey of South-West Ward*, No. 24.
[21] *Collections*, loc. cit.

SERJEANT-MAJOR (later LIEUTENANT-COLONEL SIR) WILLIAM LEIGHTON OR LAYTON

According to Wood,[1] he was a near relative of Sir William Leighton, poet and composer (fl. 1603-1614), of Plaish, Shropshire.[2] William was possibly the son of Henry Leighton, Sir William's half-brother, and himself a son of William Leighton (1533-1607), by his second wife.[3]

Before the year 1639 Leighton served in foreign parts.[4] He served throughout the Civil War in the Lifeguard of Foot, and played his part in the events described on pp. 37-43. He fought at Edgehill, where he is said to have been wounded, but he signed for ammunition, as a major, 4 November 1642.[5] He took part in the storming of Cirencester 2 February 1642/3, fighting with the detachment from the Oxford garrison under Sir Lewis Kirke. On 18 February 1642/3 he signed a receipt, again as major, at Oxford for arms and equipment for the Lifeguard.[6] He was with Prince Maurice at Little Dean, 11 April 1643.[7] He was already lodging, together with two men, at Croke's house in June 1643.[8] He served in the Cornish campaign of 1644 and signed the letter to Essex on 8 August. Leighton was promoted lieutenant-colonel by 3 January 1644/5. He was created D.C.L. of Oxford University 22 April 1645. He fought at Naseby but, although the regiment of which he was lieutenant-colonel was annihilated, he himself escaped. He was knighted at Hereford 5[9] September 1645 and took part in the defence of that place. Walker calls him a vigilant and faithful commander.[10]

In 1648 Leighton was among the defenders of Colchester, and was taken prisoner 12 June.[11] He appears to have been in the King's service abroad in 1654.[12] He is mentioned as commanding Fleetwood's troops in the Swedish service in 1656 and 1657.[13]

Leighton was involved in the Royalist plot of 1658 and was arrested on 15 May. He was imprisoned in the Tower from May 1658 to February 1658/9.[14] He was an Indigent Officer[15] after the Restoration. On 17 March 1663/4 he was commissioned as a captain in the King's Regiment of Footguards under Colonel John Russell [q.v.], late Henry Washington's Company. He retired 18 October 1665.[16]

[1] *Fasti*, Vol. II, p. 88.
[2] See *D.N.B.*
[3] See *Transactions* of the Shropshire Archaeological Society, Vol. II (1879), p. 293.
[4] National Library of Wales, Chirk Castle MS. F. 7442.
[5] *R.O.P.*, Part I, p. 160.
[6] Ib., p. 199.
[7] *The Vindication of Richard Atkyns.*
[8] St Aldate's Defaulters, MS. Add. D. 114, f. 24v. No answer was received from them.
[9] Symonds says 4 September.
[10] P. 129.
[11] P. Morant, *Essex*, Vol. I (1768), p. 59.
[12] *C.C.S.P.*, Vol. II, pp. 359 and 382.
[13] Ib., Vol. III, p. 116 and *Nicholas Papers*, Vol. IV, p. 26.

[14] MS. Rawlinson A. 57, ff. 101 and 413: see also W.C. Abbott, *Writings and Speeches of Oliver Cromwell,* Vol. IV (1947), p. 803.
[15] *I.O.*, col. 90. He was of London and Westminster.
[16] Dalton, Vol. I, pp. 37 and 43.

MR JOHN SMYTH, M.P.
(1609-1657)

Maltster. The third and youngest son of Alderman Oliver Smyth, brewer, by his first wife, Anne Bussey (see under his eldest brother, Thomas Smyth). He was baptized at St Aldate's 23 February 1608/9,[1] and matriculated from Wadham College 6 February 1623/4. He was admitted a freeman and chosen a bailiff in 1630, being junior bailiff in 1631. An active member of the city government, he became mayor in 1639 and was a member of the mayor's council in 1640, but was turned out in 1648.[2]

On 30 November 1640 Smyth was elected one of the two M.P.s for Oxford City vice Lord Andover.[3] He was at first hostile to the King, as appears from two interesting letters written by himself and his fellow member for Oxford, John Whistler (they had both withdrawn from Westminster), 3 and 5 September 1642, to Speaker Lenthall.[4] The first letter describes the condition of Oxford in mid-August 1642, and recounts a visit of Sir Richard Cave [q.v] about the proposed fortifications, the scheme for which was much disliked by the writers. They reported that: 'Both of us have of late been publicly scorned and derided and direfully menaced, and Mr Smith hath received some blows for no other reason but because he is of the Parliament'. On the advice of their friends both men had left Oxford and retired to Abingdon. Smyth was still in Oxford at the time of Sir John Byron's entry 28 August for one of Bailiff Heron's charges was that 'Mr Burges Smith and his wife were assaulted' by the soldiers and scholars.[5]

Nevertheless, Smyth and Whistler sat in the Oxford Parliament of 1643/4, although neither of them was disabled, and both signed the letter to Essex of 27 January 1643/4. It is likely that Smyth may subsequently have withdrawn from Oxford, as his name does not appear in any of the St Aldate's parish taxation lists for 1645 and 1647, or in the Subsidy of 1648. But on 12 November 1646 he petitioned to compound on the Oxford Articles, and on 3 December 1646 was fined £220.[6] His fine was accepted on 26 September 1648.[7]

Smyth married 14 October 1627 Elizabeth (died 1673), daughter of Henry Bosworth, brewer, of St Giles' parish.[8] He died 4 November 1657,[9] and was buried at St Aldate's on 7 November.[10] The churchwardens received 6s. 8d. for his grave.

In his Will he mentions his wife, whom he appointed his executrix, his sons, John and Henry, and two daughters. His capital messuage was in Kennington and Radley, Berkshire: he also had property at Garsington, Oxfordshire. The Kennington property had been left to him under his father's Will.[11]

[Will: P.C.C. 1657: 472 Ruthen: made 28 October 1657: proved 25 November 1657].

Smyth's house was the smaller entity of the Old Palace (see under Unton Croke), and was known as Hither Friers. In the Hearth Tax of 1665 Elizabeth Smyth, his widow, is entered as living in this smaller entity (nine hearths).[12] He was of Oxford at the time when he made his Will, and in this he mentions the 'goods and househould stuffe in the house I now dwell in', but he did not bequeath the house. His lodger, Montague Bertie, Earl of Lindsey [q.v.], paid all the taxes of 1645, and in one case the entry reads: 'The Earle of Lindsies howse'.

(There is brief account of Smyth [Smith] in Keeler, p. 340. She does not mention the letters to Lenthall)

[1] Wood, *C. of O.*, Vol. III, p. 199.
[2] *O.C.A.* 1626-1665, pp. 25, 29, 36, 87, 94, and 155.
[3] Ib. p. 98.
[4] H.M.C., *Portland*, Vol. I, pp. 56-9 and 59-60: see also *C.J.*, Vol. II, p.

754.
[5] *The Manuscripts of the House of Lords*, Vol. XI, New Series, p. 326.
[6] *C.C.C.*, p. 1563.
[7] *C.J.*, Vol. VI, p. 33.
[8] Wood, *C. of O.*, Vol. III, p. 202.
[9] Wood, *L. and T.*, Vol. I, p. 231.
[10] Wood, *C. of O.*, Vol. III, p. 208.
[11] P.C.C. 82 Goare.
[12] *S. and T.*, p. 192.

MONTAGUE BERTIE, second EARL OF LINDSEY
(1608?-1666)

He held the office of Lord Great Chamberlain. He was appointed a Gentleman of the Privy Chamber in 1634 but does not appear as such in 1641.[1] He was colonel of the King's Lifeguard and was taken prisoner at Edgehill, where his father, the first Earl, was slain, being detained until 11 August 1643, when he was exchanged. He was appointed a Gentleman of the Bedchamber in that year, and remained one until 1649. On 26 December 1643 he was made P.C. He sat in the Oxford Parliament of January 1643/4, and signed the letter of the Lords to Essex written at Oxford on 27 January. He was wounded at the Battle of Naseby,[2] and was at Oxford when it surrendered in June 1646. He compounded on the Oxford Articles 22 September 1646, and was fined £5,372 13s. 6d. and £1,200.[3]
(For full accounts see *C.P.* and *D.N.B.*)

[1] L.C. 3/1.
[2] Bulstrode Whitelocke, *Memorials*, Vol. I (1853), p. 449.
[3] *C.C.C.*, pp. 1501-4.

ANNE, LADY LAKE
(died c. 1656)

The third daughter of Francis Plowden (died 1652), of Shiplake, Oxfordshire, and Plowden, Shropshire, by his wife, Mary, daughter of Thomas Fermor, of Somerton, Oxfordshire, and sister of Sir Richard Fermor.[1] She married, as his second wife, Sir Arthur Lake, second son of Sir Thomas Lake, Secretary of State to James I. He, who was born c. 1598, was of New College, Hart Hall, and the Middle Temple. He was knighted in 1617, was M.P. for Minehead in 1624 and Bridgwater 1625-6: he died in Drury Lane in December 1633.
The Lakes' only child, her father's heiress, was Mary Lake, who must have been born c. 1626, as she was seven years old in 1633.
On 8 January 1644/5 Lady Lake and her daughter were of Covent Garden, when the mother was assessed at £250 and the daughter, on 27 January 1644/5, at £100. Lady Lake was respited until sequestration was taken of her estate, and Mary Lake was discharged on affidavit that she had not £100.[2]
Lady Lake was a recusant.[3] Great Dunmow rectory, Essex, had been her jointure, but it had been sequestered on account of her recusancy (see Nicholas Copley). On 19 June 1654 the granting of a pass for Lady Lake and a servant to go beyond sea was moved and denied.[4] But on 7 November 1654 it was stated that she had been absent from England.[5]. Her claim to the house and grounds at Dunmow (the only home that she had) was allowed. She was dead by 3 December 1656.[6]

[1] See Le Neve, *Knights*, Harleian Society Vol. VIII (1873), p. 243 and *Visitation of Oxfordshire*, p. 277.

[2] *C.A.M.*, p. 499.
[3] Her case is printed in *C.C.C.*, p. 2369.
[4] *C.S.P.D.* 1654, p. 214.
[5] *C.C.C.*, p. 2369.
[6] *C.S.P.D.* 1656-7, p. 185.

In June 1643 John Smyth had lodging with him 'The Lord Spenser & 4 servants he thought not fitt that Noblemen should pay, but when others did he would'.[1]

HENRY SPENCER, third BARON SPENCER OF WORMLEIGHTON and first EARL OF SUNDERLAND (1620-1643)

The eldest son of William Spencer, second Baron Spencer, by his wife, Penelope Wriothesley, eldest daughter of Henry Wriothesley, third Earl of Southampton, he was born at Althorp and baptized at Brington 23 November 1620. He matriculated from Magdalen College, Oxford, 8 May 1635, and graduated M.A. 31 August 1636, on the occasion of the King and Queen's visit to Oxford. He succeeded his father 19 December 1636.

Spencer was nominated Lord Lieutenant of Northamptonshire by Parliament 5 March 1641/2, but joined the King in August and served in the Royalist army 1642-3. He was present at Edgehill. On 14 January 1642/3 he 'mustered and trained . . . one half of this country here' [i.e. Northampton].[2] On 5 June 1643 various letters written from Oxford to Lady Spencer were intercepted at Wycombe.[3] On 6 June 1643 he was created Earl of Sunderland at Oxford.

In July Sunderland was with the King's Horse before Bristol. On 9 August he was back again at Oxford. He served at the siege of Gloucester, whence he wrote to his wife: 'I shall endeavour to provide you better lodgings at Oxford, and will be careful to furnish them according to your desire'.[4]

He married in 1639 Dorothy Sidney, eldest daughter of Robert Sidney, second Earl of Leicester. He was killed at the First Battle of Newbury 20 September 1643.
[Will: P.C.C. 1646: 191 Twisse: proved 2 December 1646].
(For a full account see *C.P.*)

[1] St Aldate's Defaulters, Bodleian MS. Add. D. 114, f. 24v.
[2] H.M.C., *Portland*, Vol. I, p. 89.
[3] *C.J.*, Vol. III, p. 115.
[4] Mrs Henry Ady, *Sacharissa* (1901), p. 96.

WIDOW WIXON

Unidentified. Her name appears in all the St Aldate's parish taxation lists of 1645. It is just possible that she is the 'vidua Wixon' who owed Oriel College two years' rent at 4s. 4d. per annum in 1646 and one year's rent in 1647, no location being specified.[1]
Her house was presumably on the west side of Grandpont.

[1] Oriel College Muniments I.E.I, Rentals 1647-1729.

FRANCIS LANE

He heads the section on Wheelwrights in the List of the Train of His Majesty's Artillery 12 February 1643/4:[1] 'ffr. Lane Peter Norrey Mr Wheelwrights'. The names of fifteen ordinary wheelwrights follow. On 7 April 1644 he signed for two hammers and a 'pincher' from the King's stores.[2] He must be the 'Fra: Lane Carpenter' included in a 'Bye Trayne of 2 Peeces of Brasse Ordinance to attend an Army of 1500 foote' 6 November 1642.[3]

[1] S.P. 16/500/40 A, f. 7. We are indebted for this reference to Dr Ian Roy.
[2] *R.O.P.*, Part I, p. 125.
[3] Ib., p. 161.

JOHN MASTON, TAILOR TO EDWARD SACKVILLE, fourth EARL OF DORSET (1590-1652)

Unidentified.
Lord Dorset was made a P.C. in 1626 and Chamberlain to the Queen in 1628. He joined the King at York, and was present at Edgehill. He was Lord Chamberlain from 21 January 1643/4 to 27 April 1646, and early in 1644 was made Lord Privy Seal and President of the Council. He sat in the Oxford Parliament and signed the letter of the Lords to Essex written at Oxford on 27 January. He was one of the signatories of the capitulation of Oxford in June 1646. He petitioned to compound on the Oxford Articles 24 September 1646, and was fined £4,360, but this sum was reduced to £2,415 on 25 March 1647.[1] His son Edward married the daughter of Edward Wray [q.v.].
(For full accounts see *C.P.* and *D.N.B.*)

[1] *C.C.C.*, p. 1509.

MR THOMAS SEYMOUR
(c.1601-1669)

Manciple of Corpus Christi College, yeoman. His family was descended from the Seymours of East Garston, Berkshire. He was uncle of Elizabeth Seymour, first wife of Christopher Wood, a younger brother of Anthony Wood.[1] On 5 April 1622, at the age of twenty-one, he was entered as a privileged person of the University: he is described as 'Berks pleb. f' and 'famulus Dris Anyan'.[2] Dr Thomas Anyan was President of Corpus from 1614 to 1629. Seymour became manciple of Corpus in 1626/7.[3]

Seymour was a churchwarden of St Aldate's in 1633-4 and 1634-5. A halberd and sword were delivered by him into the King's stores on 24 April 1643.[4] Arms were delivered to him in October 1643.[5] His name appears in all the St Aldate's parish taxation lists of 1645 and 1647. He was assessed[6] at 20s. and 8s. 'in lands' in the Subsidy Lists of 1641 and at 2s. 6d. in the Subsidy of 1648.[7] He refused to submit to the Parliamentary Visitors in the latter year and was expelled on 2 October,[8] but he was restored in 1660,[9] retiring before his death. He married Jane, daughter of John Price, cook of Pembroke College (see under Abel Parne), who left her a court cupboard and 30s. in his Will proved in the Court of the Chancellor of Oxford University in August 1637.[10] 'Thomas Seymour my sonne in lawe' was appointed one of the overseers, and the grandchild, John Seymour, received a silver spoon. He died 28 December 1669,[11] and was buried at St Aldate's on 30 December.[12]

[Will: P.C.C. 1670: 65 Penn: made 10 December 1669: proved 17 May 1670. His wife was appointed his executrix].

Seymour's house was on the west side of Grandpont, No. 84 St Aldate's. It was All Souls College property. On 30 October 1630 the College leased to Thomas Seymour, of the University of Oxford, yeoman, 'one Tenement wth a backside sett lying and being in Grandpont in Oxon . . . abutting out on the east vpon the streete, and vpon the south vpon a tenemt or house of Mr Bartons [sic] and the backside running downe from the house to the River wch runneth southward behinde the same'. The lease was for twenty years and the rent 13s. 4d. per annum. Seymour's bond is enclosed, and both documents are signed by him and have a seal attached.[13] On 2 November 1638 Seymour received a second lease from the College on the same terms, but there is no signature or seal.[14] By 1653 Seymour had been succeeded in the tenancy by Thomas Hall, maltster.[15] There were five hearths in 1665.[16] Thomas Seymour and his wife are entered in the Poll Tax of 1667 as living in St Aldate's.[17]

The western part of the present structure was built probably c. 1600. It is of two storeys with attics.[18]

[1] *L. and T.*, Vol. I, pp. 27 and 30.
[2] *Register*, Vol. II, Pt. I, p. 406.
[3] Thomas Fowler, *History of Corpus Christi College*, Oxford Historical Society, Vol. XXV (1893), p. 457.
[4] *R.O.P.*, Part I, p. 83.
[5] City Archives E. 4. 5, ff. 55-55v.
[6] Ib. B. 1. 4. c.
[7] *S. and T.*, p. 169.
[8] *Register of the Visitors*, p. 193.
[9] Wood, *Annals*, Vol. II, Pt. ii, p. 605.
[10] Hyp. b. 31.
[11] Wood, *L. and T.*, Vol. II, p. 180.
[12] Wood, *C. of O.*, Vol. III, p. 209.

[13] All Souls College Leases 57 (a) and (b).
[14] All Souls Leases 63.
[15] All Souls Rentals 14, 1653.
[16] *S. and T.*, p. 192.
[17] Ib., p. 264.
[18] The house is fully described in R.C.H.M. *City of Oxford*, p. 175: an early seventeenth-century panelled over-mantel is illustrated on Plate 19. See also *Survey of South-West Ward*, No. 23, but Salter is mistaken in stating that Seymour received a further lease in 1651.

MRS JULIAN ELLYOT
(died 1663)

She was the mother of Thomas Ellyot [q.v.] who in 1643/4 was a servant of Prince Charles. Research has shewn (what has not previously been known) that he was the eldest son of James Ellyot, servant to Charles I as Prince of Wales,[1] and a Groom of his Privy Chamber as King. James Ellyot was buried at Richmond, Surrey, 21 October 1634,[2] his Will being proved in the P.C.C.[3] by his 'deare and loving wife Julian', whom he appointed residuary legatee.

Julian Ellyot received a warrant as His Majesty's sempstress on 17 December 1635.[4] She appears as sempstress for His Majesty's person in 1641.[5] She was buried at Richmond 8 July 1663.[6]

James and Julian Ellyot had at least four daughters: Elizabeth, baptized at St Margaret's, Westminster, 16 November 1615;[7] Mary, baptized there 22 March 1619/20; Magdalen baptized there 17 November 1621, buried at Richmond 19 February 1671/2; and Ursula, living in 1680. Elizabeth had her mother's post in reversion in 1641[8] so that she is likely to have been one of the two sisters lodging in Seymour's house in 1643/4. She was buried at Richmond 27 September 1680.[9]

From Elizabeth Ellyot's Will it emerges that she was in the service of Catherine of Braganza: 'And if in case the Arrears which are due vnto me from the Queene shall be had and Received then I doe give and bequeath to my Neice Charlott Ellyot the sume of one hundred pounds' in addition to the £100 already left to her. Among many bequests of plate etc. to nephews and nieces, Charlotte's legacies from her aunt included 'my brother Thomas Ellyot's picture'.

[Will: P.C.C. 1680: 116 Bath: made 4 September 1680: proved 25 September 1680].

[1] *C.S.P.D..* 1611-18, p. 444.
[2] *Registers*, ed. J. Challenor C. Smith, Vol. I (1903), p. 190.
[3] 88 Seager.
[4] *C.S.P.D.* 1635, p. 571.
[5] L.C. 3/1.
[6] *Registers*, Vol. I, p. 216.
[7] *Registers*, p. 91.
[8] L.C. 3/1.
[9] *Registers*, Vol. I, p. 233.

MR THOMAS ELLYOT
(1612-1677)

He was himself lodging, together with his man, at Seymour's house in June 1643, when they were both reported to be out of town.[1] He was baptized at St Margaret's, Westminster, 29 April 1612.[2] He was a page to Charles I by 1633,[3] and a Groom of the Privy Chamber by 1639.[4] He appears in 1641 as a Groom,[5] but his name was afterwards crossed out. On 3 February 1641/2 he was said to have been declared an enemy of the State.[6] In May 1642 he was employed by the King to fetch the Great Seal from Lord Littleton to York.[7] Later he was transferred to the service of Prince Charles, and on 28 January 1648/9 was described as a Gentleman of the Bedchamber.[8]

As Prince Charles' servant Ellyot wrote to Prince Rupert in May, June, and October 1644.[9] He was sent by Charles I to France[10] in order to prevent his attendance on Prince Charles in the West, and he reached the Queen in February 1644/5, remaining for a time in France. He was besieged with (Sir) Edmund Wyndham and his wife, Christabel (Pyne), at Bridgwater in July 1645. Mrs Wyndham had been the Prince's nurse. Ellyot was taken prisoner but was exchanged in August 1648.[11] He rejoined his master (now Charles II) at The Hague in 1649, and remained with the King during his exile. After the Restoration he continued as Groom of the Bedchamber and was appointed Master of the Harrier Hounds and Keeper of the King's House at Newmarket.[12]

Ellyot married Elizabeth (c. 1630-post 1680), second daughter of (Sir) Edmund Wyndham, who became Knight Marshal after the Restoration. Thomas had been a protégé of Christabel Wyndham. After her husband's death, Elizabeth married a certain Walker.[13] Ellyot died between 26 July and 14 August 1677.

In his Will he mentions his sons, Thomas (residuary legatee and executor), Edmund, and Lyonell, and his daughters, Charlotte and Mary. In the memorandum he ordained that each daughter should receive an extra £300 'to be paid out of the ffirst moneys that shalbe received from the King.'

[Will: P.C.C. 1677: 83 Hale: made 6 January 1674/5, with memorandum of 26 July 1677: proved 14 August 1677].

Ellyot left his 'loveing wife . . . my house with the Gardens Stables and howses and appurtenñcs . . . in St James streete . . . Comonly called by the name of Cobblers Hall wherein I now live'. Thomas held a lease from Henry Jermyn, Earl of St Albans dated 1 April 1661 for thirty years from Michaelmas 1660 of 'One Messuage a Stable a Coach-house and wash house in St James Street'.[14] He received a grant of ground in Old Spring Garden for building a house 31 January 1661/2.[15]

[1] St Aldate's Defaulters, Bodleian MS. Add. D. 114, f. 24v.
[2] *Registers*, p. 83.
[3] *C.S.P.D.* 1633-4, p. 220.
[4] Ib. 1639, p. 139.
[5] L.C. 3/1.
[6] *C.S.P.D.* 1641-3, p. 274.
[7] Clarendon, Bk. V, §§ 203 note, 212, and 214.
[8] *C.C.C.*, p. 1897.
[9] B.M. MS. Add. 18, 981 and S.P.D.: the latter contain a letter of 17 June 1644 dated from Burford (seal with Arms).
[10] A letter from Charles I to the Queen, written from Oxford in December 1644, is endorsed on the copy 'by *Tom Elliot*' (*Reliquiae Sacrae Carolinae* (1650), p. 248).
[11] *C.J.*, Vol. V, p. 668.
[12] *C.T.B.*, passim.
[13] See P.C.C. 116 Bath.
[14] B.M. MS. Add. 22,063, item 83. We owe this reference to Mr Francis Sheppard, General Editor of the L.C.C. *Survey of London*, of which see Vol. XXX (1960), p. 295.
[15] *C.S.P.D.* 1661-2, p. 259.

In June 1643 'Thomas Clutterbooks house' is entered after that of Thomas Seymour. THOMAS CLUTTERBOOK is unidentified, and so is his lodger RALPH MARSH, 'one of the court: his wife answered that when the king payd her husband, he should pay'.[1]

[1] St Aldate's Defaulters, Bodleian MS. Add. D. 114, f. 24v.

MR WALTER CAVE
(died 1663)

Mercer and brewer. The second son of Thomas Cave, of St Helen's, Worcester, by his wife, Katharine, daughter of Walter Jones, of Witney, Oxfordshire, whom he married in 1592.[1] Thomas matriculated from St Mary Hall, Oxford, 11 October 1587, aged seventeen. His elder son was Sir Richard Cave [q.v.].
On 7 July 1619 Walter Cave, described as the son of Thomas Cave, late of Witney, was apprenticed to Thomas Cooper, of Oxford, mercer:[2] he obtained his freedom 13 September 1639.[3] He was admitted to brew by the University 20 December 1638.[4] He was elected senior bailiff 17 September 1639 and thereafter held many civic offices.[5] They included those of keykeeper, member of the mayor's council (he was chosen as assistant in August 1648 in place of the ejected Leonard Bowman),[6] and mayor in 1650.[7] He appears to have been suspected by the Royalist party in Oxford in 1642 since late one night in September, following the arrival of Sir John Byron, his house was searched by the mayor and Vice-Chancellor.[8] But he conformed during the King's occupation, and gave £5 when the city presented Charles with £520 on his entry after Edgehill.[9] He was supervisor for St Aldate's for work on the bulwarks 9 October 1643.[10] He contributed £5 towards the loan to the Lords Commissioners in October 1645,[11] and on 27 April lent them £50 for the payment of the soldiers of the Oxford garrison.[12] His name, bracketed with that of his partner in the brewing business, Mr [William] Banting, appears in all the St Aldate's parish taxation lists of 1645 and 1647. They were assessed at 9s. 6d. in the Subsidy of 1648.[13] On 26 October 1658 Cave was one of those chosen to wait on Richard Cromwell with an address of congratulation.[14]
The Brasenose Junior Bursar's Book of 1644[15] shews that Cave was one of the three brewers (the other two being Thomas Smyth and Edward Carpenter, qq.v.) who supplied the College with beer. He signs several receipts at the end of the book. His name also occurs in the St John's Buttery Book for 1642-3 and in the Magdalen Bursar's Books for the 'forties and 'fifties.
Cave married twice; first, Alice, daughter of Thomas Williams, of the Star Inn, Oxford; secondly, Jane, daughter of . . . Clemson, of Abingdon.[16] He had a numerous family.
Cave 'died in his house in Grandpoole' 21 February 1662/3.[17] He was buried at St Aldate's 23 February.[18] Jane appears as living in St Aldate's in the Hearth Tax of 1665, when there were nine hearths in her house,[19] and in the Poll Tax of 1667, together with her two sons and three daughters.[20] She was still alive in 1680.[21]
[Will: P.C.C. 1663: 76 Juxon: made 30 June 1662: proved 2 June 1663 by his widow].
Cave's house was on the west side of Grandpont, Nos. 82 and 83 St Aldate's. It was his own property. On 14 February 1638/9 Richard Hannes of Holywell (see under William Pearson), and his wife, Jane, confirmed a grant made on 20 July 1638 whereby they sold to Walter Cave, mercer, and William Banting, tanner, 'All that their . . . Capitall Messuage or Tenemt wherein the said Richard and Jane did lately inhabite & dwell and wherein the said Walter Cave and William Banting doe now dwell And the Brewhouse, Maulthouse, buildinges, fuell houses, Courts Backsides' etc. 'to the said Messuage belonginge scituate . . . in Grampoole als Grampond in the pishe of St Aldates . . . on the West side of the kinges high streete there And alsoe all that their Messuage or Tenemt called little Morehall wth all houses, bbuildinges' etc. 'to the same Messuage belonginge scituate . . . in Grampoole . . . adioyninge to the South pte of the said Capitall Messuage whereof pte was lately in thoccupacon of the said Richard Hannes And was occupied with

the said Capitall Messuage And the residue of the same other Mesuage called little Morehall is now in the occupacon of one Richard Stringer Cooper . . . All the bargained messuages and premises are scituate together betweene the Lane in the said pishe called Mill Lane on the south And a Tenemt of Alsoules Colledge in Oxon on the North [Seymour's house] And Abuttinge Eastward vppon the said streete and Westward vppon the little streame Ryver or watercourse runn'ige betweene the backyardes . . . of the said Messuages and the wall of the late black fryars'.[22] The property had been the inheritance of the late Alderman Richard Hannes. Rent was due on Littlemore Hall to Magdalen College.[23]

The house was built in the fifteenth century, but was largely remodelled in the first half of the seventeenth century. It is of two storeys with attics.[24]

In his Will Cave devised the 'Inheritance of the Messuage Brewhouse and all and singular outhouses and appertenances whatsoever to the said premises belonginge or in any way appertaining being now in my own possession and occupac̄on within the parish of St Aldates in the Citty of Oxford or the Suburbs or Liberties thereof and also the Enheritance of my Messuage and Maltehouse . . . wherein my sonn in Law Matthew Treadwell [see under Mrs Joan Tredwell] doth now inhabite in the said parrish of St Aldates . . . vnto my Loveinge Wife Jane Cave'.

Jane Cave continued the brewing business, and together with Treadwell and other Oxford brewers, got into trouble in 1666 for 'making undue entries and mixing beer with other warts' after it had been gauged and for abusing the gauger. Jane and Matthew had to pay to the Farmer of Excise of Oxfordshire moneys due from them for excise, their books being submitted for arbitration to Sergeant Holloway [q.v.], plus £40 for the Farmer's expenses in the case.[25]

[1] *Visitation of Worcestershire* 1682-3, ed. W.C. Metcalfe (1883), p. 29: Cave of Evesham.
[2] City Archives L. 5. 2, f. 58.
[3] Ib., no folio number.
[4] *Register*, Vol. II, Pt. I, p. 330.
[5] See *O.C.A.* 1626-1665, passim.
[6] Ib., p. 155.
[7] Ib., p. 175.
[8] *The Manuscripts of the House of Lords*, Vol. XI, New Series, p. 326.
[9] *O.C.A.* 1626-1665, p. 379.
[10] Op. cit., loc. cit.
[11] City Archives E. 4. 6, ff. 1-2: *O.C.A.* 1626-1665, p. 453.
[12] *O.C.A.* 1626-1665, p. 459.
[13] *S. and T.*, p. 169.
[14] *O.C.A.* 1626-1665, p. 236.
[15] A. 8. 11*.
[16] Wood, *L. and T.*, Vol. I, p. 469. He mistakenly calls Jane 'Elizabeth', as he took the burial of Elizabeth, wife of Cave's son Walter, at St Aldate's on 21 November 1668, to be that of the elder Cave's widow.
[17] Op. cit., loc. cit.
[18] Wood, *C. of O.*, Vol. III, p. 208.
[19] *S. and T.*, p. 192.
[20] Ib., p. 261.
[21] *Cart. H. St J.B.*, Vol. III, p. 328.
[22] City Archives A. 5. 4, ff. 32v-33.
[23] *Cart. H. St J.B.*, Vol. III, p. 328 and Wood, *C. of O.*, Vol. I, p. 301: he describes it as a brewhouse. See also *Survey of South-West Ward*, Nos. 21 and 22.
[24] It is fully described in R.C.H.M. *City of Oxford*, pp. 174-5: the exterior is illustrated on Plate 12 and two early seventeenth-century plaster ceilings on Plate 40. There is a drawing by J.C. Buckler (1811) in the Bodleian (MS. Don.

a. 2 (8)).
[25] *C.T.B.*, Vol. I, pp. 716 and 724.

SIR GEORGE BENYON
(died c. 1669)

The second son of John Benyon, of Whitchurch, Shropshire, by his wife, Katherine, daughter of Henry Evanson, of Ash, Shropshire. By trade George Benyon was a mercer, sometimes styled a 'silkman', and was Queen's mercer in the reign of Charles I. He was a very wealthy man. He was of Cheapside and Muswell Hill, and before the outbreak of the Civil War was Receiver of Crown Lands for Northamptonshire and Rutland, where he had property.

Benyon was the leading spirit of the revolt against the Militia Ordinance, and presented a petition against it as overruling the municipal authority of the lord mayor of London 24 February 1641/2. He was imprisoned 26 February. He was then impeached, the engrossed articles against him being read 29 March 1642. He was sentenced by the Lords on 8 April 1642 to be disfranchised, pronounced incapable of holding any office in the City, and assigned to Colchester gaol for two years, with a fine of £3,000.[1]

Benyon was pardoned by the King from York 14 June 1642, and the sentence was quashed. He joined Charles I, and was knighted at Beverley 28 July 1642. In 1660 he complained that in 1642 his official Receiver's papers and his other goods had been stolen from his house in Cheapside.[2] In August of that year £4,000 or £5,000 in gold which was ready to be dispatched to the King at York by Benyon, was found and diverted to Guildhall.[3]

Benyon was involvd in Waller's plot in May 1643. He was in charge of the city stores at Oxford, and was one of the two overseers of provisions for 'strangers' in St Aldate's.[4] He lent money to the King there 'to relieve the pressing occasions'.[5] He was sequestered[6] and assessed at £2,000 14 February 1644/5.[7] He was one of those who bound themselves for repayment of moneys lent on the Oxford Engagement for the King's service.[8]

After the Restoration Benyon resumed his Crown Receivership in Northamptonshire and was also an Excise Commissioner.[9]

He married Alice (living 1651), daughter of Francis West, of London.[10] He had four daughters, Alice, Elizabeth, Sarah, and Mary, all of whom married. It is not possible to say which daughter was with her parents in Oxford. Benyon died about November 1669.[11] In a printed pedigree[12] his Will is stated to be dated 1669, but it was not proved in the P.C.C.

[1] Clarendon, Book V, § 51: *C.J.* and *L.J.* (his defence): V. Pearl, *London and the Outbreak of the Puritan Revolution* (1961).
[2] *C.T.B.*, Vol. I, p. 100.
[3] *C.S.P.D.* 1641-3, p. 368.
[4] MS. Harleian 6084, f. 173.
[5] *C.T.B.*, Vol. I, p. 241: a warrant for £450 to be paid to him is dated 4 May 1661.
[6] *C.C.C.*, pp. 2421-2.
[7] *C.A.M.*, pp. 345-9.
[8] Ib., p. 996.
[9] *C.T.B.*, passim.
[10] *Visitation of London* 1634, Harleian Society, Vol. XV (1880), p. 65: *Familiae Minorum Gentium*, Harleian Society, Vol. XXXVII (1894), p. 413.
[11] *C.T.B.*, Vol. III, p. 316.
[12] See *Familiae Minorum Gentium.*

SIR RICHARD CAVE, M.P.
(c. 1593-1645)

The elder brother of Walter Cave [q.v.], he was probably born c. 1593. Nothing is known of his early life, but he may have been the R. Cave who was one of Prince Charles's officers in 1622/3.[1] He appears to have been in the service of Charles Louis, Elector Palatine, before 1636, since, on the latter's visit to Camridge in 1635/6, Cave was created M.A. He was knighted before 28 July 1637.[2] From 1637 to 1641 he was the Elector's agent, sometimes at Westminster and sometimes abroad, and he was also in the confidence of Elizabeth, Queen of Bohemia. There are many references to him in the *C.S.P.D.* 1637 to 1641-3, where numerous letters written by him to Sir Thomas Roe and Sir Henry Vane are printed.[3]

In 1640 he was proposed as burgess for Windsor,[4] but he did not obtain a seat in the Long Parliament until he was elected for Lichfield 12 August 1641. On joining the King, he was disabled 30 August 1642.[5]

On 11 August 1642 Cave met representatives of the city and University to discuss plans for the fortification of Oxford.[6]

At the beginning of April 1643 he was sent from Oxford[7] by the King to wait on Prince Maurice in his expedition against Sir William Waller in Gloucestershire and Herefordshire. After initial success, he surrendered Hereford, and on his reaching Oxford with news of the disaster, was arrested and summoned before a court martial. He made a convincing defence, and was honourably acquitted 26 June 1643.[8] Cave was present at Exeter in September 1643, when he was one of the parties to the Articles agreed upon for the surrender of the city to Prince Maurice.[9] He was at Milton, near Oxford, with Maurice in October 1643, when the latter was dangerously ill and attended by Dr William Harvey [q.v.]. He sat in the Oxford Parliament, and signed the letter to Essex of 27 January 1643/4. He was with the King in the Cornish campaign in August 1644,[10] and signed the letter of 8 August to Essex. He was killed at Naseby 14 June 1645.[11]

Cave married 30 September 1641[12] Elizabeth, daughter of Thomas Bartlett, of Saintbury, Gloucestershire, by his wife, Mary, daughter of Sir John Dauntesey, of Daunton Episcopi, Wiltshire: she bore him a son, Henry.[13] His widow married as her second husband Dr Thomas Yate, Principal of Brasenose (died 1681): she herself died in Oxford aged eighty or over 11 January 1688/9, and was buried beside Yate in the lobby north of Brasenose chapel.[14]

(See Keeler, pp. 128-9. There is also a short, but inaccurate, notice in J.C. Wedgwood, *Staffordshire Parliamentary History*, Vol. II (1920), p. 85: this gives Cave as unmarried and without issue)

[1] H.M.C., *Cowper*, Vol. I, p. 135.
[2] *C.S.P.D.* 1637, p. 336.
[3] See also H.M.C., *Portland*, Vol. I, p. 24 and *Cowper*, Vol. II, which contains letters from Cave to Sir John Coke.
[4] *C.S.P.D.* 1640-1, p. 248.
[5] *C.J.*, Vol. II, p. 744.
[6] H.M.C., *Portland*, Vol. I, p. 57: see also *Oxoniensia*, Vol. I (1936), p. 166.
[7] On 24 April 1 decayed musket was received from him for the King's stores (*R.O.P.*, Part I, p. 80).
[8] For full particulars see T.W. Webb, *Memorials of the Civil War in Herefordshire*, Vol. I (1879), pp. 251 et seq., 262, 272-84.
[9] H.M.C., Appendix to IVth *Report*, p. 314.
[10] H.M.C., *Portland*, Vol. I, p. 183.
[11] Symonds, p. 193.
[12] *C.S.P.D.* 1641-3, p. 134.
[13] *Visitation of Gloucestershire*, Harleian Society, Vol. XXI (1885), p. 204.
[14] Wood, *L. and T.*, Vol. II, pp. 289 and 539.

JOHN DUNTE
(died c. 1647)

Basketmaker. He obtained his freedom 18 February 1600/1.[1] He helped to take the Inventory of the goods of John Miles 4 February 1644/5 (see under Richard Miles). He appears in all but one of the St Aldate's parish taxation lists of 1645, being called 'Goodman' in one of them. The Churchwardens' Accounts record the payment of 6d. to Goodman Dunte for a basket in May 1646. In June 1647 Goodman Dunt and his wife received 1s. Thereafter only Goody Dunt received (very numerous) payments. It is therefore probable that John died about this time. Dunte's house was on the east side of Tower Hill, and it belonged to Christ Church. It was one of two adjoining tenements which, together with other property, had been leased by the Dean and Chapter in 1593 and 1597 to a baker, Peter Pory, who matriculated as a servant of the Warden of All Souls in 1576.[2] Pory died 20 November 1610,[3] and on 22 December 1610 Elizabeth Pory, his widow, was granted a lease of them by the Dean and Chapter. They are described as 'all those Two Tenements adioyning togeather wth the garden grounds cellars Sollars Easemts and all other Commodities wth thappurtenñcs whatsoeu' to the same belongeing situate . . . wthout the Southgate of the Cittie of Oxford aforesaid in the Suburbes of the same Cyttie and in the pish of St Aldates betweene the gate called Cutlers gate and the passage or way leading to the Stables and Backside of the said Deane and Chapter on the Southside and the Southwall of the Lodginge and garden belonging to John Weston Doctor of Lawe one of the Prebendaries of the said Cathedrall Church on the Northside One heade or end thereof abutteth vppon the kings highway or streete leading to South Bridge towards the Weste And another head or end thereof abutteth vppon another little garden grounde belongeing to the Lodginge of the said John Weston towards the Easte Of wch two tenemts last before demised thone is in thoccupacon of Williã' Poyner Cooke of merton Colledge and thother is in thoccupacon' of one John Dunte both of them being the vnder-tennants of one John Hodgins'.[4]
Elizabeth Pory died 7 June 1621,[5] and on 25 July 1623 the Dean and Chapter granted a lease to one of her sons by her first marriage, Abraham Tillyard, apothecary, of St Albans. Poyner (or Poynard) had left his tenement, and was replaced by Robert Wixon [q.v.]: he and Dunte were the under-tenants of William Dewey, M.A. [of Christ Church].[6]
On 23 December 1637 the tenements were leased to John Wheeler, Chapter Clerk, Wixon and Dunte being the under-tenants as before, but their neighbour on the north was now John Morris, Doctor of Divinity.[7] Dunte's tenement was 'lately in ye occupacon of Nicholas Robbinson Coop' in 1660/1.[8]
The tenements survived until after the War of 1914-18. Cutler's Gate and the lane leading through it from the back part of Christ Church to St Aldate's (Grandpont) are mentioned by Wood,[9] and still exist.
In the St Aldate's taxation lists of 1645 Dunte is always entered next to Widow Wixon (the relict of Robert). It seems that for some reason Heath, the compiler of the 'Accompt', either crossed the street and retraced his steps for some way at this point, or that, more likely, he met Dunte after leaving Walter Cave's house and took the particulars on the spot. Dunte's is the most misplaced of all the houses.

[1] City Archives L. 5. 1, f. 258.
[2] *Register*, Vol. II, Pt. I, p. 390.
[3] M.I. in St Mary's Church.
[4] Ch. Ch. MS. xx. C. 3, ff. 185-6: Register III.

[5] M.I. in St Mary's Church to her and her two husbands, William Tillyard and Peter Pory.
[6] Ch. Ch. MS. xx. c. 3, ff. 582-3.
[7] Ch. Ch. MS. xx. c. 4, ff. 45-6: Register IV.
[8] Ch. Ch. MS. xx. c. 5, ff. 42-3: Register V.
[9] *C. of O.*, Vol. I, p. 298.

JAMES PINNELL

Tanner. He was admitted a freeman 21 February 1631/2.[1] He became a common councillor in 1645,[2] junior chamberlain in 1646,[3] and was a keykeeper in 1650.[4] He was still a chamberlain in 1661.[5] He contributed £2. 10s. 0d. to the loan to the Lords Commissioners in October 1645.[6] His name appears in all the St Aldate's parish taxation lists of 1645 and 1647. He was assessed at 20s. and 8s. 'in lands' in the Subsidy Lists of 1641[7] and at 3s. in the Subsidy of 1648.[8] He had five hearths in the Hearth Tax of 1665.[9] The James Pinnell who figures in the Poll Tax of 1667 with four children is probably his son.[10]
Pinnell's house was on the west side of Grandpont. Salter[11] considers that it probably occupied the site of Nos. 69-71 St Aldate's. It has not been possible to find out whether Pinnell owned or rented the house, which appears to have been private property.
The house is misplaced in the 'Accompt'.

[1] *O.C.A.* 1626-1665, p. 38.
[2] Ib., p. 131.
[3] Ib., p. 138.
[4] Ib., p. 176.
[5] City Archives A. 5. 7, f. 294: Council Book C.
[6] Ib. E. 4. 6, ff. 1-2: *O.C.A.* 1626-1665, p. 453.
[7] Ib. B. 1. 4. c.
[8] *S. and T.*, p. 169.
[9] Ib., p. 193.
[10] Ib., p. 262.
[11] *Survey of South-West Ward*, No. 11.

MR JOHN LUMLEY
(died 1658)

The only son of Richard Lumley, first Viscount Lumley, of Waterford, by his first wife, Frances, second daughter of Henry Shelley, of Warminghurst, Sussex, and widow of William Holland, of Chichester whom she married in 1614.[1] Lord Lumley, who was a zealous Royalist, and a colonel of foot, held the estate of Stanstead, Sussex. John Lumley was an Esquire of His Majesty's Body Extraordinary in 1641.[2]
In August 1646 father and son petitioned to compound, stating that in January 1643/4 they left Stanstead, in the Parliament's quarters, to join the King, but never bore arms or contributed to his service.[3] Lord Lumley did not sit in the Oxford Parliament. Stanstead was in rebel hands when attacked by Sir Ralph Hopton in December 1643. It fell to the Royalists shortly afterwards, but surrendered to Waller in January 1643/4.[4]
On 18 September 1646 John Lumley was fined £1,800 on the Winchester Articles.[5] On 15 June 1658 he, with his wife, two children, a gentlewoman, a maid, and three men, had a pass to go to France.[6] He was buried at St Martin-in-the-Fields 10 October 1658.[7] He married Mary, elder daughter of Sir Henry Compton, K.B., of Brambletye, Sussex (c. 1585-1648), by his second wife, Mary, daughter of Sir George Browne, of Wickham, Kent, and widow of Thomas Paston, of Thorpe, Norfolk. Mary Compton was baptized at East Grinstead 5 October 1626. On 6 March 1650/1 it was stated that, on his marriage, a generous settlement was made on John Lumley by his father, and that he had a generous portion with his bride.[8] She was living 4 October 1667. John and Mary were

recusants.
They had two sons and three daughters: the elder son, Richard, was created Viscount Scarborough. Mary Lumley's half-sister, Cecily Compton, was the wife of Henry, third Lord Arundell of Wardour [q.v.], and widow of Sir John Fermor of Somerton (died 1625), who was first cousin of Anne, Lady Lake [q.v.]. John Lumley's step-mother, Elizabeth, was a sister of Sir Frederick Cornwallis [q.v.]: her first husband was Sir William Sandys.
[Will: made 2 October 1658: proved 12 March 1662/3: (not in P.C.C.)].

[1] For Lord Lumley see *C.P.*: the account in *D.N.B.* is inaccurate.
[2] L.C. 3/1.
[3] *C.C.C.*, pp. 920-1: see also *C.A.M.*, p. 388.
[4] See G.M. Godwin, *The Civil War in Hampshire* (1882), pp. ccxv and ccxvi; C. Thomas-Stanford, *The Civil War in Sussex* (1910), p. 72.
[5] *C.C.C.*, loc. cit.
[6] *C.S.P.D.* 1658-9, p. 577.
[7] M.I. in the chancel no longer extant: see E. Milner and E. Benham, *Records of the Lumleys* (1904), p. 114.
[8] *C.C.C.*

In June 1643 James Pinnell had lodging with him THOMAS, LORD WENTWORTH (q.v. under Oliver Smyth's house) and four of Wentworth's servants, who refused to pay, 'saying they are souldiers'.[1]

[1] St Aldate's Defaulters, Bodleian MS. Add. D. 114, f. 24v.

ELIZABETH MOTLEY, WIDOW

Her name, as Widow Motley, appears in all the St Aldate's parish taxation lists of 1645 and 1647. She was assessed at 9d. in the Subsidy of 1648.[1] Motley was not an Oxford name nor is it a common one. It is therefore possible that Elizabeth was the widow of Edward Motley, of the parish of St Michael le Querne, London, whose Will was proved in the P.C.C. 12 April 1624.[2] In this he made his 'welbeloved wife Elizabeth' one of his executors, the other being his son, Edward. The three children, Edward, Elizabeth, and Margaret were all under age in 1623.

Mrs Motley's house was on the west side of Grandpont, south of Overee's Lane (now Speedwell Street), on the site of Nos. 76, 77, and 78 St Aldate's, which in 1772 had a frontage of twenty yards.[3] It belonged to Thomas Smyth [q.v.]. On 8 November 1642 John Smyth, son and heir of Thomas Smyth, of the City of Oxford, baker, granted to Thomas Smyth, son and heir of Alderman Oliver Smyth, for the sum of £20, 'All that Messuage or Tenemt: Backside garden ground' etc. . . . 'scituate . . . wthin the psh of St Aldates . . . in a c'ten streete there called Grandpont on the west side of the said streete next betweene the Messuage or Tenemt of Humphry Whistler on the south side and a Messuage or Tenemt of the said Thomas Smyth late in the tenure of John Yate gent deceased on the North side and abutteinge & extendinge westwards vnto & vppon the streame or watercourse runeinge along by the ground called the fryars . . . All wch said bgained Messuage or Tenemt' etc. 'are now in the tenure possession or occupacõn of Elizabeth Motley widdowe her assigne or assignes'.[4] On 28 April 1646 Oliver Smyth, son and heir of Thomas Smyth, handed over to his maternal grandfather, John Wilmott [q.v.], and his mother, Margaret Smyth, for the sum of £5, certain properties, including 'All that messuage or tenement called or knowne by the name of Motleys howse'.[5] On 2 October 1648 he set aside those messuages, of which 'Motleys howse' was one, towards paying a debt of £800 incurred by his father to the latter's two brothers.[6] On 4 December 1648 Oliver Smyth demised these three tenements for £95 to John Savage, of the City of London.[7]

[1] *S. and T.*, p. 169.
[2] 33 Byrde.
[3] *Survey of South-West Ward*, No. 14.
[4] City Archives A. 5. 4, f. 35.
[5] Ib., f. 39.
[6] Ib., f. 58.
[7] Ib., f. 62.

MR THOMAS CHASE
(1610-1658)

Case is an error for Chase. Thomas Chase was yeoman of the King's 'Backhouse' in 1638.[1] He is probably to be identified with Thomas Chase, fifth son of Matthew Chase, of Chesham, Buckinghamshire, by his wife, Elizabeth, daughter of Richard Bowle, of Chesham, and sister of John Bowle, Bishop of Rochester (died 1637).[2] Thomas' uncle Stephen Chase was Apothecary to Prince Charles: [3] another uncle, Ralph Chase, had his Will proved at Oxford in 1644/5.

Thomas was baptized at Chesham 20 February 1609/10: he was educated at Eton and Mr Crimpshaw's at Windsor. He was admitted a pensioner of Sidney Sussex College, Cambridge, 3 July 1628. He was married as he mentions his wife in his Will. He died between 8 May and 25 May 1658, and was buried at Stone, Kent.
[Will: P.C.C. 1658: 264 Wootton: made 8 May 1658: proved 25 May 1658].

[1] S.P. 16/386/97, f. 1994.
[2] *Visitation of Buckinghamshire* 1634, Harleian Society, Vol. LVIII (1909), p. 24.
[3] MS. Harleian 3791, f, 109.

WIDOW PHILLIPS

Unidentified, but possibly the widow of Thomas Phillips, servant of Dr John Weston (see under John Dunte), Student of Christ Church, who appears in the Assessment Lists of Privileged Persons of the University, as of St Aldate's parish, from 1590 to 1607.
Mrs Phillips' house must have been on the west side of Grandpont, and was clearly commodious. It may have been rented by her from Alderman Humphrey Whistler, baker, mayor of Oxford in 1640 and 1658, who died in 1660. In 1642 his house is described as lying on the south of that of Elizabeth Motley [q.v.], but he appears from the Subsidy of 1648 to have resided himself in the parish of St Giles.

DRUM-MAJOR FRANCIS BARNES

Drum-Major Francis Barnes, of Surrey, was an Indigent Officer in 1663.[1] Although merely placed under 'Scout-Masters' in the 1663 list, he may well have been drum-major to the Lifeguard of Foot.
A Francis Barnes was living in the parish of St Martin-in-the-Fields in 1634 when, on 18 September, Elizabeth, daughter of Francis and Maria was baptized.[2] In the Surrey Hearth Tax of 1664 Francis Barnes appears as having one hearth in Blackman Street, Newington (not chargeable) and three in Epsom.[3]

[1] *I.O.*, col. 158.
[2] *Registers* 1619-1636, p. 107.
[3] Surrey Record Society, Vols. XLI and XLII (1940).

JANE WARRING

A Jane Wareing made her Will, as of St Dunstan's in the East, London, 22 May 1660: it was proved 13 July 1660.[1]
Her money, linen, bedding, brass, pewter, household stuff were all bequeathed to her son Arthur Denis, whom she made her executor.
A possible indication that the testatrix is to be identified with the Royalist laundress is the fact that she dates her Will 'the two and twentieth day of May in the twelueth yeare of the Raigne of our Soveraigne Lord Charles the Seconde', although the King had not actually returned.
Jane Wareing was buried at St Dunstan's as Jane 'Warin' 30 May 1660.[2]

[1] P.C.C. 156 Nabbs.
[2] *Registers*, Part II, p. 76: Harleian Society (1955).

PHILIP BOURNE

He was sworn a Messenger Extraordinary 'at large' 6 June 1631.[1] He is mentioned as a Messenger of the Chamber 1 October 1633,[2] and there are references to him as a Messenger in *C.S.P.D.*[3] On 27 May 1635 three bonds of Philip Bourne, gentleman, were given.[4] He is entered in 1641 as a Messenger Extraordinary.[5]
On 8 December 1643 there was received into the King's stores at New College from 'Mr Phillipp Bourne one of his mats messengers being by him brought from Wittney' a considerable quantity of ammunition, weapons, and equipment.[6]

After the Restoration Bourne was still in the Royal service. In 1660 he is entered as a Messenger of the Chamber in Ordinary, sworn before 1644:[7] he is elsewhere described as 'old Messenger Honest:'[8] in another list the words 'at Queen Hith' appear against his name.[9] In September 1664 he was still functioning as before.[10]

Possibly the Gerard Bourne who was admitted a Messenger to the Excise Office 26 October 1665 was Philip's son.[11] A petition from him was presented 16 November 1669.[12]

The Philip Bourne who married Elizabeth Carter at St Margaret's, Westminster, 16 March 1645/6 may have been the Messenger, *en secondes noces*, or a son of his. Stephen Bourne, son of Philip and Elizabeth, was baptized at St Margaret's 26 July 1647.

[1] S.P. 16/387/6, f. 8.
[2] *C.S.P.D.* 1633-4, p. 226.
[3] 1638-9, p. 34; 1639-40, p. 217.
[4] Ib. 1635, p. 88.
[5] L.C. 3/1.
[6] *R.O.P.*, Part I, p. 121.
[7] S.P. 29/1/63.
[8] S.P. 29/1/65.
[9] S.P. 29/1/66.
[10] S.P. 29/102/14 I, f. 268: see also *C.S.P.D.* 1661-2, p. 461.
[11] *C.T.B.*, Vol. I, p. 684.
[12] Ib., Vol. III, p. 158.

TWO OF LORD WENTWORTH'S GROOMS

See under Lord Wentworth.

JOAN EWEN, WIDOW
(died c. 1646)

The widow of John Ewen, yeoman, of Yarnton, Oxfordshire, manciple of New Inn Hall, Oxford. On 25 August 1626, under *Seruientes*, he was matriculated as a privileged person of the University, his age being given as forty.[1] The baptisms of the seven children of John and Joan Ewen — Elizabeth, Anna, John, Ellen, Joan, Robert, and Constance — are entered in the Yarnton Parish Registers between 1620 and 1634.[2] John Ewen's Will, as of Yarnton, was made 28 April 1637 and proved in the Court of the Chancellor of Oxford University 4 January 1637/8.[3] In this he left legacies to all his children and provided for his wife, who had all the crop of corn and grain both at Yarnton and at his copyhold property at Marston, Oxfordshire, as well as all his household stuff. An Inventory relating to the house which he leased at Yarnton was made 9 October 1639 and exhibited 12 November in the Chancellor's Court.[4] His total assets amounted to £731. 19s. 6d.

'Mrs Ewens house' is entered in all the St Aldate's parish taxation lists of 1645 except the first, when the entry is 'The children of Mrs Ewen'. She was probably dead by 1647, as her name does not appear in the lists of that year.

Mrs Ewen's house was on the west side of Grandpont and may have been on the site of Nos. 66, 67, and 68 St Aldate's, which in 1772 had a frontage of sixteen yards.[5] On 30 October 1630 John Ewen, described as yeoman, of Yardington (Yarnton), purchased from a father and son of the name of Thomas Bolte, for the sum of £250, 'All that Messuage or Tenemt Garden and Backside wth thappurtennces situate . . . in the pshe of St Aldate in a certen street there called Graundpont on the West side of the said streete next between a Messuage or Tenemt of William Goode Chaundler on the North side and a Messuage or Tenemt now or late of John Towie on the south pte Togeather with all houses edifices' etc.[6] The property had been bequeathed to Dorothy, née Flexney, wife of Thomas Bolte the elder, by her grandfather, Thomas Smyth. In his Will John Ewen describes himself as seized of a 'messuage or tenement with the appurtenances in Grandponde or Grampoole in Oxford wch I latelie purchased of one Thomas Bolt deceased'. He arranged that 'Joane my welbeloved wife for her livelihoode and mainetenance shall have hold and enioye . . . the saide Messuage or tenement wth appurtenances in Oxford for and duringe the natural life of her the saide Joane'. The copyhold messuage at Marston was to be Joan's only until John Ewen the younger had reached the age of twenty-one, when the executors were to pay her £140.

On 21 July 1649 John Ewen the younger sold to Joanna Fifeild, of Oxford, for £204, the St Aldate's messuage, which is described as lying between that of James Pinnell, tanner [q.v.] on the north and a messuage in the occupation of Widow Saunders on the south. It was 'now or late' in the occupation of Thomas Penn, who appears in the Subsidy of 1648.[7]

[1] University Archives S P 2, f. 347: 'Johēs Ewen Oxoñ: ex Hospitio Nouo Mancip̃: annos nat' 40'.
[2] Transcripts: MS. Top. Oxon. c. 165.
[3] Hyp. B. 24.
[4] Hyp. B. 12.
[5] *Survey of South-West Ward*, No. 10.
[6] City Archives A. 5. 4, f. 22v.
[7] Ib., f. 59v.

WILLIAM WHITE
(died 1658)

An entry in the Wardens' Accounts of the Poulters Company of London records that on 30 March 1637 there was 'Recd of Wm White servant to Mr Thomas Rayment for his admittance 1/8 and in leiw of a spoone 6/8'.[1] White's name does not appear in the list of members of City Companies in the return of the poll tax in 1641.[2] After the fall of Oxford he returned to London: on 16 February 1647/8 the Wardens' Accounts record that there was 'Recd of Mr White for opening of his shoppe 6/8' and for 'arrears of quarteridge 8/-'.[3] The shop was almost certainly situated in the parish of St Clement Danes, where White was residing at the time of his death. On 12 February 1650/1 there was received of White 'for the presentment of his apprentice Nicholas Bland 1/8' and for his own 'Whood money' 6/8.[4] On 11 February 1656/7 there was received 'for yee presentment of his apprentice William White 1/8'.[5] jA marriage licence for William White and Cicely Bland, who was a widow, was issued by the Bishop of London in December 1640.[6] Her husband's apprentices Nicholas Bland and William White were respectively her sons by her first and second marriages. William White the elder was buried 3 November 1658 at St Clement Danes.[7] In his Will he mentions his wife and three children, William, Elizabeth, and Rebeccah: also his son-in-law (step-son) Nicholas Bland. The son, William the younger, was King's Poulterer in 1662.[8]
[Will: P.C.C. 1658: 627 Wootton: made 12 October 1658: proved 13 November 1658 by his relict Cicely].
After her husband's death Cicely White carried on his business: there is mention of an apprentice of hers in 1661.[9] She was buried at St Clement Danes 25 December 1673.[10] In her Will she describes herself as aged. She mentions her son Nicholas Bland and his children, the sons of her son William White, and the daughter of her daughter Elizabeth Spooner, whose husband, Abraham, a vintner of St Bride's parish, was appointed co-executor with her son William, 'poulterer of the parish of St Clement Danes'.[11]
[Will: P.C.C. 1674: 13 Bunce: made 18 October 1673: proved 13 January 1673/4].

[1] MS. 2150/1. We are indebted for this and the subsequent references from the Accounts to Mr P.E. Jones, Deputy Keeper of the Records of the Corporation of London.
[2] We are indebted to Mr Godfrey Thompson, Guildhall Librarian, for this information.
[3] MS. 2150/1.
[4] Ibid.
[5] Ibid.
[6] *Calendar of Marriage Licence Allegations*, Vol. 1 (1937), p. 213.
[7] Registers, Vol. 3, f. 179v: Burials 1653-73. He is described as poulterer.
[8] S.P. 29/60/65, f. 122.
[9] P.E. Jones, *The Worshipful Company of Poulters of London*, 2nd edn. (1965), p. 208.
[10] Registers, Vol. 4, f. 5: Burials 1673-1700. She is described as 'poultress'.
[11] See also Jones, op. cit., loc. cit., where gifts to three of Cicely White's grandchildren are recorded.

XLIII

DOROTHY MOORE, WIDOW
(died 1650)

The widow of Roger Moore (More), cook of Merton College. His name appears in the Taxation Assessments of Privileged Persons from 1594 to 1610 as under-cook, living in St Thomas' parish.[1] In the Assessment List for 1624-5 he appears as 'Mr Roger more Mr Cooke of martin [sic] Colledge', living in the parish of St Aldate's and assessed at 12d.[2] He left no Will and the date of his death is unknown.
The churchwardens of St Aldate's paid 4s. for a 'Shrowde for a Souldier that died at the widow Moores 14th Januarie 1644' [i.e. 1645]. Her name does not occur in any of the St Aldate's parish taxation lists for 1645 and 1647. She died between 8 March 1649/50 and 1 April 1650.
In her Will Mrs Moore left her grandchild Katherine Moore the 'bedstead in the Chamber wherein I now lodge'. She also left Katherine 'other gear in a Chest att Mr Langleys[3] and all the peweter in the same Chest' as well as the 'great presse in the Hall'. Her daughter-in-law Bridgett Hayes was left the 'large table in the Hall', also the 'bedsted in the Chamber wherein she lodgeth'. Her grandchild Roger Moore was out of the country. She appointed her grandchild John Cooke, of Newbury, her residuary legatee and executor.
[Will: Court of the Chancellor of the University of Oxford: Hyp. B. 30: made 8 March 1649/50: proved 1 April 1650].
Mrs Moore's house must have been on the west side of Grandpont, but there is no evidence to shew its exact location, or who owned it. It may have been on the site of part of No. 65 St Aldate's.

[1] University Archives W.P. γ 25 (5) and W.P. γ 28 (6), passim.
[2] Ib. W.P. γ 28 (7).
[3] Matthew Langley the elder [q.v.].

MR THORNELL

It has not been possible to discover his Christian name, but in June 1643, when he was lodging at the house of Matthew Langley the elder [q.v.], he was described as 'surgeon to the lifeguard': no answer was received from him.[1]
It may be worth noting that a John Thornill was a Groom of the Chamber Extraordinary in 1641.[2]

[1] St Aldate's Defaulters, Bodleian MS. Add. D. 114, f. 24v.
[2] L.C. 3/1.

In June 1643 MR BIGFORD and another servant of Sir Frederick Cornwallis [q.v.] were lodging with Mrs Moore.[1]

[1] St Aldate's Defaulters, Bodleian MS. Add. D. 114, f. 24v.

WILLIAM HORNE
(c. 1568-1646)

Tailor. The son of William Horne, tailor, of Whittlebury, Northamptonshire, he was apprenticed to William Pyckover, tailor, of Oxford, 2 November 1580.[1] He was admitted a freeman 15 May 1593.[2] He is mentioned as a tailor in 1609.[3] On 24 April 1643 three weapons were received from him for the King's stores.[4] His name occurs in all the St Aldate's parish taxation lists of 1645.
[Will: 3 November 1646: MS. Wills Oxon. 307, f. 44: Caveat Book].
Horne's house must have been on the west side of Grandpont, but there is no evidence to shew its exact location or who owned it. It may have been on the site of part of No. 65 St Aldate's.

[1] City Archives A. 5. 3, f. 301.
[2] *O.C.A.* 1583-1626, p. 79.
[3] Ib., p. 196.
[4] *R.O.P.*, Part I, p. 84.

WILLIAM LOE, A TAILOR AND SERVANT TO SECRETARY (SIR EDWARD) NICHOLAS
(1593-1669)

Unidentified. He was already lodging at William Horne's in June 1643, when he refused to pay.[1]
Nicholls is, of course, a slip for Nicholas. Sir Edward Nicholas was appointed Secretary of State and knighted in 1641. He lodged at Pembroke College: (see Mr Nicholas, possibly the Secretary's father, under Thomas Smyth's house). Sir Edward conducted the surrender of Oxford in 1646.
(For a detailed study of his career see Donald Nicholas, *Mr Secretary Nicholas* (1955))

[1] St Aldate's Defaulters, Bodleian MS. Add. D. 114, f. 24v.

A SERVANT OF SIR FREDERICK CORNWALLIS

See under Cornwallis.

TWO WOMEN BELONGING TO HENRY HUNCKS

A son of Sir Thomas Huncks, who came of an armigerous family in Warwickshire, and was knighted in Dublin in 1605. His mother was Catherine, second daughter of Sir John Conway (died 1603), of Arrow, Warwickshire, Governor of Ostend, and sister of Edward, first Viscount Conway (died 1631). Henry was a brother of Sir Thomas Huncks (knighted in 1626), Francis Huncks, Colonel Sir Fulk Huncks, and Hercules Huncks, all soldiers like himself. The last-named was a colonel in the Parliamentarian service, who was in command of the guard at Cotton House during the trial of Charles I, and served in Ireland.
Henry was an ensign, promoted to lieutenant and then captain, in Ireland in 1626.[1] In 1628 he was stationed in Hampshire.[2] On 11 March 1635/6 he is mentioned by his mother (then resident in Ireland), together with Fulk, in a letter to her nephew the second Viscount Conway.[3] He was Governor of Barbados

from 1639 to 1641,[4] and was an Esquire of His Majesty's Body Extraordinary in the latter year.[5]

Henry Huncks was lieutenant-colonl of foot, Earl of Northampton's Regiment 16 November 1642.[6] He was knighted 1 January 1642/3. He was Lieutenant-Governor of Banbury Castle 22 March 1642/3,[7] and had been in command at Banbury in the absence of Northampton 22 January 1642/3.[8] He was dismissed about 2 May 1643 for correspondence with the rebels.[9] Huncks was sent to Prince Rupert to defend himself, and Major Anthony Green was appointed in his stead. He was still in Banbury Castle on 26 June 1643.[10]

Huncks held some command in the Western army (he was possibly lieutenant-colonel to Sir Fulk) by the time of the Tuke court martial in 1645, when he was a member of the Council of War.[11] He addressed a petition, as of Portlinch, Devonshire, 14 May 1646. In September 1648 it was reported that he was a commissioner to raise money against Parliament and had surrendered on the Exeter Articles (13 April 1646). His proposed fine was £327.[12]

Huncks proved the Will of his mother, Dame Catherine Huncks, 12 July 1646.[13] In this Will, which was made 13 June 1635, Dame Catherine mentions her five sons and two of her three daughters. Henry is described as sergeant major, was left £500, and made residuary legatee and executor. By a later Will, made 2 July 1641, and proved in the P.C.C. 15 June 1652,[14] this earlier Will was revoked and her nephew Lord Conway nominated executor. Henry Huncks (now styled captain) had been given £100. His daughter Elizabeth was bequeathed 40s. When the new Will was proved, the 'pretended' Will proved by the 'pretended' executor, was declared null and void.

[1] *C.S.P.I.* 1625-32, pp. 82, 83, 90, and 145.
[2] *C.S.P.D.* 1628-9, pp. 69, 107, and 246.
[3] Ib. 1635-6, p. 289.
[4] *Calendar of State Papers, Colonial Series* 1574-1660, pp. 291, 299, 305, and 317.
[5] L.C. 3/1.
[6] *R.O.P.*, Part I, pp. 164-5.
[7] Luke, p. 40.
[8] MS. Harleian 6851, ff. 105 and 106.
[9] Bodleian Library, Firth MS. c. 6, f. 171: cf. Luke, p. 72: 9 May 1643.
[10] Ib., p. 105.
[11] Sir Richard Bulstrode, *Memoirs*, p. 143.
[12] *C.C.C.*, p. 1283.
[13] P.C.C. 112 Twisse.
[14] 134 Bowyer.

FIVE SOLDIERS OF THE LIFEGUARD

It is not unlikely that these were GEORGE TURNER, THOMAS JONES, THOMAS LEE, CHRISTOPHER LOE, and ROBERT EARNEY, who were lodging with William Horne in June 1643 and would not pay.[1] But since the Lifeguard had suffered casualties at First Newbury in the interim, there may have been some changes among Horne's lodgers.

[1] St Aldate's Defaulters, Bodleian MS. Add. D. 114, f. 24v.

XLV

JOHN SAVORY
(c. 1581-c. 1653)

Rabbit seller and poulterer. The son of Thomas Savory, of Wheatley, Oxfordshire, he figures in the Will of his kinsman William Saverie, yeoman, of St Aldate's, made and proved in 1614, of which he was appointed executor.[1] In addition to a bedstead and its furniture, John was to have 'my biggest brasse pott saving one, it having broade bryms the biggest kettle wth an iron handle and all my weareinge apparrell hereafter mencoẽd that is to say my best doublet my best coate & my best breeches'.

In the Assessment of Privileged Persons for 1624-5 Savory is described as 'Poulterer to the Vniversitie' and also as a 'Carrier allowed by the Vniversitie', living in St Aldate's: he was assessed at 10d.[2] But it was not until 2 October 1635 that, at the age of fifty-four, he was matriculated.[3] The University College Bursar's Journal shews that he was supplying that society during the Civil War. On 24 April 1643 a long pike and gorget were received from him for the King's stores.[4] He was a churchwarden of St Aldate's in 1628-9, 1629-30, 1641-2, 1642-3, and 1643-4. His name appears in all the St Aldate's parish taxation lists of 1645 and 1647. He paid 20s. and 8s. 'in lands' in the Subsidy Assessment of 1641[5] and he was assessed at 2s. 6d. in the Subsidy of 1648.[6] On 11 June 1650 'John Savery, senior, who hath lived and traded in this Citty for many years selling of Rabbitts' was admitted a freeman.[7]

Savory married twice. The name of his first wife is unknown: his second was Judith, widow of Walter Fowler, a Devon man, who at the age of twenty-four, in 1610, as *promus Aulae Lateportensis* (steward of Broadgates Hall in St Aldate's), was matriculated as a privileged person of the University.[8] His administration bond, dated 8 May 1626, together with an Inventory, is preserved among the records of the Court of the Chancellor of Oxford University.[9] By 1628 Fowler's widow was in part ocupation of the house in Pennyfarthing Street which in 1643/4 was leased to Thomas Wright [q.v.]. In 1631 the St Aldate's feoffees leased the house to Judith, who must have married Savory in 1633 or 1634, as in the Churchwardens' Accounts for 1633-4 she appears for the first time as Mrs Savory. That Savory had previously been married is proved by the fact that his eldest son, Richard, was bound apprentice 11 November 1635.[10]

Savory died between 26 September 1652 and 7 July 1653. In his Will he says: 'I give vnto my wife Judith the bedd Bedsteade and furniture as it standeth in my Lodginge Roome', and she was also to have everything that had belonged to her before her marriage to Savory. The daughters, Joane Eldridge and Anne Chacock, and Anne's son, John, were left legacies, and the sons, Richard, William, and Charles, were made residuary legatees and executors.

[Will: P.C.C. 1653: 79 Brent: made 26 September 1652: proved 7 July 1653].

Judith Savory survived until January 1669/70. She expressed the wish to be buried in the church or churchyard of St Aldate's. Her daughter Ann Wild (probably the child of her first marriage), wife of George Wild, joiner, was to have the lease of the parish house in Pennyfarthing Street where John Wild the elder was then living.[11] Ann was named her mother's residuary legatee and executrix.

[Will: MS. Wills Oxon. 149/2/27: made 8 January 1669/70: proved 29 January 1669/70. An Inventory was exhibited 21 January 1669/70].

Savory's house was on the west side of Grandpont. Salter hazarded the suggestion that he occupied part of the former Nos. 62, 63, and 64 St Aldate's which, in 1772, had a frontage of nearly seventeen yards.[12] Savory's eldest son and his wife were living there in 1667 when they paid 2s. for their polls. Savory's house was private property and he probably rented it.

Savory leased from Magdalen a house on the west side of Fish Street, on the site of the former No. 103 St Aldate's (see under Ursula Collier). He also paid the churchwardens of St Aldate's a rent of £1. 13s. 4d. per annum for property in St Peter-le-Bailey parish 'at the west end of Butcherrowe'.[13]

[1] MS. Wills Oxon. 59/2/23.
[2] University Archives W.P. γ 28 (7), ff. 4, 7, and 11.
[3] Ib., S P 2, f. 338v: 'Johẽs Savory: priviliegatus sub sigillo Cancellarij affixo Instrument' gerent dat' Augustj i° Anõ Dm̃: 1635, Oxon fil: Tho: Savorye de Wheatley in Com̃ p'd: pleb: an. nat' 54.'
[4] *R.O.P.*, Part I, p. 83.
[5] City Archives B. 1. 4. c.
[6] *S. and T.*, p. 169.
[7] *O.C.A.* 1626-1665, p. 169.
[8] *Register*, Vol. II, Pt. I, p. 401.
[9] Hyp. B. 39 and 12. Judith was administratrix.
[10] City Archives L. 5. 2, f. 248v.
[11] Judith was living with the Wilds in this house in 1667, when she paid 2s. for her poll (*S. and T.*, p. 259: her name is misprinted 'Sanery').
[12] *Survey of South-West Ward*, No. 7. This seems likely, but it must have been a different house from that for which Richard Horne paid for four hearths in 1662 and 1666.
[13] Churchwardens' Accounts.

MR ADRIAN MAY
(c. 1604-1670)

The second son of John May (died 1631), of Rawmere in Mid-Lavant, Sussex, by his wife, Elizabeth Hill. The seventh son was Hugh May, the architect (1622-1684). Adrian was a nephew of Sir Humphrey May, Chancellor of the Duchy of Lancaster.[1] He matriculated from St John's College, Oxford, 16 November 1621, aged seventeen. On 22 September 1628, as a Groom of the Privy Chamber, he was granted a pension of 200 marks per annum on the surrender thereof by his uncle Hugh May.[2] On the same day he received warrants for payment of a fee of 20 marks per annum as Groom and a yearly livery.[3] On 20 January 1637/8 he and Richard May (the fourth brother) received a grant in reversion of the office of Clerk of the Statutes.[4] In 1641 he was entered as a Groom of the Privy Chamber.[5] In 1642 he was in trouble with the House of Commons.[6] In June and July he was employed as a messenger from the King to the Fleet.[7]

By 4 April 1643 May was a prisoner at Coventry.[8] He was evidently allowed to go to Oxford, for, on 11 April 1643, it was ordered that 'Mr *May* be enjoined forthwith to return to *Oxon* with one Man; and that he shall have Mr Speaker's Warrant with Caution that he carries neither Monies, Jewels, Letters, nor Ammunition, and that they be searched'.[9] A like order was issued for Sir Frederick Cornwallis [q.v.].[10] Cornwallis had brought a Message from the King to both Houses enclosed in a letter from Lord Falkland dated Oxford 9 April 1643. On 21 April 1643 it was ordered that 'Mr *Adrian May* shall have a pass to go to *Oxford*, with his Man and Two Horses'.[11] On 25 April 1643 it was ordered that 'Captain *Bullmer* who apprehended and staid Mr *May* upon the Highway, shall have Fifty Pounds of the hundred Pieces taken about him . . . and that Mr *May* be referred to the Committee for Examinations, and that he be kept in Custody in the mean time'.[12] On 27 May 1643 the House of Lords being informed that 'Mr *May*, that came from *Oxford* with a Message from His Majesty, and having the order of this House to return to *Oxford*', had been taken by the Lord General's scouts, instructed their Speaker to write to the Lord General to pay May £10 to carry him to Oxford and to have his horse and saddle returned to him.[13]

There are three references to May in Ashburnham's *Accompt:* these include: 'To Mr May for money lost by yor Matie' £20.[14]
Adrian May who, in 1643/4, was serving the Lord Treasurer, Francis, Lord Cottington [q.v.], must have been closely involved in the Wartime Messenger Service. 'James Candry allegeth that he was sworne at Oxford & did service there wch wilbee Justified by Mr Adrian May'.[15]
On 7 August 1644 it was resolved that 'Mr *Adrian May* shall be forthwith committed Prisoner to the *Tower* for adhering to the Party in Arms against Parliament'.[16]
On 30 April 1646 he begged to compound,[17] and on 18 June 1649 he was admitted by Parliament to do so on the Oxford Articles.[18] On 28 June 1649 he begged to compound, as of Little Dunmow, Essex: on 1 September his fine was reduced from £572 to £252, and on 21 October the fine was paid and the estate discharged.[19]
On 20 April 1661, May received a warrant for his pension as by Letters Patent on 26 September 1628.[20] On 10 December 1661 he received a warrant to be supervisor of the French gardeners employed at Whitehall, St James's, and Hampton Court, with a salary of £200 per annum.[21] On 30 September 1669 he received a patent appointing him conservator of all the waters belonging to Hampton Court.[22] In addition he held the post of Groom of the Privy Chamber to Charles II. On 26 April 1670 a correspondent informed (Sir) Joseph Williamson that 'Adrian May went to bed last night and was found dead in the morning'.[23] On 29 June 1671 a Privy Seal order for £1,945. 6s. 5½d. was made to Hugh May, administrator of Adrian May.[24]

[1] Le Neve, *Knights*, pp. 229-30.
[2] *C.S.P.D.* 1628-9, p. 334.
[3] Ibid.
[4] Ib. 1637-8, p. 173.
[5] L.C. 3/1.
[6] *C.J.*, Vol. II, pp. 415, 593, 598, 602-3, 604.
[7] Clarendon, *Life*, p. 172, *History*, Book V, § § 377-80, where he is described as the King's page.
[8] *L.J.*, Vol. V, p. 690 and *C.J.*, Vol. III, p. 29.
[9] *C.J.*, Vol. III, p. 39.
[10] Ibid.
[11] *L.J.*, Vol. VI, p. 14.
[12] *C.J.*, Vol. III, p. 58. For the character of the notorious scoutmaster Captain George Bulmer see *Mercurius Aulicus*, 2 May 1643.
[13] *L.J.*, Vol. VI, p. 19: for further information about the mare and saddle see pp. 24 and 38, and the money pp. 42 and 64.
[14] P. xxviii.
[15] S.P. 29/1/63: May 1660.
[16] *C.J.*, Vol. III, p. 582.
[17] *C.C.C.*, p. 1243.
[18] Ib. and *L.J.*, Vol. VI, p. 236.
[19] *C.C.C.*, p. 1243.
[20] *C.T.B.*, Vol. I. p. 237.
[21] *C.S.P.D.* 1661-2, p. 175. For May as Surveyor of the Royal Gardens see also *C.S.P.D.* 1663-4, pp. 57, 126, 281, and 311, 1664-5, pp. 193 and 475, and numerous other references in *C.S.P.D.* and *C.T.B.*
[22] *C.S.P.D.* 1668-9, p. 508.
[23] Ib. 1670, p. 186.
[24] *C.T.B.*, Vol. IV, p. 886.

MR PETER MABER
(c. 1591- after 1662)

In July 1628 he received a warrant for payment as one of the servants to the Keepers of the Council Chamber.[1] In the Ashburnham *Accompt* a payment to him of £5 is recorded.[2] His name appears in the 1660 list of Messengers of His Majesty's Chamber in Ordinary as having been 'sworne at Oxford'.[3] He was attached to the Lords Commissioners appointed for the defence of Oxford.
From a series of petitions which Maber presented to Charles II and Sir Edward Nicholas in September (?) 1662[4] we learn further facts about his career. He became waiter at the Council Board in the reign of James I, and as doorkeeper of the Council removed the Council books and records to York in 1642, being ordered £20 for his expenses. He was made a Messenger of the Chamber in 1643, and served Charles I until the surrender of Oxford. He was seventy-one years old and had lost his sight five years previously. In spite of being 'a dark man', he had hoped to be confirmed in his position as a Messenger of the Chamber at the Restoration, as he could have filled it by deputy, but on account of his blindness, another had been put in his place by the Lord Chamberlain. He petitioned for a pension and maintenance for life on account of his long services. Maber told Nicholas that he had hoped that the Lords whom he had known at Oxford and elsewhere would have noticed him and interfered for him, but hitherto he had been unable to get his petition read.

[1] *C.S.P.D.* 1628-9, p. 240.
[2] P. xxvii.
[3] S.P. 29/1/63.
[4] *C.S.P.D.* 1661-2, p. 486: S.P. 29/59/47, 48, 49, 50, and 50.1.

THOMAS LAPWORTH

Probably a carrier. His name appears in all the St Aldate's parish taxation lists of 1645 and 1647. He was assessed at 6d. and 1s. 6d. in the Subsidy of 1648.[1] In 1648-9 the churchwardens of St Aldate's paid him 2s. for 'caringe the amonition'. On 20 September 1652 Thomas Lapworth, St Aldate's parish, having been long resident there, was admitted a freeman.[2] As of Grandpont, he and his wife were assessed at 2s. in the Poll Tax of 1667.[3]

Lapworth's house was on the west side of Grandpont, probably one part of the site of No. 61 St Aldate's, which in 1772 had a frontage of thirty-four feet.[4] It was private property and was probably rented by Lapworth. There were six hearths in 1665,[5] but Lapworth's share was probably small (see under Richard Horne).

[1] *S. and T.*, p. 169.
[2] *O.C.A.* 1626-1665, p. 191.
[3] *S. and T.*, p. 261.
[4] *Survey of South-West Ward*, No. 6.
[5] *S. and T.*, p. 193.

RICHARD HORNE

Brewer. He was admitted a freeman 15 February 1616/17,[1] and was admitted to brew by the University 21 December 1626.[2] He was a churchwarden of St Aldate's 1619-20, 1620-1, 1639-40, and 1640-1. His name occurs in all the parish taxation lists of 1645 and in one list of 1647. He was assessed at 1s. in the Subsidy of 1648,[3] paid for four hearths in the Hearth Tax of 1665,[4] was assessed at 1s. in the Poll Tax of 1667,[5] and at 2s. 6d. in the Subsidy of 1667.[6]
On 14 June 1643 it was stated under 'Hornes house' that 'John Horne is a troop[er] and went forth on service vpon munday last'.[7] John was probably Richard's son. The *Journal of Sir Samuel Luke* under date Monday 12 June 1643 records the departure of troops from Oxford.
Horne's house was on the west side of Grandpont and probably occupied the larger part of the site of No. 61 St Aldate's (see under Thomas Lapworth). Judging by the number of his lodgers, Horne's portion was fairly commodious. The Lincoln College Treasurer's Computus Books shew that in 1641, 1642, and 1646 he leased a garden in 'Grandpoole' from the College at a rent of 6s. 8d. per annum. The rent was paid by his neighbour Oliver Smyth [q.v.] in 1643, 1644, 1645, and 1647. He was living across the way, in the house later occupied by John and Jane Hawkes [q.v.], as early as 1614 and is wrongly described as still being there as late as 1635. He paid 20s. and 4s. 'in lands' in the South-East Ward in the Subsidy of 1621.[8]

[1] *O.C.A.* 1583-1626, p. 263.
[2] *Register*, Vol. II, Pt. I, p. 329.
[3] *S. and T.*, p. 169.
[4] Ib., p. 193.
[5] Ib., p. 262. Edith Horne also paid 1s.
[6] Ib., p. 341.
[7] St Aldate's Defaulters, Bodleian MS. Add. D. 114, f. 24v.
[8] City Archives B. 1. 3. b.

MR HENRY KEYME

He was the most senior of the four Royal Messengers lodging in this house. He had been in the service at least as early as 1620.[1] His name occurs constantly in the *C.S.P.D.* from this date until 1640, as receiving warrants from the Council and the Lords of the Admiralty to arrest persons up and down the country. In 1635 he and some other Messengers were suspended for four months on an erroneous charge of delaying delivery of writs and letters concerning shipping and petitioned about the matter.[2] On 19 June 1636 he received a warrant for his lodging during his travels on the King's service.[3] On 19 September 1636 he was appointed deputy clerk of the Check.[4] On 2 January 1639/40 the Council of War sitting at Whitehall appointed Keyme and another to attend upon the Council.[5] There are also many certificates, receipts, etc. connected with Keyme in the *C.S.P.D.* for the period up to 1640. In 1641 he is entered as one of the forty Messengers 'in ffee'.[6] It would be natural for him to serve the Council of War at Oxford. On 6 November 1645 he was described as a 'delinquent in arms'.[7] Henry Keyme had a nephew and namesake who was sworn on 7 June 1637 'To attend ye Coms of ye Admiralty as a deputy and assistant to Robert Smith'.[8] Smith, the elder Keyme's colleague, had asked for the younger Keyme's appointment as a Messenger Extraordinary in the above capacity on 25 April 1637, and the young man's uncle had engaged that his kinsman should discharge the employment faithfully.[9] Henry Keyme the younger is entered in 1641 under Messengers in Peculiar Places as deputy to Smith.[10]

The elder Henry Keyme died before the Restoration. There is a note in the list of Messengers of the Chamber sworn before 1644, drawn up in May 1660, which runs as follows: 'Henry Keyme Nephew to old Henry Keyme for whose debts he hath suffered even to Ruine hee was sworne a Messenger ex. ãy & attended ye Admlty & Navy in ye yeare 1637.'[11] In May (?) 1660 he petitioned to be made a Messenger of the Chamber, to which he was sworn in 1637, to attend the Admiralty and Navy Court. He claimed not to have acted since the Earl of Northumberland laid down his commission — actually the Earl was dismissed by Charles I on 28 June 1642 — and mentioned that his uncle was a Messenger to the last two Kings.[12] In fact, the younger Keyme appears to have joined the rebels. On 7 February 1642/3 Henry Keyme, 'long a servitor to the Navy, which employment now fails him, was recommended by the Commissioners of the Navy to be Clerk of the Cheque in one of the merchant ships.'[13] It seems likely, moreover, that he is the Henry Keyme who served as a volunteer in the *Victory*.[14] Nevertheless, his petition must have been granted as there is a warrant to Henry Kyne [sic] dated 24 January 1661/2.[15]

[1] *C.S.P.D.* 1619-23, p. 202.
[2] Ib. 1635, p. 444.
[3] Ib. 1635-6, p. 571.
[4] Ib. 1636-7, p. 131.
[5] Ib. 1639-40, p. 295.
[6] L.C. 3/1.
[7] *C.A.M.*, p. 623.
[8] S. P. 16/387/6, f. 9.
[9] C.S.P.D. 1637, p. 25.
[10] L.C. 3/1.
[11] S. P. 29/1/63.
[12] C.S.P.D. 1660-1, p. 22.
[13] Ib. 1641-3, p. 556.
[14] Ib. 1652-3, p. 513.
[15] Ib. 1661-2, p. 253.

MR HUGH PEACHIE

The baptism of one of this name is recorded in the *Registers* of St Margaret's, Westminster, 20 July 1595. He may have been the son of Hugh Peachie whose name is included in a List of Messengers of the Council or Chamber in 1601, and whose 'beat' was Bedfordshire, Cambridgeshire, Huntingdonshire, and Hertfordshire.[1] Hugh Peachie's name appears frequently in the *C.S.P.D.* from 1627 to 1640[2] as a Messenger of the Chamber receiving warrants from the Council to travel all over the country, often with the object of making arrests. In 1634 he was sent to Montgomery and Carmarthen and received an allowance for his expenses: [3] in 1638 he was ordered to arrest disturbers of the Earl of Bedford's scheme of the Great Level[4] and was also at Newcastle.[5] On 20 June 1636, and again in 1638 (?), his horse was stolen.[6] On 21 June 1636 he received a warrant for his lodging during his travels on the King's service.[7] He is entered in 1641 among the forty Messengers 'in ffee'.[8] At Oxford he was put at the disposal of the Council of War. As Hugh Peachie's name does not appear in the post-Restoration lists of Messengers, it is clear that he must have died before 1660. A Mr Hugh Peachie was buried at St Margaret's, Westminster, 17 June 1656.

[1] *Acts of the Privy Council*, Vol. XXXII, 1601-4, p. 225.
[2] 1627-8, p. 383: 1640, p. 166.
[3] Ib. 1634-5, pp. 86 and 173.

[4] Ib. 1637-8, p. 438.
[5] Ib. 1638-9, p. 19.
[6] Ib. 1636-7, p. 5 and 1638-9, p. 269.
[7] Ib. 1636-7, pp. 8-9.
[8] L.C. 3/1.

MR NICHOLAS COPLEY
(died c. 1684)

The fourth son of Thomas Copley, of Norton, Worcestershire, by his wife, Margaret, daughter of Thomas Hanford, of Wollashull.[1] Nicholas, who was of Yorkshire descent, is described in 1634 as 'of London'.

He was a Messenger by 21 May 1640.[2] He is entered in 1641 as one of the forty Messengers 'in ffee'.[3] On 12 November 1646, as one of the King's servants in ordinary, he begged to compound on the Oxford Articles, being at Oxford on its surrender, and to free his estate from sequestration.[4]

Copley's name appears on the list of Messengers of the Chamber sworn before 1644, drawn up in May 1660,[5] as 'old Messenger Honest',[6] and 'in Tutle Street Westminster'.[7] In 1664[8] he was functioning as before. There are several references to him as a Messenger in *C.S.P.D.*, the last reference being to a bill sent by him on 1 November 1668.[9] He is mentioned as having given a bond for Lady Lake,[10] and, in connexion with the tithes of Dunmow, there is a reference to Copley's services and sufferings for Charles I and Charles II, on 31 December 1661.[11]

Copley married Elizabeth . . . , who was buried in the north cloister of Westminster Abbey 27 April 1672.[12] He himself was buried there 31 January 1683/4[13] (according to the wish expressed in his Will).

In his Will he mentions his sons, Charles and Henry, and his daughters, Luce Copley and Jane Ringrose, among his relatives.

[Will: P.C. 1684: 13 Hare: made 25 November 1681: proved 8 February 1683/4, as of St Margaret's, Westminster].

[1] *Visitation of Worcestershire* 1634, Harleian Society, Vol. XC (1938), p. 25.
[2] *C.S.P.D.* 1640, p. 192.
[3] L.C. 3/1.
[4] *C.C.C.*, p. 1562. See also p. 2369 where he appears, in 1654, as the lessee of the rectory of Great Dunmow, Essex, the property of Anne, Lady Lake [q.v.].
[5] S.P. 29/1/63.
[6] S.P. 29/1/64.
[7] S.P. 29/1/66.
[8] S.P. 29/102/14 I, f. 262.
[9] *C.S.P.D.* 1668-9, p. 137.
[10] *C.T.B.*, Vol. I, p. 319.
[11] *C.S.P.D.* 1661-2, p. 196.
[12] *Registers*, p. 176.
[13] Ib., p. 208.

MR HENRY NORTHROP

His name is entered in 1641 among the forty Messengers 'in ffee'.[1] The *Registers* shew that he was living in the parish of St Margaret, Westminster, by 31 July 1636, when a daughter, Catherine, was baptized there. A daughter, Jane, was baptized there 1 January 1638/9, a son, Henry, 25 March 1641 (buried 6 March 1642/3), and another son, Henry, 31 May 1643. His wife's name was Katherine . . . As a necessitous servant of Charles I he received a warrant for £30 on 10 October 1651 under the second list, allowed by Parliament on 13 August 1651: the receipt is dated 23 May 1654.[2]

Northrop's name appears in the list of Messengers of the Chamber sworn before 1644 which was drawn up in May 1660.[3] But in May (?) he was petitioning for confirmation of his place as Messenger of the Chamber granted him by the late King; when he was with Charles I at Oxford, the Messengers were reduced to such extreme necessity that of the forty, only he and another had horses for service, and they did the whole business; yet although wounded and plundered in the service, he is now refused admission on the ground that the number is full.[4] He was evidently admitted, for there are several subsequent references to him as a Messenger in the *C.S.P.D.* and *C.T.B.*: the last is in the latter on 8 December 1663.[5]

It is probable that the Mr Northrope whose name appears in all the St Aldate's taxation lists of 1645 is Henry Northrop: he must have rented a house at a date subsequent to the 'Accompt'.

[1] L.C. 3/1.
[2] S.P. 28/283 and S.P. 28/350/9, f. 31: No. 770.
[3] S.P. 29/1/63.
[4] *C.S.P.D.* 1660-1, p. 22.
[5] Vol. I, p. 562.

MR OLIVER SMYTH
(1606-1663)

Brewer. He was the second son of Alderman Oliver Smyth, by his first wife, Anne Bussey, and brother of Thomas and John Smyth [qq.v.]. He was baptized at St Aldate's 3 July 1606.[1] He was admitted by the University to brew 17 November 1621.[2] He matriculated from Wadham College 25 June 1624. He married, first, Elizabeth . . . (died 1631), and secondly, Christian (died 1670), daughter of . . . Lyford, of Reading, probably a niece of his step-mother, Christian Smyth (née Lyford). As Mr Oliver Smith Senior his name appears in all the St Aldate's parish taxation lists of 1645 and 1647. He was assessed at 3s. in the Subsidy of 1648.[3] He died 20 March 1662/3,[4] and was buried at St Aldate's 23 March 1662/3.[5]

Smyth's house was on the west side of Grandpont, 'in the farther end',[6] and probably occupied the site of No. 60 St Aldate's, which in 1772 had a frontage of thirteen yards: there were nine hearths in 1662 and 1666.[7] It appears to have been owned by Smyth, but was not bequeathed to him by his father, who left him lands in Berkshire, etc. For the garden in Grandpont which Smyth rented from Lincoln College see Richard Horne.

[1] Wood, *C. of O.*, Vol. III, p. 199.
[2] *Register*, Vol. II, Pt. I, p. 329.
[3] *S. and T.*, p. 169.
[4] Wood, *L. and T.*, Vol. I, p. 470 and *C. of O.*, Vol. III, p. 133.
[5] Ib., p. 208.
[6] Wood, *L. and T.*, Vol. I, p. 470.
[7] *Survey of South-West Ward*, No. 5.

THOMAS WENTWORTH, fifth BARON WENTWORTH
(1613-1665)

The eldest son of Thomas, fourth Baron Wentworth, created Earl of Cleveland in 1626, by his wife, Anne, daughter of Sir John Crofts, of Little Saxham, Suffolk. He was baptized at Toddington, Bedfordshire, 2 February 1612/13.

Wentworth was captain of a troop of horse in the two Bishops' Wars against the Scots 1639-40.[1] In the Short Parliament of 1640 he was M.P. for Bedfordshire. In November 1640 he was summoned, as Lord Wentworth, to the House of Lords. He was with his friend Goring at Portsmouth from August to September 1642, and joined the King at Oxford after Edgehill. He took part in raids in Buckinghamshire in December 1642 and May 1643. On 14 June 1643 he was lodging, together with four servants, in the house of James Pinnell [q.v.]: they all refused to pay on the ground that they were soldiers.[2] Mr Philip Nicholas, another servant, was lodging at Oliver Smyth's house at the same time and refused to pay.[3] On 26 June Wentworth was a member of the court martial of Sir Richard Cave [q.v.].[4] He was with Hopton in Sussex and Hampshire in December 1643.[5]

On 4 January 1643/4 Jane Bingley wrote to her daughter Susan: 'Your father is with his old master, Lord Wentworth, at Oxford.'[6] Wentworth sat in the Oxford Parliament in January 1643/4, and signed the letter to the Earl of Essex on 27 January 1643/4. In February 1643/4 he was appointed colonel of the Prince of Wales's Regiment in place of Sir Thomas Byron. In addition he was Sergeant-Major-General of the Horse to the 'Oxford' army. In 1644 he was present at Cropredy Bridge (29 June) and operations round Lostwithiel (August to September). On 8 August he signed the letter to Essex. He was almost certainly present at the Second Battle of Newbury (27 October). In 1645 he served as Marshal of the Field under Goring in the West, and was present at the defeat of the Royalists at Langport on 10 July. In September Wentworth was sent by Goring to the Prince of Wales at Launceston, with certain demands.[7] He settled into winter quarters round Exeter, and was president of the Council of War on the affair of Samuel Tuke. When Goring departed to France in November, he left his army under the command of Wentworth, a 'very lazy and inactive Man'.[8] On 9 January 1645/6 his Brigade (five regiments) was beaten up, three regiments at Bovey Tracey and two at Ashburton.[9] On 15 January he was made General of the Horse under Hopton. He signed the declaration of Goring's officers on 21 January.[10]

Thereafter Wentworth followed the fortunes of Charles II as Prince and as King, and was a Gentleman of the Bedchamber from 1649 until his death. He was made a P.C. in 1654. In 1656 he became colonel of the Royal Regiment of Guards (now the Grenadier Guards) in Flanders. He was reappointed in 1660 and served until his death.

He married before March 1657/8 Philadelphia, fifth daughter of Sir Ferdinando Carey. He died 1 March 1664/5. There is a M.I. at Toddington.

[Administration, as of St Giles-in-the-Fields, 24 May 1665].

(See *C.P.*; also Allan Fea, *The Loyal Wentworths* (1928), ch. II, pp. 9-31).

[1] *C.S.P.D.* 1640-1, pp. 5, 257-8; 1641-3, p. 261; H.M.C., *Rutland*, Vol. I, p. 506.
[2] St Aldate's Defaulters, Bodleian MS. Add. D. 114, f. 24v.
[3] Ibid.
[4] Webb, op. cit., Vol. I, p. 284.
[5] Sir R. Hopton, *Bellum Civile*, ed. C.E.H. Chadwyck-Healey, Somerset Record Society, Vol. 18 (1902), pp. 63, 74.
[6] *C.S.P.D.* 1644, p. 1. For his grooms see under Widow Phillips.
[7] Clarendon, Bk. IX, § 78, and Sir Richard Bulstrode, *Memoirs* p. 141.
[8] Bulstrode, op. cit., p. 149.
[9] British Museum Thomason Tract E. 316.
[10] Clarendon, S.P., Vol. 27, No. 2101.

ROBERT WILSON
(died 1663)

Brewer. The son of Robert Wilson, cooper and maltster, of St Aldate's, of which he was a churchwarden in 1618-19. On 12 July 1592 the elder Wilson, described as son of Robert Wilson, of Kettlewell in the county of York, blacksmith, was bound apprentice to Robert Bland, of Oxford, cooper.[1] The Blands also came from Kettlewell in the West Riding: on 20 November 1585 William, son of Anthony Bland, of this one-time market town, was bound apprentice to an Oxford glover.[2] The elder Wilson was admitted a freeman of Oxford 30 December 1600.[3] On 23 July 1605 he was granted a lease of one of the shops under the Guildhall for twenty-one years at a rent of 13s. 4d. per annum.[4] In 1611 he was chosen a constable,[5] and in 1629 was made a common councillor,[6] a position which he filled until his death. This occurred between 24 December 1640, when he made his Will, in which he is described as maltster, and 2 January 1640/1, when it was proved.[7] His 'loveinge wife Anne Wilson' is almost certainly the 'widow Wilson' whose house is entered as being on the east side of Fish Street in 1643.[8] She may have been a second wife: she was certainly a recusant: in the Subsidy Lists of 1641 she was assessed at 8d. and 16d. 'for her Pole'.[9]

Among the bequests enumerated in the elder Wilson's Will was one to the mayor and bailiffs of Oxford of £20 which was to be lent free of charge for periods of seven years in three or four equal portions to citizens of Oxford or their widows. Wilson named the first three beneficiaries, one of them being Anthony Bland [q.v.], the son of his former master. His son, Robert Wilson the younger, was named residuary legatee and executor.

The younger Robert Wilson and his father-in-law, Timothy Doyly (for whom see later), were among those accused by Bailiff Heron in September 1642 of assisting Sir John Byron after he entered the city on 28 August.[10] He was clearly a keen Royalist, for he was later certified as a Delinquent.[11] On 5 December 1644 he was admitted to brew by the University.[12] He followed his father in being chosen a common councillor, in 1644,[13] and he was junior bailiff in 1645.[14] As Mr Bayley Wilson he contributed £5 to the loan to the Lords Commissioners in October 1645.[15] Wilson's name does not appear in the list of bailiffs for 1648 so he was evidently removed in the 'purge' of that year. He was, however, restored 1 October 1660,[16] and was a bailiff in the list of 1661, but not in that of 1662. His name appears in all the St Aldate's parish taxation lists of 1645 and 1647. He was assessed at 9s. 6d. in the Subsidy of 1648.[17]

Wilson married a member of an ancient family, Anne, elder daughter of Timothy Doyly, of Stadhampton, Oxfordshire.[18] She died in 1652/3, aged thirty-six, the mother of four sons and four daughters.[19] When Robert Wilson senior made his Will, there were only two grandchildren, Robert and Marie, who were each to receive £100 at the age of eighteen: Robert was also left the lease of his grandfather's Guildhall shop, and was renting it in 1658.[20] The elder Wilson made 'my brother Mr Timothye Doilie' an overseer of his Will.

Robert Wilson the younger was buried at St Aldate's 13 June 1663.[21] The churchwardens received 6s. 8d. for his grave.

[Will: MS. Wills Oxon. 307, f. 113, 22 June 1663: Caveat Book].

Wilson's brewhouse (where he lived) was on the west side of Grandpont, immediately north of Folly Bridge. It was the property of New College (to which, as the 'Long Books' shew, he supplied beer). On 28 November 1643 an indenture was made between the College and Robert Wilson, of the parish of St Aldate's 'bearebrewer', by which the tenement or brewhouse, stated to be in the 'Suburbes of the Citie of Oxford in the County of Berks', was let to him. It is described as 'lying . . . betweene the kings highway leading from the Bridge called the South

Bridg towards the said Citty of Oxford on the East side and the Common River or Stream water [sic] running under the said South Bridge on the West side of the North p'te or end thereof abutting vppon the water course or Lake called Sheare Lake parting or dividing the said Counties of Berks and Oxon and the south pte or end thereof abutting vppon the said Common River or Streame of Water running Vnder the South Bridge aforesaid'. The lease was for forty years and the rent was £3. 6s. 8d. per annum. Wilson was to keep the property in repair.[22]

[1] City Archives L. 5. 1, f. 22.
[2] Ib. A. 5. 3, f. 337.
[3] *O.C.A.* 1583-1626, p. 138.
[4] Ib., p. 168.
[5] Ib., p. 216.
[6] *O.C.A.* 1626-1665, p. 22.
[7] P.C.C. 8 Evelyn.
[8] St Aldate's Defaulters List, Bodleian MS. Add. D. 114, f. 26.
[9] City Archives B. 1. 4. c. and B. 1. 4. d. It would seem probable that the widow Bridgett Wilson, recusant, who was living in the South-West Ward in 1641 and was assessed at 8d. and 12d. 'for her Pole' (B. 1. 4. c. and B. 1. 4. d.) and from whom a Welsh bill and a head piece were received for the King's stores on 24 April 1643 (*R.O.P.*, Part I, p. 85), was a relative, but she is not mentioned in Robert Wilson's Will.
[10] *Manuscripts of the House of Lords*, Vol. XI, New Series, p. 326.
[11] City Archives F. 5. 9, f. 101.
[12] *Register*, Vol. II, Pt. I, p. 330.
[13] *O.C.A.* 1626-1665, p. 123.
[14] Ib., p. 131.
[15] City Archives E. 4. 6, ff. 1-2: *O.C.A.* 1626-1665, p. 453.
[16] City Archives A. 5. 7, f. 281v.
[17] *S. and T.*, p. 169.
[18] See *Visitation of Oxfordshire* 1574 and 1634, p. 272.
[19] M.I. in St Aldate's church: see also Wood, *C. of O.*, Vol. III, p. 136.
[20] *O.C.P.*, p. 11.
[21] Wood, *C. of O.*, Vol. III, p. 208.
[22] New College Muniments Registrum Dim. ad Firm. 9, ff. 419-20.

CAPTAIN JOHN BEETON

He belonged to the Lifeguard of Foot. As a lieutenant in June 1643 he was lodging at the house of John Horne [q.v.]. He declared that 'he would not pay till the king payd him'.[1] He may be assumed to have fought at the siege of Gloucester and at First Newbury. Captain Benton [sic] was taken prisoner at Naseby on 14 June 1645.[2] Captain John Beeton was an Indigent Officer from Berkshire in 1663.[3]

[1] St Aldate's Defaulters, Bodleian MS. Add. D. 114, f. 26.
[2] Peacock, p. 95.
[3] *I.O.*, col. 90.

CAPTAIN FORSTER

He belonged to the Lifeguard of Foot. He is described as a captain, but was actually a captain-lieutenant. In June 1643, as a lieutenant, he was lodging across the street at the house of [Richard] Farmer, when no answer was obtained from him.[1]

[1] St Aldate's Defaulters, Bodleian MS. Add. D. 114, f. 24v.

ROBERT PANTING
(died c. 1658)

Boatman. In June 1643 he and one man were reported to be 'boatmen & were then vpon service for the king for the Cannons running'.[1] They are entered under 'mr farmers house' and it is probable that they were in the employment of Richard Farmer (see below).

On 19 February 1646/7 Panting was admitted a freeman on payment of £10,[2] but on 11 March this large sum was reduced to £6. 13s. 4d.[3] In the City Audit Book there are numerous entries in the year 1647 to Panting for 'worke done about the Waterworkes' for which he received substantial sums.[4] His name occurs in all the St Aldate's taxation lists for 1645 and 1647. He paid 1s. 6d. in the Subsidy of 1648.[5] On 24 January 1652/3, Henry Vaughan [q.v.] having died, he was chosen to have the remains of Vaughan's £10 of Dr Wilkinson's money for the rest of the time.[6] He was dead by 19 March 1657/8, when administration of his goods was granted.[7]

Panting's house was the Wharf House: there is still a Wharf House on the site. It was situated on the east side of Grandpont, on Lombard's or Lumbard's land on the north side of the Thames, in Berkshire.[8] He rented his house from the city. In the Chamberlains' Accounts for the year Michaelmas 1638 to Michaelmas 1639 there is an entry that there was received of Richard Farmer rent of wharfage and profits of the barges for nine months £22. 10s.[9] In the following year Farmer paid £30 as one year's rent for the Wharfage house and Wharfage place,[10] and again in the year 1643 to 1644.[11] His Will, as of Oxfordshire, was proved at Oxford in October 1643.[12] Under the heading 'Allowances of Rents' in the Chamberlains' Accounts for 1644-5 occurs the entry 'Mrs Farmer and Panting for the Wharfe, £30'.[13] Panting must have been sharing the rent with Richard Farmer's widow. In 1645-6 the Chamberlains received £5 from him as rent of the Wharf House.[14] On 27 September 1647 it is recorded that 'The Executrix of Mr Richard Farmer, who died in debt to the City for the sum of £60 for the rent of the Wharf at the South Bridge, asks for an abatement of the rent, since owing to these troublous times the benefits from it are less than they would otherwise have been. It is . . . agreed that if the executrix will pay £30 and the expenses already incurred, the City will be satisfied and discharge the said executrix of payment of the rent of £60'.[15] Panting's rent was unpaid in the year 1647-8, but he produced his £5 in 1648[16] and one year's arrears in 1650.[17] He was still living at the Wharf at the time of his death.[18]

[1] St Aldate's Defaulters, Bodleian MS. Add. D. 114, f. 24v.
[2] *O.C.A.* 1626-1665, p. 143.
[3] Ib., p. 144.
[4] City Archives P. 5. 2, ff. 265-6.
[5] *S. and T.*, p. 169. Mr [sic] Farmer was assessed at 10d.
[6] *O.C.A.* 1626-1665, p. 197.
[7] P.C.C. 1658, f. 78.
[8] Wood, *C. of O.*, Vol. I, p. 307.
[9] *O.C.A.* 1626-1665, p. 422.
[10] Ibid.
[11] Ib., p. 426.
[12] P.C.C. *Calendar* 1640-4.
[13] *O.C.A.* 1626-1665, p. 428.
[14] Ib., p. 429.
[15] Ib., p. 150.
[16] City Archives P. 5. 2, f. 272v.

[17] Ib., f. 278v.
[18] Administration.

In June 1643, under Farmer's house, as Panting's then was, it is recorded that 'three retourned as his servants are foot souldiers'. He also had lodging with him 'Captaine Min & 1 man' and 'Leiftenant forster' [q.v.], from neither of whom an answer was received.

THOMAS MINN or MYNNE
(died 1672)

The senior lieutenant (captain-lieutenant?) in Sir Arthur Aston's Regiment of Foot in 1640.[1] His younger brother, John Mynne, was the junior ensign of the same regiment. On 25 March 1641 'Tho: Myn' was captain-lieutenant to the regiment of Colonel Richard Feilding, Aston's Regiment having been disbanded by this time. Ensign 'Jo: Mynn' had also transferred to this regiment. Captain Minn fought at Cirencester 2 February 1642/3, under Colonel Lewis Kirke, whose command consisted of contingents from the Oxford garrison.[2] On 23 April 1643 he signed for 133 long pikes[3] and on 16 March 1643/4, as captain, he signed for ammunition for the Lifeguard of Foot.[4]
Thomas Mynne was the eldest son of Thomas Mynne, Knight Harbinger to James I and Charles I, who died in 1638, by his wife, Anne Lovell, who came from Lincolnshire. The Will of the elder Thomas Mynne was proved in the P.C.C. 24 December 1638.[5] He only mentions his wife and eldest daughter, Elizabeth, but both Thomas and John and their sister Frances are mentioned in the Will of their uncle Sir Henry Mynne, of Whissendyne, Rutland, which was proved in the P.C.C. 2 January 1651/2.[6] Sir Henry had been Paymaster to the Gentlemen Pensioners from 1608 to 1619. He and his family were recusants, and it is probable that his brother and nephews were also, which would make it natural for Thomas and John to serve under Sir Arthur Aston, who was himself a Roman Catholic. Thomas Mynne died in October 1672.
Mynne named his brother-in-law Sir George Wakeman, Physician in Ordinary to Queen Catherine, and also a Roman Catholic, his sole executor. As Sir George's widowed mother, Maria Wakeman (died 1676), does not mention any Mynne grandchildren in her Will, it is to be presumed that he had married a sister of Thomas Mynne and that she was the Jane Wakeman who acted as a witness to Mynne's Will. One of Sir George's younger brothers, John Wakeman, was born at Oxford in 1643, so that Mynne could have known the family there in the War. The eldest brother, Richard Wakeman, was a major in the Royalist army, and raised a troop for the King.
[Will: P.C.C. 1672: 139 Eure: made 17 October 1672: proved 26 October 1672, as of St Martin-in-the-Fields].

[1] Rushworth, Vol. III, p. 1246.
[2] *Bibliotheca Gloucestrensis*, Pt. I, p. 169: 'A Particular Relation of the Action before Cyrencester'.
[3] P.R.O., W.O. 55 423/95v.
[4] Ib., 423/121.
[5] 174 Lee.
[6] 11 Bowyer.

JOHN RICHARDSON

Boatman. He was admitted a freeman 25 June 1604.[1] He was a churchwarden of St Aldate's in 1623-4. In 1646 he was paid 5s. 6d. by the city 'for plancks in Christ Church Meade for boating Mr Mayor on the Meadow and the boatemen for the viewing the waters for the ffranchises'.[2] In 1648 he received 1s. 'for lyering a planck in Christ Church Meade' for the franchises.[3] His name occurs in all the St Aldate's parish taxation lists of 1645 and 1647. He was assessed at 6d. in the Subsidy of 1648.[4] His sons, John and Matthew, were ardent Royalists.[5] John Richardson the younger was admitted a freeman 16 April 1661.[6]
Richardson's house was on the east side of Grandpont and appears to have lain a little way north of the Wharf House. It is not possible to say whether it was owned or rented by him: probably the latter.

[1] *O.C.A.* 1583-1626, p. 161.
[2] City Archives P. 5. 2, f. 263v.
[3] Ib., f. 274v.
[4] *S. and T.*, p. 169.
[5] For the incident of 29 September 1642 see Wood, *L. and T.*, Vol. I, p. 66.
[6] *O.C.A.* 1626-1665, p. 280.

MR WILLIAM (?) WARDE

Perhaps William Warde, a servant of George Villiers, first Duke of Buckingham, who together with two other of his servants, petitioned the Duke on 23 February 1625/6.[1] He is not mentioned in the Duke's Will.
George Villiers, second Duke of Buckingham (1628-1687) joined Charles I at Oxford in 1642 and served under Prince Rupert at Lichfield in 1643. He was present with the King at the siege of Gloucester.[2] He was still quartered at Oxford just before Christmas 1643.[3] He did not sit in the Oxford Parliament, perhaps because he was a minor.
By April 1645 the Duke and his brother, Lord Francis, had gone to France,[4] and they were expected at Rome in June.[5]

[1] *C.S.P.D.* 1625-6, p. 259.
[2] Luke, p. 145.
[3] Ib., p. 222.
[4] *C.A.M.*, p. 528.
[5] *C.S.P.D.* 1644-5, p. 604.

THREE MAIDS OF KATHERINE VILLIERS, DUCHESS OF BUCKINGHAM (died 1649)

The widow of George Villiers, first Duke of Buckingham, and mother of George Villiers, second Duke [q.v.]. She was the daughter and heiress of Francis Manners, sixth Earl of Rutland. In 1635 she married, as her second husband, Randall MacDonnell, second Earl of Antrim, who was created Marquess of Antrim by Charles 1 26 January 1644/5. She died at Waterford in 1649.
The Duchess was herself lodging in Brasenose College in 1644 according to a Buttery Book of that year in which her name is bracketed with that of Elias

Ashmole as owing a small sum to the Bursar for battels.[1] Unfortunately, this book has since disappeared.

[1] *B.N.C. Quatercentenary Monographs,* Vol. II, Pt. I, Monograph XI (1909), p. 36, Oxford Historical Society and *Register,* p. 180.

ELIZABETH BURT, WIDOW

Widow of John Burt or Birt, brewer. He was the elder son of Thomas Burt, Birte or Byrte, blacksmith, of Buckland, Berkshire, by his wife, Alice . . . Thomas Burt's Will was made 27 December 1600 and proved 28 January 1600/1.[1] To his elder son he left 'my full and whole living whereof I am now possest' as well as many special bequests of furniture and bed-gear, and 'my fornace pan in the malt house and my malt mill . . ; in the said roome'. John was also to have the 'four acres of grounds the wch I have wholy to my selfe this yeare, and he to inioye the crop thereof to himselfe'. The value of Thomas Burt's goods was £122. 2s. 7d. Both sons were under age, and it was not until 13 February 1609/10 that John was apprenticed to Richard Paynter, fellmonger, of Oxford.[2] He obtained his freedom 4 July 1617.[3] On 21 February 1619/20 he was admitted to brew by the University.[4] He was a churchwarden of St Aldate's in 1627-8. An Inventory of his goods was taken 20 May 1633,[5] and administration was granted to Elizabeth 28 September 1633.[6]

Mrs Burt's name appears in three of the St Aldate's taxation lists of 1645, in which year she probably died. She had at least two sons, Thomas and Henry, who, as sons of 'John Birt late of the Citty of Oxon Ale-Brewer deceased', were respectively bound apprentice 6 August and 11 November 1633.[7] Henry Burt, entered as out of town, was living in his mother's house in June 1643.[8] The name of Richard Birt occurs in one of the lists of 1645: by 1647 the tenement was in the possession of Robert Tapping.

Mrs Burt's house was on the east side of Grandpont, on the site of the former No. 35 St Aldate's: it was situated immediately south of Denchworth Bow, the arch which crossed the Shire-Lake between Nos. 34 and 35. This tenement was the property of the city, to which it had belonged since the fifteenth century,[9] and was leased to Thomas Smyth [q.v.], who was Elizabeth Burt's landlord. Thomas' uncle Robert Jones[10] (died 1614), brewer, maltster, and B.A. of Oxford, had had leases granted him in 1603 and 1613,[11] and so had Thomas' father in 1626 and 1636.[12] In his Will, dated 26 February 1632/3, Alderman Oliver Smyth gave 'vnto my said sonne Thomas . . . All that my messuage or tenement with thappurtences, which I hold by lease of the said Maio' Bailifs and Commonalty nowe in the occupacoñ of John Birt scituate and beinge in Grandpont neere Denchworth bowe within the Suburbes of the Citty of Oxon and all my brewinge vessells vtensills implements and goods whatsoever in the same messuage or tenement.'[13] In the lease of 1636 it is stated that the tenement was once in the 'occupacon of Robert Jones Brewer and afterwards of John Birt now deceased and now in thoccupacon of Joane [sic] Birt Widdowe'.[14] Let with the tenement was the 'Orchard Backside and garden ground to the said Messuage . . . belonging . . . scituate on the east and south ptes of the said demised Messuage . . . and conteyninge in length at the north or end from Shearlake there called denchworth Bowe on the north side to the south of the same orchard, Backside', etc. 'three and fforty foote And a [edge torn] the upper end thereof next to the said Messuage three Poles . . . And in length from the gate entringe into the said Orchard', etc. 'on the west pte to the Crosse streame into wch the said Sheare Lake called denchworth Bowe doth runne on theast pte Tenne Poles lacking [tear] foote of the measure as aforesaid Togeather allsoe wth all edifices buildings' etc.

The Inventory of Robert Jones, dated 20 June 1614, mentions 'the Hawle', 'Roomes over the parlor & hawle', 'the Parlor', and 'the Brewhouse'.[15]

[1] Bodleian Library, MS. Wills Berks. 13, ff. 638v-40.

[2] City Archives L. 5. 1, f. 180.
[3] Ib., L. 5. 2, no folio number.
[4] *Register*, Vol. II, Pt. I, p. 329.
[5] MS. Wills Oxon, 295/3/48.
[6] Ib. 107, f. 22: Act Book B.
[7] City Archives L. 5. 2, ff. 272 and 276v.
[8] St Aldate's Defaulters, Bodleian MS. Add. D. 114, f. 24v.
[9] *O.C.P.*, p. 105.
[10] He married in 1589 Joane, daughter of Thomas Smyth and sister of Alderman Oliver Smyth: she died in 1619. A copy of his Will is in the University Archives Reg. G. G. 5, ff. 108v-109.
[11] See *O.C.P.*, pp. 105-6.
[12] Ibid.
[13] P.C.C. 82 Goare.
[14] City Archives D. 5. 6, f. 1. The lease was for forty years and the rent was 27s. per annum.
[15] University Archives Hyp. B. 20, ff. 27-27v. The lease of the house was valued at £21.

ENSIGN MASTERMAN

Unidentified. He probably belonged to the Lifeguard of Foot, but he was not among the officers taken at Naseby.

In June 1643 Mrs Burt had lodging with her a MR BARNSHAM and a MR WOODDARD, both of whom were 'out of towne'.[1] They are unidentified.

[1] Bodleian MS. Add. D. 114, f. 24v.

LIII

ELIZABETH (?) TREDWELL, WIDOW

This is possibly the Elizabeth Tredwell, widow, who paid 1s., as of St Aldate's, in the Poll Tax of 1667[1] and who was buried at St Aldate's 7 August 1678,[2] although her name does not occur in the parish taxation lists of 1645 and 1647 or in the Subsidy of 1648. It is possible that Widow Tredwell had been the wife of John Tredwell, cordwainer, who, as an apprentice of Alexander Tredwell, was admitted a freeman 15 June 1613.[3] Tredwell became a constable in 1619,[4] a common councillor in 1621,[5] a chamberlain in 1623,[6] and was chosen junior bailiff in 1633.[7] In 1634 he and the other ex-bailiff were involved in a disgraceful scene over their claim on the fee-farm.[8] His name appears as bailiff for the last time in September 1642, and it is therefore of significance that Goowife Tredwell paid 6s. 8d. for her husband's grave in St Aldate's in 1642-3.[9] It is probable that Matthew Tredwell (brewer?), who was a churchwarden of St Aldate's in 1666-7, and married a daughter of Walter Cave [q.v.], was John's son.

Mrs Tredwell's house was on the east side of Grandpont, being the present No. 34 St Aldate's, immediately north of Denchworth Bow. It was private property and had been conveyed in 1545 by Robert Hethe, of Shelswell, Oxfordshire, to Robert Parrett (Perrot) of Oxford. The deed, dated 3 June 37 Henry VIII, described the property as a 'tenement and garden in Grandpont in "thest" part of the street between a certain water called Denchworth bowe and the Shire lake on the South part and a tenement of the Dean and Canons of S. Frydeswide on the North'.[10] In his Will, proved in 1550,[11] Robert Perrot left 'Vnto Alice my Wife all my landes yt I bought of Robr̃t Heathe . . . and after her decease I do bequeath it to Leonarde Parret my sone his heirs and assignes for ever'. Leonard, the fourth son of Robert Perrot, was of Drayton, Oxfordshire. In his Will, proved 5 June 1594,[12] Leonard stated: 'Item I will and devise that the Rents and proffitts of my Tenement lying . . . in Grampole . . . late in the tenure of Sr Robert Jones Bachelor of Arts[13] . . . being of the yearely Rent of forty three shillings and foure pence shalbe and remaine for theis three yeares next after my decease to my Executors . . . Afterwardes I devise and bequeathe the same Tenement to my sonne Leonard Perrot, and to his heirs and assignes for ever.' Leonard Perrot the younger, his father's fourth son, was of Eynsham, Oxfordshire. He had a son, Richard, and a grandson, Francis:[14] the latter was married at St Cross, Oxford, in 1640. Either Francis or his father would have been Mrs Tredwell's landlord.

The house was built in the sixteenth century, two storeys high, of coarse rubble, containing one room on each of two floors.[15]

[1] *S. and T.*, p. 263. The Elizabeth Tredwell, widow, who figures in the Subsidy of 1621, for the South-East Ward, was perhaps her mother-in-law.
[2] Parish Registers.
[3] *O.C.A.* 1583-1626, p. 226.
[4] Ib., p. 287.
[5] Ib., p. 303.
[6] Ib., p. 321 and 322.
[7] *O.C.A.* 1626-1665, pp. 47 and 49.
[8] Ib., pp. xviii and 59.
[9] Churchwardens' Accounts.
[10] W.P. Ellis and H.E. Salter, *Liber Albus Civitatis Oxoniensis* (1909), No. 330. See also *Survey of South-East Ward*, No. 171.
[11] Registrum Simon Parret, MS. Trin. Coll. B. 83, f. 12.
[12] P.C.C. 45 Dixy.
[13] For Robert Jones see under Elizabeth Burt. He moved from No. 34 to No. 35 St Aldate's, probably when his father-in-law, Thomas Smyth, acquired the lease of the latter in 1593 (*O.C.P.*, p. 105).

[14] Bodleian MS. Wood D. 7, f. 14.

[15] For a full description and plan see *Oxoniensia*, Vols. XXVI/XXVII (1961/2), pp. 323-5 and Plate XLII B.

JOHN MASSEY
(c. 1582-after 1648)

Parchment maker. He was of Wiltshire origin. In 1626 he was matriculated as a privileged person of Oxford University, his age being given as forty-four.[1] He helped to take the Inventory of Alexander Hill, of St Aldate's (see under Widow Margaret Hill).[2] In June 1643 Massey's man was stated to have gone into St Clement's parish.[3] In 1643-4 the churchwardens paid 5s. 'for a Souldier that died in the howse of John Macie and burying of him'. In 1644-5 they paid 4s. 'for a Shrowde and a gravesmaking for a Souldier that died at John Massies 8 of ffebruary 1644' [i.e. 1645]. This was probably the corporal of the Lifeguard. Massey's name appears in all the St Aldate's taxation lists of 1645 and 1647. In 1647 he was admitted a freeman.[4] He was assessed at 2s. 6d. in the Subsidy of 1648.[5]
Massey's house was on the east side of Grandpont being the present No. 33 St. Aldate's. It belonged to William Hawkes (see under Mrs Jane Hawkes). It was first built in the mid or late sixteenth century, two storeys high, containing one room on each of two floors.[6]

[1] University Archives S P 2, f. 337: 'Johẽs Massy, Pergamenus, Wiltoñ: pl: an: nat' 44'.
[2] MS. Wills Oxon. 298/1/44.
[3] St Aldate's Defaulters, Bodleian MS. Add. D. 114, f. 24v.
[4] City Archives P. 5. 2, f. 267v.
[5] *S. and T.*, p. 170.
[6] For a full description and plan see *Oxoniensia*, Vols. XXVI/XXVII (1961/2), pp. 323-5 and Plate XLII B.

MRS JANE HAWKES
(died c. 1663)

Butcher. The widow of John Hawkes, a prosperous butcher of St Aldate's, her maiden name was Crouchloe, as we learn from her husband's Will. John Hawkes, the second son of Thomas Hawkes, butcher and freeman of Oxford, was admitted a freeman in 1612.[1] He was elected to the Common Council in 1625[2] and a bailiff in 1629.[3] In 1631 he was appointed one of the flesh-viewers (inspectors of the meat-market).[4] He paid £3 and 23s. in the Subsidy of 1641.[5] He made his Will 23 April 1642, and this was proved at Oxford 12 September 1642, his widow and his eldest son, William, being named executors and William Tompson [q.v.] an overseer. John Massey [q.v.] was a witness.[6] Mrs Hawkes paid 6s. 8d. for her husband's grave in St Aldate's church.[7]

On 24 April 1643 Jane Hawkes sent a corselet and a pike to the King's stores.[8] She contributed £2. 10s. 0d. to the loan to the Lords Commissioners in October 1645.[9] Her name appears in all the St Aldate's parish taxation lists of 1645 and 1647. She paid 4s. in the Subsidy of 1648.[10] The Churchwardens' Accounts of 1663-4 contain the entry: 'Item for breaking ground in the body of the church to bury Mrs Hawkes Sr' 6s. 8d. It would seem that Jane was a second wife as 'Jane wife of Mr John [Hawkes] bayliff of the citie' was buried at St Aldate's 9 June 1635.[11]

Mrs Hawkes' house was on the east side of Grandpont, being Nos. 31 and 32 St Aldate's. It was described in 1626, in the lifetime of John Hawkes, as lying south of two tenements (the former Nos. 29 and 30) in the occupation of Miles Godfrey and William Stevens [qq.v.]. In his Will John Hawkes arranged that Jane should have the 'Vse and Occupacon of the Two Cocklofts in the howse wherein I now live with the beddinge and furniture therein duringe her widdowhoode and the lower Roome called the Hall and the butrey and likewise the Vse of the Backside therevnto adioyninge with free liberty of Ingresse, egresse, and regresse att all tymes convenient into and from the same Provided allwayes . . . that William Hawkes my Sonne shall vppon all necessary occasions have the vse of the said Hall with my said Wife'. 'I give to William Hawkes my Sonne my howse wherein I now dwell in the psh of St Aldats aforesaid and the next howse therevnto adioyninge now in the Occupacon of John Masey' [q.v.]. William appears to have relinquished the house to his step-mother. He probably lived on the Marston property bequeathed to him by his father in trust.

Nos. 31 and 32 St Aldate's, 145 yards north of Folly Bridge, is of three storeys: the walls are timber-framed and the roofs slate-covered. It was built early in the seventeenth century.[12]

[1] *O.C.A.* 1583-1626, p. 223.
[2] Ib., p. 336.
[3] *O.C.A.* 1626-1665, p. 21.
[4] *Register*, Vol. II, Pt. I, p. 255.
[5] City Archives B. 1. 4. c. He paid 20s. and 4s. in 1628 (B. 1. 3. e).
[6] MS. Wills Oxon. 32/2/16.
[7] Churchwardens' Accounts 1642-3.
[8] *R.O.P.*, Part I, p. 83.
[9] City Archives E. 4. 6, ff. 1-2: *O.C.A.* 1626-1665, p. 453.
[10] *S. and T.*, p. 170.
[11] Wood, *C. of O.*, Vol. III, p. 207.
[12] The house is described in R.C.H.M. *City of Oxford*, p. 174 and *Oxoniensia*, Vols. XXVI/XXVII (1961/2), pp. 323-5, with plan, and illustration, Plate XLII B.

COLONEL DAVID SCRYMGEOUR
(died 1644)

The third of the five sons of Sir John Scrymgeour, of Dudhope, Forfarshire (1570-1643), created Viscount Dudhope in 1641, hereditary Constable of Dundee, by his wife, Margaret, daughter of Sir David Seaton, of Parbroath (the *Scots Peerage* calls him George Seaton), whom he married in 1596.

On 27 December 1639 Patrick, Lord Ruthven (afterwards Earl of Forth and Brentford, q.v.), Governor of Edinburgh, wrote to Charles I recommending for the post of Under-Constable of the Castle a Gentleman of the Privy Chamber, Lt. Colonel Scrimsure, a highly experienced soldier.[1] He entered the King's service at Edinburgh Castle 1 January 1639/40,[2] receiving 15s. per diem. On 5 January 1639/40 the King's assent was given to the appointment.[3] On the surrender of Edinburgh Castle in September 1640, Scrymgeour accompanied Ruthven to Berwick by coach.[4] He was Adjutant-General of the Horse for Scotland. His name does not appear in L.C. 3/1.

Scrymgeour was doubtless one of the twenty-two Scots officers who accompanied Ruthven to England in October 1642 to join the Cavaliers. 'Colonell Scrimsour, generall adjutant of the horse', led the forlorn hope consisting of twenty-five of Prince Rupert's Lifeguard, into the town at the storming of Cirencester 2 February 1642/3.[5] He was described as captain on 14 June 1643, when he was already lodging, together with three men, at Mrs Hawkes' house, and no answer could be obtained from them.[6]

A Colonel Skirmshay (Scrimgeour) was captured by Waller at Evesham with important letters 18 June 1644.[7] If he was exchanged quickly, he could have been Colonel David. The latter signed the letter to Essex written on 8 August 1644 and the Old Horse Petition,[8] so that he was in Cornwall in August.

David Scrimgeour married Joan Cockburne (living 1 December 1654), and had two daughters. He was buried in the Church of St Mary the Virgin, Oxford, 2 December 1644.[9]

[Will: Edinburgh Testaments: 1 June 1647].

Scrimgeour's eldest brother, James, second Viscount Dudhope, was in command of the Infantry under Lord Leven at Marston Moor, where he was wounded: he died 23 July 1644.

[1] *C.S.P.D.* 1639-40, p. 182.
[2] *Ruthven Correspondence*, p. 68.
[3] *C.S.P.D.* 1639-40, p. 303.
[4] Ib. 1640-1, p. 135.
[5] *Bibliotheca Gloucestrensis*, Pt. I, p. 169.
[6] St Aldate's Defaulters, Bodleian MS. Add. D. 114, f. 24v.
[7] *C.S.P.D.* 1644, p. 247.
[8] Warburton, Vol. III, p. 17.
[9] Wood, *C. of O.*, Vol. III, p. 17.

In June 1643 Mrs Hawkes also had lodging with her SERGEANT MAJOR LUGWOOD (LOCKWOOD?) and one man.[1] It has not been possible to identify him, but he was possibly a Scot, serving in the same regiment as Scrymgeour.

[1] St Aldate's Defaulters, Bodleian MS. Add. D. 114, f. 24v.

MILES GODFREY

Blacksmith. The son of Cyprian Godfrey, blacksmith, of St Aldate's, whose Will, made 22 January 1618/19, was proved at Oxford 1 October 1619.[1] In this Miles was left 'the lease of my house after my decease wholie during the terme of the said lease'. His brother John received his father's shop for ten years 'and all my workinge tooles wch doth belonge and appertayne vnto my said shoppe whatsover for ever'.

Miles Godfrey was admitted a freeman by his father's copy 24 September 1618.[2] In the St Aldate's Churchwardens' Accounts for 1631-2 there are entries of payments for the burial of his wife (5s.) and the nursing of his child (£2. 14s. 0d.). The latter item (but only 2s.) recurs in 1632-3. The name of Michael Godfrey [sic] occurs in all the St Aldate's parish taxation lists of 1645 and 1647. He was assessed at 1s. 6d. in the Subsidy of 1648.[3] He was a churchwarden of St Aldate's in 1646-7 and 1647-8. From 1646 until 1666-7 there are numerous entries relating to him in the Accounts for work done by him for the church, e.g. bells, keys, and locks.[4]

Godfrey's house was on the east side of Grandpont, being on the site of the southern part of Nos. 29 and 30 St Aldate's. It belonged to the parish, which had acquired it in 1523.[5] In 41 Elizabeth (1598-9) it was said to be 'late in the tenure of Alice Godfrey, widow,'[6] probably Cyprian Godfrey's mother, and in 3 James I (1605-6) the tenement was occupied by Cyprian himself at a rent of 20s. per annum and was worth £3 per annum.[7] On 2 February 1613/14 the St Aldate's feoffees leased to 'William Atwell als Stevens [q.v.] All that their Messuage or Tenemt Backside garden ground & Orchard wth all & singlar̃ howses . . . therevnto belonging Scytuate . . . in Grandpont . . . abutting Westwards vppon the kings highestreet there and Eastward vppon a Streame or Water runing by Mountagues Meade towards the Thames and next betweene the Tenemt of Richard Horne [q.v.] on the sowth and Mathew Langley [q.v.] on the north and now in the tenure or occupacõn of Ciprian Godfrey his assignes or Assignees'.[8] The lease was for thirty-one years and the rent £6 per annum.

Whether Stevens immediately occupied part of the house there is no evidence to shew. In 1626 the property was divided into two tenements, which were occupied by Miles Godfrey and his landlord, Stevens.[9]

[1] MS. Wills Oxon, 25/4/49.
[2] *O.C.A.* 1583-1626, p. 275.
[3] *S. and T.*, p. 170.
[4] See also Old Documents 1400-1662, f. 55, in Parish Chest.
[5] *Survey of South-East Ward*, No. 168.
[6] Ibid.
[7] P.R.O. Charitable Uses Inquests: Bundle 2, No. 27. quoted in *Survey*.
[8] Lease in Parish Chest.
[9] *Survey of South-East Ward*, p. 241. Dr Salter gives no source for this statement which we have been unable to check.

MR WILLIAM PETMAN ?
(died 1676)

Pettyman is an uncommon name. It seems probable that the person meant is William Pitman or Petman, yeoman pricker of the Privy Buckhounds, especially as he was lodging next door to John Cary [q.v.], Master of the Buckhounds to Prince Charles. He appears as Pitman, yeoman pricker, 18 and 24 December 1638,[1] and

1641 as Petman.[2]
Petman must have been loyal, as on 27 August 1669 £750 was ordered to be paid to William Pitman, Serjeant of the King's Buckhounds, for three years' arrears.[3] [Will: as William Pittman, Serjeant of H.M. Privy Buckhounds of Putney: P.C.C. 1676: 143 Bence: made 20 October 1676: proved 6 November 1676. This is quite uninformative].
It may be noted that in three of the St Aldate's parish taxation lists of 1645 the name 'Mr Pitman' occurs not far from that of Stevens, which suggests that he may later have rented a house for himself, although the name Pitman does appear elsewhere in Oxford in the seventeenth century.

[1] *C.S.P.D.* 1638-9, pp. 175 and 187, warrant for livery of 76s. per annum.
[2] L.C. 3/1.
[3] *C.T.B.*, Vol. III, p. 274.

MR DODSON

Unidentified.

In June 1643 the house is entered as 'Michael' Godfrey's and he is described as having two of the King's farriers lodging with him. The name of one of these is erased, the other being FRANCIS WINDRESSE. They stated that they would pay if others of their degree did the same.[1] Windresse is a Lancashire name. A William Windress, of Nether Wyersdale, was in arms for the King in 1643.[2] The printed St Margaret's, Westminster, Registers shew that another William Windresse and his wife, Joan, were living in the parish between 1664 and 1671: he may have been a son of Francis.

[1] St Aldate's Defaulters, Bodleian MS. Add. D. 114, f. 24v.
[2] *C.C.C.*, p. 2899.

MR WILLIAM STEVENS alias ATWELL
(died c. 1658)

Butcher. He was elected a common councillor in 1611,[1] a chamberlain in 1618,[2] junior bailiff in 1635,[3] and was a bailiff from 1637[4] until his death. He was appointed one of the flesh-viewers 12 June 1635.[5]

The Brasenose College Junior Bursar's Book for 1644[6] shews that Stevens was the butcher who supplied the College with meat. The receipts at the end are signed with his mark.

Stevens contributed £5 to the loan to the Lords Commissioners in October 1645.[7] His name appears in all the St Aldate's parish taxation lists of 1645 and 1647. He was assessed at 20s. and 8s. 'in lands' in the Subsidy Lists of 1641,[8] and at 4s. in the Subsidy of 1648.[9] In 1658 he paid £1. 10s. 0d. rent to the city for the first shop in Butcherow.[10] In the Churchwardens' Accounts for 1658-9 occurs the entry: 'received for breakeinge vpp the grounde in the body of the churche for the buryinge of Mr Stevens' 5s. 4d.

Stevens' house was on the east side of Grandpont, being on the site of the northern part of Nos. 29 and 30 St Aldate's. It was parish property. A description of the whole tenement, extracted from the first lease granted to Stevens, on 2 February 1613/14, is printed under the account of his tenant of the southern part, Miles Godfrey [q.v.]. The lease was for thirty-one years and the rent was £6. A second lease was granted to Stevens on 25 January 1623/4, and a third on 22 April 1635.[11] The Churchwardens' Accounts describe it as 'lyeinge att the Lower end of Grandpond'. The property measured, together with the garden ground, 'from the backside of Christ Church Meade' in length 'Sixty Seaven yards & in breadth ffowerteene yards & Two feet'.[12] In the lease of 1635, as in that of 1613/14, Stevens' neighbour on the south is described as being Richard Horne [q.v.], who had however by 1626 moved across the street, his tenement being acquired by John Hawkes [q.v.].

[1] *O.C.A.* 1583-1626, p. 218.
[2] Ib., p. 276.
[3] *O.C.A.* 1626-1665, p. 61.
[4] City Archives A. 5. 7, f. 78.
[5] *Register*, Vol. II, Pt. I, p. 255.
[6] A 8 11*.
[7] City Archives E. 4. 6, ff. 1-2; *O.C.A.* 1626-1665, p. 453.
[8] City Archives B. 1. 4. c. He paid 20s. and 4s. in 1628 (B. 1. 3. e).
[9] *S. and T.*, p. 170.
[10] *O.C.P.*, p. 15.
[11] All these leases are in the Parish Chest.
[12] A Particular of the St Aldate's parish messuages in 1670 (Parish Chest).

MR JOHN CARY
(1612-1686)

The eldest son of Sir Philip Cary, of Berkhamstead, Hertfordshire, and Cardington, Bedfordshire (who was buried at Aldenham, Hertfordshire, 16 June 1631), by his wife, Elizabeth (died 1623), daughter and heir of Richard Bland, of Carleton, Yorkshire. Sir Philip was a younger brother of Henry Cary, first Viscount Falkland (died 1633), and John was thus a first cousin of Lucius Cary, the second Viscount (1610-1643).

John Cary was baptized 23 October 1612 at St Olave's, Silver Street. In 1622 his father's maternal uncle Sir Thomas Knyvet left him one moiety of his estate at Stanwell, Middlesex, granted by James I. On 7 March 1622/3 he was granted by patent the reversion for life of the Keepership of Marylebone Park.[1] Cary matriculated from St John's College, Oxford, 12 October 1627, aged fifteen. In 1641 he was a Gentleman of the Privy Chamber.[2] He was also Master of the Buckhounds to Prince Charles.[3]

Cary attended Charles I to Oxford and was created M.A. 1 November 1642. His name appears twice in Ashburnham's *Accompt.*[4] He was already lodging, together with four men, with William Stevens in June 1643: no answer could be obtained from him.[5] He surrendered to Colonel Fleetwood before 1 May 1646. On 20 April 1649 he compounded for Delinquency, when he stated that, being a sworn servant in ordinary to His Majesty, he attended him to Oxford, and in other garrisons held against Parliament, but was never in arms. On 18 June 1649 he was admitted to compound on the Oxford Articles, as of Marylebone Park, and on 7 July he was fined at 1/10, £600.[6]

In June 1660 Cary received grants of the office of Master of the Harthounds and of the Privy Buckhounds.[7] In August (?) 1660 he appealed about the custody of Marylebone Park, long held by his ancestors, of which he was deprived in 1642 for waiting on the King at Oxford.[8] On 9 August 1664 he received a warrant for payment as keeper of the Park.[9]

Cary married twice. His first wife was Mary, third daughter and co-heiress of Sir Charles Montagu (died 1625), and widow of Sir Edward Baeshe (died 1653), of Stansted, Hertfordshire, whose mother, Frances Baeshe, was a daughter of Sir Edward Cary and aunt of John Cary. She was buried 24 December 1657 at Stanwell, where John resided. He married, secondly, Lady Katherine . . . She was buried at Stanwell 1 September 1673. By a deed dated 1 August 1673 she gave £100 to be distributed to six poor widows of Windsor at the discretion of her husband and another. John Cary, in 1679, by a deed dated 20 December, charged an annuity of £6 on his inn the Catherine Wheel at Colnbrook in Stanwell in satisfaction of this. She also gave £6 per annum to be distributed among six poor widows at Stanwell. Cary died in 1686.

In his Will he expressed the wish to be buried at Stanwell, and mentioned money due to him from Charles II for his salary and wages.

[Will: P.C.C. 1686: 89 Lloyd: made 10 September 1685: proved 1 September 1686].

(For a full abstract see *Miscellanea Heraldica et Genealogica*, Vol. III (1880), pp. 133-5. For his pedigree see Table III, p. 142)

[1] *C.S.P.D.* 1619-23, p. 515.
[2] L.C. 3/1.
[3] *C.S.P.D.* 1661-2, p. 64.
[4] Pp. vi and xxiii.
[5] St Aldate's Defaulters, Bodleian MS. Add. D. 114, f. 24v.
[6] *C.C.C.*, pp. 1402-3.
[7] *C.S.P.D.* 1660-1, p. 75: see also several references in 1661-2.
[8] Ib., 1660-1, p. 239.
[9] *C.T.B.*, Vol. I, p. 616.

LIEUTENANT WEBSTER

Unidentified. He was already lodging at Stevens' house in June 1643, when no answer was received.[1] He probably served in the Lifeguard of Foot, and in that case would have been through the campaign of Gloucester and First Newbury.

[1] St Aldate's Defaulters, Bodleian MS. Add. D. 114, f. 24v.

MR MATTHEW LANGLEY THE ELDER
(died c. 1652)

Tanner. He had a son of the same name, also a tanner, who was mayor of Oxford in 1651-2. Langley was admitted a freeman 6 December 1599.[1] He was elected a common councillor in 1619,[2] and a chamberlain in 1623,[3] and he remained one until 1644, when he was chosen junior bailiff.[4] He remained a bailiff until his death, being junior bailiff until 1648.[5] On 24 April 1643 a long pike was received from him for the King's stores.[6] Together with John Holloway and Edward Carpenter [qq.v.] he was appointed to take care of infected persons in St Aldate's parish.[7] He contributed £5 in October 1645 to the loan to the Lords Commissioners.[8] His name occurs in all the St Aldate's parish taxation lists of 1645 and 1647. He was assessed at 20s. and 8s. 'in lands' in the Subsidy Lists of 1641[9] and at 6s. 6d. in the Subsidy of 1648[10] Langley died between September 1651[11] and Easter 1652. The Churchwardens' Accounts for 1651-2 record that there was received 'of Mr Mayor for the making of the grave of Mr Matthew Langley, the elder in the body of the Church of St Aldates' 6s. 8d.

Langley's house was on the east side of Grandpont, being on the site of the demolished No. 28 St Aldate's. On 24 January 1621 it was described as his 'new dwelling house in the parish of St Aldate's near Oxford'.[12] It appears to have been his own property. On 1 June 1648 Oliver Smyth, son and heir of Thomas Smyth [q.v.], and his mother, Margaret Smyth, sold him a garden in his occupation 'Betweene a Tenemt lately in thoccupacoñ of John Birt on the North pte A Tenement in thoccupacoñ of John Richardson on the south the kings high waye there on the west And a Streame or River betweene a Meadow called Christchurch Meade and the same garden on the east part'.[13]

[1] *O.C.A.* 1583-1626, p. 30.
[2] Ib., p. 287.
[3] Ib., pp. 321 and 322.
[4] *O.C.A.* 1626-1665, pp. 119 and 120.
[5] Ib., p. 151.
[6] *R.O.P.*, Part I, p. 86.
[7] Bodleian MS. Add. D. 114, f. 89.
[8] City Archives E. 4. 6, ff. 1-2: *O.C.A.* 1626-1665, p. 453.
[9] City Archives B. 1. 4. c. He paid 20s and 4s. in 1628 (B. 1. 3. e).
[10] *S. and T.*, p. 170.
[11] His name is in the list of bailiffs 30 September 1651 (A. 5. 7, f. 202v.).
[12] *Liber Albus Civitatis Oxoniensis*, No. 379.
[13] City Archives A. 5. 4, f. 50.

MAJOR WILLIAM LEGGE
(c. 1607-1670)

The eldest son of Edward Legge, sometime Vice-President of Munster, by his wife, Mary, daughter of Percy Walsh, of Moyvalley. He was born c. 1607. His father having died in 1616, William was brought over to England for his education. He served on the Isle of Rhé Expedition in 1627, in Holland, etc. By 12 June 1635 he was in the Royal service.[1] He became Captain and Master of the Armoury, and was Master of the Armoury and Lieutenant of the Ordnance for the first Scottish War.

Legge was taken prisoner at Southam 23 August 1642, but he escaped from the

Gatehouse on 4 October and rejoined the King at Shrewsbury. He had first met Prince Rupert at Nottingham. 'While the Prince was at Nottingham in bed, Lord Digby being then governor, came with an order from the King, who had gone to Coventry, for two petards out of the arsenal. He knew not what it meant, and came to the Prince to inquire, and then went down into the arsenal, where they found two great apothecaries' mortars, which Colonel [sic] Legge made into a kind of petard; and from thence they were sent to the King'.[2] Thereafter Legge attached himself to the Prince, acting as his Brigade major as well as sergeant-major of his Regiment of Horse.

Legge was present at the taking of Cirencester, when his lieutenant, Noland, was killed by a shot from a house;[3] the first attempt on Bristol, the siege of Lichfield Close, Caversham Bridge, Chalgrove Field, and the First Battle of Newbury, all in 1643. He was probably also present at the siege of Gloucester in the same year.

Legge was in Oxford as Master of the Armoury by 20 November 1643, when he set up a sword factory at Wolvercote,[4] and he was still there 26 February 1643/4.[5] In March he was at the relief of Newark. As sergeant-major he was appointed temporary Governor of Chester in May 1644, and in January 1644/5 was made Governor of Oxford vice Sir Henry Gage, whose tenure of that appointment had been so brief that it had made little impact on the country people who came to market in Oxford. They had dreaded the testy and heavy-handed Sir Arthur Aston, who had been removed after his leg was amputated. They would ask the sentinel 'who was governor of Oxon?', and being told 'one Legge', replied 'A pox upon him! Is he governor still?'[6]

On 18 March the city made Legge a freeman with the title of alderman, and the right to vote in the Council House.[7] He was made a Groom of the Bedchamber 12 April 1645,[8] but was removed when Rupert surrendered Bristol. He reconciled the King and Rupert and was restored to favour. On 12 November 1646 he compounded on the Oxford Articles and was fined at 1/10, £40, 2 February 1648/9.[9]

Legge left England but returned in 1647 and waited on the King to the Isle of Wight. He was apprehended and imprisoned in Arundel Castle 19 May 1648, and was not allowed to attend Charles I at Newport. He was released, but was recaptured on his way to Ireland in 1649. In 1653 he was allowed to go abroad. At the Restoration he was installed in his former posts — Groom of the Bedchamber, Master of the Armoury, Lieutenant-General of the Ordnance.

Legge married Elizabeth, eldest daughter of Sir William Washington, of Pakington, Leicestershire, who purchased the manor of Wyke, Isleworth, in 1638, and was buried at St Martin-in-the-Fields 22 June 1643. In his Will, made 6 June 1643 and proved 1 March 1648/9,[10] he appointed Elizabeth his sole executrix. The marriage licence is dated 16 March 1641/2.[11] They had three sons and two daughters, their eldest child, Mary, not being born until 1644 or 1645. Legge died 13 October 1670, and was buried in Holy Trinity, Minories, near the Tower, in which parish he died.[12]

[Will: P.C.C. 1671: 23 Duke: made 11 October 1670: proved 18 February 1670/1].

Legge had two brothers who served in the Royal army. Major Robert Legge served in Prince Maurice's Regiment from 1643 until the end of the War.

[1] *C.S.P.D.* 1635, p. 122.
[2] Warburton, Vol. I, App. C. 'The Life of Prince Rupert'. Legge was then a captain or major at the most.
[3] *Bibliotheca Gloucestrensis,* Vol. I, Pt. I, p. 170.
[4] *C.S.P.D.* 1641-3, p. 501.
[5] Ib. 1644, p. 27.
[6] Wood, *L. and T.*, Vol. I, p. 110.
[7] *O.C.A.* 1626-1665, p. 128.

[8] Dugdale, p. 78: his name has been added on L.C. 3/1.
[9] *C.C.C.*, p. 1563.
[10] P.C.C. 29 Fairfax.
[11] *Marriage Licences issued by the Bishop of London*, p. 264.
[12] M.I. in Le Neve, *Monumenta Anglicana* 1650-79 (1718), p. 144: his age is given as sixty-three.

In June 1643 Langley had lodging with him 'Collonel vavisor & 1 man Mr Thornel Surgeon to the lifeguard . . . noe answere'.[1]

COLONEL (SIR) WILLIAM VAVASOUR, BARONET (died 1659)

The younger surviving son of Sir Thomas Vavasour, of Copmanthorpe, Yorkshire, and Skellingthorpe, Lincolnshire, by his wife, Mary, elder daughter and co-heiress of John Dodge, of Mannington, Norfolk. He was the younger brother of Colonel Sir Charles Vavasour [q.v.].

Vavasour's military experience included service in the second Scots War in 1640 when he had been colonel of the XII Regiment of Foot. At Edgehill he was lieutenant-colonel of the King's Lifeguard of Foot under Lord Willougby of Eresby, like whom he was captured. Imprisoned for a time in Warwick Castle, he was transferred to Windsor whence he succeeded in escaping about 10 April to Reading. He arrived at Oxford on 13 April.[2] In all probability he commanded the Lifeguard at Caversham Bridge (25 April). He did not, however, remain long in command of the regiment, for before the release of his colonel (now the second Earl of Lindsey) in August, he had received another appointment. On 14 June, the very day on which he was entered as lodging in St Aldate's, he was commissioned as Commander-in-Chief of all forces raised or to be raised in the counties of Hereford, Monmouth, Glamorgan, Brecon, and Radnor.[3] He was further appointed Governor of Hereford. On 17 July he was created a baronet and received a commission to raise a regiment of 500 horse. He commanded a brigade of Welsh at the siege of Gloucester and at First Newbury. He then returned to Hereford as Commander-in-Chief of the counties of Gloucester and Hereford.

Vavasour was appointed Field-Marshal and Governor of Hereford in August 1644 by Prince Rupert with whom he was when Bristol was besieged and when it surrendered in September 1645. He was a prisoner in October and received a pass to go beyond seas in December.

Vavasour made his peace with the Commonwealth. He was killed at the siege of Copenhagen 18 February 1658/9.

(For a full account see Stevens, pp. 40-42)

[1] St Aldate's Defaulters, Bodleian MS. Add. D. 114, f. 24v.
[2] *Mercurius Aulicus*, p. 187.
[3] Bodleian MS. Dugdale 19, f. 20.

For SURGEON THORNELL see under Widow Dorothy Moore's house.

MR WILLIAM TOMPSON
(died c. 1652)

College servant. He was formerly a butler (*promus*) of Christ Church, later manciple of another college, probably Pembroke. He was of Yorkshire origin. His name first appears in the Christ Church Disbursement Books for the academic year 1611-12, where he is entered in the list of *Famuli* for the second term as 'Tomsun 4 pmus'.[1] In the book for 1619-20 (the books for 1617-18 and 1618-19 are missing) he is entered as 'Tompson pm 3'.[2] Both as third and fourth butler he received 5s. for the four academic terms and a livery allowance (*vestes liberatae*) of 10s. per annum. The last book in which his name appears is that for 1626-7: 1627-8 is missing, and he had left by 1628-9. He probably became manciple of Pembroke College, where one Tompson is entered as being absent on 22 February 1641/2.[3] He had retired before the Parliamentary Visitation of 1648.[4] In 1642, as an overseer of the Will of John Hawkes (see under Mrs Jane Hawkes), he is described as 'manciple'.

On 13 March 1617/18, at the age of thirty, Tompson was matriculated as a privileged person of the University.[5] He must, however, have been older than this, as in June 1643 he is entered as 'aboue 60 yeares'.[6] In the Assessment of Privileged Persons in 1624-5,[7] Tomson, entered under manciples, was assessed at 2s. 6d. and 3s. 0d. In 1641 he was assessed in the Subsidy Lists at 20s. and 8s. 'in lands'.[8]

He was a churchwarden of St Aldate's in 1626-7. In 1643-4 the churchwardens received 6s. 8d. for his wife's grave in the body of the church, and in 1651-2 they received the same sum for making his grave there. His administration was granted on 2 March 1651/2 to Thomas Kirby, his sister's son, Tompson being a widower.[9] Kirby was clerk of St Aldate's parish in March 1661.[10]

Tompson's house was on the east side of Grandpont, but it is not possible to say exactly where it stood. In the Assessment of Privileged Persons in 1624-5 he was of St Aldate's.[11] He appears to have given up the house by 1645 as in four of the St Aldate's parish taxation lists there is entered a 'Mr Thomson at Carters', who is probably to be identified with him. Henry Carter kept the Bull Inn near the top of the east side of Fish Street, on the site of No. 8 St Aldate's: in one of the 1647 lists he is entered as 'Mr Carter at the Bull'. That is of interest, as Salter in his notes on this Christ Church property in his *Survey of the South-East Ward* (No. 134), says 'we do not know when this name began'. Carter had been paying rent for the house since 1641-2 at least. It is odd that he had no strangers lodging with him in 1643/4.

[1] Ch. Ch. MS. xii. b. 56.
[2] Ch. Ch. MS. xii. b. 64.
[3] *Oxfordshire Protestation Returns*, Oxfordshire Record Society, Vol. XXXVI (1955), p. 109.
[4] The Archivist of Pembroke College has been unable to supply us with any information about him.
[5] University Archives S P 2, f. 335: 'Gulielmus Tomson: Eboracensis Promus AEdis Christi annos natus 30'.
[6] St Aldate's Defaulters, Bodleian MS. Add. D. 114, f. 24v.
[7] University Archives W.P. γ 28 (7).
[8] City Archives, B. 1. 4. c.
[9] P.C.C. 1652, f. 38.
[10] Wood, *L. and T.*, Vol. I, p. 385.
[11] University Archives W.P. γ 28 (7), f. 4.

SIR FREDERICK CORNWALLIS, M.P., afterwards first BARON CORNWALLIS (1610-1662)

The third son of Sir William Cornwallis, of Brome, Suffolk; the only son by his second wife, Jane, daughter of Hercules Mewtas, and nephew of Sir Charles Cornwallis, Treasurer of the Household to Prince Henry. Frederick was born in 1610, and succeeded his elder half-brother in the family estates in 1626. He was created a baronet 4 May 1627 and knighted 1 December 1630.

Cornwallis is said to have been in the Household of Charles I as Prince and he was servant to him as King.[1] He was a lieutenant in the King's Bodyguard with the army in the North 1639-40. In 1641 he was a Gentleman Usher of the Privy Chamber.[2] He was M.P. for Eye in the Short Parliament, April to May 1640, and was again elected in November 1640, being disabled 23 September 1642 because 'he entertaineth and sendeth over Officers from Holland to England against the Parliament'.[3]

He was lieutenant of horse in the Captain-General's troop and Regiment, and was with the King at Oxford by 10 April 1643, when he brought a Message from Charles I to the two Houses enclosed in a letter from Lord Falkland dated Oxford 9 April.[4] On 11 May he had an order for a pass to return to Oxford[5] in spite of which he was imprisoned for a week.[6] He was already lodging, together with two men, at Tompson's house in June 1643, when they were entered as defaulters. The men would not pay 'because their mr a Courtier and hazards his life and estate' for the King.[7] Two other servants were lodging at the house of Widow Dorothy Moore [q.v.]. By ,April 1644 he had moved to All Saints' parish.[8] He is mentioned in a letter to Rupert written from Oxford 28 October 1643 as having misunderstood the King's directions to Sir Lewis Dyve about Newport Pagnell.[9] Cornwallis sat in the Oxford Parliament, signed the letter to Essex of 27 January 1643/4, and attended the Queen to Avebury and Bath on her journey to the West in April 1644. He rescued Lord Wilmot at Cropredy Bridge (June).[10] It is possible that he was in the King's Lifeguard of Horse, which distinguished itself on this occasion. On 28 July 1644 he was assessed at £1,000.[11] On 13 July 1646 he begged to compound on the Exeter Articles. He stated that, being a servant to the King, he was called into the North to attend his person. Afterwards, being sworn a servant to the Prince, he was commanded to the West, but falling sick in Exeter, he remained there until the surrender [April 1646], and then came to London and took the Negative Oath. His creditors pressing hard, he was obliged to leave the Kingdom. Although he deserted Parliament, he never took up arms against it. On 10 June 1651 he was fined £100.[12]

Cornwallis followed Charles II into exile and returned with him. He was Treasurer of the Household from 30 May 1660 until his death. On 6 July 1660 he was made P.C., and on 20 April 1661 was created Baron Cornwallis of Eye.

He married twice. His first wife, whom he married c. 1630, was Elizabeth, daughter of Sir John Ashburnham and sister of 'Jack' Ashburnham: she died at Oxford before 23 January 1643/4 and was buried at Christ Church. His second wife, whom he may have married at Oxford early in 1645, was Elizabeth, daughter of Sir Henry Crofts, of Saxham, Suffolk. The first Lady Cornwallis was a Lady of the Queen's Bedchamber,[13] and the second was also in her service at Oxford, where Cornwallis would have known her.[14] She was assessed, as of Southwark, at £400 on 21 July 1645.[15] She was in France by April 1646 and was described as lately married to Cornwallis on 30 October 1646, both being Delinquents.[16] Her Administration is dated 1674.[17]

Cornwallis died of apoplexy in January 1661/2, and was buried at Brome 18 January (M.I.). Pepys calls him a 'bold profane talking man'.[18] His Administration (lost) was granted in February 1661/2.

[1] *C.S.P.D.* 1635-6, p. 433.
[2] L.C. 3/1.
[3] *C.J.*, Vol. II, p. 779.
[4] *L.J.*, Vol. V, p. 709.
[5] *C.J.*, Vol. III, p. 39.
[6] Ib., pp. 40 and 52.
[7] Bodleian MS. Add. D. 114, f. 24v.
[8] Ib., f. 59v.
[9] Warburton, Vol. II, p. 322.
[10] *Mercurius Aulicus*, p. 1059.
[11] *C.A.M.*, p. 424.
[12] *C.C.C.*, pp. 1389-90.
[13] *C.S.P.D.* 1636-7, p. 303.
[14] *Letters of Queen Henrietta Maria*, ed. M.A.E. Green (1857), p. 242.
[15] C.A.M., p. 565.
[16] Ib., p. 696.
[17] The official accounts, *Peerages and Baronetages*, wrongly state that she was a half-sister of William, Lord Crofts, and that her marriage took place before 1641.
[18] *Diary*, 16 January 1661/2.

SERGEANT BENFEILDE

Unidentified, but probably Lifeguard of Foot.

Tompson also had lodging with him in June 1643 'mr Godwin clerke' from whom no answer was received.[1] This is probably MORGAN GODWYN, son of Francis Godwyn, Bishop of Hereford. He matriculated from Christ Church 8 June 1621 aged eighteen, graduating B.A. 14 June 1621 [sic]. He graduated B.C.L. from Pembroke 6 July 1627 and LL.D. of Trinity College, Dublin, 5 October 1637, being incorporated at Oxford 11 February 1642/3. He became Archdeacon of Salop and a Prebendary of Hereford in 1631, rector of English Bignor, Gloucestershire, 1639, and Lydney, also in Gloucestershire, 1641. Godwyn was among those who surrendered to Waller at Hereford 25 April 1643. He probably came to Oxford as, on 6 December 1645, he was cited by the Committee for Plundered Ministers on the charge of deserting his cure and betaking himself to the forces against Parliament. He was schoolmaster of Newland, Gloucestershire, in 1653. His death occurred before May 1660.

[1] St Aldate's Defaulters, Bodleian MS. Add. D. 114, f. 24v.

THOMAS HAWKES

Whitebaker. He was admitted by the University to bake 24 September 1628.[1] His name occurs in the Magdalen College Bursar's Books for the Civil War period under the heading of 'Impensae Panis' as supplying bread to that society. On 24 April 1643 several weapons were received from him into the King's stores.[2] On 3 August 1648 he was certified as a Delinquent.[3] His name appears in all the St Aldate's parish taxation lists for 1645 and 1647. He was assessed at 20s. and 8s. 'in lands' in the Subsidy Lists of 1641[4] and at 2s. 6d. in the Subsidy of 1648.[5]

Hawkes married Lettice . . ., as appears from an indenture between himself and Thomas Cooke of Lincoln College dated 4 December 1632 relating to property in St Mary Magdalen parish.[6]

His house was on the east side of Grandpont, probably on the site of the demolished No. 25 St Aldate's. In an indenture of 9 August 1650 concerning the messuage or tenement known as 'ye White Lyon' (see under Widow Margaret Hill) the latter was said to have a 'Messuage or Tenemt now or late in ye Tenure of Occupacoñ of Thomas Hawkes Baker on ye South pte'.[7] The house was private property and may have been owned by Hawkes.

[1] *Register*, Vol. II, Pt. I, p. 339.
[2] *R.O.P.*, Part I, pp. 87 and 88.
[3] City Archives F. 5. 9, f. 101.
[4] Ib., B. 1. 4. c.
[5] *S. and T.*, p. 170.
[6] City Archives A. 5. 4, ff. 28v-29.
[7] Ib., f. 60.

COLONEL SIR CHARLES VAVASOUR, BARONET
(died 1644)

The third, but eldest surviving, son of Sir Thomas Vavasour, of Copmanthorpe, Yorkshire, and Skellingthorpe, Lincolnshire, by his wife, Mary, elder daughter and co-heiress of John Dodge, of Mannington, Norfolk. He was the elder brother of Sir William Vavasour, baronet, Royalist commander [q.v.]. His father, who was Knight Marshal to James I, died in 1620, and Charles proved his Will. He appears to have been knighted by then.

On 8 January 1625/6 Vavasour was recommended for a Company vacant by the death of Captain Groves.[1] On 27 March 1627 Secretary Conway was informed that it was the King's pleasure that Sir Charles Rich's Company in the Low Countries should be conferred on Vavasour.[2] On 17 October 1630 he wrote to Secretary Dorchester reminding him of a letter from the Queen of Bohemia on his behalf and praying for employment in Sweden or Venice.[3] On 27 October Bishop Morton of Lichfield and Coventry wrote to Dorchester on behalf of Vavasour who had been commended to him by 'a royal mouth'.[4] In 1631 (?) he is referred to as 'one of the Denmark commanders'.[5] On 22 June 1631 he was created a baronet, with precedence of 29 June 1611.

'Sr Charles Vavoser Kt' appears in the list of officers who returned 1639 (?) to help their King. On 21 February 1638/9 a suggestion was mentioned that he might have been colonel for County Durham.[6] He was colonel of the XIIth Regiment of Foot in the Scottish Expedition of 1640, and there are references to the regiment in *C.S.P.D.* 1640.[7] He then became colonel of a regiment of foot in Ireland. Sir John Leake on 4 March 1641/2 referred to him as a 'nobil gentillman', and on 10

March 1641/2 wrote that 'My Lord President with his one and the regiment of Sir Charles Vavisor have rescued Dungarvan with the castell from the rebells'.[8] On 16 October 1643 Taafe wrote to Rupert: 'Sir Charles Vavasour takes shipping on Wednesday next, and brings two thousand of the forces in Munster along with him'.[9] Hopton in *Bellum Civile*[10] notes: 'About this time [autumn 1643] there came into Bristoll two Regiments from Ireland commanded by Sir Charles Vavaser and Sir Jo: Paulet, they both might make between 4. and 500 foote, bold, hardy men, and excellently well officer'd'. Hopton employed the Irish regiments in Wiltshire.[11]

Vavasour died, unmarried, in Oxford at the end of February 1643/4, and was buried in the Church of St Mary the Virgin 29 February.[12] His Regiment passed to his lieutenant-colonel, Matthew Appleyard.

[Administration dated 1 April 1662 and 11 March 1664/5].

[1] *C.S.P.D.* 1625-6, p. 217.
[2] Ib. 1627-8, p. 111.
[3] Ib. 1629-31, p. 361.
[4] Ib. p. 392.
[5] Ib. 1631-2, p. 236.
[6] Ib. 1638-9, p. 490.
[7] Pp. 286, 446, and 592.
[8] *Verney Memoirs*, Vol. II (1892), pp. 48 and 51. See also *C.C.C.*, pp. 1242 and 1879.
[9] Warburton, Vol. II, p. 320.
[10] P. 62.
[11] See pp. 63 and 65.
[12] Wood, *C. of O.*, Vol. III, p. 245. Dugdale (p. 62) gives 1 March.

In June 1643 Hawkes had lodging with him Colonel John Russell [q.v.] under Widow Margaret Hill's house, and Mr Dudley Smith, who gave 'noe answere'.[1]

MR DUDLEY SMYTH
(died 1643)

The son and heir of the deceased Sir Samuel Smyth, of London and Dublin, who had been a trusted servant of Lady Arbella Stuart. He was described by the Council in 1611, when she was in the Tower, as 'employed by her ladyship in the managing of her private estate'.[2] On 29 July 1614 Smyth had been employed concerning licences for the retailing of wines upon Lady Arbella's grant from James I.[3] He appears in 1617 as an agent for wine and aqua vitae licences in Ireland.[4] He was knighted by Viscount Falkland in Ireland 25 September 1622. In 1624 there are mentions of licences to him and a patent to his wife and son for aqua vitae which involved a quarrel between Falkland and Chancellor Loftus.[5] The last reference to Smyth occurs in 1628. His Will, as of Chichester House in or near Dublin, was proved in the Prerogative Court of Ireland in 1635 (destroyed).

Dudley Smyth was admitted to the Inner Temple in November 1631.[6] On 20 September 1639 Thomas Sheppard, J.P. for Middlesex, certified that Dudley Smith of Dublin had this day voluntarily taken the oath of allegiance before him. On 30 September a minute was made for a pass for Dudley Smith to travel into foreign parts, for three years, from this date, taking with him one servant, with the proviso not to go to Rome.[7]

He was killed at Roundway Down 13 July 1643. Clarendon writes of him: 'the loss to the King's party was less; for in this there were slain very few, and of name none but Dudley Smith, an honest and valiant young gentleman, who was always a volunteer with the lord Wilmott and amongst the first upon any action of danger'.[8]

[1] St Aldate's Defaulters, Bodleian MS. Add. D. 114, f. 26.
[2] B.C. Hardy, *Arbella Stuart* (1913), p. 300: see also p. 324.
[3] *C.S.P.I.* 1611-14, pp. 490 and 492.
[4] Ib. 1615-25, pp. 152 and 170.
[5] Ib., pp. 532, 540, and 547.
[6] *Admissions* 1547-1660, p. 270.
[7] *C.S.P.D.* 1639, pp. 527 and 536.
[8] Bk. VII, § 119.

MARGARET HILL, WIDOW

The widow of Alexander Hill, cordwainer. Alexander was the son of Alexander Hill, brewer, of Oxford, and was apprenticed to John Phillips, cordwainer of Oxford, 5 May 1601.[1] He was admitted a freeman in 1611[2] and was frequently one of the searchers of leather between 1615 and 1638. In 1621 he was elected a chamberlain,[3] but he had ceased to be one by 1638. The surviving Christ Church Receipt Books for the sixteen-thirties shew that Hill leased a brew house in St George's parish from the Dean and Chapter. He probably died in 1639, as on 14 June of that year an Inventory of his goods and chattels was taken by Thomas Elroy, Thomas Allen, John Horne [q.v.], and John Massey [q.v.] and exhibited 27 September, the total value amounting to £10. 18s. 10d.[4] The same day administration of his goods was granted to his relict, Margaret: he is described as of the parish of St Aldate's. Margaret's account was presented 20 November 1639. She was possibly dead by 6 May 1645, as her name does not appear in the St Aldate's parish taxation list of that date.

Mrs Hill's house was on the east side of Grandpont, probably on the site of the demolished No. 24 St Aldate's. Plomer Hall had previously stood there. It was now known as the White Lyon, and had acquired its sign in 1615.[5] It had belonged to John Hawkes (see Mrs Jane Hawkes), who gave to his youngest son, John, by his Will, dated 23 April 1642, 'my howse in the psh of St Aldate aforesaid called and known by the name of the White Lyon now in the tenure of Widow Hill'.[6] On 14 March 1644/5 Powdrell Smith, of Southrop, Gloucestershire, sold to John Earle [q.v.] and his wife, Margaret, a messuage in Grandpont, in Earle's tenure, situated 'betweene a Messuage or Tenemt then of John Hawkes called the white lyon nowe in the occupacon of Margarett Hill widdowe . . .'[7] A Mr Hill (probably Margaret's son) was in occupation of her house in 1648, where he was assessed at 1s. 6d. in the Subsidy of that year.[8] Alexander, son of Alexander Hill, was apprenticed to a fellmonger in 1630/1[9] and was admitted free in 1638.[10] On 9 August 1650 John Hawkes, chirurgeon, of London, sold to John Kibblewhite, gentleman, of Oxford, and his wife, Edith, for £290 'All that his Messuage or Tenement with thappurtenances situate . . . in ye pishe of St Aldates comonly called or knowne by ye name of ye White Lyon now in ye tenure or Occupacõn of him ye said John Hawkes or of his Assigne or Assignes Tenant or Tenants next betweene a Messuage or Tenemt now or late in ye Tenure or Occupacõn of one John Earle [q.v.] on ye North pte And a Messuage or Tenemt now or late in ye Tenure or Occupacõn of Thomas Hawkes Baker [q.v.] on ye South pte And abuttinge on ye highe Street on ye West and a river or streame of water on theast'.[11]

Alexander Hill's Inventory shews that the house contained the following rooms: 'the Parlor', 'the Hall', 'the Hall Chamber', 'the Chamber over the parlor', 'the highest Chamber of the howse', 'the chamber ouer the entry', 'the Seruants Chamber', and 'the highest Chamber ouer the Shopp'.

[1] City Archives L. 5. 1, f. 105.
[2] *O.C.A.* 1583-1626, p. 218.
[3] Ib., p. 303.
[4] MS. Wills Oxon. 298/1/44.
[5] *Survey of South-East Ward*, No. 163.
[6] MS. Wills Oxon. 32/2/16.
[7] City Archives A. 5. 4, f. 35v. Her name is misleadingly printed 'Mary' in the *Survey*.
[8] *S. and T.*, p. 170.
[9] City Archives L. 5. 2, f. 203v.
[10] *O.C.A.* 1626-1665, p. 80.
[11] City Archives A. 5. 4, f. 60v.

TWO SERVANTS OF THE LORD HIGH CHAMBERLAIN

See Montague Bertie, second Earl of Lindsey, under Mr John Smyth's house.

A SERVANT OF COLONEL JOHN RUSSELL, M.P. (1620-1687)

The third son of Francis Russell, fourth Earl of Bedford, and brother of Edward Russell [q.v.]. He was born in 1620. He matriculated from Magdalen Hall, Oxford, 8 July 1634. Probably he is to be identified with the Lieutenant John Russell who was serving in the Earl of Barrymore's Regiment in 1640. In 1641 he inherited estates from his father and was elected (June) M.P. for Tavistock, being disabled 22 January 1643/4 for Royalism.[1] He was imprisoned for three weeks in September 1642.[2]

Russell fought at Cirencester 2 February 1642/3. In June 1643 he was lodging, together with four men, at the house of Thomas Hawkes [q.v.], when they were all entered as defaulters. The men would not pay 'because their mr spends life & estate here in kings service'.[3] He was in the Chalgrove Raid (17/18 June), being then lieutenant-colonel of Lord Wentworth's Dragoons. (For Wentworth see under Mr Oliver Smyth's house). He assumed command of Prince Rupert's Bluecoats when the Prince took over that regiment after Colonel Henry Lunsford was killed at the first siege of Bristol. On 22 December 1643 he wrote to Rupert to report the death of Captain Ventris.[4] He sat in the Oxford Parliament.

Russell commanded the Bluecoats at the storming of Leicester, in which he was prominent, in May 1645,[5] and was wounded at Naseby. He was at Bristol later in the year. On 25 April 1646 he begged to compound for Delinquency in being in arms against Parliament, as of Covent Garden, and Shingay, Cambridgeshire. On 24 September he was fined £7,000, but on 2 October 1648 he produced a certificate that he had deserted the Oxford garrison before its surrender, and on 23 November the fine was reduced to £2,204. 3s. 0d.[6]

Russell was an active Royalist conspirator during the Commonwealth, being a member of the Sealed Knot.[7]

On 23 November 1660 Russell was commissioned as colonel of a second Royal Regiment of Guards (for the first see under Lord Wentworth), which he raised, and when, on Wentworth's death in 1665, the two regiments were incorporated into a single regiment (later known as the Grenadier Guards), he commanded it until 1681.[8] He was appointed major-general in the expedition against the United Provinces in 1673.

Russell was in temporary disgrace in 1664/5.[9] He was made Chief Forester of Chingford Walk in Waltham 15 January 1666/7.[10] On 19 May 1671 he was appointed a commissioner for the accounts of the loyal and indigent officers.[11] He was often commissioned to command in chief the troops left in London during Charles II's absence from the capital.[12]

Russell died unmarried, and was buried at Chenies 25 November 1687.

[1] *C.J.*, Vol. III, p. 374.
[2] Ib., Vol. II, pp. 748, 761, and 781.
[3] Bodleian MS. Add. D. 114, f. 26.
[4] British Museum MS. Add. 18,980, f. 116.
[5] Symonds, pp. 165 and 180.
[6] *C.C.C.*, pp. 1208-9.
[7] D. Underdown, *Royalist Conspiracy in England* (1960), passim, esp. p. 81.
[8] Dalton; *C.S.P.D.*, passim; 1680-1, pp. 610 and 616 for his resignation.
[9] *C.S.P.D.* 1664-5, pp. 229 and 281.

[10] *C.T.B.*, Vol. I, p. 160.
[11] *C.S.P.D.* 1671, p. 255.
[12] Ib., passim.

THREE GROOMS AND ONE FOOTMAN OF MR HENRY MURRAY

The eldest son of Thomas Murray (1564-1623), Provost of Eton, successively tutor and secretary to Prince Charles, afterwards King Charles I, by his wife, Jane, daughter of George Drummond, of Blair.[1] Henry was a first cousin of William Murray, first Earl of Dysart (1600?-1651). He was educated at Eton from 1623 to 1625. Appointed a Groom of the Bedchamber to Charles I, on 15 February 1635/6 a warrant was issued to pay him £250 for the half-year ended the previous Michaelmas upon a pension of £500 per annum granted in 1634.[2] In 1635 he was sent to visit the Queen of Bohemia after her illness.[3] His name is entered as a Groom in 1641.[4]

Murray was allowed to attend the King 26 July 1647[5] and waited on him as a Groom at Newport 13 September 1648.[6]

He married in 1635 Anne Bayning, second daughter of Paul, first Viscount Bayning of Sudbury, and sister-in-law of Henry Pierrepont, Viscount Newark [q.v.]: she died in 1678, having married as her second husband Sir John Baber. The Murrays had four sons and five daughters. He died between 5 April 1669 and 24 September 1672. He was of the parish of St Paul's, Covent Garden, but he is not buried in the church. His wife was appointed his heir and executrix.

[Will: P.C.C. 1672: 112 Eure: made 5 April 1669: proved 24 September 1672].

[1] Wills: P.C.C. 64 Swann, 1623 and 195 Fines, 1647.
[2] *C.S.P.D.* 1635-6, p. 229.
[3] Ib. 1635, pp. 93 and 127.
[4] L.C. 3/1.
[5] *C.J.*, Vol. V, p. 258.
[6] *C.S.P.D.* 1648-9, p. 278.

In June 1643 Mrs Hill had lodging with her 'William Gattacar, he sayth he hath no mony. 2 of Ld Dungarvens men gonne out of towne on Saterday last. 1 of Sr John Scidmores men, his mr he sayth must pay for him 2 of Ld mordents men. noe answere'.[1]

WILLIAM GATACRE

Unidentified. Gatacre is a very uncommon name, however, and he is possibly the third of the eight sons of William Gatacre, of Gatacre, Shropshire (1561-1615), who was appointed Cockmaster to James I in 1607, by his wife, Anne, daughter of James Corbet.[2]

[1] St Aldate's Defaulters, Bodleian MS. Add. D. 114, f. 26.
[2] See *Visitation of Shropshire* 1623, Harleian Society, Vol. XXVIII (1889), p. 198.

RICHARD BOYLE, LORD DUNGARVAN, afterwards second EARL OF CORK AND first EARL OF BURLINGTON, M.P. (1612-1698)

The second, but first surviving, son of Richard Boyle, first Earl of Cork, by his second wife, Catherine, daughter of Sir Geoffrey Fenton, Principal Secretary of State for Ireland. He was brother-in-law of Arthur Jones, second Viscount Ranelagh [q.v.]. He was born at Youghal 20 October 1612, and was known as Viscount Dungarvan until his father's death on 15 September 1643. He raised a troop of horse for the expedition to Scotland in 1639. He was M.P. for Appleby in the Long Parliament until 10 November 1643 when he was disabled.[1] At first he co-operated with Pym, and he did not oppose Strafford's attainder. On 25 August 1641 he was granted leave of absence to go to Ireland, and in November was authorized to take a command there. He distinguished himself at the Battle of Liscarroll in 1642.

Dungarvan landed at Padstow, Cornwall, 18 November 1642.[2] He was possibly one of the Committee for Ireland which attended the King at Oxford at the end of the year.[3] He was back in Ireland by 15 September 1643.[4] On 19 February 1643/4 Sir George Radcliffe wrote from Oxford to Ormonde: 'The earl of Cork would be lord treasurer of Ireland. It is very probable that the earl of Cork will buy the presidentship of Munster of lord Portland'.[5] So he was in Oxford by then.

On 4 November 1644 Dungarvan was created at Oxford Baron Clifford, of Lanesborough, Yorkshire. On 25 July 1644 he was assessed at £5,000.[6] On 7 September 1646 he begged to compound on the Oxford Articles for Delinquency in siding with the King's party in the War. He was fined at 1/10, £1631, 28 November 1646.[7]

He was created Earl of Burlington 20 March 1663/4. He married in 1634 Elizabeth Clifford, *suo jure* Baroness Clifford (died 1690/1), daughter of Henry Clifford, fifth Earl of Cumberland. He died 13 January 1697/8.

[Will: P.C.C. 1698: 259 Lort].

(For full accounts see *C.P.* and *D.N.B.*)

[1] *C.J.*, Vol. III, p. 307.
[2] *C.S.P.D.* 1641-3, p. 408.
[3] Carte, Vol. V, p. 470.
[4] Ib., p. 469.
[5] Ib., Vol. VI, pp. 38-9.
[6] *C.A.M.*, p. 423.
[7] *C.C.C.*, p. 1474.

SIR JOHN SCUDAMORE
(1600-before 1644)

The eldest of the five sons of William Scudamore, of Ballingham, Herefordshire (died 1649), by his wife, Sarah, daughter and heir of Anthony Kyrle, Surveyor of the Works to Queen Elizabeth I, of the Kyrles of Walford Court, Herefordshire. John was baptized 2 August 1600. He was knighted at Oxford 22 March (February ?) 1642/3 and was created a baronet 23 June 1644. He married Penelope (twin with her sister Frances), third daughter of Sir James Scudamore, of Holme Lacy, Herefordshire, and sister of John, first Viscount Scudamore and Sir Barnabas Scudamore, Governor of Hereford. Sir John died before 1649.

(*C.B.*: C.J. Robinson, *The Mansions and Manors of Herefordshire* (1873), p. 21)

HENRY, LORD MORDAUNT, afterwards second EARL OF PETERBOROUGH
(1623-1697)

The eldest son of John Mordaunt, first Earl of Peterborough, by his wife, Elizabeth, daughter and heir of William Howard, Lord Howard of Effingham. He was baptized

18 October 1623, and was educated at Eton 1635-8 and in France. He served on the Parliamentarian side at the beginning of the Civil War, commanding his father's troop of horse. He joined the King at Reading in April 1643, and fought for him at the sieges of Bristol and Gloucester and the First Battle of Newbury, where he was wounded. He succeeded his father as second Earl of Peterborough 19 June 1643. Although a minor, he sat in the Oxford Parliament in January 1643/4 and signed the letter from the Lords and Commons to the Earl of Essex on 27 January. He fought at Cropredy Bridge and Lostwithiel in 1644, commanding in the West the regiment which he had raised. He withdrew from Oxford and went abroad early in 1645. He was assessed at £2,000 on 12 November 1645.[1] On 25 April 1646 he petitioned Parliament to be received into favour in memory of his father's faithful service, from which he had departed in his minority. On 23 June 1646 he was fined at 1/3, £6,337.[2] He took part in the Second Civil War under Lord Holland and fled from England. He compounded for further Delinquency 29 May 1649, and was fined at 1/6, £1,677.[3]
Peterborough married in the winter of 1644-5 Penelope, daughter of Barnabas O'Brien, fifth Earl of Thomond. He died 19 June 1697, and was buried at Turvey, Bedfordshire, 29 June. [Will: P.C.C. 1698: 146 Pyne].
(For details of his later career see *C.P.* and *D.N.B.*)

[1] *C.A.M.*, p. 654.
[2] *C.C.C.*, pp. 1207-8.
[3] Ib., p. 1208.

In June 1643 'mr Robortons house' is entered after that of Widow Margaret Hill and before that of Widow Sara Neale.

MR REYNOLD ROBOTHAM
(c. 1573-c. 1646)

On 20 June 1629 Reynold Robotham, *generosus*, of London, aged fifty-six, collector of the rents of Corpus Christi College, Oxford, was matriculated as a privileged person.[1] On 19 May 1632, as collector of the rents of Lincoln College, he was again matriculated, his age being given as sixty.[2] In his Will he mentions his freehold lands at Merstham in Surrey, and he made his 'very lovinge Cozen John Earle' [q.v.] one of his two residuary legatees and executors. As his Will was first proved at Oxford 18 April 1645, he was dead by that date.
[Will: P.C.C. 1646: 152 Twisse: made 16 August 1644: proved 20 November 1646].
Robotham's house was the messuage in the tenure of John Earle sold to him and his wife by Powdrell Smith, of Southrop, Gloucestershire, 14 March 1644/5,[3] to which reference is made under Widow Margaret Hill, Widow Sara Neale, and John Earle himself. It was on the east side of Grandpont, on the site of the demolished 23 (?) St Aldate's, formerly St Frideswide's Hall or domus Solman.[4] In addition to stating that the tenement lay between those of John Hawkes (Margaret Hill) and George Hilliard (Sara Neale) the indenture describes it as 'abuttinge eastward vppon a streame or water-course com̃only called Trilmilbowe and Westwards vppon the kings high streete'.
Earle must have installed his cousin in the house at some date subsequent to 2 November 1642, when Robotham's Will shews that he was lodging in the parish of St Giles. The unpleasant experience which the old man then underwent there is worth recording in full for the vivid light which it throws on conditions in Oxford after the King's entry following the Battle of Edgehill. He records:
'It is knowne how vnconscionably I have bine vsed and most vniustly wronged by

Lievtenant Colonel Lunsford and Captain Henry Hall who came one [sic] the second day of November One thousand sixe hundred forty two about the Kings first comeing to Oxoñ to the house where I lodged in St Giles parish accompanied wth sixe or more souldiers haveing muskets and pistols ready charged vseing thundering and terrifieing speeches to the amazement of the Inhabitants of the house where I lay, putting vs all in danger and fear of our lives calling for a barrell of Gunpowder to blow vp the house, and in this terrifieing manner did violently without cause take from me my plate gold and gold rings to the value of about three hundred pounds so esteemed which as yet is not restored or any satisfaction made A note of all the perticulars they have and I a Coppy thereof in one Boxe or other in my Truncke'. Robotham desired his executors to try by every possible means to recover his property, adding 'they [Lunsford and Hall] being men of Estates sufficient to make satisfaction And it is well knowne it is not his Maties Will any of his true Subiects should be so wronged Nor was I ever but truely Loyall to my King'.

The villains of the piece were Lieutenant-Colonel Herbert Lunsford, lieutenant-colonel of the Regiment of the Lord General, the Earl of Forth [q.v.], and Henry Hall, who was a captain in the regiment, probably the senior one six months later.[5] It is surprising both that the Lord General's officers were so ill-disciplined and that he did nothing to right such a flagrant wrong.

[1] University Archives S P 2, f. 337: 'Reynoldus Robotham: Collector Redituũ Col. Corp. Christj London: Generosi conditionis an: nat' 56'.
[2] Ib., f. 338: 'Reynold: Robotham, Generosus Collector Redituũ pro Coll: Lincolniensi sub Chyrographo Doris Hood Rectoris ejusdem Collegij: an: nat' 60'.
[3] City Archives A. 5. 4, ff. 35v-36.
[4] *Survey of South-East Ward*, No. 162.
[5] P.R.O., W.O. 55/1661.

In June 1643 in addition to an Oxford boatman 'Wiłł Giles', who 'shewed a warrant whereby he was commanded with his boate to goe on the water on the Kings service', Robotham's house was credited with another defaulter, 'One of Mr Grants men gonne away'.[1]

MR WINTER GRAUNT
(died c. 1660)

The son of John Graunt, of Northbrook, Warwickshire, by his wife, Mary Winter, of Huddington, was at the time Waggon-Master-General to King Charles I. A Proclamation of 5 January 1642/3 required that arms sold or lost by his soldiers and horses illegally bought from them should be brought to Graunt or his deputies at '*Iohn* [sic] *Robotham's* house in *Granpoole* in our City of *Oxford*', so that it is clear that both Robotham and Graunt were established there by the beginning of the year. Graunt, who as early as 1638 is described as a servant to the King,[2] is entered as a Gentleman Usher of the Privy Chamber in 1641.[3] He delivered a considerable quantity of weapons and arms into the King's stores 25 April 1643.[4] He ceased to be Waggon-Master in the autumn of 1643 when he was posted at Pendennis, and he continued to be active in the West in 1644. His Will was proved in the P.C.C.[5] in 1660. He was presumably Roman Catholic.

[1] Bodleian MS. Add. D. 114, f. 26.
[2] *C.S.P.D.* 1637-8, p. 472.
[3] L.C. 3/1.
[4] *R.O.P.*, Part I, p. 92.
[5] 311 Nabbs.

SARA NEALE, WIDOW

Her name, as Mrs Neale or Widdow Neale, appears in all the St Aldate's parish taxation lists of 1645.

In her Will[1] she left bequests to her daughters, Anne, Mary, and Sara, and to her sons, John, Richard, James, and Thomas. This has no date of when it was made or proved, but adminisration was granted to Sara's daughter Mary 13 September 1645.[2]

Mrs Neale's house was on the east side of Grandpont, perhaps on the site of the demolished No. 22 St Aldate's.[3] It belonged to George Hilliard, butcher, brother-in-law of John Lambe [q.v.]. On 14 March 1644/5 Powdrell Smith, of Southrop, Gloucestershire, sold to John Earle [q.v.] and his wife, Margaret, a messuage in Grandpont situated 'betweene a Messuage or Tenemt there of John Hawkes called the white lyon nowe in the occupacon of Margarett Hill widdowe [q.v.] on the south pte And a messuage or Tenemt of George Hilliard nowe in the occupacõn of Sara Neale widdowe on the north'.[4] In his Will proved 5 March 1668/9,[5] Hilliard bequeathed to his wife 'All that my messuage or Tenement in Grand Pond in the parish of Saint Aldates in the Suburbs of the Cittie of Oxon now divided into several Tenements'.

[1] MS. Wills Oxon. 47/4/18.
[2] Ib. 107, f. 87v: Act Book B.
[3] *Survey of South-East Ward*, No. 161.
[4] City Archives A. 5. 4, f. 35v.
[5] P.C.C. 33 Coke.

SIR ROBERT LEE
(c. 1602-1659)

The eldest son of Sir Robert Lee, of Billesley, Warwickshire (whom he succeeded in 1637/8). His mother was Anne, eldest daughter of Sir Thomas Lowe, lord mayor of London in 1604-5. He was born c. 1602.[1] He may have been the Robert Leigh who was a Gentleman of the Privy Chamber in 1641.[2] He was knighted at Stoneleigh 21 August 1642. He perhaps served in the Lifeguard of Horse, and he may have been present at Edgehill. He was created D. Med. of Oxford 31 January 1642/3.

In June 1643 Lee was already lodging, together with four men, at Sara Neale's house, when they were entered as defaulters. The man who was in answered 'no reason his mr should pay haveinge a troope of horse and ventured his life'. The three other men were troopers and away on service.[3]

Lee was in garrison at Worcester when it surrendered 20 July 1646,[4] having previously been nominated to treat for the soldiers.[5]

Lee married Frances, eldest daughter of Sir William Cope, second baronet, of Hanwell, Oxfordshire. They had one child, Anne, who married, first, in 1656, Sir Edward Barkham, first baronet, of Waynflete, Lincolnshire (died 1669); secondly, in 1671 or 1672, John Hodges, of the Inner Temple, Recorder of Ipswich. Her marriage licence, dated 21 December 1671, gives her age as about twenty-eight: she would thus have been a 'small childe' in 1643/4. Sir Robert died in 1659, aged about fifty-seven.

[1] *Visitation of Warwickshire* 1682-3, Harleian Society Vol. LXII (1911), p. 71.
[2] L.C. 3/1.
[3] Bodleian MS. Add. D. 114, f. 26.

[4] *C.S.P.D.* 1645-7, p. 456.
[5] *Diary of Henry Townshend*, Vol. I, p. 144: Worcester Historical Society (1915-20).

JOHN HORNE
(died c. 1675)

Brewer. He was a churchwarden of St Aldate's in 1637-8. His name occurs in all the St Aldate's parish taxation lists of 1645 and 1647. On 11 March 1646/7 he was admitted a freeman.[1] He was assessed at 1s. 8d. in the Subsidy of 1648.[2] He paid for three hearths in the Hearth Tax of 1665,[3] 2s. in the Poll Tax of 1667,[4] and 2s. 10d. in the Subsidy of 1667.[5] He married Margaret . . . He died between 17 April 1672 and 26 March 1675, when an Inventory of his goods (worth £38. 0s. 10d.) was taken.

In his Will he mentions his son John (living in the Barbados), his son William, and two daughters, Edith, married to Matthew Leech, and Margaret, married to Nathaniel Vnett. His wife was appointed executrix.

[Will: MS. Wills Oxon: 132/2/9: made 17 April 1672: proved 16 April 1675].

Horne's house was on the east side of Grandpont, on the site of the demolished Nos. 17 and 18 St Aldate's. It was the property of Magdalen College. On 16 December 1635 the College demised to 'John Horne of the Cittie of Oxford Brewer All yat yeir Tenemt in Grampoole . . . late in ye tenure or occupacōn of Thomas Hollowaie gent and Johane his wife . . . scituat . . . betweene a Tenement' of the College [this is an error] 'now or late in the tenure of Ralphe Flexnie Butcher on the southside, and a Tenemt late Anne Bentlies on the north; And also a Garden belonginge and adioyninge to the foresaid Tenemt shootinge vpon Christ Church walkes on theast bearing ye breadth the foresaid Tenemt yroughout, (yat is to saie) eight yeards from the high streete on ye west wheareon the foresaid Tenemt abutteth euen to the waters side wch parteth the said garden & the said Walke'. The lease was for forty years at a rent of 8s. per annum.[6] It was renewed to Horne on the same terms on 15 January 1657/8[7] and 18 August 1670.[8]

In his Will Horne directs: 'I give and bequeath vnto my sonn William Horne ymediately after myne and my wifes decease, the house out-houses garden' etc.: 'Which house I hold by lease from Magdalen Colledge in the Vniversity of Oxford'. The Inventory enumerates 'ye Hall', 'ye kichen', 'ye Chamber ouer ye shop', 'ye Chamber of ye hall', 'ye Chamber ouer ye kichen', 'ye vper Chambers', 'ye celler', 'ye backside'.

Horne's widow, Margaret, made her Will on 3 April 1676: it was proved at Oxford 1 August 1683.[9] In the Inventory of her goods (worth £19. 13s. 6d.), made after her death on 9 February 1682/3, the following rooms are listed: 'the purple chamber', 'the street chamb one [sic] the sam fflore', 'the 1st chamb one ye ffirst fflore one the Left hand vp one paire of staiers', 'the 2d Chamb one ye ffirst fflore', 'the Hall', 'the Kitching'.

[1] *O.C.A.* 1626-1665, p. 144.
[2] *S. and T.*, p. 170.
[3] Ib., p. 194.
[4] Ib., p. 263.
[5] Ib., p. 342.
[6] Magdalen College Lease Ledger M, f. 156.
[7] Lease Ledger P, ff. 30v-31.
[8] Lease Ledger Q, ff. 243v-244v. See also *Cart. St J.B.H.*, Vol. II, p. 196 and *Survey of South-East Ward*, No. 159.
[9] MS. Wills Oxon. 34/2/8.

MRS AUBREY

In 1640 one Auberry was the senior ensign in Sir John Meyrick's Regiment of Foot.

From the muster roll of 25 March 1641, when he was still ensign of his colonel's Company, we learn that his name was Antho: Awbray. The surname is not common, and since the officers of the Lifeguard, to which we can safely assign him, would be selected from men of some military experience, there can be little doubt that Mrs Aubrey was his widow.

By June 1643 Aubrey had received a step in rank, as one would expect, for we find 'Leifetenant awbry' lodging with one man in John Horne's house. He is in the Defaulters List where he is noted as remarking that 'he would pay if other souldiers did'.[1] He was presumably a casualty of the Gloucester-Newbury campaign. It is sad to reflect that his wife and two young children cannot have joined him at Oxford more than a few weeks before his death.

[1] Bodleian MS. Add. D. 114, f. 26.

ANTHONY BLAND

Cooper. The eldest son of Robert Bland, cooper, of Oxford, by his wife, Ursula . . . , who survived him. The Blands originally came from Kettlewell, in Yorkshire (see under Robert Wilson). Anthony was apprenticed to his father 15 April 1620.[1] On 31 August 1626 he was admitted a freeman by his father's copy.[2] An Inventory of Ursula Bland's goods, as of St Aldate's, was taken 11 February 1627/8 by William Bland, Matthew Langley [q.v.], and John Yeats, the total value amounting to £5. 0s. 2d.[3] Administration was granted to her son Anthony, who exhibited the Inventory, 4 March 1627/8.[4] In 1640 he was named a beneficiary under the Will of Robert Wilson senior, who had been apprenticed to Robert Bland.

On 24 April 1643 some weapons were received into the Saltpetre house at Oxford for the King's use from Bland.[5] His name does not appear in any of the St Aldate's parish taxation lists of 1645 and 1647: in the latter year Goodman [Matthew] Wildgoose appears to have been occupying his house, and Bland was probably dead by then.

Bland's house was on the east side of Grandpont, on the site of the demolished No. 16 St Aldate's.[6] It was privately owned, and almost certainly rented by Bland. In 1609 it belonged to William Bust, surgeon, who in his Will proved in that year in the Court of the Chancellor of Oxford University,[7] let to 'Jone Bust my [youngest] daughter my house and garden grounds situate . . . in Grandpole als Grandpond . . . in wch house one Richard Parsons now dwelleth to her and to her heires for ever'. Joan was also left 'the lease or terme of yeares . . . not yet expired of the house next to the house Richard Parsons now dwelleth in and wch I holde of magdalen Colledge in Oxon . . .' (i.e. the house of John Horne [q.v.] immediately to the south). Bust's widow, Anne, the mother of Joan, subsequently married John Bentley, M.D., of Newcastle-upon-Tyne.[8] Anne and Joan received leases of the Magdalen house in 1609 and 1611, but Anne appears to have kept the house north of it until her death: administration of her goods was granted to Joan (now Synedayle) in 1626/7. On 11 December 1628 Thomas Holloway and Joan his wife (Joan Bust evidently married twice) received a lease of the house from Magdalen, but whether the tenement described in Horne's lease as 'late Ann Bentlies on the north' came to the Holloways also and whether, if so, they retained it or sold it, there seems to be no evidence to show.

Ursula Bland's Inventory lists the following rooms: 'the Chamber over the Hall', 'the chamber over the shopp', 'the Hall', and 'the Shopp'.

[1] City Archives L. 5. 2, f. 65v.
[2] *O.C.A.* 1583-1626, f. 342.
[3] MS. Wills Oxon. 160/3/20.
[4] Ib. 106, f. 157: Act Book A.
[5] *R.O.P.*, Part I, p. 82.
[6] *Survey of South-East Ward*, No. 158.
[7] Hyp. B. 22.
[8] Will proved in the P.C.C. in 1618.

TWO OF DR WILLIAM HARVEY'S MEN

The famous Dr William Harvey (1578-1657), discoverer of the circulation of the blood, was appointed Physician Extraordinary to James I in 1618 and Physician in Ordinary, with an annuity of £300, to Charles I (to whom his *De Motu Cordis et Sanguinis* (1628) was dedicated) in 1630. In 1641 he was given as third of three physicians 'for ye person of his Matie', the other two being Sir Theodore de Mayerne and Sir Matthew Lister.[1]

Harvey left London with the King early in 1642 and was present at the Battle of Edgehill in October. On 7 December he was incorporated M.D. of Oxford, and he remained at Oxford until the surrender of the garrison in June 1646, when he returned to London. In an undated list of Royal servants charged with payments towards the Oxford city works, probably belonging to the summer of 1643, 'Dcõr harvy' is entered as owing 15s. for six weeks. The answer which he gave to Richard Poole, the official deputed to extract the money, was that he 'pleads priviledge as Phisition gnãll to ye Army & ought not to be charged'.[2] On 9 April 1645 he was elected Warden of Merton College, holding the post until the following year.[3]

Harvey's two men were already lodging in Bland's house in June 1643, when no answer was received from them as defaulters.[4]

[1] L.C. 3/1.

[2] MS. Harleian 6804, f. 229.

[3] See Louis Chauvois, *William Harvey His Life and Times* (1957), pp. 137-49, Sir Geoffrey Keynes, *The Life of William Harvey* (1966), pp. 291-314, and Merton College Register 1567-1731, 3. 1, ff. 355-60.

[4] Bodleian MS. Add. D. 114, f. 26.

MR GEORGE LOCKSMYTH
(c. 1604-c. 1644)

Manciple of Christ Church. The son of George Locksmyth, gentleman, of Twickenham, a member of the Royal Household,[1] he was matriculated as a privileged person of Oxford University 23 October 1635, his age being given as thirty-one.[2] The younger George Locksmyth's name first occurs in the Christ Church Disbursement Books, at the head of the list of *Famuli*, for the third term of the academic year 1622-3.[3] His salary as *obsonator* was £1. 13s. 4d. for each of the four university terms. On 28 January 1625/6 he was granted a lease of two messuages in St Mary's parish by Christ Church, when he is described as 'of the University of Oxford, gent'.[4] He was chosen sub-bedell of theology 9 December 1635.[5]

Locksmyth was a defaulter in June 1643, when it was reported that 'he refuseth to pay till he speaks with the vicechancelor, being one of the bedles'.[6] His name appears for the last time in the Christ Church Disbursement Books for the first term of the academic year 1643-4.[7] On 20 February 1643/4 his successor as sub-bedell was appointed.[8] He may have died of the plague. The churchwardens of St Aldate's received in 1643-4 'for the grave of Mr George Locksmith in the body of the said church' 6s. 8d.

He married Edith, daughter of Anthony Findall, butcher, afterwards grazier, mayor of Oxford in 1620-1, who was buried in St Aldate's 31 December 1650. They had a son, Anthony, and three daughters, Edith, Meriall, and Alice (all mentioned in their paternal grandfather's Will, Edith being appointed executrix and proving the Will). Their mother made her Will on 4 October 1651, and it was proved in the P.C.C.[9] on 15 January 1651/2 by her executrix, Meriall. She left 'Mr Seamer' (Thomas Seymour [q.v.]) 10s.

Administration of Locksmyth's goods was granted on 4 November 1645 to his widow in the Court of the Chancellor of Oxford University,[10] an Inventory having been taken on 29 October 1645.[11] His assets, including debts due to him, amounted only to £10. 15s. 8d.

Locksmyth's house was on the east side of Grandpont, on the site of the demolished Nos. 15 and 15a St Aldate's. It belonged to Magdalen College. On 27 July 1605 a lease was granted to Anthony Fyndall, yeoman, and his wife, of two messuages in Grandpont for forty years at a rent of 20s. per annum.[12] The lease was renewed to the Fyndalls on 31 July 1616 on the same terms.[13] On 20 December 1631 the College granted a further lease, for forty years, at the same rent, to 'Anthony Ffyndall of the Cittie of Oxford yeoman and Alice his wife' . . . of 'All yose yeir twoe tenements in Graundpoole . . . & twoe gardens to the said twoe Tenemts belonginge & adioyninge as yey are scituat . . . betweene a Tenemt late in the tenure of Thomas Dennyngton Esquire[14] on ye south and a Tenemt nowe in ye tenure of John Willmott [q.v.] on the north, and abuttenth vpon the meadowes of Christ Church Colledge on theast and the high streete leadinge to south bridge on ye west'.[15] On 6 August 1651 the College granted to Edith Locksmith, 'widdowe', the same two tenements on the same terms.[16]

The Locksmyths were living in Findall's house in 1643/4, but in the St Aldate's parish taxation lists of 1645 and 1647 and in the Subsidy of 1648 Mr Findall's name occurs. He must have left the lease to his daughter. In her Will she says: 'I give and bequeath vnto my sonne Anthony Locksmith the sum̃e of thirty pounds to be paid vnto his vse vnto Mr John Hopkins his hand vpon the sale of the Lease of my howse which is now mortgaged vnto the said John Hopkins . . . My Will and meaning is that my lease of my howse which I hold of the President and schollars of Magdalen Colledge in Oxford shalbe sould by my executrix hereafter named with as much convenient speed and to the best vallue that may bee'.

No. 15a became the Wheatsheaf and Anchor in the early eighteenth century.

[1] His Will was proved in the P.C.C. (54 Pembroke) 17 April 1650.
[2] University Archives S P 2, f. 338v: 'Georg: Locksmith: Manceps AEdis Christj middles: fil: Georgij Locksmith de Twickenham in Com̃. p'd: familij Regis 31'.
[3] Ch. Ch. MS. xii. b. 67.
[4] *Cart. Oseney Abbey*, Vol. I, p. 169.
[5] *Register*, Vol. II, Pt. I, p. 258.
[6] Bodleian MS. Add. D. 114, f. 26.
[7] Ch. Ch. MS. xii. b. 87.
[8] *Register*, loc. cit.
[9] 9 Bowyer.
[10] Hyp. B. 41.
[11] Hyp. B. 15.
[12] Magdalen College Lease Ledger J, f. 153v.
[13] Lease Ledger K, f. 92v.
[14] Will proved in 1598.
[15] Lease Ledger M, ff. 13v-14.
[16] Lease Ledger O, ff. 187-187v. See also *Cart. H. St J.B.*, Vol. II, p. 240, and *Survey of South-East Ward*, No. 157.

MR EDWARD WRAY
(1589-1658)

There is no Wray peerage. The person intended must be Edward Wray, third son of Sir William Wray, first baronet, of Glentworth, Lincolnshire, by his first wife, Lucy, eldest daughter of Sir Edward Montagu, of Boughton, Northamptonshire. He was baptized at Louth 9 November 1589, and was admitted a Fellow Commoner of Sidney Sussex College, Cambridge, in June 1602. He was admitted to Lincoln's Inn 7 November 1605, and was a Groom of the Bedchamber to James I from 1617 to 1622. On 27 March 1622 Wray married Elizabeth Norreys, *suo jure* Baroness Norreys, of Rycote, Oxfordshire, for which act he was imprisoned until 1622/3. In July 1625 he entertained Charles I at Rycote. Through his wife he acquired the manor of Wytham, Berkshire, as well as Rycote.

Information was supplied that in 1643 or 1644 he left home and went to the King's garrison at Oxford, and sent two horses, men, and arms there to the King. When in Oxford he invited and feasted the Earl of Lindsey, the Earl of Dorset [qq.v.], and Dorset's son.[1] His wife died shortly before 10 October 1645 and was buried in Westminster Abbey 28 November 1645. Their daughter, Bridget Wray (1627-1656/7), succeeded her mother as Baroness Norreys.[2] Wray died at Fritwell, Oxfordshire, 20 March 1658.

[Administration was granted in the P.C.C. 10 July 1658: 1658, f. 193].

[1] *C.A.M.*, p. 1221.
[2] For her marriages see *C.P.*

JOHN WILMOTT
(c. 1573-1647)

Whitebaker. The son of John Wilmott, of Stadhampton, Oxfordshire, yeoman, he was a member of the armigerous family of Wilmott of that place.[1] On 30 November 1585 he was apprenticed to Edward Jennynge, whitebaker, of Oxford.[2] On 26 September 1595 he was admitted a freeman.[3] He was admitted by the University to bake 23 July 1598.[4] The Magdalen College Bursar's Books of the Civil War period, under the heading 'Impensae Panis', shew that he was supplying that society with bread. He was elected a common councillor in 1602,[5] a chamberlain in 1606,[6] junior bailiff in 1612,[7] and he remained a bailiff from 1613 until his death. In 1613 he was chosen a millmaster,[8] and he was a member of the mayors's council from 1618 to 1638.

Wilmott married in 1595 Elizabeth (died 1633), daughter of John Daniell, carpenter, of St Aldate's.[9] Their daughter, Margaret, was the wife of Thomas Smyth [q.v.] His name appears in the Subsidy List of 1624 as 'gent':[10] he paid 20s. and 8s. 'in lands' in the Subsidy of 1641.[11] A halberd for the King's stores was received from him 24 April 1643.[12] His name appears in all the St Aldate's parish taxation lists of 1645 and 1647. He died 17 February 1646/7,[13] and was buried in St Aldate's church the same day.[14] The churchwardens received of 'Mrs Margaret Smith widow for a grave for mr John Willmott in the body of the church' 6s. 8d.

Wilmott's house was on the east side of Grandpont, on the site of the demolished No. 14 St Aldate's, formerly Rack Hall.[15] It was the property of Balliol College, which leased it on 8 March 1588/9 to Wilmott's father-in-law, John Daniell.[16] On 1 October 1599 the property was leased to John Wilmott and his wife, Elizabeth, for forty years at a rent of 16s. per annum. It is described in the indenture as 'all their Tenement or howse scituat . . . in Grampound in the parishe of Snt Alldates in the suburbes of the Citye of Oxford together wth A Garden backside and Orchard therevnto belonginge And wth all other howses edifices & buildings wth all other Commodities pfitts appurtenñcs whatsoever they bee therevnto belonginge or in any wise apperteyninge All wch p'misses are nowe in the tenure & occupacon of the said John Willmott'.[17] The lease was renewed to John and Elizabeth on the same terms 21 November 1611,[18] and 22 March 1627/8.[19] After Wilmott's death, the tenancy of the house passed to his daughter, Margaret Smyth, and her son Oliver Smyth the younger, who, on 8 September 1649, were granted a lease by Balliol for forty years at a rent of 16s. per annum. The premises are described as being 'nowe in the tenure & occupacon of the said Margaret Smyth or her Assignes'.[20] The house was described by Wood in the early 1660s as being opposite to Littlemore Hall and 'now a new house lately built'.[21] It was no longer tenanted by the Smyths.

[1] The Arms of Wilmott of Stadhampton were displayed on his M.I. in St Aldate's church and are to be seen on the house built by his son-in-law, Thomas Smyth [q.v.]. For the Wilmotts of Stadhampton see *Visitation of Oxfordshire* 1574 and 1634, pp. 301-2. It is not possible to say exactly where John Wilmott fits into the pedigree. A John Wilmott, of Stadhampton, husbandman, had his Will proved at Oxford in 1573 (MS. Wills Oxon, Series I, Vol. 8, 206), but he is unlikely to have been our John Wilmott's father, who is not described as dead until 1588, when a younger son, Robert, was apprenticed in Oxford. The husbandman had three sons, Richard, executor with his mother, Anne, and curiously enough, two younger sons, John and Robert, both under age in 1573.

[2] City Archives A. 5. 3, f. 334v.

[3] *O.C.A.* 1583-1626, p. 95.
[4] *Register*, Vol. II, Pt. I, p. 338.
[5] *O.C.A.* 1583-1626, p. 148.
[6] Ib., p. 177.
[7] Ib., p. 223.
[8] Ib., p. 229.
[9] Wood, *C. of O.*, Vol. III, pp. 201 and 207.
[10] City Archives B. 1. 3. c.
[11] Ib. B. 1. 4. c.
[12] *R.O.P.*, Part I, p. 88.
[13] Wood, *C. of O.*, Vol. III, pp. 133-4: his M.I. is printed there.
[14] Ib., p. 208.
[15] *Survey of South-East Ward*, No. 155.
[16] Balliol College Leases B. 13. 2 and 3.
[17] Ib. B. 13. 4 and 5.
[18] Ib. B. 13. 6 and 7.
[19] Ib. B. 13. 8.
[20] Ib. B. 13. 9 and 10. See also *The Oxford Deeds of Balliol College*, ed. H.E. Salter, Oxford Historical Society, Vol. LXIV (1913), p. 195.
[21] *C. of O.*, Vol. I, p. 301.

In June 1643 Wilmott had lodging with him '2 of Sr Richard Hubbards men, they put them of to their mr in Oriall Coll.'[1]

SIR RICHARD HOBART, HUBERT or HUBBARD

Of Langley, Buckinghamshire, he was Groom Porter to Charles I and Charles II. He was already Groom Porter when he was knighted (as of London) at Greenwich 5 August 1633. He appears as Groom Porter in 1641.[2]
On 18 July 1643 Hobart was assessed at £150, and was noted as being with the King.[3] On 6 November there is mention of a silver cistern that had been seized from him.[4]
His name appears in the Oriel College Buttery Books from 1643 to 1645. He was in Oxford when the Articles were agreed upon on 22 June 1646 before the city surrendered.[5] On 14 March 1647/8 his fine of £400, at 1/10, on his estate of £200 per annum was accepted by the House of Commons and an order was passed for pardoning him and taking off his sequestration. His offence was that he assisted the forces raised against Parliament. On 9 May 1649 he was assessed at £250, but on 30 May he was discharged as he had compounded.[7]
On 6 November 1661 an order was made for the grant to Hobart of the office of Groom Porter in any of the King's houses.[8] On 13 November a warrant was made for the grant to him of the office of Cockmaster of England and the grant was confirmed on 30 November.[9] He was dead by 31 May 1665.[10]
Hobart married Dorothy, third daughter of John King, Bishop of London, and sister of Henry King, Bishop of Chichester, who lived in Hobart's house at Langley from 1643 to 1651. Lady Hobart died in 1658.[11] The second son, Richard, was a Gentleman of the Privy Chamber to Charles II.[12]

[1] St Aldate's Defaulters, Bodleian MS. Add. D. 114, f. 26.
[2] L.C. 3/1.
[3] *C.A.M.*, p. 197.
[4] *C.S.P.D.* 1641-3, p. 497.
[5] Ib. 1645-7, p. 486.
[6] *C.J.*, Vol. V, p. 496.

[7] *C.A.M.*, p. 1070.
[8] *C.S.P.D.* 1661-2, p. 137.
[9] Ib., pp. 144 and 164.
[10] Ib. 1664-5, p. 397.
[11] M.I. at Langley: see G. Lipscomb, *History of Buckinghamshire*, Vol. IV (1847), p. 536.
[12] Ibid.

MR JOHN EARLE
(c. 1615-c. 1673)

Mercer. The son of John Earle, yeoman, of Clack, Wiltshire, he was apprenticed to Robert Cockram, mercer, of Oxford, 17 December 1627.[1] He was subsequently apprenticed to a Mrs Townshend, and was admitted a freeman 16 January 1637/8.[2] The (defective) records of the Oxford Mercers Company shew that he was one of the 'Cominalty' from 1648 to 1659 and an Assistant from 1660 to 1673.[3] On 27 August 1640 he was granted for ten years £25 of Sir Thomas White's money.[4] He was elected a member of the Common Council in 1642,[5] and a bailiff in 1645,[6] continuing to hold this office until 1672. He contributed £5 to the loan to the Lords Commissioners in October 1645.[7] His name appears in all the St Aldate's parish taxation lists for 1645 (where reference is made to both his houses) and in those for 1647. He was a churchwarden of St Aldate's in 1648-9 and 1649-50. He was assessed at 2s. 8d. in the Subsidy of 1648,[8] paid for five hearths in the Hearth Tax of 1665,[9] was assessed at 6s. for himself, his wife, and four children in the Poll Tax of 1667,[10] and at 3s. 8d. in the Subsidy of 1667.[11]

Earle married twice. By his first wife, Elizabeth, daughter of Robert Saunders [q.v.], he had a daughter of the same name: his second wife was Margaret, widow of John Whetham, by whom she had a son of the same name.[12]

The churchwardens of St Aldate's received 6s. 8d. in 1673-4 for a grave for Mr 'Yearle'.

Earle's house was on the east side of Grandpont, on the site of the demolished No. 13 St Aldate's. It had once been a St Frideswide's tenement, but had been freehold property for nearly a century.[13] By 1645 Earle had moved to his other house, lower down the same side of the street, bought by him 14 March 1644/5 when already in his tenure, and occupied in 1643, as has been seen, by Earle's cousin Reynold Robotham. In 1647 Earle's northern house was occupied by Edward Crawford, or Crafford, whitebaker, to whom he must have sold it. Crawford, whose freehold is mentioned as being north of the later No. 14 in a lease dated 30 December 1668,[14] on 28 September 1674 granted it for the sum of £208 to John Paynton.[15] It is there described as 'All that Messuage or Tenement Bake house Garden Ground and ffuell houses situate . . . in Grandpond in the Suburbs of the City of Oxford on the East side of the streete there betweene A pc̃ell of Land belonging to Allsoules Colledge in Oxon now in the Occupac̃on of John Lambe [q.v.], Maulster of the North pte And a Messuage or Tenement & Backside belonging to Balliol Colledge in Oxon . . . on the south Abutting vpon a Little Streame or Watercourse running betweene Christ Church Walkes and the p'mises on the East And the Streete or Highway on the West And Conteyning in Length from East to West seaventy & two yards or thereaboutes And in Breadth from North to South att the West ende Thirteen yardes & one ffoote or Thereaboutes And in Breadth from the North to South Att the East ende thirteen yards & one ffoote alsoe or thereaboutes togeather with the Great Gateway & passage and all other waies etc.'. In 1569 the situation of the tenement is given as being opposite to Littlemore Hall,[16] which places it exactly.

[1] City Archives L. 5. 2, f. 160.
[2] *O.C.A.* 1626-1665, p. 78.
[3] City Archives G. 5. 4. Mercers Company 1572-1815: there is a gap from 1576 to 1648.
[4] *O.C.A.* 1626-1665, p. 93.
[5] Ib., p. 110.
[6] Ib., p. 131.

[7] City Archives E. 4. 6, ff. 1-2: *O.C.A.* 1626-1665, p. 453.
[8] *S. and T.*, p. 170.
[9] Ib., p. 193.
[10] Ib., p. 263.
[11] Ib., p. 341.
[12] City Archives A. 5. 4, ff. 35v-36.
[13] *Survey of South-East Ward*, No. 154.
[14] *Oxford Deeds of Balliol College*, p. 195.
[15] City Archives A. 5. 4, ff. 101v-102.
[16] *Liber Albus Civitatis Oxoniensis*, No. 368.

SERGEANT-MAJOR JOHN or ROBERT MARKHAM (?)

The person intended is almost certainly either John or Robert Markham, sons of Abraham Markham, of Tumby Woodside, in the parish of Revesby, Lincolnshire, by his wife, Jane, daughter of Robert Eyre, of Armitage, Staffordshire. Abraham Markham belonged to a cadet branch of the Markhams of Sedgebrooke, Lincolnshire, and was a cousin of Sir Robert Markham, of Sedgebrooke, a Royalist, who was created a baronet by Charles I 15 August 1642. Abraham was an Esquire of His Majesty's Body Extraordinary in 1641.[1] Under the Will of Abraham's cousin Gervase Markham, of Dunham, Nottinghamshire (proved at York 1636/7), Jane Markham received £20 per annum and a gift of £50 as well as half his household goods. Her sons John and Robert each received £20 per annum, and a younger son, Francis (born c. 1624), and two daughters, Elizabeth (born c. 1617) and Ellen (born c. 1627), are also mentioned. Francis was ejected from Christ Church in 1648 by the Parliamentary Visitors.

Jane, John, and Robert Markham all appear in *C.C.C.*[2] in connexion with their legacies from Gervase. These annuities were allowed 7 November 1650. Jane is erroneously described in the heading as the widow of Gervase. From *C.C.C.* it emerges that John Markham begged to compound on the Oxford Articles for repairing thither to assist the King, 19 November 1646. He was fined £120, and is styled as of Westminster. Robert Markham also begged to compound on the Oxford Articles on 1 December 1646: he was in the city at its surrender. He was fined £25, and is styled as of Christhead, Lincolnshire (Kirkstead, a short distance from Tumby Woodside). He is described in the Markham pedigrees as a serjeant-at-law, and his wife's name is given as Mary, daughter of Robert Peirson. His nuncupative Will was made 16 May 1659 and proved 22 November 1659 in the P.C.C.[3] He was then of Graby, Scremby, Lincolnshire (Scrimby-cum-Grabby). In this he appoints 'my brother Henry Fines of Christhead Esq' an executor. Henry Fines (alias Clinton) of Kirkstead, was the husband of Markham's sister Jane. The Fines had evidently given Robert a home after the War. He mentions his four children.

The Royalist Major Markham was in the King's Lifeguard of Foot. He probably fought at Edgehill, and very likely as a captain. He was a captain at Oxford by 18 February 1642/3.[4] He was probably the senior captain by this time, being next in seniority to William Leighton [q.v.]. He was probably at Caversham Bridge (April). As 'Captaine markham' he was already lodging at John Earle's house in June 1643, when he was a defaulter and returned no answer.[5] He was a major by 13 November 1643.[6] On 29-30 May 1644 one hundred and sixty muskets were received from him into the King's stores.[7] He was at Cropredy Bridge and in the Cornish campaign. On 30 November 1644 he was ordered to march with the Lifeguard Regiment from Faringdon to Oxford.[8] On 8 January 1644/5 his lieutenant, Richard Edmonds [q.v.],[9] received arms for the Lifeguard.[10] He was in the Naseby campaign.[11] On 18 December 1645 Charles I, writing to William Salesbury by Sir Edward Nicholas, mentions that letters of 2 December 1645 had been sent to Salesbury by Major Markham.[12]

[1] L.C. 3/1.
[2] P. 1569.
[3] 480 Pell.
[4] P.R.O., W.O. 423/93.
[5] Bodleian MS. Add. D. 114, f. 26.
[6] W.O. 55.
[7] *R.O.P.*, Part I, p. 136.
[8] MS. Harleian 6802, f. 316.
[9] See W.O. 55.
[10] P.R.O., W.O. 423/208.
[11] Symonds, p. 194.
[12] *Calendar of Salusbury Correspondence* 1553-c. 1700, ed. W.J. Smith, p. 355: University of Wales Board of Celtic Studies, History and Law Series, No. 14 (1954).

MONSIEUR DU MOULIN

The Christian name of the French Agent Du Moulin is unknown. He was secretary to the French Ambassador to England, the Comte de Tillières, and was charged with correspondence during his absence from August to October 1623. On 9 August 1623 Du Moulin issued a pass for John Mitchell, tailor to Charles, Prince of Wales, who was going to Spain with clothes for his master.[1] Early in 1624 Du Moulin was sent to France in connexion with the French marriage project for Prince Charles, returning in July. He stayed on after the departure of Tillières, but was recalled in August.[2]

Du Moulin accompanied the Duc de Bassompierre on his mission to England to effect a reconciliation between King Charles and Queen Henrietta in the autumn of 1626. On Bassompierre's departure in December, he left Du Moulin in charge.[3] In March 1627 he was invested by Louis XIII with the title of Secretary. In July 1627, when he was ordered by Charles I to leave, Henrietta shed tears.[4] He was back in England in June 1629,[5] and in 1631.[6]

Thus Du Moulin was no stranger to this country when he accompanied the Sieur de Grécy to England in June 1643. On 10 July 1643 he received a pass to go to Oxford and return.[7] On 7 August 1643 it was reported that 'Cressi will depart by the post tomorrow leaving here M. de Molin, with the title of ordinary resident, the one [M. de Bure] left by the Ambassador Fertante [D'Estampes] being recalled'.[8] On 26 August it was ordered that 'M. du Moulin shall have Mr Speaker's warrant for a Servant of his to go to Oxon, with some letters to the Queen'.[9]

There are various references in the *L.J.*, *C.J.* and *C.S.P.V.* and one in the Baschet Transcripts in the Public Record Office[10] to Du Moulin in London. He appears to have gone to Oxford in January 1643/4. On 23 February 1643/4 there is a reference to letters taken in his passage to Oxford.[11] But he was back in London by 21 January, on which date he wrote two letters to Paris, one directed to Monsieur du Boys, Maître d'Hôtel de Monsieur St Vaudreuil, the other to Monsieur de Monteforte, Maître des Comptes.[12] In the former he urges his return to France and asks for his extraordinary expenses: in the latter he reports the opening of letters by Parliament. On 22 January it was decided to recall him, and Grécy was left as sole French Agent in England. In 1646-7 Du Moulin was sent on a mission from France to the Irish.

Between 11 August 1643 and 11 February 1643/4 Du Moulin addressed eighteen letters from England to Henri-Auguste, Comte de Brienne (1595-1666), Minister and Secretary of State. A list of these is printed in Appendix III.

It is curious that neither Sir Charles Firth in his *Notes on the Diplomatic Relations of England and France* 1603-1688 (1906) nor Armand Baschet in his *Lists of*

French Ambassadors &c in England 1509-1714 (1876) mentions that Du Moulin was French Resident in 1643-4.

[1] *C.S.P.D.* 1623-5, p. 49.
[2] *C.S.P.V.* 1623-5, passim.
[3] Ib. 1626-8, p. 39.
[4] Ib., p. 298.
[5] Ib. 1629-32, p. 103.
[6] H.M.C., *Cowper*, Vol. I, pp. 423 and 424.
[7] *L.J.*, Vol. VI, p. 126.
[8] *C.S.P.V.* 1643-7, p. 4.
[9] *C.J.*, Vol. III, p. 220.
[10] P.R.O., 31. 3/73, ff. 110-110v.
[11] *C.J.*, Vol. III, p. 405.
[12] *C.S.P.D.* 1644, pp. 5-6.

SIR WILLIAM SAINT-RAVY or RAVIE

He was brought up in the entourage of the House of Rohan[1] and was servant to Benjamin de Rohan, Seigneur de Soubise (1585-1642), brother of Henri de Rohan, first Duc de Rohan, the godfather of Charles I. Soubise visited England in 1608 and in 1622. St Ravy was in command of two Rochellese men-of-war which captured the *Croissant* of Calais in March 1623. He was at Newmarket that month.[2]
St Ravy attended James I on his hunting during the summer of 1623 and was knighted by him then.[3] On 16 October 1623 he was to be presented with a jewel by the King and to have a pension of £200 per annum.[4] On 25 October 1623 he was granted letters of denization.[5] In November 1628 he received a grant as a Gentleman of the Privy Chamber of a pension of £200 per annum.[6]
St Ravy was employed and paid for secret service by Charles I. He was sent to France in October 1635;[7] in September 1638 to congratulate Louis XIII and Anne of Austria on the birth of the Dauphin;[8] and in October 1640 to congratulate the King and Queen of France on the birth (21 September) of Prince Philip.[9] His brother had been sent to England to congratulate her King and Queen on the birth (8 July 1640) of Prince Henry.
In 1642-3 he received £200 from the King.[10] On 11 July 1643 it was ordered that he should have a pass to go into France to condole on the death of Louis XIII.[11] The same day the Lords desired the Commons to concur in the granting of the pass, but they refused. 'Resolved that the person of Sir William St Ravy shall be forwith seized and apprehended and kept in safe custody by the Serjeant at Arms; as an Enemy to this State, and one who has been in actual war against the Parliament'. He was accused of plundering persons of quality.[12] On 7 August 1643 it was reported: 'To respond to his [Du Moulin's] office H.M. has chosen the Sieur de St Ravi, his chief huntsman, a Frenchman, but a Protestant, with the title of gentleman. He has asked for a passport here, but has failed to get it, so he will have to go incognito by another route'.[13] On 11 September 1643 it was reported: 'M. de San Ravi has crossed the sea and arrived at the French Court to respond to the office performed by Cressi [Grécy], and to take some commissions from the Queen here to H.M.'[14] He had evidently returned to England by January 1643/4. A letter of Charles I to the Queen, dated from Oxford 4 May 1645, and taken among his private papers at Naseby, is endorsed on the copy 'By *Malin St Ravy*'.[15] In March 1648 his name appears among those sequestered for Delinquency in Westminster.[16]
During the Commonwealth St Ravy was evidently in Holland. On 23 March 1651/2 Charles II recommended his claims to Mary, Princess of Orange. On 4 April 1653 Henrietta Maria also recommended him: 'He is a person who has long served with

fidelity and affection'.[17].

On 7 November 1660 a grant was made to St Ravy and John Cary [q.v.] of £1,000 for His Majesty's service [imprest of deer].[18] On 13 November 1661 a warrant was issued for payment of £100 to St Ravy for his expenses in transporting red and fallow deer from Germany and elsewhere to replenish Windsor and Sherwood Forests.[19] In 1663 he was employed by Charles II to escort a present of livestock to Louis XIV.[20] On 19 June 1663 it was reported: 'He [Charles II] is sending to the Most Christian by Saint Ravi, a Huguenot gentleman, who distinguished himself in the armies of England by his sword for thirty-five years, a very great quantity of deer, Indian ducks, pelicans and other extraordinary animals to put in the park at Versailles.'[21] In June 1668 a grant was made to Prince Rupert 'during pleasure' of the Upper Spring Garden in possession of Sir William St Ravy.[22] St Ravy had negotiated the purchase of the Spring Garden for Charles II in 1662,[23] and helped to furnish it.[24] On 6 February 1670/1 he received a legacy of £210 from the Queen Mother.[25] He was still alive 16 March 1674/5, when the last mention of the payment of his pensions occurs.[26] Both his pensions of £200 per annum continued after 1660. He was dead by 22 January 1679/80.[27]

[1] *C.S.P.D.* 1623-5, p. 109.
[2] Ib. 1619-23, p. 535.
[3] Ib. 1623-5, p. 83: 25 September 1623.
[4] Ib., pp. 96-7.
[5] Shaw, p. 36.
[6] *C.S.P.D.* 1628-9, p. 373.
[7] Ib. 1635, pp. 412, 438, 444.
[8] Ib. 1638-9, pp. 11-12 and *C.S.P.V.* 1636-9, pp. 449, 456, 458, and 466.
[9] *C.S.P.V.* 1640-2, p. 87.
[10] Ashburnham's *Accompt*, p. xxxiv.
[11] *L.J.*, Vol. VI, p. 128.
[12] *C.J.*, Vol. III, p. 162. Cf. *Oxoniensia*, Vols. XI and XII (1946-7), p. 134: Edward Perrot, of Northleigh, Oxfordshire, feared St Ravy, who hated him.
[13] *C.S.P.V.* 1643-7, p. 4.
[14] Ib., p. 17.
[15] *Reliquiae Sacrae Carolinae* (1650), p. 244.
[16] *C.C.C.*, p. 93.
[17] *C.Clar. S.P.*, Vol. II, pp. 452 and 454.
[18] *C.T.B.*, Vol. I, p. 81 and Vol. VI, p. 409.
[19] *C.S.P.D.* 1661-2, p. 143: see also 30 November 1661, p. 163.
[20] Ib. 1663-4, pp. 95, 96, 114, 118, and 122.
[21] *C.S.P.V.* 1661-4, p. 250.
[22] *C.S.P.D.* 1667-8, p. 467.
[23] *C.T.B.*, Vol. I, p. 391.
[24] *C.S.P.D.* 1661-2, p. 302.
[25] *C.T.B.*, Vol. III, p. 779.
[26] Ib., Vol. IV, p. 708.
[27] Ib., Vol. VI, p. 409.

QUARTERMASTER BENJAMIN STONE

Stone was in the Lifeguard Regiment of Foot by 31 January 1642/3.[1] In June 1643 'Beniamen Stone a quartermr' was already lodging with John Earle and said that 'he [would] not pay till the king pay him'.[2]

It is likely that the Quartermaster is to be identified with Benjamin Stone, swordmaker. The latter was a somewhat unruly member of the Cutlers Company and their chief competitor in supplying swords to the Tower. As early as 1620 he was accused of 'goeinge to Sturbridge fayre unsearched'. In 1629/30, and again in 1630/1, his claim to the mark of a Bunch of Grapes was refused.[3] He established a manufactory of blades, of exceptional quality, at Hounslow, and probably another at Birmingham. He lived in Bartholomew Lane.

In 1636 Stone was appointed His Majesty's blademaker to the Ordnance Office. He tried to get the monopoly of supplying blades to the Royal stores. In this he was opposed by Captain William Legge, Master of the Armoury [q.v.]. During the years 1636 to 1640 he had a lengthy dispute with the Cutlers Company.[4] Stone had much influence at Court, and the decision, in the handwriting of Secretary Nicholas [q.v.], was that 'the petitioner is to make as many swords as he can, and they shall be all taken off if they be serviceable and good'.

The withdrawal of Charles I from London at the beginning of 1642 left Stone without protectors, and with a stigma of 'malignancy upon him in the midst of enemies'.[5] After the War his factory passed to other hands.

(See *D.N.B.* and Welch, op. cit.)

[1] P.R.O., W.O. 457/60/67.

[2] St Aldate's Defaulters, Bodleian MS. Add. D. 114, f. 26.

[3] Charles Welch, *History of the Worshipful Company of Cutlers*, Vol. II (1923), pp. 22 and 346.

[4] See *C.S.P.D.* 1636-7, pp. 45, 305; 1637-8, p. 105; 1638-9, p. 236; 1639-40, pp. 134, 317, 349.

[5] *D.N.B.*

LXVIII

FRANCIS WEST

College servant. He was the second butler of Christ Church. His name first appears in the list of *Famuli* in the Disbursement Books for the academic year 1641-2 as second butler (*promus*),[1] but as there is no book extant between 1631-2 and this, he was probably appointed earlier. He received 10s. for each of the four academic terms and 13s. 4d. livery allowance (*vestes liberatae*). His name is entered in the book for 1644-5, but by 1659 (the next book extant) his name has disappeared. West's name occurs in the St Aldate's parish taxation lists of 1645, but not in those of 1647, nor does he figure in the Parliamentary Visitation of 1648.
It is possible that West was the father of Francis West, cook of Pembroke College, who was a cornet of horse in the Royalist army.[2]
West's house was on the east side of Grandpont, but its exact position is uncertain. It was probably on the site of the demolished No. 9 St Aldate's.

[1] Ch. Ch. MS. xii. b. 85.
[2] D. Macleane, *A History of Pembroke College, Oxford*, p. 237, quoting Bodleian MS. Wood F. 28, f. 24, A List of Royalist Officers from Pembroke.

MR EDWARD MILLS

Miles must be a mistake for Mills. Edward Mills was yeoman of the Pantry in 1638.[1]

[1] S.P. 16/386/97, f. 184v.

JOHN KING
(died 1644)

Slatter or plasterer. On 24 April 1643 a halberd and two flasks were received from him for the King's stores.[1] He is mentioned as being 'sick in his bed' in June 1643.[2] He was one of the two constables of St Aldate's in October 1643, Thomas Wright [q.v.] being the other.[3] In the St Aldate's Churchwardens' Accounts for 1643-4 occurs the entry: 'Paid to John King the slatter for mending the roffe of the Church' £1. 0s. 5d. He married Mary . . . He died 15 August 1644. Administration of King's goods was granted at Oxford to his widow 17 February 1644/5.[4] John Savory [q.v.] was one of those who took the Inventory. His goods were valued at £18. 8s. 4d.

King's house was on the east side of Grandpont and occupied the site of the demolished No. 8a St Aldate's. It was built on the garden called Trillmillbowe, which belonged to Christ Church, having been purchased from the town in 1544. This piece of land lay between Trillmill Stream and the entrance to Christ Church Meadow. 'The name is incorrect, for the "bow" was the arch by which the road crossed Trillmill stream, but the name was applied in a loose way to a piece of land near the arch'.[6]

This garden, with the tenement upon it, went with the tenements of John Dunte and Robert Wixon [qq.v.]. When, on 25 July 1623, they were leased by the Dean and Chapter to Abraham Tillyard, apothecary, of St Albans, the garden was in the tenure or occupation of John Wheeler 'Bearebrewer', and the tenement was in the tenure or occupation of Joanne Sparrow, widow.[7] On 23 December 1637 the Dean and Chapter granted to John Wheeler, Chapter Clerk, together with the tenements of Dunte and Wixon, 'all that their garden ground wth thappurtennes called Trillmillbowe and all the tenements now builded or standing vpon the same scituate . . . within the said pish of St Aldats betweene a Comon river or watercourse there on the South side, and the said gate called Cutlers gate and the said passage or way leadeing to the said stables & backside of the said Deane & Chapter on the North side one head or end thereof abutting vpon the kings high way or streete leadinge vnto South bridge towards the west and the other head or end thereof abbutting vpon a garden grounde or Orchard belonging to the said Deane & Chapter now in the tenure or occupacon of Richard Gardyner Doctor of Diuinity one of the Prebendaries of the said Cathedrall Church towards the East wch said demised garden ground called Trillmillbowe is now in the tenure or occupacon of George Jacob Brewer and the said Tenemt now builded or standing vpon the same is now in the tenure or occupation of John King Slatter'.[8]

In King's Inventory mention is made of 'the best chamber' and 'the cocke lofte'.

No. 8a St Aldate's was still standing in 1925, but was then demolished as being one of the houses on the site of the projected Christ Church War Memorial Garden.

[1] *R.O.P.*, Part I, p. 80.
[2] St Aldate's Defaulters, Bodleian MS. Add. D. 114, f. 26.
[3] City Archives E. 4. 5, f. 167v.
[4] MS. Wills Oxon 107, f. 81: Act Book B.
[5] Ib. 298/4/20.
[6] *Cart. Oseney Abbey*, Vol. III, p. 1.
[7] Ch. Ch. MS. xx. c. 3: Register III, ff. 582-3.
[8] Ch. Ch. MS. xx. c. 4: Register IV, ff. 45-6.

DR JOHN HEWETT or HEWIT
(1614-1658)

The fourth son of Thomas (William?) Hewett clothworker.[1] He was born at Eccles, Lancashire, in September 1614, was admitted sizar of Pembroke College, Cambridge, 13 May 1633, and matriculated 4 July 1633.
'Dr Hewett was born a gentleman, and bred a scholar, and was a divine before the beginning of the troubles. He lived in Oxford and in the army till the end of the war'.[2] He was created D.D. of Oxford University 17 October 1643. He is said to have been chaplain to Charles I, but his name is not included in L.C. 3/1, and he is called here chaplain to the Lifeguard. Later he became chaplain to Montague Bertie, second Earl of Lindsey, Lord Chamberlain [q.v.]. He was vicar of St Gregory's by St Paul's c. 1653-8. He was the author of devotional works.
Hewett married first a daughter of Robert Skinner, of St Botolph, Aldersgate, Merchant Taylor; and secondly Lady Mary Lindsey, fourth and youngest sister of his patron, Lord Lindsey. He was beheaded on Tower Hill for conspiracy 8 June 1658, despite the intercession of Cromwell's favourite daughter, Elizabeth Claypole, who is said to have reproached her father for Hewett's execution on her death-bed (August 1658).
(For full accounts see *D.N.B.*, and David Underwood, *Royalist Conspiracy in England*, esp. pp. 211-12)

[1] T. Hunter, *Famulae Minorum Gentium*, Harleian Society, Vol. XXXVII (1894), p. 1030.
[2] Clarendon, Bk. XV, § 101.

In June 1643 King had lodging with him three of 'Coll: Herberts men'.[1]

RICHARD HERBERT, second LORD HERBERT OF CHERBURY, M.P.
(1600?-1655)

The eldest son of Edward Herbert, first Lord Herbert of Cherbury, by his wife, Mary, daughter and heir of Sir William Herbert, of Julians. He succeeded his father in 1648.
In 1639 Herbert commanded a troop of horse in the Scottish Expedition; and he was also on service in the North in 1640.[2] In July 1641 his troops were among those ordered to be disbanded.[3] He was M.P. for Montgomery Borough from 1640 until his disablement as a Royalist 12 September 1642.[4]
Herbert was commissioned by the King at Nottingham 3 September 1642 to raise a regiment of 1200 Foot and was appointed Governor of Bridgnorth. While he was there, Charles sent him a commission as captain of a troop of eighty horse. He conducted the Queen from Bridlington to Oxford in 1643, and so would have been absent from Oxford in June. He sat in the Oxford Parliament in January 1643/4 (a fact not mentioned by Keeler). He was described as Colonel Herbert in March 1643/4, when he was at Sudeley Castle.[5] In 1644 he joined Prince Rupert at Shrewsbury, and was appointed Governor of Aberystwyth Castle 20 April 1644.
On 6 June 1647 Herbert begged to compound. He declared that he had long since submitted in a letter to the Earl of Northumberland. On 30 June 1648 he was fined at 1/3, £2,574.[6]
Herbert married Mary Egerton, daughter of John Egerton, first Earl of Bridgewater. He died 13 May 1655.
(For full accounts see *C.P.*; *D.N.B.*; and Keeler)

[1] St Aldate's Defaulters, Bodleian MS. Add. D. 114, f. 26.

[2] *C.S.P.D.* 1640-1, passim.
[3] *C.J.*, Vol. II, p. 220.
[4] Ib., p. 762.
[5] Stevens, p. 24.
[6] *C.C.C.*, p. 1682.

ROBERT WIXON
(c. 1598-1645)

Cooper. The son of Robert Wixon, yeoman, of Tiddington, Oxfordshire, he was apprenticed to Marmaduke Brooke, cooper, of Oxford, 9 December 1610.[1] He was admitted a freeman 26 September 1617.[2]
Wixon married Elizabeth . . . who, as Widow Wixon, figures in the St Aldate's parish taxation lists of 1645. In 1644-5 the churchwardens of St Aldate's received 6s. 8d. for the grave of Robert Wickson in the body of the church.
Administration of his goods was granted to his widow at Oxford 15 May 1645.[3]
Wixon's house was on the east side of Tower Hill, and it belonged to Christ Church. On 25 July 1623 the Dean and Chapter granted it, together with the adjoining tenement occupied by John Dunte [q.v.], to Abraham Tillyard, apothecary, of St Albans. Wixon and Dunte were the under-tenants of William Dewey, M.A., of Christ Church. Dunte had been an under-tenant of John Hodges when the tenements were leased to Tillyard's mother, Elizabeth Pory, in 1610, and their precise situation, as described in her lease, will be found in the account of Dunte. 'Robert Wixon Coop' appears for the first time in the lease of 1623, his tenement having been 'latelie in thoccupacon of William Poyner Cooke of Merton Colledge'.[4]
The Dean and Chapter also granted to Tillyard 'all that ther Tenem' or little Shoppe wth thappurtenncs erected or built against the Southwest Tower of the sayd Lodginge of the sayd John Weston ['Doctor of Lawe One of the Prebendaries of the said Cathedrall Church'] and is situate on the North side of Thentry or way leadinge into the sayd Tenemt now in the occupacon of the sayd Robert Wixon wthout the sayd South gate in the sayd pishe of St Aldats and now is in thoccupacon of the sayd Robert Wixon or of his assignes'.[5]
On 23 December 1637 the two tenements and the shop were leased to John Wheeler, Chapter Clerk, Wixon and Dunte being the under-tenants as before, but their neighbour on the north was now John Morris, Doctor of Divinity.[6]
Elizabeth Wixon, as has been seen, continued to live in the tenement, and on 3 January 1660/1, in a lease of the two granted by the Dean and Chapter to Thomas Keyt, it is stated that 'one is or lately was in the occupacon of Elizabeth Wixon widow'.[7]
The tenement survived until after the War of 1914-18.

[1] City Archives L. 5. 1, f. 193.
[2] Ib. L. 5. 2, no folio number.
[3] MS. Wills Oxon. 107, f. 83: Act Book B.
[4] Ch. Ch. MS. xx. c. 3: Register III, ff. 582-3.
[5] Ibid.
[6] Ch. Ch. MS. xx. c. 4: Register IV, ff. 45-6.
[7] Ch. Ch. MS. xx. c. 5: Register V, ff. 42-3.

In June 1643 there was reported as a defaulter in Wixon's house 'Mr Del Roy, of the pastry to the king' who 'answeres he serves the king there'.[1]

It is likely that DEL ROY was one of the two 'kings pastrymen' lodging with Wixon in January 1643/4. In 1638 John Dellroy is entered as first of two yeomen of the Pastry with Arthur Dellroy (probably his son) as his servant.[2] In 1662 Arthur Dellroy is entered as third yeoman of the pastry.[3] If John Dellroy was one, Arthur Dellroy is likely to have been the second of Wixon's pastrymen lodgers.

[1] Bodleian MS. Add. D. 114, f. 26.
[2] S.P. 16/386/97, f. 190.
[3] S.P. 29/60/65, f. 122.

LXXI

JOHN BOLTE

Tailor. The son of John Bolte, tailor, of Witney, Oxfordshire, he was apprenticed to Richard Palmer, tailor, of Oxford, 14 February 1612/13.[1] He obtained his freedom 18 June 1620.[2] As his name does not occur in the St Aldate's parish taxation lists of 1645, he was probably dead by then. The name of a lodger in part of his house in 1643/4, Sir William Howard [q.v.], occurs in one of the 1645 lists. Bolte must have been a man of some substance, as he lodged not only Howard, with four men, but the King's apothecary, with his son and servant.
Bolte's house must have been on the east side of Fish Street, perhaps occupying the site of a house called 'ye Longhouse' which is mentioned in seventeenth-century leases of the Bull (see under William Tompson) as lying south of that tenement. If this is so, Bolte would have lived immediately north of Christ Church.

[1] City Archives L. 5. 1, f. 223.
[2] Ib. L. 5. 2, no folio number.

JOHN WOLFEGANG RUMLER

A native of Augsburg, on 20 July 1604 a grant was made to him of the office of apothecary to Queen Anne, Prince Henry, and the rest of the Royal children for life.[1] On 7 November 1607 he was appointed apothecary to the King for life.[2] In the Roll of New Year's Gifts for 1605/6 'John Vulp' received a box of Indian plums.[3] On 20 July 1610 he was naturalized as John Wolfgang Rumbler, Apothecary in Ordinary to the King and Queen, together with Anna Wolfgang Rumbler, alias Anna de Lobell, born in Middlesborough in Zeeland, his wife, and any children born or to be born to them.[4]
When James I granted a charter to the Apothecaries Company in December 1617, the name of 'Mr Wolfe' headed the list of Assistants. He was Master of the Company in 1622-3 and 1636-7.[5]
Rumler is mentioned in the Epilogue to Ben Jonson's masque *The Gypsies Metamorphosed* (1621) as 'Master Wolfe the Court Lycanthropos'.
There are many references to him in the *C.S.P.D.* of James I and Charles I. Soon after the accession of the latter, as apothecary to the Household, Rumler, on 8 October 1625, received a grant for life of the office of compounding and serving all sweet waters, powders, and other oderiferous things for the service of the King and Queen with a fee of 20 marks per annum. On 6 November 1627 he received a grant for life of the office of Apothecary in Ordinary to the King, with a fee of £40 per annum as granted to Jolliffe Lowndes deceased.[7] In 1633 (?) he is mentioned as appointed 'to deliver all physical and oderiferous parcels for the household' and as resigning his post of apothecary,[8] and on 6 March 1638/9 as Apothecary in Ordinary to his Majesty.[9] In 1641 he is entered under Apothecaries as 'John Woolfgang Romler for his Mats person'.[10]
In June 1643 Rumler was already lodging with Bolte together with two men. He answered he was 'the King's Apothecary & must attend to that'.[11] His son's name was Frederick: he was granted administration of his father's goods.
[Administration, as of Isleworth: P.C.C. 1650: 28 May 1650, f. 81].
Frederick Rumler, described as 'ye executor of Wolfe Gang Rumler', received a warrant for the payment of £1,400 dated 10 October 1651 upon the second list of Charles I's necessitous servants and creditors, allowed by Parliament 13 August 1651. Frederick petitioned one of the Treasurers appointed for the sale of Charles I's pictures, etc.: 'Mr Hunt I pray the Contents of this warrant to Mr William Geere & his acquittance shalbe a good discharge as witnesse my hand ffr. Rum'. Geere

signed the receipt 8 November 1651.[12]

[1] *C.S.P.D.* 1603-10, p. 134.
[2] Ib., p. 379.
[3] J. Nichols, *Progresses of James I*, Vol. I (1828), p. 597.
[4] Shaw, p. 16.
[5] See C.H. Cameron and E.A. Underwood, *A History of the Worshipful Society of Apothecaries*, Vol. I, 1617-1815 (1963), passim.
[6] *C.S.P.D.* 1625-6, p. 549.
[7] Ib. 1627-8, p. 423.
[8] Ib. 1633-4, p. 378.
[9] Ib. 1638-9, p. 566.
[10] L.C. 3/1.
[11] St Aldate's Defaulters, Bodleian MS. Add. D. 114, f. 26.
[12] S.P. 28/283 and S.P. 28/350/9, f. 371, No. 919. Mr W.L.F. Nuttall, 'King Charles I's Pictures and the Commonwealth Sale'. *Apollo*, October 1965, p. 307, is wrong in describing Geare, silkman to the King and draper, as J.W. Rumler's executor.

At the end of the 'Accompt' occurs the entry 'In parte of the house where John Bolte liveth Sr William Howard & 4 Men.'

SIR WILLIAM HOWARD
(c 1600-1672)

The sixth son of Thomas Howard, first Earl of Suffolk, by his second wife, Catherine, eldest daughter and co-heir of Sir Henry Knyvett, of Charlton, Wiltshire, and widow of Richard Rich, heir of Robert Rich, second Baron Rich. He was born c. 1600 and was created K.B. 4 November 1616. He was appointed Lieutenant of the Pensioners at £300 per annum.
In 1645 Howard was paying a tax as a resident of St Aldate's parish.
On 4 April 1646 he compounded for Delinquency in attending the King at Oxford, being his sworn servant.[1] On 14 May 1646 he was fined £500, as of Tollesbury, Essex, which manor he had inherited from his brother Henry, Lord Suffolk's third son. On 5 June 1646 the House of Commons accepted this fine, 'his Offence being, Residing at Oxford, and his Estate £168 per annum in Fee'. An Ordinance for his pardon was passed and ordered to be sent to the Lords for their concurrence.[2] It was sent on 21 November 1646.[3] On 5 March 1646/7 the Lords sent a message to the Commons to let them know that 'Sir Wm Howard having paid £250 for the Moiety of his Fine for Delinquency, and is to pay £250, which this House thinks fit to remit, in regard he hath lost his Place of Lieutenant of Pensioners, worth £300 per annum given to Mr [Edward] Villiers [Howard's nephew by marriage], and was looked upon by the King's Party as a Person that adhered to the Parliament'. The Commons' concurrence was desired.[4]
Howard died unmarried between 7 July and 7 August 1672.
He appointed his brother Edward Howard, Lord Howard of Escrick, his executor and left him the whole of his estate.
[Will: P.C.C. 1672: 97 Eure: made 7 July 1672: proved 7 August 1672].
(See H.K.S. Causton, *Howard Papers* (1863), pp. 523-4 and 612*)

[1] *C.C.C.*, p 1165.
[2] *C.J.*, Vol. IV, p. 564.
[3] Ib., p. 727.
[4] *L.J.*, Vol. IV, p. 57.

In June 1643 Bolte had lodging with him 'mr Gryffin & one man'. Griffin stated tht he was 'the princes surgeon & must attend that.[1]

MAURICE GRIFFIN or GRIFFITH

In 1638 he appears as the second of two chirurgeons to Prince Charles.[2] In 1641 he is listed as the only chirurgeon:[3] in both cases his name is spelt Griffith. He was living in the parish of St Martin-in-the-Fields as early as 1626: the *Registers* record the baptisms of several children of himself and his wife, Elizabeth. The latter was dry nurse to Charles I's eldest daughter, Princess Mary, later Princess of Orange,[4] whom she accompanied to Holland in 1641/2, remaining with the Princess until the latter's death in 1660.

By 1644 Griffin had left St Aldate's, and is probably to be identified with the 'Mr Griffith' who was lodging in St Martin's parish.[5] His name is included in a list of Delinquents whose goods were sequestered in Westminster in March 1648.[6] According to a petition for a pension (which was granted) presented by his widow to Charles II in 1661, Griffin 'died in the service of the late king'.[7] One of his sons, John, baptized at St Martin-in-the-Fields in 1631/2, was page to Henry, Duke of Gloucester, whom he helped at the time of Queen Henrietta's attack on her son's religion in 1654. John remained with the Duke until the latter's death in 1660.[8]

[1] St Aldate's Defaulters, Bodleian MS. Add. D. 114, f. 26.
[2] MS. Harleian 7623, f. 9v.
[3] MS. Harleian 3791, f. 110.
[4] MS. Harleian 7623, f. 11v and MS. Harleian 3791, f. 115.
[5] Bodleian MS. Add. D. 114, f. 59v.
[6] *C.C.C.*, p. 92.
[7] *C.S.P.D.* 1660-1, p. 555.
[8] MS. List of the Duke of Gloucester's servants preserved at Rousham House.

JOHN HENSLOW or HENSLEY
(c. 1588-1669)

Yeoman and innholder. The son of John Hensley or Henslow, of Adderbury, Oxfordshire, later of St Aldate's, miller and yeoman, who was a churchwarden in 1631-2 and 1632-3. His Will, as of St Aldate's, was made 22 November 1634 and proved 5 March 1635/6.[1] His 'loveing wief Suzan Hensley' may have been a second wife. The younger John was appointed residuary legatee and executor.
In the sixteen-twenties Henslow was servant to Thomas Wood, of Postmasters Hall, the father of Anthony Wood, the antiquary.[2] On 18 October 1630 he was matriculated as a servant, being then servant to Benjamin Elliot, B.D., of Corpus Christi College, his age being given as forty-two.[3] On 24 April 1643 arms were received from him for the King's stores.[4] His name occurs in all the St Aldate's parish taxation lists of 1645 and 1647, and he was assessed at 3s. 4d. in the Subsidy of 1648.[5] In the Hearth Tax of 1665 he had ten hearths;[6] he was assessed at £100 in money and £1. 1s. 0d. pole in the Poll Tax of 1667,[7] and at 10d. in the Subsidy of 1667.[8] On 19 February 1646/7 Henslow was admitted a freeman.[9] He was a churchwarden of St Aldate's in 1648-9 and 1649-50.
From the elder John Henslow's Will we learn that the younger John was twice married. By his first wife, Dorothy Missen, who died in childbed in 1623/4,[10] he had two surviving sons, John and William: by his second wife, Joane, he had a son, Richard, and four daughters, Ann, Joane, Katherine (or Catherine) and Marie. He was buried at St Aldate's (as Hensley) 23 November 1669.[11] The churchwardens in 1669-70 received 6s. 8d. for his grave.
In his Will he left his estate to his three surviving daughters: Joane, wife of Henry Malory, Mary, wife of John Greeneway, and Anne, wife of Thomas ffreeman. The fourth daughter, Catherine, wife of Samuel Everard, M.A., of Doddinghurst, Essex, died 14 August 1662 and was buried at St Aldate's, where there was a M.I.[12]
[Will: nuncupative (as Henslow): Court of the Chancellor of the University of Oxford: Hyp. B. 27: made 19 November 1669: proved 27 August 1673].[13]
An Inventory was taken 29 June 1670,[14] the effects being valued at £828. 17s. 8d. Administration was granted 2 August 1672.
Henslow's house was on the east side of Fish Street, being situated at its junction with the south-west corner of New Lane (Blue Boar Street). It still stands as the present Nos. 6 and 7 St Aldate's. The property belonged to Christ Church. In the College Receipt Book 1631-2 there occurs among the St Aldate's rents 'Willm Bust a Tnt now Henslow'.[15] This presumably refers to John Henslow senior. In the next extant book, 1641-2, the name 'Jo. Henslowe' is entered.[16]
On 23 July 1645 the Dean and Chapter granted to 'John Hensley of the pish of St Aldats in the Citty of Oxōn . . . yeoman', a lease of 'All that their Tenemt & garden ground wth thappurtenncs scituate . . . in the pish of St Aldats in the Citty of Oxford . . . abutting vppon ye high street on ye West, & the Timber yard of ye sd Deane & Chapter on theast, & on a Tenemt now in the tenure or occupacōn of Henry Carter Inneholder on the South side and on a Lane called or knowne by the name of New Lane on the North side, together wth all & all manner of Cellars Solars Howses Easemts. Edifices whatsoever to ye same Tent. belonging in as large & ample manner as Willm Bust of London Gent latelie Deceased heretofore held & enioyed the same'. The lease was for forty years and the rent was 13s. 4d. per annum, plus 'One Couple of good fatt Capons or in lieu thereof Three shillings four pence'.[17] The lease was renewed to Henslow on 10 July 1666.[18] On 22 October 1646 he was licensed by the city to keep an inn and to hang out the sign of the Unicorn.[19] He had an open racket court (the walls of which still exist) at the back of the premises.[20] On 10 July 1635 Thomas Crosfield, Fellow of Queen's College, noted in his *Diary*: 'Dansing on ye rope at ye racket Court, by ye

blewbore',[21] the latter being the house of John Mander [q.v.]. Until recently Henslow's inn was known as the Rackett Restaurant. In his Inventory no mention is made of the rooms, but this entry occurs: 'Item the Howse & Tennis Court being holden of the Deane & Chapter of Christchurch valued at £400.00.00.'

The house is of three storeys with cellars and attic: the walls are timber-framed and the roofs slate-covered. It was probably built about the middle of the seventeenth century and was remodelled again c. 1700 and again in modern times. The first floor formerly projected on the west front which is finished with two gables.[22]

[1] MS. Wills Oxon. 132/1/22.
[2] See baptismal and burial entries (May 1620) of Henslow's son Richard in the Register of the parish church of St John Baptist (Merton College Chapel): Merton College Muniments 2. 11.
[3] University Archives S.P. 2, f. 348: 'Johẽs Hensley, Oxõn: seruiens mṛi Elliott s. s. Theol: Baccalaurej, fil: Johĩs Hensley de Atherburye in Com. p'd: Pleb: an: nat' 42.'
[4] *R.O.P.*, Part I, p. 88.
[5] *S. and T.*, p. 170.
[6] Ib., p. 194
[7] Ib., p. 264.
[8] Ib., p. 342.
[9] *O.C.A.* 1626-1665, p. 143.
[10] Merton College Muniments 2. 11: 14 January 1623/4 'Dorothy wife of John Hensley died in childbed = Buried in the church-yard.' Her maiden name comes from Bodleian MS. Wood E. 33 and the fact that Henslow was still 'servant to Master Wood' from Bodleian MS. Rawlinson B. 402a (see Alan Bott, *The Monuments in Merton College Chapel* (1964), p. 114).
[11] Wood, *C. of O.*, Vol. III, p. 209.
[12] Ib., Vol. III, pp. 134-5.
[13] See also MS. Wills Oxon. 307, f. 49, 21 and 24 November 1669: Caveat Book.
[14] Hyp. B. 13.
[15] Ch. Ch. MS. xi. b. 35.
[16] Ch. Ch. MS. xi. b. 45.
[17] Ch. Ch. MS. xx. c. 4: Register IV, ff. 164-5.
[18] Ch. Ch. MS. xx. c. 5: Register V, f. 262.
[19] *O.C.P.*, p. 340.
[20] *S. and T.*, p. 115.
[21] Ed. F.S. Boas (1935), p. 79. See also *Survey of South-East Ward*, No. 134.
[22] The house is described in R.C.H.M. *City of Oxford*, p. 174 and illustrated on Plate 12.

ARTHUR JONES, second VISCOUNT RANELAGH, M.P.
(died 1670)

The eldest son of Roger Jones, first Viscount Ranelagh (Ireland), and Baron Jones of Navan, co. Meath, by his first wife, Frances, daughter of Gerald Moore, first Viscount Drogheda.

Jones was M.P. for Sligo 1633-4 and was elected for Weobley in the Long Parliament in 1640. He was admitted to Gray's Inn 16 March 1640/1. He was active in the Long Parliament in 1641. He had leave to go to Ireland, where he was a captain of foot in the King's army in May 1642.[1] At first he sided with Parliament, but his reliability began to be suspected after the outbreak of war. He was respited from discharge and disablement from membership of the House of

Commons 22 January 1643/4, but sentence was pronounced against him for being in the King's quarters and adhering to him 5 February 1643/4.[2]
Jones succeeded his father, who died 'of the epidemicall disease then raging in Oxon', 30 October 1643.[3] He was assessed at £2,000 on 28 July 1644.[4]
He married before 1630 Katherine Boyle (1614-1691), fifth daughter of Richard Boyle, first Earl of Cork, and sister of Lord Dungarvan [q.v.]. She was allowed £6 a week for herself and her four children from the sequestration treasury at Guildhall by Parliament 6 February 1646/7.[5] She was a friend of Milton: 'eminent for her piety and suffering'.[6]
Ranelagh died 7 January 1669/70, and was buried 14 January in St Patrick's Cathedral, Dublin.
[Will: proved in P.C. of Dublin in 1670].
(For full accounts see *C.P.* and Keeler, pp. 238-9)

[1] *C.J.*, Vol. II, p. 576.
[2] Ib., Vol. III, pp. 374 and 389.
[3] Wood, *L. and T.*, Vol. I, p. 104 and *C. of O.*, Vol. III, p. 258.
[4] *C.A.M.*, p. 436.
[5] *C.C.C.*, pp. 1659-60.
[6] Ibid.

SIR JOHN PRICE, M.P.
(died 1657)

The son and heir of Edward Price, of Newtown, Montgomeryshire, by his wife, Julia, daughter of John Vaughan, of Llwydyarth, Montgomeryshire. He was created a baronet, of Newtown, 15 August 1628. In 1640 he was elected to the Long Parliament as M.P. for Montgomeryshire. At first he worked for the Popular Party and pledged two horses for the defence of Parliament in June 1642.[1] However, he attended the Oxford Parliament, and signed the letter to Essex of 27 January 1643/4. On 5 February 1643/4 he was listed among the defaulters at the call of the House of Commons, but was respited.[2] In the Balliol College Bursar's Book of Battells 1642-53, Price's name is entered for the seventh week of the second academic term of 1643-4, so he must have moved there immediately after the 'Accompt' was taken. His name recurs every week until the fifth week of the third term, when the records cease until 1649.
By the late summer of 1644, Price had gone over to Parliament again. On 26 September Sir Thomas Myddleton wrote: 'Sir John Price is with me' [at Montgomery Castle].[3] On 20 October 1645 he was disabled from sitting in Parliament.[4] On 26 December 1645 he was assessed at £2,000, but on 12 January 1645/6 he was ordered to be discharged of this, having been in arms for Parliament and much money being due to him.[5] In August 1650 he was sequestered, but he was pardoned, and the sequestration was taken off 31 March 1652.[6]
Price married Catharine, daughter of Sir Richard Pryse, of Gogerddon, Cardiganshire. He died 18 June 1657.
[Administration: P.C.C.: 1657: 1657, f. 268].
(For full accounts see *C.B.*; Keeler, pp. 314-15; Norman Tucker, *Royalist Officers of North Wales* 1642-1660 (1961), p. 51)

[1] *Notes and Queries*, Series I, Vol. 12, p. 360.
[2] *C.J.*, Vol. III, p. 390.
[3] *C.S.P.D.* 1644, p. 534.
[4] *C.J.*, Vol. IV. p. 316.
[5] *C.A.M.*, p. 664.
[6] *C.C.C.*, p. 2552 and *C.J.*, Vol. VII, p. 112.

SERGEANT-MAJOR THOMAS LINDSAY

Eldest son and heir of Bernard Lindsay, of Lochill, Haddingtonshire (East Lothian), by his wife, Barbara Logane, and grandson of Thomas Lindsay, of Kingswark in Leith, Snowdon Herald. Bernard was a favourite 'chamber-cheild' or Gentleman of the Bedchamber to King James VI and I, who heaped gifts upon him. He is mentioned in Izaak Walton's *Life of Sir Henry Wotton*. On 26 June 1610 Bernard was naturalized. There are several allusions to him in the *C.S.P.D.* and Nichols' *Progresses of James I.* His Will is recorded in the Edinburgh Commissariot, 23 February 1628/9.[1] His widow was recorded in the same commissariot 30 September 1637.[2] Bernard's brother Robert was Chief Harbinger and Comptroller of Artillery to James VI and I.

Thomas Lindsay adopted the career of a professional soldier. He was a captain by 24 April 1626, when he was commander of one of the companies returned from Cadiz. The mayor and justices of Barnstaple committed him to prison for certain words spoken.[3] He was sent up to answer before the Council.[4] On 8 September 1627 he was captain of the First Regiment at Plymouth.[5] On 16 March 1627/8 he was in command of a Company helping the Rochellois.[6] By 16 December 1634 he had undertaken the charge of a captain in a Scottish regiment in France to serve under Sir John Hepburn, its colonel, who had raised it.[7] On 9 July 1635 a warrant was issued to Captain Thomas Lindsay to transport a hundred men who had been detained, the said hundred being part of a company of two hundred levied by him.[8] In 1637 (?) he was back in England and petitioning the Council for release after being six weeks in the custody of two Messengers for supposed words which he never spoke.[9]

In 1641 Captain Thomas Lindsey is entered among the Gentlemen of the Privy Chamber Extraordinary.[10] As sergeant-major he was taken prisoner on the surrender of Chichester 27 December 1642,[11] and removed first to Lord Petre's house in London 2 January 1642/3[12] and then, 11 January 1642/3, to Windsor Castle.[13] He was accompanied (among others) by Colonel [Andrew] Lindsay (afterwards exchanged), and Captain Richard Lindsey [of Buxted, Sussex].

In November 1643 John Ashburnham received a warrant from the King to pay a sum of money to Sergeant-Major Thomas Lyndesay, Gentleman of our Privy Chamber.[14]

Lindsay's brother Robert was cupbearer to Prince Charles, afterwards Charles II.[15] One of his sisters, Helen Lindsay, married in 1627/8, as his third wife, Sir Patrick Murray, of Elibank, created Baron Elibank in 1643, a strong Royalist. On 23 June 1632 Charles I granted to Murray a portion of the Lochill estate resigned to him by his brothers-in-law Thomas and Robert Lindsay with their mother's consent.[16]

[1] Vol. 54, f. 264v.
[2] Vol. 58, f. 199.
[3] *C.S.P.D.* 1625-6, p. 318.
[4] Ib., p. 335: see also *Acts of the Privy Council* March 1625-May 1626, p. 487.
[5] Ib. September 1626-June 1628, p. 16.
[6] *C.S.P.D.* 1628-9, p. 22.
[7] *Register of the Privy Council of Scotland*, 2nd Series, Vol. V, 1633-5, pp. 443-4.
[8] Ib., Vol. VI, 1635-7, pp. 45-6.
[9] *C.S.P.D.* 1637-8, pp. 79-80.
[10] L.C. 3/1.
[11] British Museum E. 84. (22).
[12] *C.J.*, Vol. II, p. 910.
[13] *L.J.*, Vol. V, p. 590.

[14] MS. Harleian 6851, f. 217.
[15] MS. Harleian, 7623, f. 9 and MS. Harleian 3791, f. 109.
[16] *Registrum Magni Sigilli Regum Scotorum* 1620-33, No. 1997. See also Nos. 2015 and 2049.

CAPTAIN LOCKETT

It is just possible that this is Giles Lockett, of Charlton Mackrell, Somerset, who, on 26 June 1646, compounded for Delinquency. He claimed to have been a scholar at Oxford (although his name does not appear in the Matriculation Register) who, at the command of his father, at the instance of Sir John Stowell, Governor of Taunton, joined the King's forces there against Exeter. He had taken the Negative Oath. He was fined £93 on 2 July 1646.[1]
Giles' father must have been the Revd. Giles Lockett, rector of Charlton Mackrell in 1606 and West Monkton in 1644.[2] The eldest son, Henry, was a Chaplain Extraordinary to the King.[3] He matriculated from Oriel College, Oxford, 30 October 1635, aged sixteen.

[1] *C.C.C.*, p. 1361.
[2] J. Walker, *Sufferings of the Clergy* (1714), Vol. I, p. 104, Vol. II, p. 298.
[3] L.C. 3/1.

In June 1643 Henslow had lodging with him a MR REEVES who is unidentified.[1]

[1] Bodleian Add. MS. D. 114, f. 26.

In June 1643 between Henslow's house and that of John Lambe is entered 'widdow wilsons house'. She is probably 'BRIDGETT WILLSON WIDDOWE', a recusant, whose name occurs in the Subsidy Lists for 1641 in the South-East Ward (See Robert Wilson).[1] She had lodging with her 'mr Boulton at London a prisoner, mr Stanton, mr Browne, mr woods': no answer was received from the last three.[2]
Mr Stanton may be WILLIAM STAUNTON, of Staunton, Nottinghamshire, son of Anthony Staunton, by his wife, Frances Palmer. He was with Charles I at Edgehill[3] and was created M.A. of Oxford University 1 November 1642. On 6 July 1646 he compounded for Delinquency, being a colonel in arms against Parliament at Newark. He was fined £1,520.[4] On 23 December 1647 his fine was accepted.[5] He died in 1656, aged forty-eight.
[Will: P.C.C. 1658: 320 Wootton].
Mr Stanton might alternatively be Thomas Staunton, of Staunton or Stanton, Suffolk, a major of horse in the King's army, who, on 7 August 1646, begged to compound on the Faringdon Articles and was fined £160.[6] On 16 September 1647 his fine was accepted.[7] Thomas may be the Captain Stanton who was in Oxford in September.[8]

[1] City Archives B. 1. 4. c and B. 1. 4. d.
[2] St Aldate's Defaulters, Bodleian MS. Add. D. 114, f. 26.
[3] R. Thoroton, *Nottinghamshire*, Vol. I (1790), p. 309.
[4] *C.C.C.*, p. 1382.
[5] *C.J.*, Vol. V, p. 397.
[6] *C.C.C.*, p. 1448.
[7] *C.J.*, Vol. V, p. 302.
[8] Stevens, p. 32.

JOHN LAMBE
(c. 1610-1681)

Tailor, afterwards maltster. The son of Lawrence Lambe, of Godington, Oxfordshire, husbandman, he was apprenticed 2 September 1622 to William Jennings, tailor, of Oxford.[1] He was admitted a freeman 21 September 1630.[2] John's younger brother, Hugh, was apprenticed to him 6 April 1635.[3]

John Lambe was appointed constable of the South-West Ward in September 1633.[4] He was mayor's chamberlain in 1644[5] and junior bailiff in 1649.[6] He remained a bailiff from October 1650 until March 1657/8, when he became an assistant.[7] He was elected mayor 19 September 1659[8] and became an assistant again in October 1660.[9] On 6 June 1662, although he had voluntarily taken the Oath of Allegiance, he was removed by the commission for the regulation of corporations,[10] but on 9 September 1667 he was given a bailiff's place,[11] followed by that of an assistant,[12] becoming mayor for a second time on 14 September 1668[13] and assistant again in 1669, remaining so until his death.

Lambe was a churchwarden of St Aldate's in 1644-5, during which time he was 'shutt vp of the plague'. His name occurs in all the St Aldate's parish taxation lists of 1645 and 1647. As 'taylor' he contributed £2. 10s. 0d. to the loan to the Lords Commissioners in October 1645.[14] He was assessed at 3s. in the Subsidy of 1648,[15] had five hearths in the Hearth Tax of 1665,[16] was assessed at £1. 15s. 0d. for title and pole in the Poll Tax of 1667,[17] and at 6s. in the Subsidy of 1667.[18] He is described as 'maulster' in 1674 (see under John Earle).

On 8 August 1681 Wood records: 'John Lamb, one of the 13, sometimes Mayor, died in his journey from London to Oxford. A presbyterian, an enimy to Academians. He was a taylor, first, afterwards a maulster'.[19] He is mentioned as dead 15 August 1681.[20]

Lambe's house was on the east side of Grandpont and occupied the site of the demolished Nos. 10 and 11 St Aldate's, the former Trill Mill or Trentle Hall.[21] It was the first tenement on the south side of Trillmill Bow. It was private property, and up to the Dissolution paid a quit-rent of 3s. to Eynsham Abbey. On 2 April 1632 Thomas Smith, M.A., of Lincoln College sold to George Jacob, of St Aldate's, yeoman and alebrewer, 'All that his Messuage or Tenemt together wth the Brewhouses and all other singular houses . . . to the same Messuage or Tenemt belonging . . . scituate . . . in Grandpont in the pish of St Aldate . . . and late in the tenure of Richard Spicer Alebrewer deceased . . . and now in the tenure or Occupacon of him the said George Jacob his assigne or assignes, And the premises are next adioyninge to the River or streame of water Comonlie called Trill Mill Bowe on the North pte and are next betweene a garden grounde of the Warden and Colledge of the Sowles of all faythfull people deceased of Oxford on the South pte and the said River or Streame on the North pte Abutting Westward vppon the kings high street and Eastward vppon thaforesaid River or Streame'.[22] George Jacob, who had been manciple of Broadgates Hall, died intestate in 1637:[23] whether, as seems probable, Lambe acquired the property on Jacob's death, is uncertain. The house is placed out of order in the 'Accompt'.

The tenement was subject to a rent charge of 1s. per annum to the city, and this was paid by John Lambe in 1658, when it is described as a 'tenement sometimes Peter Page's [i.e. Porye's], built upon a piece of ground near Trill Mill Bow'.[24] Salter suggests that the tenement (later called the Green Dragon) projected far into the road and was removed under the Paving Act of 1772.[25]

In addition to his house, Lambe was in occupation of a piece of 'void' ground immediately south of Trillmill Hall, the site of the demolished No. 12 St Aldate's belonging to All Souls. Leases of this ground were granted by the College 1604, 1607, and 1621. On the last occasion the lessee was the Thomas Smith of Lincoln previously mentioned, when the property was described as 'one voide peice of grounde whearevpon sometimes there stood a Tenemt or messuage being in Grandpont by Oxōn contayning in Length from the East to the West Eleven poles and halfe and one foote accounting eighteene foot in everie pole being in breadth at the West end eighteene foote and att the East end twentie and one foote and tenne inches abbutting vpon the high streete which leadeth from Oxōn to Abbington on the West and vpon a little River that runeth betweene the said grounde and Christchurch als frisewides meadow on the East and on a Tenemt of Mr Nappers now of late in the tenure of Barnard Banger on the north side and vpon a peece of ground now of late belonging to Christ Church als frisewides on the South side according to a vewe taken and recorded in the towne Court'. The lease was for twenty years at an annual rent of 5s. payable on St Michael's Day.[26] The All Souls Rental of 1653 shews Lambe paying the 5s. rent for the ground, as he contined to do.[27]

[1] City Archives L. 5. 2, f. 105.
[2] Ib., no folio number.
[3] Ib., f. 267.
[4] *O.C.A.* 1626-1665, p. 49.
[5] Ib., pp. 122 and 123.
[6] Ib., p. 166.
[7] Ib., p. 227.
[8] Ib., p. 247.
[9] Ib., p. 269.
[10] Ib., p. 294.
[11] *O.C.A.* 1666-1701, p. 13.
[12] City Archives B. 5. 1, f. 57v.
[13] *O.C.A.* 1666-1701, p. 23.
[14] City Archives E. 4. 6, ff. 1-2: *O.C.A.* 1626-1665, p. 453.
[15] *S. and T.*, p. 169.
[16] Ib., p. 193.
[17] Ib., p. 264.
[18] Ib., p. 342.
[19] *L. and T.*, Vol. II, p. 550.
[20] *O.C.A.* 1666-1701, p. 140. See also for Lambe *Oxoniensia*, Vol. XXV (1960), pp. 73, 75, 76, 81.
[21] Wood, *C. of O.*, Vol. I, pp. 299-300.
[22] City Archives A. 5. 4, f. 28.
[23] Administration was granted in the Court of the Chancellor of Oxford University 10 November 1637.
[24] *O.C.P.*, p. 11.
[25] Ib., pp. 107-8. For the earlier history see *Records of the City of Oxford*, ed. W.H. Turner (1880), p. 375.
[26] All Souls College Leases 51(a), 20 April 19 James I.
[27] See also *Survey of South-East Ward*, No. 153.

LIEUTENANT RICHARD EDMONDS

He belonged to the Lifeguard of Foot and was lieutenant to Major Markham [q.v.]. On 8 January 1644/5 he received arms for the Lifeguard.[1]

[1] See P.R.O., W.O. 55.

In June 1643 Lambe had lodging with him '4 of Lord Sturton's men' from whom no answer was received.[1]

WILLIAM STOURTON, fifth BARON STOURTON
(c. 1594-1672)

The eldest son and heir of Edward Stourton, tenth Baron Stourton, by his wife, Frances, daughter of Sir Thomas Tresham, of Rushton, Northamptonshire, he was born in or before 1594. He was created K.B. in 1616. He gave the King £300 towards the Scottish War in 1639. Having succeeded his father in 1633, he had leave to be absent from Parliament 14 April 1640. He did not sit in the Oxford Parliament, being among those 'Peeres employed in His Majesties service or absent with leave'. Stourton claimed not to have been in active arms for the King, but his estate was sequestered for Delinquency 27 October 1645.[2] He was in Oxford at the surrender in June 1646, and claimed to compound on the Oxford Articles, although he was a recusant, 1 December 1646. On 19 December 1649 he was fined £556. 6s. 6d., and on 6 July 1654, £1,236. 19s. 5d., his Delinquency consisting in going to Oxford and other places in the King's quarters.[3]
He married Frances, daughter of Sir Edward Moore, of Odiham, Hampshire. He died 25 April 1672 and was buried at Stourton, Wiltshire.
[Will: P.C.C. 1672: 81 Eure].
(For a full account see *C.P.*)

[1] St Aldate's Defaulters, Bodleian MS. Add. D. 114, f. 26.
[2] *C.A.M.*, p. 615.
[3] *C.C.C.*, p. 1583.

JOHN MANDER or MAUNDER
(died 1644)

Innkeeper. On 28 September 1632 he was admitted a freeman.[1] On 15 September 1634 he was appointed constable for the South-West Ward,[2] and on 30 September 1643 was made a councillor.[3] He was a churchwarden of St Aldate's in 1633-4. He paid 20s. and 8s. 'in lands' in the Subsidy Lists of 1641.[4] On 24 April 1643 arms were received from him for the King's stores.[5] He married Dorothy . . . He was buried at St Aldate's 16 March 1643/4.[6]

In his Will Mander mentions his son, John (who was under twenty-one), and his four daughters, Sibble, Anne, Susannah, and Elizabeth (who were all under eighteen). His wife was appointed executrix and residuary legatee, and the overseers named were Thomas Seymour, John Henslow, and John Lambe [qq.v.], who were each to receive 2s. 6d. to buy gloves. John Lambe was also a witness. Mander desired to be buried at St Aldate's.

[Will: P.C.C. 1647: 9 Fines: made 3 March 1643/4: proved 13 January 1646/7].

Mander's house was on the east side of Fish Street, at its junction with the north-west corner of New Lane (Blue Boar Street). It was the former No. 5 St Aldate's (being the last house in the parish on that side going north), the site recently occupied by the Public Library, and was called the Blue Boar Inn.[7] The property belonged to New College. By an indenture dated 1 October 1638 between the College and John Maunder 'of the parish of St Aldates Innhoulder' the former 'demise graunt and to farme lett' two tenements described as 'lying togeathar within the psh of St Aldates . . . between the Guild hall of the said citty of Oxford on the North side & a tenement belonging to the Deane & Chapter of the Cathedrall Church of Christ late in the tenure or occupacon of William Bust . . . deceased & now John Hensley or of his assignes on the south side abutting vpon the High streete leading from Christ Church toward Carfax on the West & vpon a garden ground . . . on the east'. Both tenements were in the tenure or occupation of Mander and one was called 'ye Blew bore'. The lease was for forty years and the rent for the inn was 53s. per annum.[8]

In his Will Mander left the lease of the Blue Boar to his wife for her life and his son, John, was to have it after her death. Dorothy Mander was remarried by 1647[9] to Matthew Loveday, of St Aldate's (to whom she bore a son, Matthew), and was buried at St Aldate's 18 December 1676.[10] Matthew Loveday the elder was buried at St Aldate's 27 August 1666.[11] Loveday's Will, as of the University of Oxford (he matriculated as *servus* 20 March 1634/5 aged thirty-five), innholder, was proved in the P.C.C. 29 October 1666.[12] The Blue Boar was left to Dorothy for her life and after her death to their son, Matthew, of Oriel College, later a barrister of the Inner Temple, and husband of Frances, daughter of John Windebank and granddaughter of John Holloway [qq.v.].

On 20 October 1652 an indenture was entered into between New College and John Maunder, 'of the parish of St Pulchers London Salter' whereby the two tenements described in the indenture of 1638 were leased to him. Loveday is described as occupying them.[13] On 30 May 1656 a similar lease was granted to Matthew Loveday.[14]

In the schedule annexed to the indenture of 1638 the following rooms are mentioned: 'the Old Hall', 'the Parlour', 'the Newe Hall', 'the Litle Chamber over the new Hall', 'the Kitchin', 'the Chamber over the Kitchin', 'the Long Chamber', 'the Greene Chamber', 'the Chamber over the Signe', 'the Chamber at the Staireheade', 'the Milkhouse & Larder', 'the Chamber over the Office', 'the Cockloft'; also 'the New Stable', 'the Ould Stable', 'the Litle Stable', and 'the Court'.

The Blue Boar, which was an important inn in the seventeenth century, was acquired by New College early in the reign of Queen Elizabeth I, and was held by it until 1824.[15]

[1] *O.C.A.* 1626-1665, pp. 41 and 44.
[2] Ib., p. 56.
[3] Ib., p. 116.
[4] City Archives B. 1. 4. c.
[5] *R.O.P.*, Part I, p. 90.
[6] Wood, *C. of O.*, Vol. III, p. 208.
[7] 'John Manders house the Inne being blew bore', Bodleian MS. Add. D. 114, f. 26.
[8] New College Registrum Dim. ad Firm. 9, ff. 262-4.
[9] St Aldate's parish taxation lists.
[10] Wood, *C. of O.*, Vol. III, p. 209 and *L. and T.*, Vol. III, p. 7.
[11] Ib. Matthew and Dorothy Loveday were buried beside each other 'neere the great south door'.
[12] 166 Mico.
[13] Registrum Dim. ad Firm. 10, ff. 217-18.
[14] Registrum Dim. ad Firm. 11, ff. 76-7.
[15] *O.C.P.*, p. 152. See also *Survey of South-East Ward*, No. 134 and Wood, *C. of O.*, Vol. I, pp. 155-6. There is an elevation of the house as it appeared in 1806 in the City Archives (G. I. 62): this is reproduced in *O.C.P.* (opp. p. 152).

JOHN STEWART, first EARL OF TRAQUAIR
(c. 1600-1659)

The son and heir of John Stewart the younger, of Traquair, Peeblesshire, by his wife, Margaret, daughter of Andrew Stewart, Master of Ochiltree. He was born c. 1600; was made a P.C. for Scotland, and created a Baron in 1628, and an Earl in 1633. He was Lord Treasurer of Scotland from 1636 to 1641.

Traquair was accused of trimming, but Clarendon praises him highly.[1] He went with the Duke of Hamilton to York in March 1642/3, and then attended the King at Oxford until March 1643/4. On 27 March Nicholas wrote to Lord Forth [q.v.] from Oxford: 'The Earls of Kinnoul [q.v.] and Traquair go this day northward':[2] and again on 29 March: 'The Earls of Kinnoul and Traquair went two days since towards the north'.[3]

He was fined 400,000 merks by Act of the Scottish Parliament 8 March 1644/5. He took the Covenant and was pardoned at the King's request. He took part in the Second Civil War and was captured after the Battle of Preston, about 19 August 1648, and was imprisoned at Warwick Castle until 1651, returning to Scotland in 1652.

Traquair married c. 1620 Catherine, daughter of David Carnegie, first Earl of Southesk, and died 27 March 1658/9 in great poverty at Edinburgh, where he was buried.

(For full accounts see *C.P.: Scots Peerage; D.N.B.*)

[1] Bk. II, § 12.
[2] *C.S.P.D.* 1644, p. 75.
[3] Ib., p. 79.

SIX SERVANTS OF HENRY FREDERICK HOWARD, BARON MOWBRAY, afterwards third EARL OF ARUNDEL (1608-1652)

The eldest surviving son of Thomas Howard, second Earl of Arundel, whom he succeeded in 1646, by his wife, Lady Aletheia Talbot, youngest daughter of Gilbert Talbot, seventh Earl of Shrewsbury. He was born 15 August 1608, and was created K.B. 4 November 1616.

As Lord Maltravers, he sat as M.P. for Arundel 1628-9 and 1640. On 21 March 1639/40 he was summoned to the Upper House in his father's barony of Mowbray. He was among the peers who subscribed in 1642 to pay for horses for the King's service.[1] He was present at Edgehill, and was created M.A. of Oxford University 1 November 1642. He attended the Oxford Parliament and signed the letter to Essex of 27 January 1643/4. In 1648 he was fined by Parliament £6,000, and he compounded for his estate 25 November 1648.[2]

Mowbray married in 1626 Lady Elizabeth Stuart, eldest daughter of Esmé Stuart, third Duke of Lennox: she died in 1673/4. He died 17 April 1652 at Arundel House, and was buried at Arundel.

(For full accounts see *C.P.* and *D.N.B.*)

Three of Lord Mowbray's servants were already lodging with John Mander in June 1643, when they were entered as defaulters and said that 'the Constables must goe to their mr.'[3]

[1] Peacock, p. 9.
[2] *L.J.*, Vol. X, p. 609; *C.C.C.*, p. 2461.
[3] Bodleian MS. Add. D. 114, f. 26.

FIVE SERVANTS OF GEORGE HAY, second EARL OF KINNOULL (c. 1602-1644)

The second and only surviving son of George Hay, first Earl of Kinnoull, by his wife, Margaret, daughter of Sir James Haliburton, of Pitcur, and widow of Patrick Ogilvie the younger, of Inchmartin. He was born c. 1602. He was Captain of the Yeomen of the Guard 1632-5, and a P.C. for Scotland. He succeeded his father in 1634. On 24 June 1641 Sidney Bere wrote to Sir John Penington: 'Lord Morton has resigned his place of Captain of the Guard to the Earl of Kinnoull',[1] but Morton (who was Kinnoull's father-in-law) did not actually resign until 1644.

Kinnoull refused to take the Covenant. He followed the King to Oxford. On 23 March 1643/4 Charles wrote to him: 'Considering the long affection of the Earl of Kinnoul to our person and service, and his many losses and sufferings for us, and taking kindly his forebearing at this time to urge the performance of our former engagements to him, we do, on the word of a prince, promise that whenever he shall desire us we shall admit him Gentleman of our Bedchamber'.[2] He left Oxford 27 March 1644 (see under Earl of Traquair).

Kinnoull married Ann (died 1667), eldest daughter of William Douglas, seventh (or eighth) Earl of Morton. He died at Whitehall 5 October 1644, and was buried at Waltham Abbey 8 October.

(For full accounts see *C.P.*; *Scots Peerage*; *D.N.B.*)

[1] *C.S.P.D.* 1641-3, p. 24.
[2] Ib. 1644, p. 66: see also p. 67.

SIR WILLIAM WALLINGTON

Unidentified. There was no knight or baronet of this name, and we have failed to discover who is intended. William Widdrington, first Baron Widdrington (1610-1651) is a possibility.

John Mander had lodging with him in June 1643 four of the King's servants, four of the Prince's, four of Lord Mowbray's, three of Lady Dormer's, and two of Lord Herbert's.

ALICE, LADY DORMER
(died 1650)

Daughter of Sir Richard Molyneux, first baronet, of Sefton, Lancashire, by his wife, Frances, eldest daughter of Sir Gilbert Gerard, of Sudbury, Suffolk, Master of the Rolls. She married 21 February 1609/10 Sir William Dormer, of Wing, Buckinghamshire, eldest son and heir of Robert Dormer, first Baron Dormer, of Wing, who died in his father's lifetime in October 1616. Her only son, Robert, created Earl of Carnarvon in 1628, was killed at the First Battle of Newbury in 1643. Lady Dormer was a recusant. She possessed the manor of Eythrope, Buckinghamshire, in 1645. She died 2 July 1650.[1] Lady Dormer was mother-in-law of Lord Herbert (see below).

[1] F.G. Lee, *History of the Prebendal Church at Thame* (1883), p. 514.

EDWARD SOMERSET, BARON HERBERT, afterwards second MARQUESS OF WORCESTER
(c. 1603-1667)

The eldest son of Henry Somerset, first Marquess of Worcester, by his wife, Anne Russell, daughter and heir of John Russell, Lord Russell, He was probably born in 1602/3. At the beginning of the Civil War he acted as intermediary for furnishing the King with vast sums of money advanced by his father. He took part in the operations in the Forest of Dean in the autumn of 1642, and was given the command in South Wales in January 1642/3. His forces were defeated by Sir William Waller at Highnam, near Gloucester, 24-25 March 1643. In April 1643 he was appointed Lieutenant-General of South Wales and Monmouth. Clarendon says that Lord Herbert was seldom with his forces, he being at Oxford 25 March 1643.[1] From January 1644/5 to 18 December 1646 he was styled Earl of Glamorgan. On the latter date he succeeded his father as second Marquess of Worcester. His estates were sequestered.[2]

Herbert, who was a recusant, married, first, c. 1628 Elizabeth, daughter of Sir William Dormer, of Wing, by his wife, Alice (see above). She died in 1635. He married, secondly, 1639 Margaret, second daughter and co-heir of Henry O'Brien, fourth Earl of Thomond. He died 3 April 1667 and was buried 19 April at Raglan. (For full accounts see *C.P.* and *D.N.B.*)

[1] Bk. VI, §§ 291-2.
[2] *C.C.C.*, pp. 1705-15 and *C.S.P.D.* 1649-50, p. 39.

APPENDIX I

LISTS OF STRANGERS LODGING IN THE PARISHES OF ST MARTIN, ALL SAINTS, AND ST JOHN ABOUT APRIL 1644

BODLEIAN MS. ADD. D. 114, f. 59v.

St Martins
monies receaued by Henry Roe Collector
vpon the whole month*

1.	mr Heath	0	10	0
2.	Mr Tomkins pliament man	0	10	0
3.	Sr Roger Palmer	1	0	0
4.	mr Griffith	0	10	0
5.	mr Wharton†	0	5	0
6.	Sr Ed: Griffith a pliament man	1	0	0
7.	mr weston	0	10	0
8.	mr North	0	10	0
	mr Southcott	0	10	0
	mr Tunston	0	10	0
9.	mr Ryder	0	10	0
10.	mr withers	0	10	0
11.	mr Sainthill a pliament man	0	10	0
12.	mr Jane a pliamnt man	0	10	0
13.	mr King Cler	0	2	0
		8	7	0

*The date '10th Ap. 1644' occurs in some calculations in another column on the same page.
†Erased in the original.

All saints parish

		£	s	d
	mr Trustrum(?)	0	5	0
1.	sr Thomas Hamersley	0	10	0
2.	Sr Dudly Carleton	1	0	0
	mr Hayes	0	5	0
3.	Lady Whorwood	0	12	0
4.	mr Penruddock	0	5	0
5.	mr morgan pliam̃nt man	0	10	0
6.	sr Henry Spiller	1	0	0
7.	mr Watson	0	10	0
8.	mr Dobson	0	5	0
9.	mr Thornton	0	5	0
10.	Coll: weston	0	10	0
11.	Sr Henry Moody	0	10	0
12.	mris Pudsey			
13.	Sr William Palmer	1	0	0
14.	Coll: Knightly	0	5	0
15.	sr fred. Cornwallis a plia man	1	0	0
16.	mr Billingsly	0	10	0
17.	Dr frazer	0	10	0
	mr Lowen	0	10	0
18.	sr Thomas Dorrell	1	0	0
	mr Whitfeild	0	5	0

19.	mr warpoole	0 5 0
20.	mr mathewes	0 5 0
21.	Coll: Cobb	0 10 0
22.	mr Basset	0 10 0
23.	Sr Ed: Rodny	1 0 0
24.	mr Robt Heath	0 5 0
25.	mr francis Heath	0 5 0
	mr west	0 10 0
	mr Lewys	0 10 0
26.	mr Stanier	0 10 0
27.	Captaine Bill	0 7 6
	mr Hurst	0 10 0
28.	mr Bagshaw	0 10 0
		17 19 6

St Johns parish

1.	Sr John Culpepper	1 0 0
2.	sr Alexander Culpepper	1 0 0
3.	mr freak	0 10 0
		2 10 0
	The totall is	28 16 6

ST MARTIN'S PARISH

1. EDWARD HEATH (1612-1669)

See Introduction.

2. THOMAS TOMKINS (died 1674)

The fourth (but second surviving) son of James Tomkins of Monnington, Herefords., he was of Monnington and Garnstone (also Herefords.).

Admitted to the Middle Temple, 1622.

Barrister, 1631.

M.P. Weobley, Jan. 1640-22 Jan. 1643/4, when disabled (*C.J.*, Vol. III, p. 374).

Sat in Oxford Parliament, 1643/4.

Married Mary, daughter of Sir Walter Pye.

(Keeler, p. 362).

3. SIR ROGER PALMER (1577-1657)

The son of Sir Thomas Palmer, Bart., of Wingham, Kent, Gentleman of the Privy Chamber to James I, brother of Sir James Palmer, Gentleman Usher of the Privy Chamber to Charles I, and uncle of Roger, Earl of Castlemaine.

Cup bearer to Prince Henry and afterwards to Prince Charles.

Master of the Household to Charles I.

K.B., 1625/6.

Cofferer by 1632.

M.P. Newton, Lancs., 1640-22 Jan. 1643/4, when disabled (*C.J.*, Vol. III, p. 374).

Sequestered, Sept. 1643 (*C.J.*, Vol. III, p. 256; *C.C.C.*, pp. 1394-6).

Married Katherine, daughter of Sir Thomas Porter, and widow of Sir Richard Welch.

Palmer's Will was proved in 1657 (P.C.C. 453 Ruthen).

(Keeler, pp. 293-4).

4. MAURICE GRIFFIN or GRIFFITH

See p. 235.

5. MR WHARTON

Almost certainly this is Michael Warton or Wharton (1593-1645), of Beverley, Yorks.

M.P. for Beverley 1640-22 Jan. 1643/4, when he was disabled (*C.J.*, Vol. III, p. 374).

Attended the King at Oxford (H.M.C., App. to VIIth *Report*, p. 122), and sat in Oxford Parliament (late), 1643/4.

Killed at the siege of Scarborough, 1645.

(Keeler, pp. 379-80; *C.C.C.*, pp. 955-8).

It is just possible that 'Mr Wharton' is (Sir) George Wharton (1617-1681), son of George Wharton, blacksmith, of Kendal.

Raised a troop of horse for the King and joined him at Oxford in 1644.

Paymaster to the Magazine and Artillery.

Prisoner at Windsor, 1655.

From 1660 until his death, Treasurer and Paymaster of the Ordnance.

Created baronet, 1677.

6. SIR EDWARD GRIFFIN (c. 1605-1681)

The son and heir of Sir Thomas Griffin, of Braybrooke, Northants., by his second wife, Elizabeth, daughter of George Touchet, Lord Audley, and widow of Sir John Stawell, of Cotherstone, Somerset, he was of Braybrooke and Dingley (also Northants.).

Matriculated from Queen's College, Oxford, 1616.

Knighted, 1625.

Gentleman of the Privy Chamber by 1638.

M.P. Downton, Wilts., 1640-5 Feb. 1643/4, when disabled (*C.J.*, Vol. III, p. 389).

Sat in Oxford Parliament, 1643/4.

Compounded before the fall of Oxford. Fined £1,700, 1646/7 (*C.C.C.*, p. 1206).

Resumed post of Gentleman of the Privy Chamber after 1660 and later became Treasurer of the Chamber.

Married Frances, daughter of Sir William Uvedale, of Wickham, Hampshire. (Keeler, pp. 196-7).

7. RICHARD WESTON (c. 1609-1652)

The son and heir of Sir Richard Weston, Baron of the Exchequer, he was of Rugeley, Staffs.

Admitted to the Inner Temple, 1625.

Barrister, 1632.

M.P. Stafford 1640-30 Oct. 1642, when disabled (Keeler: no reference).

Sat in Oxford Parliament, 1643/4.

Slain in the Isle of Man.

(Keeler, p. 386).

8. GILBERT NORTH (c. 1597-1656)

The fourth son of Sir John North, M.P. Cambs., by his wife, Dorothy, daughter of Sir Valentine Dale.

Educated at Eton, 1610-12.

Fellow Commoner of Caius College, Cambridge, 1612.

Gentleman of the Privy Chamber (L.C. 3/1).

Compounded on Oxford Articles. Fined £32, 1646 (*C.C.C.*, p. 1577).

North's Will was proved in 1656 (P.C.C. 255 Berkeley).

9. MARK RIDER

In 1660 he petitioned for the place of Groom of the Poultry, which he did not obtain. He stated that he was employed before and during the Civil War as purveyor of poultry for Charles II when Prince of Wales and James, Duke of York; also for collecting sums of money in Oxfordshire and as surveyor of stables (*C.S.P.D.* 1660-1, p. 29). In Ashburnham's *Accompt*, occurs the entry: 'To Captain Danscoat [sic for Dabscoat] by Mr Ryder £10' (p. xxxiv).

George Rider (perhaps Mark's brother) was Yeoman of the Poultry to Prince Charles from 1638 (MS. Harl. 7623, f. 10v). George was described on 9 Jan. 1643/4 as being 'now at Oxford' (*C.A.M.*, p. 319). Both Mark and George may have been nephews of William Ryder, Gentleman Harbinger and Surveyor of the Stables to James I (died 1617), whose Will (P.C.C. 121 Weldon) mentions a brother Jacob, his wife, and children. William Ryder was the father of Mrs Whorwood (see under Lady Whorwood).

Mark Rider was living in the parish of St Martin-in-the-Fields 7 Sept. 1665, when his daughter Dorothy, aged 19, had a licence to marry Jacob Withers, of Richmond, aged 22 (*Marriage Licences issued from the Faculty Office*, Harl. Soc., Vol. XXIV, p. 90). Withers was the son of Mark Rider's neighbour in Oxford during the Civil War. (See next).

10. JACOB WITHERS (died c.1678)

In 1641 he was entered as yeoman under Harbingers in the Household of Prince Charles (MS. Harl. 3791, f. 112). In 1662 he was the first of six yeomen Harbingers to Charles II (S.P. 20/60/123).

On 31 Dec. 1639 he had a licence to marry Elizabeth Avery (*Marriage Licences granted by the Bishop of London*, Index Library, p. 196). His son Jacob had a licence to marry Dorothy, daughter of Mark Rider (see above), 7 Sept. 1665. Withers left 1s. to 'Dorothy formerly wife of my sonne Jacob Withers'.

Withers' Will was proved in 1678 (P.C.C. 72 Reeve).

11. PETER SAINTHILL (1593-1648)

The third son of Peter Sainthill, of Bradninch, Devon, by his wife, Elizabeth, daughter of Thomas Martin, D.C.L., of Steeple Morden, Cambs., he was of Bradninch.

Educated at Blundell's School, Tiverton.

Matriculated from Oriel College, Oxford, 1610.

Admitted to the Middle Temple, 1611.

M.P. Tiverton 1640-22 Jan. 1643/4, when disabled (*C.J.*, Vol. III, p. 374).

Sat in Oxford Parliament, 1643/4.

Begged to compound on Exeter Articles, 1646.

Married Dorothy, daughter and heir of Robert Packer (Parker?), of Foldhay, Devon.

(Keeler, pp. 331-2).

12. JOSEPH JANE (c. 1600-c. 1660)

The son of Thomas Jane, sometime mayor and deputy-steward of Liskeard, Cornwall, he was of Liskeard.

M.P. Liskeard, 1626.

Mayor of Liskeard, 1631 and 1635.

M.P. Liskeard, 1640-22 Jan. 1643/4, when disabled (*C.J.*, Vol. III, p. 374).

Sat in Oxford Parliament 1643/4, a fact which Mrs Keeler has overlooked.

Married first, Jane Sparker, of Plymouth; secondly, Loveday, daughter of William Kekewich, of Calchfrench, Cornwall.

(Keeler, p. 232).

13. MR KING CLER[icus]

This might be John King, curate of St Thomas', Salisbury, who confessed that he was once at Oxford with Mr Buckner and once returned money there for Mr Richard Pill. His confession was made before the County Committee 14 June 1646 (A.G. Matthews, *Walker Revised* (1948), p. 375).

ALL SAINTS' PARISH

1. SIR THOMAS HAMERSLEY (died 1653 or 1654)

The son of Sir Hugh Hamersley, alderman of the City of London, lord mayor 1627-8, governor of the Levant Company.

Knighted, 1641.

On 22 Oct. 1642 the House of Commons ordered the lord mayor and sheriffs to search the house, seize the arms, and secure the persons of Sir Thomas and Dame Mary Hamersley in Aldgate Ward, together with those of others who would not contribute to the common cause (*C.J.*, Vol. II, p. 819).

On 28 Sept. 1643, having been declared a Delinquent by the Commons, order was made for the sale of his sequestered goods (*C.J.*, Vol. III, p. 285: see also *C.A.M.*, p. 306).

He compounded on Oxford Articles. Fined £53. 6s. 8d., 1648 (*C.C.C.*, p. 1514).

Hamersley's Administration is dated 1653/4, in the Fleet Prison (P.C.C., Vol. III, f. 131).

2. SIR DUDLEY CARLETON (c. 1599-1654)

The second son of George Carleton, of Brightwell Baldwin and Huntercombe, Oxon., by his second wife, Katherine, daughter of Thomas Harrison, of Finchampstead, Berks.

Educated at Eton, 1613-15.

Scholar of King's College, Cambridge, 1615.

Fellow, 1618-24.

Secretary to his uncle Sir Dudley Carleton (later Viscount Dorchester) when the latter was Ambassador at The Hague, whence he returned in 1625.

Knighted, 1630.

Admitted to Lincoln's Inn, 1633.

A Clerk of the Council, 1637.

Carleton's Will was proved in 1653/4 (P.C.C. 341 Alchin).

3. URSULA, LADY WHORWOOD (died 1653)

The only daughter and heir of George Brome, of Holton, Oxon., and widow of Sir Thomas Whorwood, of Sandwell Hall, Staffs. and Holton, who died in 1634: his Will was proved in 1634 by his widow (P.C.C. 81 Seager). M.I. at Holton.

Lady Whorwood was a devoted Royalist. She appears in Ashburnham's *Accompt* as giving the King £158 (p. vii) and 'Three dozen Plate Trenchers, in value £89. 1s. 7d.' (p. xi). She had returned to Holton from Oxford by Dec. 1645 (*C.A.M.*, p. 648). Her son Brome's wife, Mrs Jane Whorwood (née Ryder: see under Mark Rider), was also devoted to the King (*D.N.B.*).

Lady Whorwood's Will was proved in 1654 (P.C.C. 348 Alchin).

(For the Whorwood family see *Visitation of Oxfordshire* 1634, Harl. Soc., Vol. V, p. 242, and *Miscellanea Genealogica et Heraldica*, N.S., Vol. IV (1884), p. 38).

4. (SIR) GEORGE PENRUDDOCK (died c. 1664)

Of Broad Chalke, Wilts: a friend of John Aubrey. One of the four sewers to Charles I (L.C. 3/1). Gave Charles I £160 (Ashburnham, *Accompt*, p. iv). Apparently served with the Wallingford garrison in Oct. 1646, as he sent a troop of horse from there against the enemy (*C.S.P.D.* 1645-7, p. 487).

Compounded on Oxford Articles. Fined £1,000 (*C.C.C.*, p. 1433). Pardoned.

Knighted between Sept. 1660 and Jan. 1662/3.

Penruddock's Will was proved in 1664 (P.C.C. 66 Bruce).

5. WILLIAM MORGAN (died 1649)

The son and heir of Llewellyn Morgan, of Ystradvelltrey, Brecon, he was of Ddrew or Therrow, Brecknocks.

Admitted to the Middle Temple, 1616.

Solicitor-General before President and Council of Wales, 1639.

M.P. Brecknocks, 1640-49.

Cited as a defaulter, Feb. 1643/4 (*C.J.*, Vol. III, p. 390).

Lent Charles I £100 (Ashburnham, *Accompt*, p. vii).

Charged with issuing commissions of array under Great Seal at Oxford and of contributing money, horses and arms (*C.A.M.*, p. 390).

Sat in Oxford Parliament, 1643/4, but escaped disablement.

Declared that he was made prisoner and carried to Raglan and thence to Oxford and forced to sit in the Parliament there (statement made in May 1647: H.M.C., Appendix to VIth *Report*, p. 173).

Married Elizabeth, daughter of Sir William Morgan, of Tredegar.
(Keeler, p. 279).

6. SIR HENRY SPILLER (died 1650)

He was acting as an Exchequer official early in the reign of James I with a special concern for recusants' affairs, and so continued for many years, also acting on numerous commissions in the reign of Charles I (*C.S.P.D.* 1604 and onwards, passim).

Admitted to Lincoln's Inn as of Bucks., *armiger*, 1606.

Granted manor of Laleham, Middlesex, 1612.

Knighted, 1618.

Was in trouble with the House of Commons in 1621 Parliament (*C.J.*, Vol. I, pp. 550 and 652), and at the beginning of the Long Parliament when he was sent for as a Delinquent (14 Nov. 1640) and placed in custody, but was quickly bailed (*C.J.*, Vol. II, pp. 29, 31, and 33).

Compounded for Delinquency in residing in the King's quarters, 1646.

Stated that he had gone to Hereford for recovery of his health and was there taken prisoner when the town was reduced by Parliament (Dec. 1645). He was left behind at Gloucester on account of sickness and was too infirm to attend Committee of Compounding (*C.C.C.*, pp. 1145-7 and *C.A.M.*, pp. 436-8).

Committed to the Tower but quickly released on petition, 1646 (*C.J.*, Vol. IV, pp. 597 and 620).

Fined £8,961, pardoned, and had sequestration taken off his estate, 1647 (*C.J.*, Vol. V, p. 486 and Vol. VI, p. 24).

Married twice. His second wife, Anne, who survived him, was found guilty of recusancy, 1640.

Spiller's Will was proved in 1653 (P.C.C. 298 Brent).

7. MR WATSON

Almost certainly this is Richard Watson (died c. 1653), the son of John Watson, a sea captain, of London, by his wife, Anne, daughter of Thomas Ashby, of Moulsham, Essex. He was of Ampthill, Beds.

Surgeon in Ordinary to Charles I (L.C. 3/1).

Member of the Barber-Surgeons Company.

Summoned to attend the House of Commons, Dec. 1641. On examination admitted that he had a house near Ampthill, but in the way of arms had only two fowling-pieces, crossbow, etc., and had not trained men or had confluence of people to his house. Dismissed (*C.J.*, Vol. II, p. 354).

Described as a Papist and Delinquent to whom the Barber-Surgeons Company owed £1,000, Aug. 1645 (*C.A.M.* pp. 589-91; *C.J.*, Vol. III, p. 671 and IV, p. 254).

Compounded on Oxford Articles. Fined £380. 12s., 1647.

Watson's Will was proved in 1653 (P.C.C. 45 Brent).

It is not unlikely that 'Mr Watson' is Peter Watson (died c. 1674), Gentleman Usher and Quarter Waiter to Charles I (L.C. 3/1).

After the Restoration he petitioned to be admitted to his former post, which he did not obtain, or for a place under the Queen (*C.S.P.D.* 1661-2, pp. 77 and 388).

Received a legacy of £150 from the Queen Mother, Henrietta Maria, 1671 (*C.T.B.*, Vol. III, p. 780).

Watson's Will was proved in 1674 (P.C.C. 12 Bunce).

8. WILLIAM DOBSON (1611-1646)

Portrait-painter.

Stated by Walpole in his *Anecdotes of Painting* to have been appointed Sergeant-Painter and Groom of the Privy Chamber to Charles I.

Accompanied the King to Oxford, where he painted Charles, his sons, his nephews, and a number of distinguished Royalists. According to Walpole he 'lodged in the High Street almost over against St Mary's Church, in a house where some of his work remained till of late years'.

9. SAMUEL THORNTON (died c. 1667)

The eldest son of Sir Roger Thornton, of Snailwell, Cambs. and Wratting, Suffolk, and grandson of John Thornton, of Soham, Cambs., he was of Soham.

Fellow Commoner of Emmanuel College, Cambridge, 1619.

Admitted to Lincoln's Inn, 1620.

Served as a captain in the Civil War, probably in Prince Charles's Regiment of Horse. Attended a Council of War at Banbury 24 July 1643 (*Transactions* of the Archaeological Society of North Oxfordshire, Vol. I (1853-5), p. 33).

Compounded on Oxford Articles. Fined £333 (*C.C.C.*, p. 1515).

Thornton's Will was proved in 1667 (P.C.C. 41 Carr).

10. THOMAS WESTON, afterwards 4th EARL OF PORTLAND (1609-1688)

The second son of Richard Weston, 1st Earl of Portland (1577-1635), by his second wife, Frances, daughter of Nicholas Waldegrave, of Borley, Essex.

Gentleman Commoner of Wadham College, Oxford, 1626.

M.A. Cambridge, 1629.

Gentleman of the Privy Chamber Extraordinary to Charles I (L.C. 3/1).

With Goring at the siege of Portsmouth, Aug.-Sept. 1642.

Possibly served at Powick Bridge, where Digby was wounded, 23 Sept. 1642.

Probably fought at Edgehill as lieutenant-colonel to Digby, 23 Oct. 1642.

Probably present at the siege of Lichfield, Apr. 1643.

Fought at Roundway Down, where he was probably acting as C.O. to Digby's Regiment, 13 July 1643.

Near the end of Ashburnham's *Accompt* (p. xxxiv) occurs the entry 'To Lieutenant Coll: Weston £10'.

Took over Digby's Regiment of Horse when the latter was made Secretary of State, 28 Sept. 1643.

Paid £200 under the Privy Seal at Oxford, Feb. 1643/4 (*C.S.P.D.* 1644, p. 13).

Served in the Cornish campaign and signed letter to Essex, 8 Aug. 1644 (Walker, p. 61).

His Regiment, together with Hopton's and Colonel Conquest's, routed at Buckingham, Nov. 1644 (*Luke Letter Books* 1644-5, No. 94).

Taken prisoner at Rowton Heath 24 Sept. 1645 (*Civil War Tracts of Cheshire*, Cheetham Soc., N.S., Vol. 65 (1909), pp. 139, 142, and 146).

Later went abroad.

Succeeded his nephew as 4th Earl of Portland, 1665.

Abroad again by 1683, dying at Louvain: a Roman Catholic.

Married Anne, daughter of John, 1st Baron Boteler of Brantfield, and widow of Mountjoy Blount, 1st Earl of Newport.

(For the Weston family see R.E.C. Waters, *Chester of Chicheley*, Vol. I, pp. 100-9).

11. SIR HENRY MOODY, 2nd BARONET (c.1607-c.1661)

The son and heir of Sir Henry Moody, 1st Baronet, of Garsdon, Wilts., by his wife, Deborah, daughter of Walter Dunch, of Avebury, Wilts.

Matriculated from Magdalen Hall, Oxford, 1621.

Gentleman Usher of the Privy Chamber Extraordinary to Charles I (L.C. 3/1).

D.C.L. Oxford, 20 Dec. 1642. Wood (*Fasti*, Vol. II, p. 43) says that he was 'in some esteem at court for his poetical fancy'.

Sequestrated but discharged, 'he not being worth £200', 1646 (*C.C.C.*, p. 1577).

Sold Garsdon and emigrated to Massachusetts.

Died, unmarried, in Virginia, 1661 or 1662.

12. MRS PUDSEY

This is possibly Jane, second wife of Michael Pudsey, of Elsfield, Oxon., who died in Oct. 1645, aged 84, and daughter of Nicholas Stokes of Arthingworth, Northants. She died 22 March 1654/5, aged 75.

(For the Pudsey family see *Visitation of Oxfordshire* 1634, Harl. Soc., Vol. V, pp. 248-9).

13. SIR WILLIAM PALMER (died c. 1683)

The son and heir of Robert Palmer, of Hill Manor, Old Warden, Beds., by his wife, Mary Craddocke.

J.P. Beds., 1634.

Joined the King on the outbreak of the Civil War.

Knighted at Oxford, 2 Nov. 1642.

His house threatened with plunder, Dec. 1642 (*Verney Memoirs*, Vol. II, p. 71).

Probably in Life Guard of Horse.

Reported to have been taken prisoner by the Northants. Horse 24 Mar. 1644/5 (*Luke Letter Books* 1644-5, No. 437).

Sworn Carver in Ordinary to Charles I at Weobley, 6 Sept. 1645 (*C.S.P.D.* 1660-1, p. 30).

Compounded on Oxford Articles. Fined £1,100 (*C.C.C.*, p. 1482).

Noted as a Delinquent in Westminster, Mar. 1648 (*C.C.C.* p. 93).

Reported by Major-General Boteler as a suspect, under Cromwell.

Petitioned for a place as Carver to Charles II, 1660 (*C.S.P.D.* 1660-1, p. 30).

Married first, Dorothy, daughter of Sir John Bramston, serjeant-at-law, and secondly, a daughter of Sir Thomas Gardiner, of Cuddesdon, Oxon., Recorder of London.

Palmer's Will was proved in 1683 (P.C.C. 38 Drax).

14. (SIR) JOHN KNIGHTLEY, 1st BARONET (c. 1611-1650)

The son and heir of Robert Knightley, of Offchurch, Warwicks., by his first wife, Anne, daughter of Sir John Pettus, of Norwich, he was of Offchurch.

A Roman Catholic.

Raised a troop of horse for the King.

Colonel Knightley was ordered to march his troop to Winchester and put it under the command of Colonel (Sir) Christopher Lewknor (his wife's cousin) and to obey Lord Hopton's orders, 19 Nov. 1643 (MS. Harl. 6852, f. 243).

Created a baronet for his services, July 1645.

Married Bridget, daughter of Sir Lewis Lewknor, of Selsey, Sussex, Master of the Ceremonies to James I.

Died in his father's lifetime.

15. SIR FREDERICK CORNWALLIS

See pp. 199-200.

16. FRANCIS BILLINGSLEY (died c. 1658)

The eldest son and heir of Francis Billingsley, of Astley Abbotts, Salop, by his wife, Eleanor, daughter of Thomas Kerrey, of Bewdweston, Salop, he was of Astley.

Colonel of the trained band which was on duty at Bridgnorth, Oct. 1645 (Symonds, p. 252).

Taken prisoner at Stow-on-the-Wold by Colonel Birch, Governor of Hereford, where he was so long detained that he could not compound until 1647. Fined £206. 5s.: fine later reduced to £140 (*C.C.C.*, p. 1701).

Billingsley's Will was proved in 1658 (P.C.C. 324 Wootton).

(For the Billingsley family see *Visitation of Salop* 1623, Harl. Soc., Vol. XXVIII, pp. 46-7).

17. (SIR) ALEXANDER FRAIZER

See p.93.

18. SIR THOMAS DAYRELL (c. 1603-1669)

The only son of Francis Dayrell, of Biddlesden, Bucks., by his wife, Barbara Powell, who married as her second husband Euseby Andrew, father of Colonel Euseby Andrew, who was beheaded in 1650.

Admitted to Lincoln's Inn, 1620.

Fellow Commoner of Christ's College, Cambridge, 1622.

Barrister, 1628.

Knighted, 1633/4.

Acquired property at Hinxton and Castle Camps, Cambs., where he settled.

Followed the King to Oxford where he was in charge of the men from St Thomas' parish who were working on the fortifications (Bodleian MS. Add. D. 114, f. 28).

Married Sarah, second daughter of Sir Hugh Wyndham, Baronet, of Pilsdon, Dorset.

M.I. at Hinxton giving biographical particulars.

Dayrell's Will was proved in 1669 (P.C.C. 53 Coke).

19. (SIR) JOHN WALPOLE (1612-1672)

The eldest son of Dymock Walpole, of Pinchbeck and Spalding, by his wife, Jane, daughter of Thomas Ogle, of Pinchbeck, he was of Spalding.

Pensioner of Queens' College, Cambridge, 1627.

Admitted to Gray's Inn, 1630.

A Gentleman Pensioner and cornet of the King's Troop of Horse during the Civil War.

Present at Battles of First Newbury, Cropredy, Lostwithiel, Naseby, Rowton Heath, etc. (*Genealogist*, Vol. I, p. 101).

Knighted at Cardiff, 31 July 1645 (Symonds, p. 218).

Made Standard Bearer by Charles I at Oxford, and granted augmentation of arms by Sir Edward Walker there, June 1646.

Begged to compound on Oxford Articles, 1646 (*C.C.C.*, p. 1379 and

C.A.M., p. 1073).

Admitted Standard Bearer to Band of Pensioners, 1663 (*C.S.P.D.* 1663-4, p. 286).

Appointed a commissioner for taking accounts of Loyal and Indigent Officers, 1671 (*C.S.P.D.* 1671, p. 325).

Unmarried.

Walpole's Will was proved in 1672 (P.C.C. 127 Eure).

(For the Walpole family see *Lincolnshire Pedigrees*, Harl. Soc., p. 1041).

20. WILLIAM MATHEWS (died 1647?)

Yeoman of the Slaughter House.

Compounded for Delinquency in deserting his house at Westminster and going to the Oxford garrison, 1646. Fined £108 (*C.C.C.*, p. 1457).

Possibly the William Mathews who died of the Plague and was buried at St Margaret's, Westminster, 10 June 1647.

21. SIR FRANCIS COBB (c. 1606-c. 1671)

Son and heir of Sir Francis Cobb, of Burnham, Norfolk, and Ottringham in Holderness, Yorks., by his wife, Mary, daughter of Daniel Beswicke, of Yorks. He was of Ottringham. The elder Sir Francis, who was descended from the Cobbs of Sandringham, Norfolk, was an Esquire of the Body to James I and Charles I, and was knighted by the latter.

Ensign in Colonel Jerome Brett's Regiment of Foot, 1640.

Esquire of the Body Extraordinary to Charles I (L.C. 3/1).

Claimed to have served the King from his coming to York in 1642 until the surrender of Oxford, 1646 (*C.S.P.D.* 1670, p. 295).

Knighted at Beverley, 28 July 1642.

Subscribed to the Yorks. Engagement, Feb. 1643/4 (*C.A.M.*, p. 907).

A colonel of horse and commanded a troop in Prince Rupert's Regiment of Horse at the relief of Newark, 1643/4.

Governor of Clifford's Tower during the siege of York, and present at the relief of the city (Rupert's MS. Diary).

Signed articles for the surrender of Skipton Castle, Dec. 1645.

Compounded on Oxford Articles. Fined £72, 1646 (*C.S.P.D.* 1645-7, p. 486 and *C.C.C.*, p. 1551).

After the Restoration made a Gentleman of the Privy Chamber.

Appointed Captain of the Blockhouses at Hull, 1661 (Dalton, Vol. I, p. 13).

Played an important part in the public affairs of Yorks. and was High Sheriff, 1665 and 1666.

Married Ellen, daughter of Christopher Constable, of Catfoss, Yorks.

A kinsman was the Colonel William Cobb, of Sandringham, who was sequestered for recusancy and Delinquency, 1643 (*C.C.C.*, p. 2317).

(For the Cobb family see *Visitation of Yorks.* 1666, Surtees Soc., Vol. XXXVI, p. 332).

22. WILLIAM BASSETT (1602-1656)

The son and heir of William Bassett, of Claverton, near Bath, by his wife, a daughter of Rice Davies, of Backwell, Som., he was of Claverton.

A ward of the King on his father's death, 1613.

Admitted to Lincoln's Inn, 1622.

M.P. Bath 1640-5 Feb. 1643/4, when disabled (*C.J.*, Vol. III, p. 389).

Initially worked with Popular Party, but an order was issued to apprehend him as a Delinquent, Oct. 1643 (ib., p. 38).

Sat in Oxford Parliament, 1643/4, a fact which Mrs Keeler overlooked.

Surrendered to Parliament, Oct. 1645.

Compounded, Apr. 1646. Fined £2,512. 17s., 1648/9 (*C.C.C.*, p. 1181).

Married first, Mary, daughter of Moses Tryon, of Harringworth, Northants., and secondly, Elizabeth, daughter and heir of Sir Joseph Killigrew, of Arwenack, Cornwall.
(Keeler, pp. 100-1)

23. SIR EDWARD RODNEY (1590-1657)

The eldest son of Sir John Rodney, of Stoke Rodney and Pilton, Som., by his wife, Jane, daughter of Sir Henry Seymour, he was of Stoke and Pilton.

Stated by himself to have been four years at Magdalen College, Oxford, but not so recorded.

Admitted to the Middle Temple, 1608.

A witness of the marriage of his cousin William Seymour (afterwards Marquess of Hertford) to Lady Arbella Stuart, 1610. Subsequently accompanied Seymour abroad.

Knighted on the occasion of his marriage, 1614.

M.P. Wells, 1621, 1624, 1625, and 1626.

M.P. co. Somerset, 1628.

M.P. Wells, 1640-12 August 1642, when disabled (*C.J.*, Vol. II, p. 716).

Accused of High Treason, Aug. 1642 (ib., p. 475).

Named to some committees in the early stages of the Long Parliament, but disapproved of the attack on the King and joined the Marquess of Hertford.

Gentleman of the Privy Chamber Extraordinary (L.C. 3/1).

Petitioned to be removed from Parliament granted, Jan. 1642/3 (*C.J.*, Vol. II, pp. 932-3).

His house to be disarmed, Feb. 1642/3 (ib., p. 961).

Sat in Oxford Parliament, 1643/4, a fact which Mrs Keeler has overlooked.

Named a colonel of country people in Somerset at Kingsmore, 23 July 1644 (Symonds, p. 36).

One of those commanded to 'distress' Taunton, Sept. 1644 (Walker, p. 96).

Compounded, Oct. 1645, stating that he submitted on the surrender of Bristol and that he had never borne arms (*C.C.C.*, p. 916). His statement about not having arms contradicted, no doubt correctly, by a captain and a major who had served under him (ib., pp. 916 and 1380). Fined £1,200, 1645/6 (ib., p. 916).

Ordered to be committed to Ely House and all his papers and jewels seized, Nov., 1645, but released on security, Dec. 1645 (*C.A.M.*, p. 432).

Married Frances, daughter of Sir Robert Southwell, of Woodrising, Norfolk, and a lady of Queen Anne of Denmark's Household.

Rodney's Will was proved in 1657 (P.C.C. 282 Ruthen).
(Keeler, pp. 324-5. For the Rodney family see *Genealogist*, N.S., Vol. 16, pp. 207-14 and Vol. 17, pp. 6-12 and 100-7).

24. ROBERT HEATH (1620- at least 1668)

The fourth son of Sir Robert Heath (1575-1649), of Brasted, Kent, judge and Recorder of London, by his wife, Margaret, daughter and heir of John Miller, of Tonbridge.

Fellow Commoner of Corpus Christi College, Cambridge, 1634.

Admitted to the Inner Temple, 1637.

Barrister, 1652.

Auditor in the Court of Wards.

Probably to be identified with Robert Heath the poet (see *D.N.B.*).

25. FRANCIS HEATH (1622-1683)

The fifth son of Sir Robert Heath (see above).

Entered Corpus Christi College, Cambridge, 1633.

Admitted to the Inner Temple (at his father's request), 1641.

Served as a colonel of foot at Colchester (*C.S.P.D* 1661-2, pp. 290-1).

26. ROBERT STANIER (c. 1602-1673)

The son and heir of David Stanier, merchant, of London, a native of Cologne, by his wife, Abigail, an Englishwoman. David received letters of denization in 1604 and was naturalized in 1624, but was established in London by 1597.

Matriculated from Pembroke College, Cambridge, 1619.

B.A., 1622.

Admitted to the Middle Temple, 1624/5.

Was living in the parish of St Margaret's Westminster, 1641/2.

Followed the King to Oxford.

Wrote to George, Lord Digby from Bridgnorth about the movements of the King, etc., 24 Sept. 1645 (*C.S.P.D.* 1645-7, p. 158). Digby wrote to Nicholas from Denbigh about 'all my papers which were left with Stanier, and all my other necessaries at Worcester', 26 Sept. 1645 (ib., p. 160).

Compounded on Oxford Articles. Fined £22, 1646/7 (*C.C.C.*, p. 1597).

Married Hester . . .

27. JOHN BILL II (died c. 1680)

The eldest of the three sons of John Bill I, King's Printer from 1604 until his death in 1630, by his wife, Jane, daughter of Henry Francklin.

Succeeded to his father's share in the Printing House.

Was still under age c. 1636 when Jane (née Brett), third wife of Sir Thomas Bludder, petitioned with 'John Bill, an infant', having 'by grant from His Majesty the moiety of the office of King's Printer' (*C.S.P.D.* 1636-7, p. 267).

Granted a pass to travel abroad for three years, May 1638 (ib., p. 481).

A Gentleman Waiter Extraordinary (L.C. 3/1).

Dispatched two printing presses with type to York, 1642: these were sent thence to Exeter (*C.C.C.*, p. 1191).

His goods ordered to be sequestered, June 1643 (*C.J.*, Vol. III, p. 149).

Described as *Fil. imprimat*, being second captain in Colonel John Fleetwood's Regiment of Horse of the Earl of Cleveland's Brigade, the lieutenant-colonel being John Stuart, whose major Bill later became (*I.O.*), Sept. 1644 (Symonds, p. 102). Must have served in the Cornish campaign and fought at Second Newbury.

Compounded, stating that he was major of a regiment of horse under Lord Hopton and surrendered at Truro in March, Apr. 1646. Fined £500 and £800, Sept. 1646 (*C.C.C.*, p. 1191).

Compounded for a second Delinquency, having been engaged in the Surrey insurrection with the Earl of Holland, 1649 (ib.).

Reduced to great poverty by 1651 (ib., p. 3268).

Made statement with Christopher Barker about the office of King's Printer, asserting that they had both been sequestered and plundered of their materials so that at the Restoration, while claiming the printing, they had had to put the work into other hands. Bill refused to come to terms with Barker about the profits, 1660 (*C.S.P.D.* 1660-1, p. 273).

Continued as King's Printer until his death.

Married first, a daughter of Sir Thomas Bludder, of Flanchford in Reigate, Surrey (*C.J.*, Vol. III, p. 149). Bludder was M.P. for Reigate from 1640 until disabled for attending Oxford Parliament (Keeler, pp. 109-10; no mention of the Bill connexion); secondly, Margaret, daughter of Sir Harry Vane, and widow of Sir Thomas Pelham, 2nd Baronet (Lysons, *Environs*, Vol. III, *Middlesex*, pp. 349 and 367).

Bill's Will was proved in 1680 (P.C.C. 124 Bath).

(See H.R. Plomer, *Dictionary of Booksellers and Printers* 1641-1667 (1907), p. 24).

28. EDWARD BAGSHAW (c. 1590-1662)

The second son of Edward Bagshaw, gentleman, of London, by his wife, Mary Heming, who married as her second husband Sir Augustine Nicholls, Justice of Common Pleas.

Entered Brasenose College, Oxford, 1604.

Admitted to the Middle Temple, 1608.

Barrister, 1615.

M.P. Southwark, 1640-22 Jan. 1643/4, when disabled (*C.J.*, Vol. III, p. 374).

At first Puritan in sympathy and worked closely with Pym, but later joined the King at Oxford.

Sat in Oxford Parliament, 1643/4.

Taken prisoner and sent to King's Bench, Southwark, 1644 (*C.J.*, Vol. III, p. 546).

Wrote most of his numerous works on political and religious questions in prison: released 1646.

Married and was father of Edward Bagshaw (1629-1671), divine.

(Keeler, p. 94; *D.N.B.*).

ST JOHN'S PARISH

1. SIR JOHN COLEPEPER (1600-1660)

The second and only surviving son of Thomas Colepeper or Culpeper, of Wigsell in the parish of Salehurst, Sussex, by his first wife, Anne, daughter of Sir Stephen Slaney and nephew of Sir Alexander Colepeper [q.v.], he was of Hollingbourne, Kent.

Possibly the John Colepeper who was Fellow Commoner of Peterhouse, Cambridge, 1611.

Admitted to the Middle Temple, 1617-18.

Knighted, 1621/2.

Appears to have seen military service abroad.

Sold Wigsell to his cousin (Sir) Cheney Colepeper, eldest son of Sir Thomas Colepeper, of Hollingbourne, where Sir John later resided, 1623.

Esquire of the Body Extraordinary to Charles I (L.C. 3/1).

M.P. Rye, 1640-22 Jan. 1643/4, when disabled (*C.J.*, Vol. III, p. 374).

Initially worked with Popular Party, made famous speech against monopolies, and favoured Strafford's attainder, but opposed Grand Remonstrance and Militia Bill.

P.C. and Chancellor of the Exchequer, Jan. 1641/2.

Joined the King at York, May 1642.

Present at Edgehill, 23 Oct. 1642 where he distinguished himself.

Master of the Rolls, Jan. 1642/3-Nov. 1643.

Sat in Oxford Parliament, 1643/4.

Created Baron Colepeper, of Thoresway, Lincs., Oct. 1644.

Member of Prince Charles's Council, Mar. 1645.

Accompanied the Prince to France, 1646.

Married first, Philippa, daughter of George Snelling, of West Grinstead, Sussex, and secondly, Judith, daughter of Sir Thomas Colepeper, of Hollingbourne.

Colepeper's Will was proved in 1660 (P.C.C. 235 Nabbs).

(Keeler, p. 138; *C.P.*; *D.N.B.*: the genealogical details in the two latter are inaccurate. For an accurate account of the Colepeper family see F.W. Attlee and J.H.L. Booker, 'The Sussex Colepepers', *Sussex Arch. Coll.*, Vol. XLVII (1904), pp. 47-81, with pedigree).

2. SIR ALEXANDER COLEPEPER (c. 1570-1645)

The youngest of the four sons of John Colepeper, of Wigsell, in the parish of Salehurst, Sussex, by his wife, Elizabeth, daughter of William Sedley, of Southfleet, Kent, and uncle of Sir John Colepeper [q.v.], he was of Greenway Court in the parish of Hollingbourne, Kent.

Knighted, 1621.

Married Mary, daughter of Sir Thomas Scott and widow of Anthony St Leger, of Ulcombe, Kent.

Died at Bridgwater, Aug. 1645.

The petition of his executors, dated 20 Dec. 1645, described him as 'never any housekeeper but always a sojourner'. Greenway Court was the home of his first cousin Sir Thomas Colepeper, who was also in Oxford during the Civil War. His executors further declared that he was 'about March 1643 drawn down to Oxford and Bristol; since that time he fell sick of the dead palsy and made his Will, being £1,100 in debt'. He was said never to have borne arms or aided the King against Parliament (*C.C.C.*, p. 1058).

Posthumously fined £640 (ib.).

Colepeper's Will was proved in 1645 (P.C.C. 157 Rivers).

(See article cited under Sir John Colepeper).

3. MR FREKE

Almost certainly this is William Freke (1605-1657) eighth and youngest son of Sir Thomas Freke, of Shroton, Dorset, by his wife, Elizabeth, daughter of John Taylour, Haberdasher and Alderman, of London.

Matriculated from St Mary Hall, Oxford, 1621.

Admitted to the Middle Temple, 1622.

He and his elder brother Ralph Freke (1596-1683) were inseparable and married sisters: Ralph married Cicely and William married Frances, daughters of Sir Thomas Colepeper, of Hollingbourne, their elder sister being Judith, wife of Sir John Colepeper [q.v.].

Ralph Freke was almost certainly in Oxford in 1644 as his daughter Frances was born in one of the houses belonging to Anthony Wood's mother, Mrs Mary Wood, in Butcher Row (now Queen's Street) (*L. and T.*, Vol. I, p. III). But instead of lodging with his relatives-by-marriage, the Colepepers, he is more likely to have been living in the same house as his wife.

A portrait of William Freke inscribed 'AEtatis 40, 1645' is in the Bodleian Library and may have been painted in Oxford.

Ralph and William Freke gave a collection of coins to the 'Schooles in Oxon', 1657.

The brothers built Hannington Hall, Wilts., on their joint estate there in the 1650s.

William Freke's Will was proved in 1657 (P.C.C. 464 Ruthen).

(For the Freke family see *The Ancestor*, Vol. X, pp. 179 *et seq.* and C.B. Fry, *Hannington* (1935), passim: this gives the M.I.s of William and Ralph, pp. 73 and 74).

APPENDIX II

CHRISTIAN NAMES OF THE ST ALDATE'S LANDLORDS AND LANDLADIES JANUARY 1643/4

The following is an analysis of the seventy known Christian names of the St Aldate's landlords and landladies of January 1643/4. The names of four widows are unknown.

MEN

John (16), William (9), Thomas (8), Robert (4), Richard (3), George (2), Anthony (2), David, Arthur, Henry, Abel, Andrew, Unton, Edward, Walter, James, Oliver, Miles, Matthew, Francis (1 each). Total = 57

WOMEN

Margaret (3), Elizabeth (3), Susan, Ursula, Christian, Joan, Jane, Dorothy, Sarah (1 each). Total = 13

So much for the popular idea that seventeenth century Englishmen usually had Biblical names such as Obadiah!

APPENDIX III

THE CORRESPONDENCE OF MONSIEUR DU MOULIN

A

LETTERS OF DU MOULIN TO HENRI-AUGUSTE, COMTE DE BRIENNE CONTAINED IN BRITISH MUSEUM MS. HARLEIAN 4551

1. London, 11 August 1643: received 20th (ff. 194-5).
2. London, 11 September 1643: received 16th (ff. 196-7).
3. London, 24 September 1643: received 30th (f. 198).
4. London, 1 October 1643: received 7th (ff. 200-1).
5. London, 8 October 1643: received 15th (ff. 202-3).
6. London, 5 November 1643: received 11th (ff. 204-5).
7. London, 5 November 1643: (f. 206).
8. London, 10 November 1643: received 16th (f. 208).
9. London, 10 November 1643: received 16th (f. 210).
10. London, 11 November 1643: received 19th (f. 212).
11. London, 27 November 1643: received 3 December (f. 214).
12. London, 11 February 1643/4: received 17th (ff. 216-17).
    (In this letter Du Moulin refers to his letter of
    22 January which he thinks has been intercepted).

B

LETTERS OF DU MOULIN TO HENRI-AUGUSTE, COMTE DE BRIENNE PRINTED IN *Nouvelle Collection des Mémoires relatifs à l'Histoire de France* par MM. Richard et Poujoulet*

1. London, 4 September 1643 (Vol. XXVII, p. 87).
2. London, 17 September 1643. (p. 88).
3. London, 19 November 1643: received 10 December (pp. 88-9).
4. London, 4 December 1643: received 11th (p. 89).
5. London, 17 December 1643: received 24th (p. 89).
6. No address, 14 January 1643/4: received 22nd (pp. 90-1).
   (This letter is apparently not printed in full)

*Nouvelle édition (1854). Vol. XXVII. *Comte de Brienne*, 1615-1661, publiés avec des additions inédites tirées des manuscrits autographes par MM. Champollion-Figeac et Aimé Champollion Fils.

GENERAL INDEX

INDEX OF STRANGERS

LANDLORDS OF ST. ALDATE'S PARISH